Theatre in the United States: A Documentary History

General Editor: Barry B. Witham

This is the first of two volumes of documents that describe the growth and development of theatre in the United States. The first volume goes from the beginnings of theatre in the North American colonies up to the World War I. With such an abundance of primary documents to consult, the editors have focused on three specific "tensions" that have created and sustained American theatre: commercial versus artistic values; urban versus regional theatre; and the controversy over what is American and what is "foreign" or imported. The volume is organized in three chronological sections, each with its own introduction. The documents and commentary are arranged into chapters on business practice, acting, theatre buildings, drama, design, and audience behavior. Written sources include records of business transactions, letters, newspaper reports, reviews, memoirs, and architectural descriptions. There are also numerous pictorial items.

Volume I: 1750–1915, Theatre in the Colonies and United States. Contributors: Martha Mahard, David Rinear, and Don B. Wilmeth

Volume II (forthcoming): 1915–present. Contributors: Barry B. Witham, Glen Loney, Rosemarie Bank

Theatre in the United States

Volume I

Theatre in the United States: A Documentary History

General Editor: Barry B. Witham

This is the first of two volumes of documents that describe the growth and development of theatre in the United States. The first volume goes from the beginnings of theatre in the North American colonies up to World War I. With such an abundance of primary documents to consult, the editors have focused on three specific "tensions" that have created and sustained American theatre: commercial versus artistic values; urban versus regional theatre; and the controversy over what is American and what is "foreign" or imported. The volume is organized in three chronological sections, each with its own introduction. The documents and commentary are arranged into chapters on business practice, acting, theatre buildings, drama, design, and audience behavior. Written sources include records of business transactions, letters, newspaper reports, reviews, memoirs, and architectural descriptions. There are also numerous pictorial items.

Volume I: 1750–1915, Theatre in the Colonies and United States. Contributors: Martha Mahard, David Rinear, and Don B. Wilmeth

Volume II (forthcoming): 1915–present. Contributors: Barry B. Witham, Glen Loney, and Rosemarie Bank

Theatre in the United States: A Documentary History

Volume 1: 1750–1915
Theatre in the Colonies
and United States

Edited by
BARRY B. WITHAM

1750–1810: MARTHA MAHARD
1810–1865: DAVID RINEAR
1865–1915: DON B. WILMETH

 **CAMBRIDGE**
UNIVERSITY PRESS

Published by the Press Syndicate of the University of Cambridge
The Pitt Building, Trumpington Street, Cambridge CB2 1RP
40 West 20th Street, New York, NY 10011–4211, USA
10 Stamford Road, Oakleigh, Melbourne 3166, Australia

First published 1996

Library of Congress cataloguing in publication data

Theatre in the United States: a documentary history / edited by Barry Witham.

p.   cm.

"Section one, 1750–1810: Martha Mahard; Section two, 1810–1865: David Rinear; Section three, 1865–1915: Don B. Wilmeth."

Contents: v. 1. 1750–1915, theatre in the colonies and United States.

1. Theater – United States – History – Sources. I. Witham, Barry, 1939–

PN2221.T54   1995

792'.0973 – dc20   94–39375

ISBN 0521 30858 5 / hardback

A catalogue record for this book is available from the British Library

ISBN 0521 30858 5

Contents

List of Documents

II: Acting

III: Theatre Buildings

IV: Technical Production

V: Audiences

IV: Design and Technical Production

* Illustration

Acknowledgments

Martha Mahard wishes to acknowledge Jay Matthew Korn, Deborah Field, Margaret Hennig, Ruth Shuman, Robert Wright.

David Rinear acknowledges Melissa Miller of the Hoblitzelle Theatre Arts Collection, University of Texas, and Jeanne Newlin and her staff at the Harvard Theatre Collection.

Don B. Wilmeth would like to recognize Jane K. Curry for her research assistance during the early stages of this project and his students in the development of the American theatre for their help in locating a number of potential documents. Without the financial generosity of former Dean of the Faculty at Brown University, John Quinn, and the Brown Faculty Development, it would have been impossible to do the necessary archival research. The following individuals, archivists, and librarians have been especially helpful in locating documents, gaining access to archival materials, or suggesting possible inclusions or areas of investigation: Stephen Archer, Rosemarie Bank, C. Lance Brockman, Mark Brown, Frances Bzowski, Maryann Chach, Barbara Filipac, Mary C. Henderson, C. Lee Jenner, Mary Ann Jensen, Warren Kliewer, Albert T. Klyberg, Brigitte Kueppers, Orville K. Larson, Marti LoMonaco, Douglas McDermott, Brooks MaNamara, Martha Mahard, Brenda Murphy, Jeanne T. Newlin, Levi D. Phillips, Louis Rachow, David Rinear, Jane Rubin, Robert J. Sarlós, Anne W. Schmoll, Laurence Senelick, Dorothy Swerdlove, Bob Taylor, Paul Voelker, and Daniel J. Watermeier. Indebtedness to archives and collections is indicated in the text with specific documents. Finally, Barry Witham has earned my greatest respect and affection for the care he has taken in the general editing and especially for the thoroughness of his responses and his encouragement each step of the way, which, as he knows, has been long and often thorny. He has made it much more palatable than it might have been to make difficult decisions and to accept the inevitable elimination of some absolutely "essential" documents!

Barry B. Witham would like to acknowledge all the libraries, museums, and collections which have assisted in this undertaking. He would also like to recognize the recommendations and advice of a number of scholars including Rosemarie Bank, Steve Archer, Felicia Londré, John Wolcott, and Ted Shank. And a special thanks to Sue Bruns for all her help and hard work.

Theatre in the United States: A Documentary History

General Editor: Barry B. Witham

This is the first of two volumes of documents that describe the growth and development of theatre in the United States. The first volume goes from the beginnings of theatre in the North American colonies up to the World War I. With such an abundance of primary documents to consult, the editors have focused on three specific "tensions" that have created and sustained American theatre: commercial versus artistic values; urban versus regional theatre; and the controversy over what is American and what is "foreign" or imported. The volume is organized in three chronological sections, each with its own introduction. The documents and commentary are arranged into chapters on business practice, acting, theatre buildings, drama, design, and audience behavior. Written sources include records of business transactions, letters, newspaper reports, reviews, memoirs, and architectural descriptions. There are also numerous pictorial items.

Volume I: 1750–1915, Theatre in the Colonies and United States. Contributors: Martha Mahard, David Rinear, and Don B. Wilmeth

Volume II (forthcoming): 1915–present. Contributors: Barry B. Witham, Glen Loney, Rosemarie Bank

General Introduction

BARRY B. WITHAM

The history of the American theatre is a complex story which has been prob-lematized in recent times by controversies involving periodization, gender, eth-nicity, and historiography. When we first began this study, the issues seemed relatively clear: What were the major documents which, brought together in these volumes, could provide a historical narrative of the ways in which the American theatre had been created in the colonies, survived the opposition of churches and the Continental Congress, and then flourished in the rest of the country? In a relatively brief time, however, we discovered that even the most widely accepted views of history were subject to re-examination and critique. What does "American" mean, for example, in a world which has questioned the contribution of artists and theorists outside the geographical confines of the con-stantly expanding United States? How do we deal with a traditional "history" which has frequently denied or repressed the contributions of women and minorities? And how do we address the fact that so many of our national histor-ies focus on the accomplishments of the Broadway theatre in New York City?

These questions did not lead us to answers but rather to an extensive review of the literature and eventually the formulation of an approach which shapes both the narrative and the selection of documents in these volumes. The litera-ture is impressive. We were struck by the richness of detail in Mary Henderson's *Theater in America* where she grapples with many of the problems that we encountered and finally settles on an approach which divides the material according to function (producer, director, actor, etc).[1] And we admired the breadth and intellectual grasp of Travis Bogard who describes the "central reflector" of American drama as the playwright's ongoing fascination with the land. "The American has always thought of himself as Antaeus, deriving his strength from his contact with the earth."[2]

---

[1] Mary C. Henderson, *Theater in America* (New York: Abrams, 1986).
[2] Travis Bogard, *The Revel's History of Drama in English* (London: Methuen, 1977), p. 45.

We reviewed many of the pioneering works in the field by Barnard Hewitt, Garff Wilson, and Walter Meserve and rediscovered some interesting resources like the two-part assessment of the American theatre by Richard Moody and Oscar Brockett for the National Educational Theatre Conference in 1986.[3] Professor Brockett's piece is especially noteworthy as he attempts to evaluate the impact of the Ford Foundation and the National Endowments on the organization of American theatre as well as speculate on notions of postmodernism in performance.

We concluded after numerous discussions that it might be productive not to try to reinvent categories and periods but rather to examine theatrical activity as a kind of mediation among three specific "tensions" which operated across all geographical and period lines. And these tensions became the controlling principles which guided us in our selection and discussion.

The first is that the American theatre was created and sustained by a tension between what was perceived as "commerce" and what was "art." This is illustrated in a variety of ways from the "closet" dramas of the eighteenth and early nineteenth centuries (compared with the melodramas of the same period) to the current prejudice against the popular theatre of writers such as Neil Simon and Bernard Slade, often considered inferior to their peers, Sam Shepard, David Mamet, or Irene Fornes. Although dramatists like Eugene O'Neill momentarily united these impulses – with four Pulitzer Prizes and over a million dollars at the box office – the tension continues to the present day. Despite the subsidy of the WPA Federal Theatre Project in the 1930s or the National Endowment for the Arts thirty years later, most theatres are forced into a stance where they must negotiate this tension in order to survive. Since even relatively successful regional theatres are only able to earn approximately 70% of their expenses at the box office, new and imaginative funding strategies are constantly being tested in order to insure that "art" has a commercial market.

Of course, this tension is not limited to writers; there are countless examples in the American theatre where commerce and art collide. Edwin Booth's attempts, for example, in the nineteenth century to create a temple of art for Shakespeare had to be constantly revised and subsidized by his colleague Joseph Jefferson's immensely popular presentations of *Rip Van Winkle* (Doc. 160). And the experience of the New Theatre (1909–11) still stands as testimony to the pressures and contradictions of trying to negotiate the uneasy landscape between art and commerce which has characterized much of the American theatre. (Doc. 206–7)

There is, of course, a perception that "art" had nothing to do with the Ameri-

---

[3] "The American Theatre, 1936–1961" and "The American Theatre, 1961–1986"; reprinted in *Theatre History Studies*, 7 (1987), 84–98, 99–116, respectively.

can theatre until well into the nineteenth century but that prejudice has more to do with the literary acceptability of the written word than the performance context.[4] The "art" of the actor is very much a concern in eighteenth-century America as well as the "politics" of the performance and how that will help or hinder the box office.

Second, there is a tension between what is urban theatre and what was happening in the rest of the country. Historically, theatre in the United States is often a history of the Broadway stage and we have tried in these volumes to mediate between that perception and the vast amount of activity elsewhere. The extravagant touring "Tom Shows" of the nineteenth century, the popular melodramas circulating on the Stair–Havlin "wheel" at the turn of the century and the "Little Theatre" movement in the 1920s all attest to a tradition of popular theatre in the "provinces." Eighteenth-century theatre companies toured outside of metropolitan areas during the yellow fever season; the university theatres of the mid-twentieth century became repositories of culture in numerous small communities, and the current Regional Theatre movement which exploded in the 1960s saw the creation of professional theatres in Minneapolis, Hartford, New Haven, Seattle, and elsewhere.

While it is true that much of the nation's touring theatre originated in New York City and that production there served as a kind of imprimatur for works originating elsewhere, there is a rich tradition of theatre activity throughout the country which we have drawn on for this history. E. P. Hingston's colorful 1864 account of visiting the playhouse in Salt Lake City, with Brigham Young in attendance (Doc. 122), or the rowdy crowd in Cincinnati which Frances Trollope deftly sketches (Doc. 116) provide wonderful insights into a theatre tradition that did not rely upon Manhattan for its legitimacy.

Third, there has been an ongoing tension in the theatre between what is "American" and what is "foreign." This is perhaps the most important of the three tensions because it is fundamental to the theatre experience and yet resonates differently in different eras. Prior to the institution of an International Copyright Act in the 1880s, for example, American playwrights were often just gifted translators who could go to Paris and transcribe current hits. As times changed, however, the notion of an American voice became central to the theatre. Walt Whitman and others complained about the lack of native dramatists (Doc. 133) and in the early nineteenth century the actor, Edwin Forrest, created prize competitions for plays on American subjects by American writers (Doc. 124). Eventually the idea of "American" became embroiled with the world politics of two wars and the "requirement" of being American was extended to such

---

[4] Bogard, *The Revel's History,* p. 15. The "complete professionalism" to which actors aspired is surely an index of their artistry.

vivid examples as the vetting of playwrights and performers before the House Committee on Un-American Activities and the emergence of companies like Teatro Campesino and the Negro Ensemble Company where notions of being "American" were extended beyond a traditional white, male perspective.

This tension – like the other two – has literally ebbed and flowed over the years and has precipitated numerous controversial episodes. The British star "invasions" of the early nineteenth century played a vital part in shaping the nature of American acting and also led to civil disasters such as the Astor Place Riot. More recently, Actors' Equity "quotas" on the numbers of foreign actors who can appear in Broadway casts has insured more roles for natives but has also led to increasingly restrictive immigrations laws such as those proposed by the Bush administration for visiting artists and companies.

With the controlling notions of these three tensions guiding our philosophical speculation, we then turned to the more pragmatic considerations of how to group specific documents. Since these volumes are related to a larger enterprise at Cambridge University Press (Theatre in Europe: a documentary history) we wanted to follow the categories in those volumes where possible. However, because many of the European selections (documents of control or official censorship acts) did not always have direct corollaries in the United States we had to modify the system. Moreover, each of the "periods" in the American theatre had slightly different emphases so we did not impose a completely uniform grid on them.

Consequently, each period has common chapters on such topics as business, acting, theatre buildings, and drama but not all contain information on audience. Based upon the documents which we uncovered, audience benefits from very vivid documents in some eras and a relative paucity in others. Of course, space guidelines also had a great deal to do with sorting out topics common to all eras and those unique to a certain period. Each of the contributors submitted many more documents than we were finally able to use.

The thrust of the material is chronological within each chapter. We chose to do this partly in order to conform with the other books in the Cambridge series and because we decided that this was the clearest way to present the material given the number of editors on the project. Similarly, after numerous discussions and tentative models we came back to a traditional treatment of times and "periods." And while it is possible to argue for different lines of demarcation as Walter Meserve does so persuasively in *An Emerging Entertainment*, for example, we believed that the project would be best served by traditional periodization rather than creating a new set of signposts.[5] Thus beginnings and ends are signified by

---

[5] Walter J. Meserve, *An Emerging Entertainment: The Drama of the American People to 1828* (Bloomington: Indiana University Press, 1977). Meserve argues for 1828 as a significant breaking period in American Drama because of, among other things, the election of Andrew Jackson and the launching of Edwin Forrest's playwriting competitions.

events such as George Frederick Cooke's influential tours in the nineteenth century, the American Civil War, and the constellation of forces that mark the years around 1915 as a significant place from which to view the modern.

In reprinting such a wide variety of documents we have had to deal with a host of stylistic and editing problems and I would like to acknowledge especially the help of Sarah Stanton at Cambridge University Press who has been enormously supportive of the project over the years. In the midst of struggling to obtain copyright permissions, replacing editors who had not realized the enormity of the project, or awaiting the arrival of long-sought photographs, she has been patient and helpful.

Initially, Cambridge undertook this project with the intent of allowing the documents to speak for themselves and intended a minimum of footnotes. As it evolved, however, some editors felt that more notes were needed to provide a better context or to reference recent scholarship. As a result some sections have more notes than others, although I have tried to insure that archaic, confusing, or long forgotten references have some explanation. The language of the documents has been consistently modernized in matters of spelling, punctuation, and grammatical usage for clarity – except in cases where an individual editor wants to catch the flavor of a particular letter or contract – and generous cuts have been made in a lot of the documents where material was deemed to be redundant or not illustrative of the subject under discussion. Each period contains an introductory essay and connecting commentary by the individual compilers which further amplifies what is unique about that period and its documents. The connecting statements provide a narrative and a link between individual documents.

The "history" of the American theatre is a daunting topic and selecting the documents that most clearly illuminate that story is both rewarding and controversial. We had hoped to include many more documents illustrating popular entertainments, non-traditional theatre pieces, and native American performance but page constraints forced us to eliminate many items in this volume. Each printed document excludes several others and eventually the "construction" of this history involves numerous compromises among contributors and editors. By establishing a series of mediating tensions, however, we have tried to provide a focus whereby contributors have the freedom to tell their individual stories within the boundaries of a larger narrative. Volume One traces the theatre from its earliest manifestations in Colonial America to approximately 1915. Volume Two picks up the threads of that narrative and concludes in the present with particular emphasis on the marginalized and minority voices which were discovered and recovered in the twentieth century.

1750–1810

MARTHA MAHARD

INTRODUCTION

> The first centuries of American history are a history of pioneers: pioneers in forest and field, in politics, industry, science, and occasionally in literature and the arts. Since the theatre is privileged or condemned to be a mirror of the experience of its audiences, the early history of the American stage is equally a history of pioneers.[1]

The English actors who reached Virginia in the middle of the eighteenth century came from a country where theatrical activity was tolerated but severely restricted. Actors in England had yet to shed the Elizabethan stigma of rogues and vagabonds. Laws limited the number of theatres in London and empowered local provincial magistrates to license or prohibit plays within their jurisdiction. Actors who could not find work in London were forced to tour the provinces, often under wretched conditions. The stigma and the restrictive legislation followed the actors across the Atlantic. The poor conditions, particularly in terms of accommodations and the need for constant travel in search of new audiences, were probably not drastically different from what they would have endured at home.

In the American colonies, by the mid-eighteenth century, the cities along the eastern seaboard were well-established, active commercial centers. As the citizens became more prosperous they had time for leisure activities and the climate was ready for a company of actors to provide the appropriate entertainment. The broadly based and religiously diverse demographics of the original American colonies make any generalizations about those who went to the theatre in this period extremely difficult. Yet the records clearly indicate that in the southern cities, where Puritanism had scarcely any influence, the actors were consistently welcomed. In the north the arrival of the players regularly awakened a spirited and vocal opposition. Predictably New England remained the most adamantly opposed to performances. The Puritans had been against the theatre in England, and during the Interregnum had successfully closed the theatres from 1642 to 1660. To

---

[1] Alan S. Downer, ed., *The Memoir of John Durang: American Actor, 1785–1816* (Pittsburgh: University of Pittsburgh Press, 1966), p. xi.

the Puritans, including those who had made their homes in New England, the theatre was a place of licentiousness and vice, a source of potential corruption that could not be tolerated. Their presence so dominated the social and political life of the region that Boston did not find it necessary to enact an injunction against stage plays until 1750. In New York, the Dutch settlers had brought with them no particular intolerance for the theatre on religious grounds, their objections arose more from their inability to justify spending money on pleasurable pursuits, as well as the fear that it would breed idleness among the apprentices. The Quakers and Presbyterians of Pennsylvania proved to be nearly as intolerant as their neighbors to the north. It is possible, as the historian of the Philadelphia stage, Thomas Clark Pollock suggests, that they wished to exclude stage plays, masks, revels, and other "rude and riotous sports . . . to fence their Eden as a sober precaution against riotous and alluring serpents."[2] Constance Rourke suggests that "what seemed to be prejudice on the part of religious groups perhaps really stemmed from the intuitive sense that the theater really was a free and incalculable agent whose force might disrupt the slow growth toward stability."[3] We do not know how many attempts to stage plays were made in Pennsylvania during the first part of the eighteenth century. It is, however, a matter of record that the colonial government made repeated attempts to enact anti-theatrical legislation from 1682 to 1713 and again in 1759. Each of these statues was countermanded by royal veto.

The company of actors who sailed from England with Lewis Hallam and his family already had some experience with restrictive, anti-theatrical legislation. In London the Licensing Act of 1737 had made Covent Garden and Drury Lane, the two Theatres Royal, the only officially sanctioned theatres. For ten years after the passage of this act managers of small, "illegitimate" playhouses attempted to produce plays and pantomimes under a variety of ingenious disguises. England's greatest actor of the eighteenth century, David Garrick, made his London debut in one of these theatres. Lewis Hallam's brother William, who organized the expedition to America, had managed the New Wells in Goodman's Fields, successfully defying the Licensing Act for several years. In 1747 however the management of Drury Lane, seeking to eliminate competition, called for the enforcement of the ten-year-old statute and William was forced to close his playhouse. The future course of the American theatre was shaped by his decision to send a company to the colonies rather than to the relative security of the English provinces.

Hallam's company were by no means the first actors to appear in Colonial America. Their predecessors were college students, gentlemen amateurs, and a few adventurers-turned-strolling-players. A semiprofessional company managed by Walter Murray and Thomas Kean had performed in Philadelphia, New York, and Williamsburg from 1749 to 1752, but had disbanded leaving few records. The arrival of the Hallams and their company of professional actors marked the beginning of the theatre as a cultural force in the colonies.

[2] Thomas Clark Pollock, *The Philadelphia Theatre in the Eighteenth Century* (Philadelphia: University of Pennsylvania Press, 1933), p. 4.
[3] Constance Rourke, *The Roots of American Culture* (New York: Harcourt, Brace and World, Inc., 1942), p. 99.

What is remarkable about the Hallams is that they persisted where others had not. They overcame physical and financial hardship as well as vigorous political opposition. By 1774 they had built or renovated playhouses in New York, Philadelphia, Williamsburg, Annapolis, and Charleston; they had developed and presented a diverse and popular repertory, comparable to what would have been presented in the best English provincial houses; and they had established an audience capable of sustaining them. It remained for the next generation to develop native talent (both in playwriting and performing) and to advance beyond the styles of acting that been popular in England in the mid-eighteenth century.

Actors in the pre-Revolutionary period were confronted with the job of obtaining permission to perform, winning supporters who would constitute a paying audience, and building or refurbishing suitable spaces in which to play. Although in many ways they appear to have insulated themselves against the political storm that was gathering around them, they could not remain unaffected by it. They became on occasion the victims-by-association of the colonists' resentment against the corruption and greed of the mother country. Whether the actors were justly or unjustly associated with the wealthy, Loyalist, governing class, they encountered a new vigor in the anti-theatrical voices as the conflict with England approached. Once the Continental Congress had made the prohibition of performances a matter of patriotic abstinence the players had no choice but to withdraw.

Where the colonial theatre had been enjoyed primarily by an elite group of prosperous, well-connected citizens, after the Revolution the theatre was embraced by a broad cross section of the American public; and the theatre managers appealed to this public with lavish spectacles featuring the glories of the Republic and a repertory of comedies, burlettas, and pantomimes.

Encouraged perhaps by this new atmosphere of acceptance the first distinctive voices of the American drama began to be heard. Royall Tyler's *The Contrast* was first performed in 1787, the same year in which the American Constitution was signed. The principal contrast in the play is between the foppish Anglo-American Dimple and the virtuous, if rough-hewn, patriot Colonel Manly. His triumph over the duplicitous Dimple becomes a triumph of the national identity. Two years later *The Father, or American Shandyism* by William Dunlap was successfully presented in New York. The comedy involved the American Colonel Campell, the father in the title, who believes his only child to have been a British officer killed at Bunker Hill. The usual array of flirtation, deceptions, cross-purposes, and revelations finally leads to a reunion between father and son. On September 5, 1789, the *Gazette of the United States* praised the performance and noted: "The happy allusions to characters and events, in which every friend to our country feels interested – and those traits of benevolence which are brought to view in the most favorable circumstances, conspired to engage, amuse, delight, and instruct the audience through five acts of alternated anticipations, and agreeable surprizes." Dunlap went on to write, adapt, and translate more than fifty plays, unquestionably earning the title of Father of the American drama. His adaptations from the German playwright Kotzebue, including *Pizarro, or the Virgin of the Sun* and *The Stranger*, were enormously successful. His own verse tragedy *André* (1798), although not initially well received, in a later, revised version titled *The Glory of Columbia – Her Yeomanry* (1803), became a fixture in the popular repertory. *André's* failure may be attributed to the fact that the historical events portrayed – including the execution of Major Andre, the British messenger to Benedict Arnold – were still too fresh in the public memory. The revised version enlarged the roles of the comic characters, added songs, including several verses of "Yankee Doodle," and featured a spectacular scenic finale of the battle of Yorktown with a transparency showing an eagle holding a crown of laurel over the head of General Washington.

In the last decade of the century handsome, permanent theatres were built in Charleston, Philadelphia, New York, and Boston. A final attempt to enforce the anti-theatrical statue in Boston had been instigated by Governor John Hancock in 1792. In the face of eloquent public support the statute was allowed to expire unenforced. The issue of restrictive legislation was no longer a serious threat to the actors. The monopoly maintained for so many years by Hallam and his Old American Company could no longer be preserved. Thomas Wignell established himself in Philadelphia. Thomas Wade West and John Bignall formed a company and took up residence in Charleston. John Hodgkinson eventually left New York for Boston's Federal Street Theatre, leaving Dunlap to struggle on with the financially troubled Park Theatre. There was plenty of room for expansion, and competition flourished as more competent and even distinguished performers continued to arrive from England. The new actors brought with them improvements in acting gradually replacing the mid-eighteenth century style introduced and maintained by the Hallams. The theatre in England was experiencing sweeping changes, particularly in the new, naturalistic style of acting introduced by David Garrick. But it was not until after the Revolution that the American stage began to feel the effect of Garrick's innovations.

Notable among the new arrivals was Thomas Abthorpe Cooper, recruited by Wignell for Philadelphia's Chestnut Street Theatre in 1796. When he left Philadelphia after two years to join Dunlap at the new Park Theatre in New York he began to achieve great popular recognition. He became America's eminent classical actor, excelling in a remarkable variety of Shakespearean roles. His acting style derived from Garrick's successor, the English tragedian John Philip Kemble – dignified, formal, and often statuelike – although Cooper is credited with conveying more passion than Kemble.

In addition to recruits from England, America began to produce its own generation of competent and distinguished performers. Many of the names that dominate the nineteenth-century American theatre began to appear – the Placide family, the Jeffersons, the Warrens, to name only a few. William Burke Wood, the first American-born actor to achieve distinction, made his debut with Wignell's company in 1798. In the ten years before he went into management with William Warren at the Chestnut Street Theatre in Philadelphia he had earned a solid reputation, particularly in high comedy roles. When he appeared in New York in 1810 his performance in the role of de Valmont in the melodrama *The Foundling of the Forest* inspired one critic, writing under the name "Hamlet" to write in the *Columbian*:

> Mr. Wood exhibited a superiority of acting seldom witnessed on our boards. He gave an importance and effect to the part to which we were strangers. . . . In the letter scene . . . his triumph over the audience was complete. . . . The tears, the sobs, and the agitation of the spectators, with the fainting of a lady in one

of the boxes, electrified the house with all the delicious luxury of woe, and crowned the conquest of the actor with drama's chaplet.[4]

At the end of 1810 George Frederick Cooke, one the great stars of the English stage, traveled to America, astonishing American audiences with his erratic brilliance. His appearance paved the way for a new era dominated for the first time by stars from London, including the elder Junius Brutus Booth and Edmund Kean. Although continuing its close connection with the London stage for many years the American theatre had finally become a part of American urban culture.

[4] *Columbian* (New York), September 22, 1810.

I.   The Business of Theatre

Since the business of producing theatre in Colonial America was so closely tied to winning official recognition and popular approval, the following documents illustrate the process by which professional theatre finally came to be accepted in the United States. In May 1752 a company of actors organized by William Hallam and led by his brother Lewis left England for the American colonies. After a voyage of six weeks, they arrived in Yorktown, Virginia and proceeded to Williamsburg. By the end of August they had completed the necessary alterations to the existing playhouse and obtained the Governor's permission to give performances there. Their first was *The Merchant of Venice*, presented on September 15, 1752. While performing in Virginia they apparently encountered some competition from the Murray and Kean Company, who fade from the record after this season. After receiving some encouragement to travel to New York for a season the Hallam company was unpleasantly surprised to find a more vigorous anti-theatrical prejudice prevalent in the north than they had as yet experienced. It is possible to assume that some of this opposition was the result of the poor conduct and performances of their predecessors, the Murray and Kean Company. The following document is Hallam's appeal to the public in which he airs his grievances and hopes for support.

1   Lewis Hallam's Appeal for Public Support, 1753

New York Mercury, July 2, 1753

The Case of the London Company of Comedians, lately arrived from Virginia, humbly submitted to the consideration of the public; whose servants they are, and whose protection they intreat.

As our expedition to New York seems likely to be attended with a very fatal consequence, and ourselves censure for undertaking it, without assurance of success; we beg leave, humbly to lay a true state of our case before the worthy inhabitants of this city; if possible endeavor to remove those great obstacles which at present lie before us, and give very sufficient reasons for our appearance in this part of the world, where we all had the most sanguine hopes of meeting a very different reception; little imagining, that in a city, to all appearance so polite as this, the Muses would be banished, the works of the immortal Shakespeare, and other the greatest geniuses England ever produced denied admittance among them, and the instructive and elegant entertainment of the stage utterly protested against: When, without boasting, we may venture to affirm, that we are capable of supporting its dignity with proper decorum and regularity . . . In the infancy of this scheme, it was proposed to Mr. William Hallam, now of London, to collect a company of comedians, and send them to New York and the other Colonies of America. Accordingly he assented, and was at a vast expense to procure scenes, clothes, people, etc. And in October 1750, sent over to this place, Mr. Robert Upton, in order to obtain permission to perform, erect a building, and settle everything against our arrival; for which service, Mr. Hallam advanced no inconsiderable sum. But Mr. Upton on his arrival, found here that Set of Pretenders,[1] with whom he joined, and unhappily for us, quite neglected the business he was sent about from England; for we never heard from him after. Being thus deceived by him, the company was at a stand, til April 1752, when by the persuasion of several gentlemen in London, and Virginia captains, we set sail on board of Mr. William Lee, and arrived after a very expensive and tiresome voyage, at York River, on the 28th of June following. We obtain'd leave of his Excellency the Governor, and performed with universal applause, and met with the greatest encouragement; for which we are bound by the strongest obligations, to acknowledge the many and repeated instances of their spirit and generosity. We were there eleven months before we thought of removing; and then asking advice, we were again persuaded to come to New York by several gentlemen, whose names we can mention, but do not think proper to publish. They told us, that we should not fail of a genteel and favorable reception; that the inhabitants were generous and polite, naturally fond of diversions rational, and particularly those of the theatre. Nay, they even told us there was a very fine Playhouse building, and that we were really expected. This was encouragement sufficient for us, as we thought, and we came firmly assured of success. But how far our expectations are answered, we shall leave to the candid to determine, and only beg leave to add, that as we are people of no estates, it cannot be supposed that we have a fund sufficient to bear up against such unexpected repulses. A journey by sea and land five hundred miles is not undertaken without money. Therefore, if the worthy magistrates would consider this in our favor, that it must rather turn out a public advantage and pleasure than a private injury; they would, we make no doubt, grant permission, and give us an opportunity to convince them, we were not cast in the same mold with our theatrical predecessors; or that in private life or public occupation, we have the least affinity to them.

---

[1] "Set of Pretenders" presumably refers to the Murray and Kean Company which performed at various places between 1749 and 1752 and then disappeared.

By September Hallam had succeeded in overcoming the opposition and following their season in New York the company went to Philadelphia where they again faced significant public disapproval. Having at length been granted permission to perform they presented a short season and then moved further south to the more hospitable Charleston. Hallam then took the company to Jamaica where he died in 1756. His widow married David Douglass, an actor who had come to Jamaica from London with a small company. The two troupes were merged and returned to New York in 1758. Here Douglass fitted up a new playhouse on Cruger's Wharf, offending the authorities by his failure to obtain the necessary permissions. As his predecessor had done Douglass took his case to the public.

2   David Douglass' Appeal for Public Support, 1758

New York Mercury, November 6, 1758

Mr. Douglass,

Who came here with a company of comedians, having applied to the gentlemen in power for permission to play, has (to his great mortification) met with a positive and absolute denial. He has in vain represented, that such are his circumstances, and those of the other members of his company, that it is impossible for them to move to another place; and though in the humblest manner he begged the magistrates would indulge him in acting as many plays as would barely defray the expenses he and the company have been at, in coming to this city, and enable them to proceed to another; he has been unfortunate enough to be peremptorily refused it. As he has given over all thoughts of acting, he begs leave to inform the public, that in a few days he will open

An HISTRIONIC ACADEMY

Of which proper notice will be given in this paper.

The town authorities were further offended by this attempt to avoid their "positive and absolute denial," and Douglass published the following.

3   David Douglass Disclaimer on Acting Plays, 1758

New York Mercury, December 11, 1758

Whereas I am informed, that an advertisement of mine, which appeared some time ago in this paper, giving notice that I would open an histrionic academy, has been understood by many, as a declaration, that I proposed to act plays, without the consent of the Magistracy:

THIS IS THEREFORE TO INFORM THE PUBLIC,

that such a construction was quite foreign to my intent and meaning, that so vain, so insolent a project never once entered into my head. It is an impeachment of my understanding to imagine, I would dare, in a public manner, to aim at an affront on gentlemen, on whom I am dependent for the only means that can save us from utter ruin.

All I proposed to do was, to deliver dissertations on subjects, moral, instructive, and entertaining, and to endeavor to qualify such as would favor me with their attendance, to speak in public with propriety. But as such an undertaking might have occasioned an enquiry into my capacity, I thought the public would treat me with greater favor, when they were informed that I was deprived of any other means of getting my bread; nor would that have done any more than barely supplied our present necessities.

The expenses of our coming here, our living since our arrival, with the charge of building, etc. (which let me observe, we had engaged for before we had any reason to apprehend a denial) amount to a sum that would swallow up the profits of a great many nights acting, had we permission.

I shall conclude with humbly hoping, that those gentlemen who have entertained an ill opinion of me, from my supposed presumption, will do me the favor to believe, that I have truly explained the advertisement, and that I am, to them, and the public,

A Very Humble, and Very Devoted Servant,

DAVID DOUGLASS,

Douglass and his company were finally permitted a short season in New York at the end of 1758. Whether they were able to recoup their expenses there is not recorded. From New York the company travelled to Philadelphia where the previously encountered anti-theatrical prejudice remained firm. Here, however, they were able to benefit from the influential support of the Governor of the colony who delayed approval of anti-theatrical legislation long enough to allow the company almost six months of performances. In addition to this tactic Douglass selected a site for the theatre on Society Hill, outside of Philadelphia city limits, beyond the reach of its magistrates – a ruse that actors have successfully employed since Elizabethan times.

The player's constant need to placate puritanical opponents and curry favor is clear in this prologue written by Francis Hopkinson for the opening performance at the theatre on Society Hill, June 25, 1759.

4   Prologue Spoken by Lewis Hallam, 1759

Pennsylvania Gazette, June 27, 1759

A PROLOGUE

Spoken by Mr. LEWIS HALLAM, at the opening of a Theatre at Philadelphia.

> To bid reviving virtue raise her head,
> And far abroad her heav'nly influence shed;

The soul by bright examples to inspire,
And kindle in each breast celestial fire:
For injur'd innocence to waken fear;
For suff'ring virtue swell the gen'rous tear;
Vice to expose in each assum'd disguise,
And bid the mist to vanish from your eyes,
With keener passion, that you may detest
Her hellish form, howe'er like virtue drest:
The muse to cherish, genius to inspire,
Bid fancy stretch the wing, and wit take fire –
For these we come – for these erect our stage,
And show the manners of each clime and age:
For these we come – oh! may your smiles attend
The pleasing task, and all our toils befriend.
 – Away ye senseless, ye whom nought can move,
Vice to abhor, or virtue to approve;
Whose souls could ne'er enjoy the thought sublime,
Whose ears ne'er taste the muses' flowing rhime.

But ye whose breasts the pow'rs of softness know,
Who long have learnt to feel another's woe
Nor blush to heave the sympathetic sigh,
Or drop the pious tear from pity's eye;
Attend our work, and may you ever find
Something to please and to improve the mind:
That as each diff'rent flow'r that decks the field
Does to the bee mellifluous sweetness yield:
So may each scene some useful moral show;
From each performance sweet instruction flow.
Such is our aim – your kind assent we ask,
That once obtain'd, we glory in the task.

From Philadelphia Douglass took the company south, playing in Annapolis, Williamsburg, and Charleston. In the summer of 1761 they traveled north to Newport, Rhode Island. The announcement of their intention to perform demonstrates that they had taken some pains to anticipate and deflect potential public opposition to their performances.

5   Announcement of the Douglass Company, 1761

Newport Mercury, August 11, 1761

The company of comedians propose to entertain the town for a short time with theatrical performances. As they have been at considerable expense, they humbly hope that the inhabitants will grant them their protection; and, if they are so happy as to meet with encouragement, they propose to give a benefit night for the support of the poor. The following recommendation, copied from the original, was signed by the Governor, Council, and near one hundred of the principal gentlemen of Virginia:

> Williamsburg, June 11, 1761
>
> The company of comedians under the direction of David Douglass have performed in this colony for near a twelvemonth; during which time they have made it their constant practice to behave with prudence and discretion in their private character, and to use their utmost endeavors to give general satisfaction in their public capacity. We have therefore thought proper to recommend them as a company whose behavior merits the favor of the public, and who are capable of entertaining a sensible and polite audience.

Although the Town Council voted to deny them permission, Douglass proceeded to set up a temporary theatre where they performed for almost two months. The company's initial performance on September 7, 1761, was the first dramatic performance by a company of professional actors to be given in New England. The *Newport Mercury* reported their final performance:

6   Newspaper Report on Douglass Company, 1761

Newport Mercury, November 2, 1761

On Friday evening last, the company of comedians finished their performances in this town by enacting the tragedy of *Douglas* for the benefit of the poor. This second charity is undoubtedly intended as an expression of gratitude for the countenance and favor the town has shown them, and it can not without an uncommon degree of malevolence be ascribed to an interested or selfish view, because it is given at a time when the company are just leaving the place, and consequently can have neither hopes nor fears from the public. In return for this generosity it ought in justice to be told that the behavior of the company has been irreproachable; and with regard to their skill as players, the universal pleasure and satisfaction they have given is their best and most honorable testimony. The character they brought from the Governor and gentlemen of Virginia has been fully verified, and therefore we shall run no risk in pronouncing that "they are capable of entertaining a sensible and polite audience."

At the time when the unpopular Stamp Act was causing unrest among the colonists the theatre became a focus for some of the violent anti-royalist sentiments. At least one scheduled performance at the theatre in Chapel Street was cancelled because of the protests directed at the theatre by the "Sons of Liberty." Once news had been received of the repeal of the hated act a company of performers placed the following announcement in the *New York Mercury*:

7   Announcement of *The Twin Rivals*, 1766

New York Mercury, May 5, 1766

A COMEDY, called,
THE TWIN RIVALS.
With a SONG in Praise of LIBERTY.

To which will be added an Entertainment, called,
The *King* and the *Miller* of *Mansfield*.

Tickets to be had of H. Gaine, and of Philip Miller, watchmaker, at the Old Slip. The Doors to be opened at three o-clock, and the play to begin precisely at six. No person upon an account, will be admitted behind the scenes.

BOXES 8s.   PIT 5s.   GALLERY 3s.

N.B. *As the packet is arrived, and has been the messenger of good news relative to the repeal, it is hoped the public has no objections to the above performance.*[1]

[1] Refers to the arrival of the packet, a passenger boat carrying mail and cargo on a regular schedule, with news of the repeal of the Stamp Act.

Apparently even the insertion of the "Song in Praise of Liberty" at a prominent place on the bill was not sufficient to placate the more hostile of the anti-royalists.

8   Newspaper Account of Theatre Riot, 1766

Weyman's New York Gazette, May 12, 1766

Our Grand Theatre in Chapel Street on Monday night last had a grand rout. When the audience was fixed, (agreeable to the assurance of performing the play of the Twin Rivals) about the middle of the first scene a more grand rout instantly took place both out and in the house, for by the usual English signal of one candle, and an huzza on both sides, the Rivals began in earnest. Those were best off who got out first, either by jumping out of windows, or making their way through the doors, as the lights were soon extinguished, and both inside and outside soon torn to pieces and burnt by persons unknown. . . . Thus ended the comedy, in which a boy unhappily had his skull fractured, his recovery doubtful; others lost their caps, hats, wigs, cardinals, and cloaks tails of smocks torn off (through mistake) in the hurry; and a certain He (who was to act the part of Mrs. Mandrake) being caught in the She-Dress,[1] was soon turn'd topsy-turvy and whipped for a considerable distance.

[1] Apparently refers to an unidentified actor in female costume.

In 1774 while the American Company was enjoying its most successful season since 1766, the British fleet was blockading Boston Harbor. The citizens of Charleston had raised money and sent supplies to the people of Boston, and the newspapers were filled with reports of special meetings and patriotic appeals. Once again the presence of a company of actors gave offense to some "serious minded" citizens who made an unsuccessful effort to close the theatre.

9   Grievance against Players, 1774
South Carolina Gazette, February 28, 1774

The following are the two presentments of the grand jurors at the last session for this district which were quashed, and therefore not ordered to be published amongst the rest – and are here inserted by particular desire:

"We present as a grievance the company of players; a play house in Charleston being unfit for the present low estate of the province; for although there is great want of money to procure the conveniences and even the necessities of life, yet large sums are weekly laid out for amusements, these by persons who cannot afford it; and is a means of promoting the frequent robberies that are committed and of vice and obscenity.

We recommend that the legislature may suppress the same, tending to the corruption of youth and the injury of many families." . . .

By the time war declared with England, David Douglass and his American Company of Comedians had accomplished a great deal. They had established permanent theatres in Philadelphia, New York, and Charleston; they had promoted a loyal and enthusiastic following among the people. They had even tested, albeit without much success, the receptivity of New England colonies. That theatrical performances were prohibited during the war should not be regarded as a defeat for the players nor as a continuation of the anti-theatrical opposition to their performances. Rather, as Pollock suggests, it was "a clearing of the social decks for action as the conflict with the mother country approached war."[1]

[1] Pollock, *The Philadelphia Theatre*, p. 32.

10   Resolution Passed by the Continental Congress, Philadelphia, 1774

Quoted in *Documents of American History*, ed. Henry Steele Commager, 8th ed. (New York: Appleton-Century-Crofts, 1968), p. 86

That we will in our several stations encourage frugality . . . and discourage every species of extravagance and dissipation, especially all horse racing, and all kinds of gaming, cock fighting, exhibition of shows, plays, and other expensive diversions and entertainments.

With the war over, the state of emergency passed, the company of actors returned from their self-imposed exile in Jamaica. In 1784 Lewis Hallam petitioned the General Assembly of Pennsylvania for the repeal of the existing law prohibiting performances. He failed but the company remained in Philadelphia, acting under the ruse of presenting concerts or lectures on various subjects. The company left for New York in August 1785. In their absence the Assembly altered the form of the law, extending the prohibition to include pantomime, and adding a fine of two hundred pounds for each offense. In 1787 Hallam's company made another brief attempt to reestablish themselves in Philadelphia, using more ingenious ruses, including renaming the Southwark Theatre the Opera House, and in March 1788 Hallam and the actor John Henry renewed their petition. A committee appointed to investigate the matter returned a recommendation that a theatre be licensed. The motion was, however, tabled. The players were somewhat emboldened by this near success and the following summer presented a short season of plays only thinly disguised. (For example, *The School for Scandal* was announced as "A Lecture on the Disadvantages of Improper Education, Exemplified in the History of TONY LUMPKIN.") In the fall Hallam and Henry asked that the recommendation of the committee be considered and a license to perform granted. The opponents of the drama continued their vocal resistance until a group of eminently respectable citizens formed a Dramatic Association "for the Purpose of obtaining the Establishment of a Theatre in Philadelphia under a liberal and properly regulated plan." Pollock called the Dramatic Association "a civic movement, the voice of the best liberal element in the growing city, of those interested in the arts and in political rights," and described their statement of rights as "one of the most important social landmarks of America."[1] This document was presented to the Assembly on February 16, 1789.

[1] Pollock, *The Philadelphia Theatre*, p. 46.

11   Proposal for a Theatre in Philadelphia, 1789

Pennsylvania Packet, February 17, 1789; quoted in Pollock, *The Philadelphia Theatre*, p. 47

To the Honorable the General Assembly of Pennsylvania. The subscribers being a committee of the Dramatic Association on behalf of themselves and the many citizens who have prayed for a repeal of any law or part of a law, that prohibits dramatic entertainments, beg leave, with the utmost respect, to submit the following representation: . . .

The Drama is now a subject of earnest discussion; from a topic of private discussion, it has become the object of legislative decision, and contending parties are formed, on the one hand denying and on the other asserting, the propriety of tolerating the stage. . . .

Those who wish the establishment of the Drama, desire a thing, which it is in the power of their opponents, deeming it an evil, to avoid, even after it is established; and which, at all events, intrudes upon no right and interferes with no privilege. But those who wish the prohibition of the Drama seek to deprive their opponents of what they consider as a rational enjoyment, and by their success, will abridge the natural right of every freeman to dispose of his time and money, according to his own taste and disposition, when not obnoxious to the real interests of society. . . .

The petition of favor of the theatre, offers to the legislature an opinion of upwards of two thousand citizens (who think the business of life requires some recreation) that the Drama, divested of every other consideration, is a rational amusement. At the same time it is respectfully, and temperately, intimated, that it is not just to call on the subscribers to sacrifice that opinion, merely in compliance to the prejudice of those of their fellow citizens, who think [Drama] . . . contrary to the laws of conscience and virtue.

But the petition against the theatre, in a spirit less gentle and conciliatory, unequivocally declares that the toleration of a theatre would be impolitic, and injurious to the virtue, happiness, and productive of many vices and mischiefs: thence necessarily leading to this inference, that every man of a contrary opinion (expressed by signing the other petition) is a friend and promoter of the predicted inundation of wickedness and ruin. . . .

Here indeed, is a fair criterion to decide this controversy. An Act of Assembly has prescribed a certain test, or political obligation to be taken by every citizen. This, it is said, is incompatible with the opinions of a respectable body. An application is, therefore, made for a repeal of the law, and, we believe, every generous mind entertains a favorable wish upon the subject, for the members of the same community, certainly owe a mutual deference and respect to the sentiments, and even to the conscientious weaknesses of each other. But let us suppose that a petition was presented, stating that allegiance is a debt, which every man incurs, as a necessary consequence of the protection that he receives from the government, and picturing a cloud of visionary evils, which might result from allowing these persons to partake in the administration of public affairs, who were adverse from giving a solemn and unequivocal mark of their attachment to the Commonwealth. What should be said of a petition of this kind? Precisely what may be said of the petition against the theatre; with this difference only, that, in one instance, the pretense would be for the sake of the political safety, as it is in the other, for the sake of the moral happiness of the people. Neither of which would, in fact, be endangered by the repeal of the said law, or the establishment of the Drama.

From these premises, we think, the following inferences are fairly deducible:

1st. That whether the theatre is, or is not, a proper institution, rests, on this occasion, merely upon the opinion of the respective subscribers.

2d. That, it is thought to be advantageous by men, whose profession best enables them to judge upon the subject; by parents, on whom it is most encumbent to suppress every real instrument of corruption, and by citizens whose experienced patriotism, and extensive interest in the state, entitle them to the consideration of the legislature.

3d. That if a theatre is tolerated, no man sustains an injury, no man is deprived of a means of recreation from the toils and cares of life; nor anyone compelled to act contrary to his principles, or his prejudices.

4th. That if a theatre is not tolerated, many respectable citizens will be disappointed in their reasonable hopes, a source of rational amusement will be destroyed, and every freeman must incur a forfeiture of a natural right, which he ought to possess – the right of acting as he pleases, in a matter perfectly indifferent to the well-being of the community. . . .

On March 2, 1789, the Assembly enacted the repeal of "any act or part of an act which prohibits theatrical representations within the city of Philadelphia and the neighbourhood thereof."

In New York the success of the John Street Theatre was threatened by a dispute between Thomas Wignell and the managers. Wignell, on whose popularity as a performer much of the company's success depended, wished to become part of the management. Hallam and Henry were determined to exclude him primarily for financial reasons. Seeing no way to resolve matters to his satisfaction Wignell withdrew from the company and left New York to establish a rival company in Philadelphia. William Dunlap, who later entered the management of the John Street Theatre himself, recounts the substance of the disagreement.

12   William Dunlap's Account of Thomas Wignell Dispute, 1792

William Dunlap, *A History of the American Theatre* (New York: J. and J. Harper, 1832), I: 90–92

In the year 1792, this important division of the American Company took place. The writer knew, four years before, that discord and jealousy existed between

Henry and Wignell. Hallam, who was Wignell's cousin, and had sent him out in 1775, sided with the latter in 1788. Thus the managers, Hallam and Henry, were at variance. Hallam through life professed to be guided by two maxims in the management of a theatre. They were, "keep down the expenses," and "divide and govern." The first may be right according to circumstances, as a general rule it is wrong. The second is always wrong. It is the base resource of the weak to govern by fraud and falsehood, when they find that they have not the ability to govern by truth and justice. It is the Machiavellian policy of tyrants. Hallam could divide, but could not govern, and the two more powerful minds took the reins of government into their own hands and divided the kingdom. The following statement of the immediate cause of the separation was communicated to the writer by Wignell, in 1802, and in the main agrees with Hallam's account of the transaction. The reader will see where they would necessarily differ, each stating his own case.

By recurring to the early account of the division of shares, it will be seen that the manager had a share as such, and another as performer. Two managers enjoyed the same source of emolument, each having his share as such, and Wignell, knowing himself to be at this time the favorite of the public, aspired to a share in the management and the advantages belonging thereto. Henry had given him repeated promises of taking him into the firm; Hallam appearing to wish for the same. In the winter of 1791–2, it had been considered necessary by the sharers to send an agent to England for the purpose of engaging performers. The sharers, it appears, were occasionally called together as a council to the joint kings, and they saw that the American public began to call for more than satisfied the colonies of England, or the exhausted and jealous states immediately after their independence. In addition to more actors, scene painters, musicians, machinists, and a better wardrobe was wanted. Wignell requested that he might be the company's agent, and it had been promised to him. He had in consequence written to his friends, that after an absence of fifteen years he should see them again in London. In this stage of the business he had a more than usually violent quarrel with Henry, who threatened him that "his reign should not be long."

In 1792, while the company were playing in Philadelphia, the following paragraph appeared in one of the papers. "We have authority to say that John Henry, one of the managers of the old American Company, will soon embark for England, for the purpose of engaging performers for the company." On seeing this, Wignell called upon Hallam, and asked him if he knew of, or had sanctioned that paragraph. He replied, "No." "Who then authorized it?" The reply was, "Henry, I suppose, as it is in his usual way."

Wignell asserted his right to go home as agent, mentioned the promise given to him, and his desire to visit his friends. Henry persisted in his determination to take the business on himself, and as appeared by the sequel, had Hallam's assent to the plan. A meeting of the sharers was called to choose their agent for this important mission. When all were assembled, Hallam . . . expatiated on the condition of the company, the growth of the country, the demands of the public, the necessity of satisfying these demands that the company might prevent opposition, that for these reasons an agent must be sent to England to procure performers, as well as make purchases, and establish such a correspondence as would further their views, concluding with these words, "Mr. Henry is willing to go, and Mr. Wignell is anxious to go. If Mr. Henry goes, we can continue playing and maintain ourselves. If Mr. Wignell goes, we must shut up." . . .

[Wignell] proceeded thus. "This was the first idea I had of Hallam's duplicity, and I immediately saw my situation. I represented to the meeting the promise given to me, and the arrangement I had made in consequence of that promise. I repeated the threat of Mr. Henry to destroy me, and the mode in which I understood he intended to accomplish it, by bringing out an actor to supersede me in my business, which, by keeping me out of the management, he could effect, as by casting new plays, he could bring a new performer into public favor, and thereby ruin me in my profession. I therefore demanded either to be made a joint partner, purchasing at their own price, and without asking credit, or to be appointed the company's agent. Both demands were positively refused by the two managers, and the meeting of sharers broke up without electing their agent."

The next day another meeting was called, "which," said Wignell, "as I knew all had been previously determined, I declined to attend." Wignell resigned his situation in the company; Henry was appointed the agent, and soon after embarked.

The plan of a new theatre in Philadelphia, probably long contemplated by many, was now matured without loss of time. Mr. Reinagle, a professor of music, entered into partnership with Wignell. Their friends furnished such additional funds as were necessary. The site of the present theatre in Chestnut Street, not then as now in the center of the city, was purchased before the opponents of theatrical establishments knew for what purpose it was to be used, and while an elegant theatre was building, Wignell followed Henry to England with power and inclination to engage such a company and such additional aids as would overwhelm his long-time enemy, Henry, and his ex-friend and cousin, Hallam.

Following his bitter quarrel with the managers of the New York company, Wignell entered into management in Philadelphia, now the capital of the country, with musician Alexander Reinagle. William Wood, who joined Wignell's company as an actor in 1798, described the difficulties this alliance presented.

13   William Wood on Thomas Wignell, 1855

William B. Wood, *Personal Recollections of the Stage* (Philadelphia: Henry Carey Baird, 1855), pp. 92–95

With all his skill and judgment Mr. Wignell, it must be confessed, committed an error of management at his outset, to which he himself attributed nearly as deep an injury as that which he sustained by the recurrence of the pestilence for many years, a matter I have already spoken of. The error of management was this: the founders and patrons of the new house were chiefly of a class familiar with music, and were desirous of placing it on an equal rank with the drama. As a subordinate part of the establishment it had always been favored; but Wignell, who, at the instance of these persons, had associated himself with Reinagle, a professional musician and composer, was unfortunately induced to rely chiefly on this portion of his attractions for the support of the whole. The musical part of the entertainment being now made so prominent, greatly swelled the expenditures. These included the enormous charge of a perfect orchestra of instrumental performers of undoubted abilities, carefully selected from the great theatres abroad. The musical instruments of all kinds (then the property of the manager), including two grand pianos and a noble organ, swelled this sum yet more. Then again the skeleton of a chorus, to be constantly kept and filled up as wanted, formed another item. The orchestra music (afterwards destroyed by fire), was obtained at an expense of nearly two thousand dollars. . . . A full ballet corps under the direction of Byrne added largely to the salary list. Such was Wignell's reliance on his musical force, that the first performance given by his new theatre in America was an opera, *The Castle of Andalusia*. Hitherto the public had been satisfied with as much music as could be heard from an operatic farce – enriched by the compositions of Shield, Arnold, and other popular composers. A few days clearly proved where the superiority in management lay.

It is needless to state that the discords among the singers proved a great addition to the poor manager's cares. As most of the operas had been composed with a view to the peculiar powers and voices of some original representative, it frequently happened that these pieces were not suited to the ability of later singers, and it became necessary to omit much of the composer's music, substituting such popular and approved airs as were most certain of obtaining applause. As a natural consequence, each artist insisted on a share of this privilege, until the merciless introduction of songs, encored by admirers of the several singers, protracted the entertainment to so late an hour, as to leave the contending songsters to a show of empty benches, and a handful of tired-out hearers; the audience preferring to retire at a reasonable hour. . . . To show how badly the union of the two entertainments affected the manager, Mr. Wignell used to refer in later times the advocates of the junction to his book of receipts, which presented such contrasts as *Love in a Village, Robin Hood,* or *Artaxerxes* (all musical dramas), performed to audience of one hundred to one hundred and fifty dollars; while the *Revenge, Romeo and Juliet, Alexander,* or almost any other tragedy, seldom fell below a receipt of from five hundred to seven hundred dollars. My own management confirms his views. I myself remember listening to one of the best operas, and well sung, which yielded a receipt of only forty dollars. On a more successful occasion it reached sixty dollars; and it is a fact, which the book of my treasurer proves, that *Speed the Plough, Poor Gentleman, John Bull,* and *Foundling of the Forest,* realized more real profit to our theatre than all the operas produced during twenty-five years.

After the close of the regular season at the John Street Theatre in June 1797 Hallam retired from the management, selling his share to John Hodgkinson and Dunlap. He continued as a salaried actor in the company, as did his wife. This transaction was completed at length, with much bitterness and ill will on all sides, due in part to old grievances, Mrs. Hallam's continued drunkenness, Hodgkinson's acquisitiveness, and Hallam's inability to manage. Hodgkinson published his own account of his quarrel with Hallam, appealing to the public for sympathy. In this pamphlet he provides an interesting outline of the responsibilities which had devolved upon him at that time.

14   Recollections of John Hodgkinson, 1797

John Hodgkinson, *A Narrative of his Connection with the Old American Company from the fifth September, 1792, to the thirty-first of March, 1797* (New York: J. Oram, 1797), pp. 14–15

. . . I had frequently conversed with Mr. Dunlap, respecting my situation, and the torture I labored under, and as I knew him to be attached to the theatre, in one of our conversations, I offered to sell him half my share, if he would undertake the acting management; for that I had more labor than the mind or body could possibly sustain. I had applied to Mr. Hallam, to know what he meant to allow me for my extraordinary fatigue, and he had peremptorily refused any compensation; which I thought hard, because, on the first commencement of theatrical business after our partnership, we had paid a gentleman one hundred pounds for acting as treasurer and bookkeeper only ten weeks. And here I hope it will not be deemed an unnecessary digression, if I mention what my situation exactly was. I had to cast and arrange the business of every play brought forward. I had the various tempers, rivalships, and ambitions of thirty or forty people to encounter and please. I kept all the accounts; I made all disbursements, and was made, in all money transactions, solely responsible. My professional labors were extreme, and I never finished them for the evening that I did not attend to take the state of each night's receipts. Nay, instead of enjoying my comfortable hour of social intercourse with my family, on my arrival home, I had a check account to take, and to make the regular entries in my books. I wrote and corrected every playbill for the printer. I planned and copied every scene plot for the carpenter. I attended every rehearsal, to give directions. I went through a varied and extensive line of characters on the stage. I found principally my own wardrobe for them; and my salary, for all this, was twenty dollars per week, paid only when we performed! Mr. Hallam received the same, and had no share in the fatigue. His answer to me, on application to know what he would allow me, was, that "he would quit the theatre the moment any man received a shilling more than him." An idea exceedingly unjust; for at the time of his purchase from John Henry, the shares were, Mr. Henry four and a half, Mr. Hallam three and a half, and when Mr. Hallam agreed with me, he reserved the difference: for the whole property being equally divided between us, Mr. Hallam gained a sixteenth; as he paid Mr. Henry no more for four and a half shares, than I did him (Mr. Hallam) for four shares.

To return to my narrative: Mr. Dunlap seemed inclined to treat with me, and finally was introduced, as Acting Manager, into the theatre, with the concurrence of Mr. Hallam, and to receive my assistance. I flattered myself I was now some little distance removed from my disquiets; but I was disappointed. Mr. Dunlap's inexperience compelled me still to be the director in the stage department, according to agreement, and I never gave an order in Mrs. Hallam's hearing that she did not pointedly ridicule and insult me. My wife never passed her, that she was not treated with every mark of contempt; and those who may lack information on this part, or labor under a different impression, I here inform, that she never made one word of reply.

Wood's purchase of a partnership in the management of the Chestnut Street Theatre in Philadelphia in 1809 merely formalized a previously existing arrangement. Wood had served as treasurer under Wignell's management. After Wignell's death in 1803 his widow (Anne Merry) married the actor William Warren, who assumed the administration of the theatre. The Warren-Wood partnership was extremely successful and continued at the Chestnut Street Theatre until 1826.

15   William Wood on Management, 1855

Wood, *Personal Recollections*, pp. 129–31

In the autumn of the year 1809, Mr. Benjamin C. Wilcocks, of Philadelphia, and some other friends, proposed to me the plan of a purchase from Warren of a share in his property and management, the heaviest burden of which I had borne for some years with much care and small remuneration. The means of payment were generously provided, terms adjusted, and an equal partnership formed. The purchase included one-half of Warren's interest in the Philadelphia,

Baltimore, and Washington theatres. One express stipulation proposed by him was, that the entire active management should be assumed and executed by me. I have already intimated that Warren, although an industrious actor, felt always an extreme dislike to the fatiguing details of the director, which his difficulty with Webster and others had rather increased. The new plan, as carried out, succeeded perfectly, and in a way which it could not have possibly done under a double and equal rule. Hitherto my services as aid to the management had been silent and unannounced.

Notwithstanding the increasing prosperity of the drama for several years past, and many hopeful prospects for the future, which now began to show themselves, I could not enter upon my charge of manager without feelings of the deepest anxiety. A long and hard service of ten years in the acting line, aided by the generous approbation of the public, had elevated me to a respectable rank in that department, notwithstanding it was pursued with the disadvantages of ill health, and among successful rivalry, and I had held at the same time the invidious and half-responsible situation of assistant or subdirector. Many of the difficulties, incident to my course, had driven me to the verge of abandoning so thorny a path. A gleam of hope would urge me on, and a feeling of honest pride forbade me to withdraw under any circumstance which might give to my retirement the least aspect, either to myself or the public, of my having withdrawn in any way defeated. I hope that a point of respectable mediocrity might be confessedly attained, when a graceful retirement from the profession could be affected. So gradual was a progress to this point, that I actually reached my humble wish before I myself perceived it. When I did, a new, delightful feeling of the possibility of fame, in addition to pecuniary advantages, combined to detain me in a pursuit for which I never felt any romantic partiality. I now entered on the CAREER of MANAGEMENT, and surely no aspirant ever entered upon his duty with fairer prospects, public or private.

II.   Acting

Acting in Colonial America was based on the English traditions in which the Hallams and their contemporaries had been trained. It involved the possession of parts and the standard "lines of business" and was enriched by "benefit" performances for those who had sufficient drawing power. Salaries ranged between four and fifteen pounds per week and two benefits might increase an actor's income by as much as a third. Records of acting during this period are largely reminiscences of fellow performers or occasional newspaper accounts. When David Douglass returned to Philadelphia in 1766 with the American Company, he had augmented their personnel and acquired new scenery from London. An anonymous "Gentleman Contributor" wrote the following review of Isaac Bickerstaffe's comic opera *Love in a Village* commenting on the players.

16   Review of *Love in a Village*, 1767

Pennsylvania Gazette, January 22, 1767

As the practice prevails in our Mother Country, I hope you will have no objections against inserting in your paper the observations that any gentleman may decently make concerning the actors in our little theatre here.

I do not rely wholly upon my own delicacy of judgment in the following remarks, for I have gathered and compared the sentiments of many others, who have had good opportunities of improving their taste of both plays and players. The practice of altering the author's expressions is so universally condemned by all men of sense, and leaves no excuse for the vanity or neglect of the actor; and I hope this little hint will be sufficient to guard our actors against anything of the like Nature for the future. For they ought to consider that one indecent, unguarded, ill judged expression, will do them inconceivable mischief in this country, and that no advantage can arise from taking such a liberty. But if they clearly avoid this rock, and are prudent in the choice of plays, the rational entertainment must, and will succeed, agreeable to the highest wishes of those who are concerned in it.

I am sorry Mr. Hallam, who is genteel in his person and actions, could not take copy from the inimitable Garrick, and speak plain English, whenever he assumes a character that may be supposed to understand the language. There is no necessity of destroying the least articulate beauty of language, through fury, eagerness, or passion. Miss Cheer never loses the sweetest accent, or faulters in the clearness of expression, from any or all those causes, though I believe she is equally delicate, and capable of feeling the force of passion.

I am not alone when I pronounce her one of the best players in the empire. She appears to me, from that ease of behavior which always shines through every action, to have been much among people of fashion, for she well fits the highest character she ever assumes.

I must beg leave to inform the public, that the pleasing *Love in a Village* is done here beyond expectation, and must give real delight to every person void of ill nature. . . . Miss Wainwright is a very good singer, and her action exceeds the famous Miss Brent. Mr. Hallam exceeds everything in the character of Hodge; and Mr. Woolls almost equals Beard in Hawthorn. Miss Hallam deserves universal applause and encouragement. I could wish to see the house better filled whenever this justly applauded entertainment is exhibited.

17   Nancy Hallam as Imogen Disguised as Fidele in *Cymbeline*, by Charles Willson Peale, 1771

Courtesy of Colonial Williamsburg Foundation; oil on canvas, 127 × 102.9 cm.

When Nancy Hallam (a cousin of Lewis Hallam the younger) appeared as Imogen in Shakespeare's *Cymbeline* at Annapolis in September 1770 she inspired an outpouring of enthusiasm. One admirer wrote: "She expected my utmost idea! Such delicacy of manner!

Such classic strictness of expression! The music of her tongue – the vox liquida, how melting!"[1] A poem in the same issue of the *Maryland Gazette* called on the "self-tutor'd Peale" to preserve for posterity "the nameless Grace that ev'ry Heart can charm." The painter obliged the following year with this exquisite portrait. Charles Collman Sellers, a descendant and biographer of Peale, has suggested that Peale may have painted scenery for the Douglass company while in Annapolis. He further suggests that the background in the portrait reflects that work.[2]

At the age of fifteen John Durang left Philadelphia to travel to Boston as an assistant to an itinerant performer whose repertoire he described as consisting of a "miscellaneous collection: transparencies, the magic lantern, sea fights in machinery, singing – all bad enough, but anything was thought great in those days." They "exhibited" for almost two months in Boston with Durang performing on "several instruments of music," dancing, and helping with the machinery. Not long after his return to his family in Philadelphia Durang's ability as a dancer came to the attention of Lewis Hallam. The following excerpts recount Durang's audition for Hallam and his subsequent debut at the John Street Theatre in New York.

[1] *Maryland Gazette,* September 1770.
[2] Charles C. Sellers, *Charles Wilson Peale* (New York: Scribners, 1969).

18   Excerpts from John Durang's *Memoir,* 1785

The Memoir of John Durang: American Actor, 1785–1816, ed. Alan S. Downer (Pittsburgh: University of Pittsburgh Press, 1966), pp. 17–24

Mr. Hallam wish'd me to rehearse my hornpipe in the morning on the stage, to get used to it – I expect a desire on his part to see a specimen of my talents. When I came on the stage, Mr. Hallam introduced me to Mr. and Mrs. Allen. The presence of them sitting in the front of the stage to see me rehearse robbed me of my best powers. A kind of fright seized me and weakened my better strength, which will always be the situation of a novice on his first examination, especially when before such sterling old actors. You dread the criticism of their judgment. Mr. Hallam played the "Collage Hornpipe" on the violin. I danced a few steps and made an apology, and hoped he would be satisfied, with my dancing at night. He encouraged me by assurance that he was already satisfied with the certainty that I would please. Mrs. Allen gave me a complete description of the suitable dress, with the advice to finish every step beating time. . . .

My dress was in the character of a sailor, a dark blue roundabout full of plated button, trousers made with 6 yards of fine linen, black satin small clothes underneath, white silk stockings, a light shoe with a handsome set buckle, a red waistcoat, a blue silk handkerchief; my hair curled and black, a small round hat gold laced with a blue ribband. . . .

With anxiety I waited the result of the night. The theatre on this occasion was crowded to see a fellow townsman make his first appearance on any stage. I had contrived a tramule behind the wing to enable me to gain the center of the stage in one spring. When the curtain rose, the cry was, "Sit down, hats off!" With the swiftness of Mercury I stood before them, with a general huzza, and danced in bursts of applause. When I went off the stage, I was encored. They made such a noise, throwing a bottle in orchestra, apple, etc. on the stage, at last the curtain was raised again and I danced a second time to the general satisfaction of the audience and managers, and gained my point. . . .

While I remained in New York, I applied my time in the practice of dancing and music. The violin and German flute were the chief instruments I made my study. I would sometimes divert myself with the octive, the flagelet, the French horn. I made an instrument of music called Pan's pipe made of reeds, which I learned to play so well on that I could play and dance at the same time. In the grand pageant of Shakespeare's Jubilee, I used to dance before the Comic Muse, playing on this pipe. The novelty had a pleasing effect. I applied much of my time in the study of the drama and vocal parts.

Mr. Hallam gave me some idea of the "Dwarf Dance," which by a little study I soon brought to perfection as I thought and introduced it to admiration, but I was convinced to the contrary when I repeated the dance in Philadelphia a year after. The body and the head of the Dwarf were tied above my hip, and the upper part of my body and head were covered by a colored petticoat gathered with my hands at the top of my head. In this concealed manner I would make my entrance. Dancing it one night I was deluded by the stage lights, which I took for the wing lights, my situation being almost blindfold. I made my exit over the spikes of the stage and orchestra. Three spikes entered my left thigh and calf, where I hung till Mr. Gibbon, our assistant tailor, extricated my leg from the spikes. I was in a swoon the whole time. I was set on my feet in the pit passage. I recovered from the swoon and did not feel my wounds but run round the theatre into the dressing room, when I only discovered I was hurt. I was laid up two months. This mischance convinced [me of] my error, which made me make the addition to change from the man Dwarf to a woman before I quit the stage; this improvement made the dance complete. The metamorphosis was from a man of 3 foot to a woman of 6 foot.

19   A Scene from *The Contrast*, 1790

Printed by subscription in 1790 with frontispiece drawn and engraved by William Dunlap;
line engraving, 12.4 × 7.9 cm.

This crude engraving from Royall Tyler's play is one of the most frequently reproduced of
early American theatrical scenes. We do not know whether Dunlap drew the characters
from life although it is tempting to assume that he did. Historian George C. D. Odell specu-
lated "if [Dunlap] had in mind the performers of the first cast then we have something
like portraits from left to right in the engraving of [John] Henry, Mrs. Morris, [Thomas]
Wignell, [Owen] Morris and Hallam [the younger]. One likes to think that the somewhat
interesting female figure does indeed suggest the dashing Mrs. Morris; certainly the figure
of Jonathan is like that of Wignell as Darby, and thereby supports the hope. And the
incredibly stiff Hallam to the right!"[1]

[1] George C. D. Odell, *Annals of the New York Stage* (New York: Columbia University Press, 1927), I: 256.

20   Thomas Wignell as Darby, 1789

William Dunlap, del., & fec. (New York, 1789); etching, 12.5 × 9.2 cm. Department of Prints, Museum of Fine Arts, Boston

Wignell arrived in America to join the company of actors led by his cousin Lewis Hallam the younger in 1774. Shortly after that the company left for Jamaica where most of its members remained until the end of the Revolutionary War. It was not until the company's

return to New York in 1785 that Wignell's popularity with American audiences was established. He achieved acclaim in the role of Darby, an irrepressible Irish soldier, in O'Keefe's *The Poor Soldier* (1785). George Washington particularly admired Wignell and attended the first performance of Dunlap's pastiche *Darby's Return* in New York on November 24, 1789. In 1792 Wignell founded his own theatre in Philadelphia where through his vigorous recruiting of new actors from London his company soon surpassed his New York rivals.

The portrait, drawn and etched by the multi-talented Dunlap, is thought to be the earliest American *etched* portrait. It is also America's first known *printed* portrait of an actor in a role.

The popular tragedy *Gustavus Vasa* by Henry Brooke was chosen for the premiere of the Federal Street Theatre in Boston in 1794. The building, designed by architect Charles Bulfinch, was opened in February 1794 under the management of Charles Stuart Powell. A reporter recorded his impressions of the company.

21   Review of *Gustavus Vasa*, 1794

Boston *Columbian Centinnel*, February 5, 1794

Mr. Baker, in Gustavus, was all that could be expected from that animated and arduous character. His powers of elocution must have been extensive, to support so important a part. The unconquerable agitation of the mind, at the opening of a new scene, in a new hemisphere, must have operated powerfully on the most experienced and veteran performer. And it is to this alone it can be attributed that a prompter was once necessary to this gentleman. We mention this circumstance the more readily, as he nevertheless, met universal approbation. Of Mr. Powell, who supported the character of Christein, we need only say, that his performance added greatly to his former celebrity. At his entre, in the Prologue, he met a most cordial welcome from the audience, and his susceptibility on the occasion, did honor to his heart. His brother, Mr. S. Powell, in the character of Arvida, true to nature, and happy in the recollection of his part, made a deep and favorable impression . . . In Trollio, Mr. Jones, as such, had not an opportunity to display the powers of which he is possessor; he nevertheless looked the rosy-cheek Prelate, anathematized like a despotic churchman, and as the honest Hibernian said, "acted death to the life." Mr. Nelson, in Anderson was spirited and correct; and though we cannot enter into a detail of the subordinate male characters, we can say, the public opinion has pronounced that much was to be applauded, and but little to be censured. Everything that the poet conceived in the character of Christina, was performed by Miss Harrison. It may be said, without adulation, that in this character, (and in this alone have we seen her) "majestic was her form – her every action dignity and grace." And we can say of Mrs. Jones, in Mariana, that her part could not have been better filled. As the mother of Gustavus, in the tender scene, Mrs. Baker's dignity of character, propriety of action, and maternal tenderness, at once charmed and affected. It needed not the heart of sensibility to be touched with the melting powers of her pathos; for many a manly eye, enraptured gazed, "unconscious of the tear, which trickled down the cheek." Nor were the tender plaints of her "little lamb" Cordelia, without their merited effect.

Of the performance of the truly humorous afterpiece, *Modern Antiques: or, the Merry Mourners*, we cannot say too much. The bursts of applause which shook every part of the house, are the best panegyric of its merit, and the merits of the performers. Mr. Jones in Cockletop, appeared the genuine son of the sock, and Mr. Baker, in Joey, made the muscles of every face, vibrate in unison with his own. . . . In Frank, Mr. S. Powell displayed the genteel comedian to great advantage. Mrs. Collins, appears to possess the naivete of a lively actress, and when Miss Baker (whom we have not mentioned before) as Mrs. Cockletop, was discovered at her toilette, a smile of general complacence was diffused on the cheeks of the audience. The graces of an elegant person, and the beautiful suavity of her features, afforded the eye of taste a luxurious banquet. . . . It is deeply to be regretted, that the amiable modesty of the woman, proved a barrier to the fine accomplishments of the actress.

> We saw her charming, but we saw not all,
> The charms her downcast modesty conceal'd.

We ought to make mention of some others of the performers; but as the parts alloted them, have not as yet been conspicuous, we hope to have an opportunity, in the course of the season, to be the herald of their merit. We shall endeavor to be just.

A letter signed "Philo Theatricus" analyzed the relative merits of the actors and actresses announced for the season and those who had left the company. Unfortunately the critic does not share with his readers the method upon which his point system is based.

22   "Philo Theatricus" on Acting, 1796

Philadelphia *Gazette of the United States,* December 16, 1796

Considering theatrical exhibition, when conducted with an earnest desire to please those, who support the theatre, by frequent attendance, as the only rational entertainment the citizens, in Philadelphia, can possibly partake of in public. After the laborious hours of business, the theatre presents itself, to smooth the varied scenes of life, to see Nature portrayed or "catch the manners living as they rise" either in the exhilarating smiles of comedy, or the impressive scenes of the tragic muse, these form "a consummation devoutly to be wished," by every admirer of the Drama.

I well remember to two seasons past, the performances have been much approved of, the performers received that indulgence and almost unbounded encouragement their respective merits entitled them to: and, at the close of each season the managers thanked the public, for their "very generous and liberal support." How then can these very managers now come forth, and affect, the very contrary to be the fact? It was then true, or if not their acknowledgments must be considered only as satirical eulogiums on a parsimonious public whom they seem inclined to force into any measure they may please to adopt.

Mr. Wignell has gratified the Philadelphians in bringing Mrs. Merry to America. Such exquisite performances as hers, must convince, even the most prejudiced that the stage can, and ought to portray nature in all the beauties of expression and action. In these Mrs. Merry answers our most sanguine expectations. Were there such helps to her as her abilities deserve and demand, the New Theatre would fully compensate the managers (even at the advanced price of admission) for their labors. Excepting this paragon, this excellent theatrical star, the present company is much inferior in numbers and abilities to any former season. How then, can the public expect to have that entertainment generally they have been used to? If we may judge from a comparative scale of the abilities of those perform-ers who have left the theatre . . . and those newly engaged, it plainly appears, the public are not benefited. I have arranged the merits, upon a ratio, making fifteen equal to the highest perfection, upon a general line of acting, of those absent, and of those engaged to supply their position; leaving the generality of the company to their own merits, several of whom are really respectable.

Performers absent			New performers		
Mrs.	Whitlock	13	Mrs.	Merry	15
	Shaw	10		Mechtler	4
	Marshall	7	Miss	L'Estrange	4
	Cleveland	5	Mrs.	L'Estrange	3
	Green	4			
	Rowson	3			
Miss	Broadhurst	10			
Mr.	Fennel	13	Mr.	Cooper	11
	Bates	12		Warren	9
	Chalmers	12		Fox	6
	Whitlock	11		L'Estrange	4
	Marshall	7			
	Cleveland	6			
	Green	5			
		119			56

From this it appears that the former companies were much superior in numbers and abilities, to the present arrangement. I have omitted several performers belonging now and formerly to the same theatre, whose performances merit, on the same scale, viz. Mr. Moreton, 13, and who undoubtedly is the only chaste male actor on the New Theatre stage. Mr. Wignell, 10, and Mr. Harwood (whom the public are happy to recognize once again), 13. Mr. Francis, 9. Mrs. Oldmixon, 14. Mrs. Morris, 8. Mrs. Warrell, 6.

The above system of merits, are more from public than private opinion; and the general receipts of the theatre will speak most feelingly to . . . the managers, and subscribers, whether the advantage this season, will be more favorable than any former one.

PHILO THEATRICUS

William Wood is described by Odell as "the first American actor to gain high distinction in an American playhouse."[1] After ten years in which he established himself as popular comedian Wood joined William Warren in the management of the Chestnut Street Theatre in Philadelphia. Wood characterized his own life in the theatre in *Personal Recollections of the Stage*, published a few years before his death, as having been passed in "unintermitted devotion to the business of actor and manager." This memoir provides vivid accounts of the actors and actresses of the late eighteenth and early nineteenth centuries. Although written as much as fifty years after the actual events described Wood's recollections were aided by letters and journal entries from the time. He noted with some regret in his introduction that "these documents will detract from the rigid unity of a narrative; but as contemporary records they will perhaps present a more animated and truthful view than would be given by a more labored effort prepared at this later day."

The following excerpt describes Wood's debut in 1798. Having decided upon a career on the stage, the nineteen-year-old Wood sought out his father's friend, the comedian and manager Thomas Wignell. Wignell and his company were then playing in Annapolis for a short season. Wood's criticism of the different actors' costumes in *Every One Has His Fault* alludes to the fact that it was customary at that time for each actor to supply his own stage wardrobe.

[1] Odell, *Annals of the New York Stage*, II: 349.

23   William Wood's Description of His Debut, 1798

Wood, *Personal Recollections*, pp. 45–58

Monday. – You cannot imagine the embarrassment I felt in making known my wishes to my father's old friend, Wignell; notwithstanding his intimacy in our family, and a complimentary allusion to my having received a prize or two at school for elocution, a matter it seems he remembered better than I did at the moment. He has appointed me an interview in the morning. After this visit to him, in his room behind the scenes, I hurried to the front. The play was *Every One has his Fault*, and the cast, with one or two exceptions, good, but the ill-dressing of the old John Street company never equalled the absurd variety exhibited on this occasion. Lord Norland was well enough in a court suit; Morris looked like the wearer of the first cut of coat and vest, when the earliest approach to modern dress was attempted. Mr. Placide walked about the streets in a black silk stockinet, full suit, trimmed and sparkling with black bugles. Captain Irwin looked like the latest edition of a modern disbanded officer, as he should. Warren as Harmony, was properly equipped, while the servants revelled in every age and variety of livery. The ladies were appropriately habited, as was the boy Edward, delightfully acted by Mrs. Marshall. Few who have witnessed her performance of this character, can have forgotten it. Bernard (the worst dresser on this stage) was as usual in the rearward of fashion at least half a century, but acted Sir Robert so well that his dress was wholly overlooked, or pardoned.

Tuesday. – The awful meeting is over. Mr. Wignell began with such a grave look, that my heart sunk within me. He requested me to recite some few passages he named, and was silent as to the execution. He doubtless perceived my extreme terror and embarrassment. So extreme indeed was it, that I feel entirely certain that no public effort can be more dreadful, than is this trial before a friend. After some occasional remarks, evidently made to give me time for rallying a little, he requested a further essay. I recited again and much better (at least not so execrably), as he said and I felt. When I had finished, he took my hand in his, and with an expression of his fine face that baffled all my efforts to explain, said very calmly, 'My dear boy, I much fear your friends at home will not be pleased with this experiment of yours. However, I well know the impetuosity of young folks in regard to our profession, and am glad you applied to me rather than to a stranger. You shall have an opportunity of trying your ability here at once, in this place, although you will have to face as intelligent an audience for its number, as can be found in America. The best discrimination and judgment will doubtless be tempered with a proportionate indulgence and kindness; for I have ever remarked the most fastidious and severe judges to be the vulgar and uneducated. To one condition you must bind yourself, should I consider your attempt hopelessly bad – you must return to your friends, and give up all thoughts of the stage.' I made him this promise and will keep it. He has given me a list of ten or twelve characters to choose from, not one of which I like, but dare not say so, for I am fully assured he is anxious for my success. After some pause, I decided on George Barnwell. One or two that I preferred, he discouraged at once, frankly giving as his reason, that Moreton had been very happy in them, and that a comparison could not fail to be injurious, if not fatal to me. I have seen Moreton often, and feel too painfully the truth and judgment of Mr. Wignell.

Friday. – The rehearsals are over, and (shall I call it?) the performance is past. The first was perhaps as distressing nearly as the latter, although the performers all seemed kind and desirous to aid me. No one among them, surely could be so humble as to fear any rivalry from me.

"Before I go to rest, let me endeavor to recall the events and feelings of this night, on which so much of the happiness or misery of future years may depend. A large and elegant assemblage greeted my appearance, and nearly deprived me of all power to proceed. I feel that my deportment must have been deplorable; and even the few speeches, on which, from my rehearsal, I had built some slight hopes, were given either with a pitiable feebleness, or a scarcely less pitiable attempt at character, which my agitation utterly deprive me of the power to execute. Mr. Wignell is affectionate, but alarms me by his silence. Mr. and Mrs. Merry have been kind and encouraging, pointing out some of my most prominent faults, while they promise me future counsel. This 'future' seems to say they do not consider it quite a lost cause. I feel most sensibly the difficulties and dangers of my attempt. If the liberal forbearance and indulgent kindness of these generous Marylanders have scarcely enabled me to proceed through my first effort, what will be my terror and insufficiency when brought to face elsewhere a larger audience, wholly uninfluenced by the kind feelings which my youth and favorable private introduction have procured for me here?"

John Howard Payne was a prolific playwright and is still remembered for his lyrics to "Home, Sweet Home." He had been fascinated with the stage from an early age. His initial theatrical aspirations, however, were as an actor. He made his acting debut on the American stage, at the age of nineteen, in a conscious imitation of the popular English child actor, Master Betty (William Henry West Betty). Payne enjoyed a success similar to Master Betty's in the roles of Hamlet, Young Norval in John Home's *Douglas*, and Rolla in Sheridan's *Pizarro*. Despite his early success he could not sustain the competition with more skillful performers such as Thomas Abthorpe Cooper. He eventually gave up acting and went to London where he spent almost twenty years as a playwright. Wood witnessed some of Payne's first performances and recalled their extraordinary effect.

24   **William Wood on John Howard Payne, 1855**

Wood, *Personal Recollections*, pp. 127–28

On my return to the United States, in October 1809, I found Master Payne in the full tide of popular favor at Baltimore, where the enthusiasm for his acting was perhaps more intense than in another city. I speak particularly of his first engagement, for such a furor could not be expected to last. He appeared as Young Norval, Hamlet, Romeo, Tancred, Octavian, Frederic, Rolla, Achmet, and Zaphna, to large and brilliant audiences. His benefit proved a crowning triumph. On this memorable night, the receipts touched the extraordinary amount of $1160. It must here be remarked that the house when filled at other times to its utmost capacity, had never yet produced $800. Where then, it may be asked, did we contrive to stow away $1160? This is the answer. Great numbers of tickets were paid for at high prices, and without the intention of being used. One gentleman I know gave his check of $50 for a single ticket, besides paying liberally for the box occupied by his family. Many others paid sums varying from five to twenty dollars for single tickets, and the large gallery was filled with box tickets, failing to obtain seats below. Some very ridiculous circumstances attended Master Payne's performances, where, from his child-like figure, a physical absurdity could not fail to strike an unsophisticated auditor. A learned judge who, when crowded out of the boxes by the ladies, sought refuge in the gallery, related the following: Master Payne was enacting Rolla [in Sheridan's *Pizarro*] while a knot of youngsters were sitting together, some of whom were not particularly interested in what was going on before them. When they were coming to the scene in which Rolla seizes the child of Cora (who in Master Payne's instance happened to be nearly as large as Payne himself) and runs across the bridge with him (a very effective scene where the Rolla is a large and powerful man), one of these youngsters called his companions to order, and as an inducement to them to leave their talking, urges; "Now, boys! look out, and presently you will see one of those little fellows shoulder the other, and run away with him over that plank," pointing to the bridge.

George Frederick Cooke was the first actor of real distinction to come to America. His appearances were greeted with tremendous excitement. Despite his erratic behavior and frequent bouts of inebriation and temperament, his performances drew record-breaking audiences. His first performance in New York on November 12, 1810, in the character of Richard III, was enthusiastically reviewed.

25   Review of George Frederick Cooke, 1810

Columbian, November 23, 1810

Mr. Cooke's style of acting is vivid, original, and impressive. It is the product of genius, improved and exalted by taste and study. His excellence is altogether from the resources of his own capacious mind. Nature has been by no means lavish in her bounties to the person or voice of this eminent tragedian. His figure is neither majestic nor symmetrically proportioned. His voice, though not deficient in compass, is neither mellow nor varied. His gesticulation is more expressive than elegant. His gait is less distinguished for grace than ease and freedom; and it may be greatly questioned whether his stage-walk is always compatible with the dignity of a hero. In what then, it may be asked, does the wonderful superiority of Cooke consist? We answer, in the force and comprehension of his genius, the boldness and originality of his manner, the significance of his gestures, the astonishing flexibility of his countenance, and the quick and piercing expression of his eye, united to the thorough knowledge, not only of the text, but the meaning of his author. Mr. Cooke, in Richard, differs not more widely from than he surpasses, every other representative of the part. . . . In all the diversified humors of the crook-backed tyrant, whether his duplicity is employed in wooing the affections of the fickle Anne, whether his daring ambition is crowned with success or thwarted by opposing accidents, where his cool malignant sarcasms are thrown out at the court-flies that surround him or his perturbed spirit wanders in a world of terrible shadows, he uniformly appears through every change and variety of scene impregnated with the genius of his author, always impressive, and always, Richard.

. . . In his first interview with Lady Anne, the deep dissembling cunning of Richard assumed an air of such perfect sincerity, that it might have deceived a mind less weak and trusting than the one whose credulity he so successfully played upon. In the same scene, where the mock-penitent tyrant demands his death from Anne, Mr. C. contrived to throw in the part a wonderful degree of force and expression. When he exclaims,

> Nay, do not pause, for I did kill King Henry,
> But 'twas thy heavenly face that set me on,
> Nay, now dispatch, 'twas I that stabb'd young Edward –

his instantaneous transition from the former to the latter part of each sentence, and his accompanying expressions of ardent attachment, displayed a mind deeply read in the language of genuine passion. The cool and settled malignity of Richard's heart in the sentence

> I can smile, and smile, and murder while I smile,

was uttered by Mr. Cooke with admirable effect. . . . His affected piety and humility before the lord mayor, and his seeming unwillingness to accept the crown, were finely portrayed. Throughout this scene he not only evidenced the deep cunning of a practiced villain, but the archness of a fiend. His burst of triumphant exultation at the success of his schemes, the energy of his manner in grasping the hand of Buckingham, and the vehemence with which he threw the prayer book from him, at the departure of the lord mayor, were highly expressive of the swelling ambition of the proud and aspiring Gloster. Mid the noise and bustle that preceded the battle, there was nothing so preeminently conspicuous as the cool, collected, and thoughtful manner of Richard. His manner of bidding good night to the lords Surrey and Norfolk, was truly inimitable. . . . Mr. Cooke was by no means as successful in the 5th as in the preceding acts. His exclamation on starting from his couch,

> Give me another horse – bind up my wounds!
> Have mercy Jesu!

were not sufficiently descriptive of the wildness and disorder which at that moment, haunted the guilty soul of Richard. In this and the following passage, where he exclaims, "a thousand hearts are swelling in my breast," there was less force and vehemence in his manner, than we have been accustomed to witness in the Richard of Cooper, and less, we think, than the character demanded. Upon the whole, however, Mr. Cooke is unquestionably the best representative of the part that has ever appeared on the American boards. It is a character which he has so profoundly studied, so happily conceived, and so masterly delineated, that perhaps taking it all in all, we shall never witness a performance so replete with beauties, so finished and so faultless.

Cooke's performances had an enormous impact on the American theatre and for a while he became the standard by which other actors were judged. John Bernard, who observed many of America's best actors, later offered these observations on John Hodgkinson, Thomas Wignell, and Thomas Cooper.

26   John Bernard on American Actors, 1887

John Bernard, *Retrospections of America, 1797–1811, from the manuscript by Mrs. Bayle Bernard*, ed. Laurence Hutton and Brander Matthews (New York: Harper & Brothers, 1887), pp. 256–58, 267–68

When I associate this actor [John Hodgkinson] with Garrick and Henderson (the first of whom I had often seen, and the latter played with) I afford some ground for thinking he possessed no common claims. I do not hesitate to say, that had he enjoyed their good fortune – the inspiration and discipline of a refined London public – he would have risen to the rank of their undoubted successor. What was his distinction? That which peculiarity stamped them – that union of a sympathetic and an imitative faculty, which, whether of humor or pathos, can draw all the forms and give all the colorings of character. Nature being full of rule, being a law as it were in action, is of course a great classifier, a worker on models, fond of species and types, and thus the old man and the young, the hero and the rogue of tragedy and comedy, being distinct types or models, actors usually come into the world with their own special aptitude; whenever, therefore, nature departs from her scheme, and forms a mind in which merges the most opposite perceptions, as colors that meet, and yet shine in a rainbow, she is evidently in one of her wonder-working moods, fantastical or wearied with her uniform labors.

Hodgkinson was a wonder. In the whole range of the living drama there was no variety of character he could not perceive and embody, from a Richard or a Hamlet down to a Shelty or a Sharp. To the abundant mind of Shakespeare his own turned as a moon that could catch and reflect a large amount of its radiance; and if, like his great precursors, it seemed to have less of the poetic element than of the riches of humor, this was owing to association, which, in the midst of his tragic passions, would intrude other images. An exclusive tragedian will always seem greater by virtue of his specialty, by the singleness of impressions which are simply poetic; while Hodgkinson had one gift that enlarged his variety beyond all competition – he was also a singer, and could charm you in a burletta, after thrilling you in a play; so that through every form of drama he was qualified to pass, and it might be said he "exhausted worlds" if he could not "invent new." I doubt if such a number and such greatness of requisites were ever before united in one mortal man. Nor were his physical powers inferior to his mental; he was tall and well-proportioned, though inclining to be corpulent, with a face of great mobility, that showed the minutest change of feeling, while his voice, full and flexible, could only be likened to an instrument that his passions played upon at pleasure.

Such was this great actor, who, dying in the prime of life of a prevailing epidemic, was prevented from reaching that distinction which must have worthily connected his memory with the drama of his country. It would be gratifying, of course, if I could enlarge as much upon the man; but his early life had been unfortunate; he had never known a due restraint, and, as he rose to fame, he attracted friends who were more willing to share his errors than to pity or condemn them; but it is right I should add that, though wholly self-educated, he had attained to taste and manners, and even evinced some skill in literature, by the production of a comedy.

[Thomas Wignell] was an excellent fellow, whose abundance of heart was unluckily accompanied by a deficiency of head, that kept him always in difficulties. . . . In a professional light he had but moderate claims. He had variety as an actor, but with limited power. He had enjoyed the good-fortune of being the first general comedian who had crossed the Atlantic; and by the side of the stiff humor of his friends, Henry and Hallam, both of whom belonged to the old school of London, he had certainly shone as a spirited actor.

[Thomas] Cooper, . . . who, after Hodgkinson's death, became our ruling tragedian, had also his distinctions. The son of an Irish surgeon, he had been educated chiefly under the care of Mr. Godwin, and so derived that independence which marked him through life. Endowed with great genius, and the highest qualifications in face, voice, and person, he had little or no art, which he never strove to acquire, being content to cover its want by his impulse and freshness. Thus, as he grew older, he failed to improve, while his luxurious habits abated his force, and left but gleams of the fire which, at first, was continuous. His history is significant. Appearing as Hamlet, at Covent Garden, when scarcely turned twenty, he produced the most signal impression, even in the face of John Kemble. But, instead of remaining, and winning his way upward by study and art, he thought America a field which he could seize without effort, and there found he had to grapple with the successor of Henderson. Thus rendered more careless, he failed in 1803, when he sought a second time to win the verdict of London; though, on returning to America, he became its great favorite, until the arrival of Cooke, whose light, though it was setting, extinguished all others. Still, with all his defects, I look back to his youth as displaying a power which I can only rank second the greatest I have seen. I still think his Macbeth was only inferior to Garrick's, and his Hamlet to Kemble's; while his Othello, I think, was equal to Barry's itself.

III. Buildings and Technical Production

Theatrical architecture as well as scenic practice was based on English models in Colonial America. Many of the records have been lost, but we do have intriguing evidence of what the theatres looked like and how the productions were mounted. The following documents illustrate both the physical nature of the theatres and conventions of technical production. Philip Schuyler was in New York at the time of the Hallam company's first performances in 1753 and his brief account in a letter to a friend in Albany is the only known report of the company's first theatre in New York.

27 Philip Schuyler Letter about Hallam Company, 1753

Benson J. Lossing, *The Life and Times of Philip Schuyler* (New York: Mason Brothers, [1860]), pp. 68–70

September 21, 1753

The schooner arrived at Ten Eyck's wharf on Wednesday, at one o'clock, and the same evening I went to the play with Phil. You know I told you before I left home that if the players should be here I should see Phil's sweetheart went with us. She is a handsome brunette from a good understanding. Phil and I went to see the grand battery in the afternoon, and to pay my respects to the governor, whose lady spent a week with us last spring. We bought our play tickets for eight shillings apiece, at Parker and Weyman's printing-office, in Beaver Street, on our return. We had tea at five o'clock, and before sundown we were in the theatre, for the players commenced at six. The room was quite full already. Among the company was your cousin Tom and Kitty Livingston, and also Jack Watts, Sir Peter Warren's brother-in-law. I would like to tell you all about the play, but I can't now, for Billy must take this to the wharf for Captain Wynkoop in half an hour. He sails this afternoon.

A large green curtain hung before the players until they were ready to begin, when, on the blast of a whistle, it was raised, and some of them appeared and commenced acting. The play was called *The Conscious Lovers*, written, you know, by Sir Richard Steele, Addison's help in writing the *Spectator*. Hallam, and his wife and sister, all performed and a sprightly young man named Hulett played the violin and danced merrily. But I said I could not tell you about the play, so I will forbear, only adding that I was no better pleased than I should have been at the club, where, last year, I went with cousin Stephen, and heard many wise sayings which I hope profited me something.

Amateur theatricals presented by the military were seldom documented in the newspapers at this time. From 1756 to 1763, the time of the French and Indian War, there were large numbers of British troops stationed in New York City and elsewhere in the colonies. The indefatigable Odell researched in vain for evidence of their activities. That such activities did indeed occur is inferred by references found in diaries and accounts from other cities as well as from a fictional account in James Fenimore Cooper's novel *Satanstoe; or, the Little page Manuscripts. A Tale of the Colony*, set in New York in 1757.

The excerpt is of interest particularly for the description of the fashionable audience and for its glimpse inside the theatre building. Odell refers to this episode in Cooper's novel as "corroborative testimony" to his supposition of the popularity of military theatricals, but notes the unlikelihood of a double bill comprising two full-length pieces such as *Cato* and *The Beaux' Stratagem*. He identifies the theatre Cooper describes as the playhouse opened by David Douglass on Cruger's Wharf in December 1758.[1]

---

[1] Odell, *Annals of the New York Stage*, I:105–6.

28   Excerpt from *Satanstoe*, 1845

[James Fenimore Cooper], *Satanstoe; or, the Littlepage Manuscripts. A Tale of the Colony* (New York: Burgess, Stringer & Co., 1845), I:114–20

Instead of going directly down Crown Street, into Maiden Lane, which would have been the nearest way to the theatre, we went out into Broadway, and round by Wall Street, the walking being better, and the gutters farther from the ladies; the center of the street being at no great distance from the houses, in the narrower passages of the town. We found a great many well-dressed people moving in the same direction with ourselves. Herman Mordaunt remarked that he had never before seen so many hoops, cardinals, cocked hats and swords in the streets, at once, as he saw that evening. All the carriages in town rolled past us as we went down Wall Street, and by the time we reached William Street, the pavements resembled a procession, more than anything else. As every one was in full dress, the effect was pleasing, and the evening being fine, most of the gentlemen carried their hats in their hands, in order not to disturb their curls, thus giving to the whole the air of a sort of vast drawing-room. . . .

At length we reached the theatre, and were permitted to enter. All the front seats were occupied by blacks, principally in New York liveries; that is to say, with cuffs, collars, and pocket-flaps of a cloth different from the coat, though a few were in lace. These last belonged to the topping families, several of which gave colors and ornaments almost as rich as those that I understand are constantly given at home. I well remember that two entire boxes were retained by servants, in shoulder-knots, and much richer dresses than common, one of whom belonged to the Lt. Governor, and the other to my Lord Loudon, who was then Commander-in-Chief. As the company entered, these domestics disappeared, as is usual, and we all took our seats on the benches thus retained for us. . . .

Great was the curiosity, and deep the feeling, that prevailed, among the younger portion of the audience in particular, as party after party was seated, that important evening. The house was ornamented as a theatre, and I thought it vast in extent; though Herman Mordaunt assured me it was no great thing, in that point of view, as compared with most of the playhouses at home. But the ornaments, and the lights, and the curtain, the pit, the boxes, the gallery, were all so many objects of intense interest. Few of us said anything; but our eyes wandered over all with a species of delight, that I am certain can be felt in a theatre only once. Anneke's sweet face was a picture of youthful expectation; an expectation, however, in which intelligence and discretion had their full share. The orchestra was said to a have an undue portion of wind instruments in it; though I perceived ladies all over the house, including those in our own box, returning the bows of many of the musicians, who, I was told, were amateurs from the army and the drawing-rooms of the town.

At length the Commander-in-Chief and the Lt. Governor entered together, occupying the same box, though two had been provided, their attendants having recourse to the second. The commotion produced by these arrivals had hardly subsided, when the curtain arose, and a new world was presented to our view! Of the playing, I shall not venture to say much; though to me it seemed perfection. Bulstrode gained great applause that night; and I understand that divers gentlemen, who had declared that his Cato would have done credit to either of the royal theatres. His dress appeared to me to be everything it should be; though I cannot describe it. I remember that Syphax wore the uniform of a colonel of dragoons, and Juba, that of a general officer; and that there was a good deal of criticism expended, and some offense taken, because the gentlemen who played these parts came out in wool, and with their faces blacked. It was said, in answer to these feelings, that the characters were Africans; and that any one might see, by casting his eyes at the gallery, that Africans are usually black, and that they have woolly hair; a sort of proof that, I imagine, only aggravated the offense.[1]

[1] In England, Othello is usually played as black, while in America he is played as a nondescript; or of no color that is ordinarily seen. It is not clear that England is nearer right than America, however; the Moor not being a negro, any more than he is of the color of a dried herring.

Apart from this little mistake, everything went off well, even to Harris's Marcia. It is true, that some evil-inclined persons whispered that the "virtuous Marcia" was a little how-came-you-so; but Bulstrode afterwards assured me that his condition helped him along amazingly, and that it added a liquid lustre to his eyes, that might otherwise have been wanting. The high-heeled shoes appeared to trouble him; but some persons fancied it gave him a pretty tottering in his walk, that added very much to the deception. On the whole, the piece went off surprisingly, as I could see by Lord Loudon and the Lt. Governor, both of whom seemed infinitely diverted. Herman Mordaunt smiled once or twice, when he ought to have looked grave; but this I ascribed to a want of practice, of later years, in scenic representations. He certainly was a man of judgment, and must have known the proper moments to exhibit particular emotions. . . .

The Beaux Stratagem . . . commenced, and Bulstrode was again seen in the character of Scrub. Those who were most familiar with the stage, pronounced his playing to be excellent – far better in the footman than in the Roman Senator. The play itself struck me as being as broad and coarse as could be tolerated; but as it had a reputation at home, where it had a great name, our matrons did not dare to object to it. I was glad to see the smiles soon disappear from Anneke's face, however, and to discover that she found no pleasure in scenes so unsuited to her sex and years. The short, quick glances that were exchanged between Anneke and Mary Wallace, did not escape me, and the manner in which they both rose, as soon as the curtain dropped, told quite plainly the haste they were in to quit the theatre. I reached their box-door in time to assist them through the crowd.

The American Company's last season of performances before the outbreak of the Revolutionary War (1773–74) has been called by historians the most brilliant dramatic season of Colonial America. It is probably not a coincidence that this season took place in Charleston, where the social climate had always been hospitable to the actors. A new theatre had been built for the company under Douglass' supervision and was opened on December 22, 1773.

29   Review of American Company, 1773

Rivington's New York Gazette, December [27?], 1773

On Wednesday last, the new theatre in this town was opened with Mr. Kelly's *Word to the Wise* and *High Life Below Stairs*, with an occasional prologue and epilogue spoken by Mr. Hallam and Mr. Douglass.

The performance gave universal satisfaction. Mr. Hallam in particular, in Captain Dormer, displayed his extraordinary theatrical talents in a most splendid manner. Indeed, all the performers did great justice to their characters, but that gentleman's superior abilities were so remarkably striking that we could not pass them over unnoticed. The house is elegantly finished, and supposed, for the size, to be the most commodious on the continent. The scenes, which are new and well designed, the dresses, the music, and, what had a very pleasing effect, the disposition of the lights – all contributed to the satisfaction of the audience, who expressed the highest approbation of their entertainment.

Before the conclusion of the Revolutionary War, Alexander Quesnay attempted to give a season of performances in the Southwark Theatre in Philadelphia. Possibly he expected that the patronage of General Washington and other dignitaries would force the local authorities to overlook his defiance of the Continental Congress' injunction against "exhibition of shows, plays, and other expensive diversions and entertainments." The following describes the theatrical "spectacle."

30   Theatre Spectacle, 1782

Freeman's Journal, or, the North American Intelligencer, January 9, 1782

On Wednesday evening . . . . , Alexander Quesnay Esq. exhibited a most elegant entertainment at the playhouse, where were present his excellency General Washington, the minister of France, the president of the state, a number of officers of the army, and a brilliant assemblage of ladies and gentlemen of the city, who were invited.

After a prologue, suitable to the occasion, *Eugenie* an elegant French comedy was first presented (written by the celebrated M. Beaumarchais) and in the opinion of several good judges was extremely well acted by the young gentlemen, students in that polite language. After the comedy was acted the *Lying Valet*, a farce, to this succeeded several curious dances, followed by a brilliant illumination, consisting of thirteen pyramidal pillars, representing the thirteen states – on the middle column was seen a Cupid, supporting a laurel crown over the motto – WASHINGTON – *the pride of this country and terror of Britain.*

On the summit was the word – Virginia – on the right – Connecticut, with the names GREENE and la FAYETTE – on the left – the word Pennsylvania, with the names WAYNE and STUBEN: and so on according to the birthplace, and state proper to each general. The spectacle ended with an artificial illumination on the thirteen columns.[1]

---

[1] A letter to the editor of the *Freeman's Journal* published the following week indicates that the illustrious audience was insufficient to keep Quesnay from being warned that further performances would not be tolerated. No further record of his performing in Philadelphia appears for that year.

A letter addressed to the Managers of the Theatre by an anonymous critic provides some interesting comments on the deficiencies of the scenery at the John Street Theatre.

31   Description of Scenery at John Street Theatre, 1787

New York Daily Advertiser, April 4, 1787

. . . Tho' we do not look for a theatre here conducted in so regular a manner as those in Europe, or the decorations so expensive and elegant, yet a proper respect to the audience, and decent and proper scenery, is an ought to be expected. . . . Surely the scenes should have as much the appearance of nature as possible; which those we generally behold at the theatre have not. For frequently where the author intended a handsome street or a beautiful landscape, we only see a dirty piece of canvas; what else can we call a sense in which the colors are defaced and obliterated? Nor is it uncommon to see the back of the stage represent a street, while the side scenes represent a wood, as if two of the most opposite appearances must be put together to cause a natural effect. – The musicians too instead of performing between the play and the farce, are suffered to leave the orchestra to pay a visit to the tippling houses, and the ladies in the meantime, must amuse themselves by looking at the candles and empty benches.

Little is known of the appearance of the John Street Theatre beyond Jonathan's [famous description] and Dunlap's note that it "was about 60 feet back from the street, having a covered way of rough wooden material from the pavement to the doors."[1]

[1] Dunlap, *History of the American Theatre,* I:51.

32   Excerpt from *The Contrast,* 1787

[Royall Tyler], *The Contrast,* a comedy in five acts written by a citizen of the United States; performed with applause at the theatres in New-York, Philadelphia, and Maryland and published (under an assignment of the copy-right) by Thomas Wignell (Philadelphia, 1790)

JONATHAN: As I was going about here and there, to and again, to find it, I saw a great crowd of folks going into a long entry that had lantherns over the door; so I asked a man whether that was not the place where they played hocus pocus? He was a very civil, kind man, though he did speak like the Hessians; he lifted up his eyes and said, "They play hocus pocus tricks enough there, Got knows, mine friend." . . .

So I went right in, and they shewed me away, clean up to the garret, just like meeting-house gallery. And so I saw a power of topping folks, all sitting round in little cabbins, "just like father's corn-cribs";

and then there was such a squeaking with the fiddles, and such a tarnal blaze with the lights, my head was near turned. At last the people that sat near me set up such a hissing – hiss – like so many mad cats; and then they thump, thump, thump, just like our Peleg threshing wheat, and stampt away, just like the nation; and called out for one Mr. Langolee, – I suppose he helps act the tricks. . . .

Gor, I – I liked the fun, and so I thumpt away, and hiss'd as lustily as the best of 'em. One sailor-looking man that sat by me, seeing me stamp, and knowing I was a cute fellow, because I could make a roaring noise, clapt me on the shoulder and said, "You are a d——d hearty cock, smite my timbers!" I told him so I was, but I thought he need not swear so, and make use of such naughty words.

JESSAMY: The savage! – Well, and did you see the man with his tricks?

JONATHAN: Why, I vow, as I was looking out for him, they lifted up a great green cloth and let us look right into the next neighbour's house. Have you a good many houses in New-York made so in that 'ere way?

JENNY: Not many; but did you see the family?

JONATHAN: Yes, swamp it; I see'd the family.

JENNY: Well, and how did you like them?

JONATHAN: Why, I vow they were pretty much like other families; – there was a poor, good-natured, curse of a husband, and a sad rantipole of a wife. . . .

There was one youngster; they called Mr. Joseph; he talked as sober and as pious as a minister; but, like some ministers that I know, he was a sly tike in his heart for all that. He was going to ask a young woman to spark it with him, and – the Lord have mercy on my soul! – she was another man's wife. . . .

JENNY: And did you see any more folks!

JONATHAN: Why, they came on as thick as mustard. For my part, I thought the house was haunted. There was a soldier fellow, who talked about his row de dow, dow, dow, and courted a young woman; but of all the cute folk I saw, I liked one little fellow –

JENNY: Aye! who was he?

JONATHAN: Why, he had red hair, and a little round plump face like mine, only not altogether so handsome. His name was Darby; that was his baptizing name; his other name I forgot. Oh! it was Wig – Wag – Wag-all, Darby Wag-all, – pray, do you know him? – I should like to take a sling with him, or a dram of cider with a pepper-pod in it, to make it warm and comfortable.

JENNY: Well, Mr. Jonathan, you were certainly at the play-house.

JONATHAN: I at the play-house! – Why didn't I see the play then?

JENNY: Why, the people you saw were the players.

JONATHAN: Mercy on my soul! did I see the wicked players? – Mayhap that'ere Darby that I liked so was the old serpent himself, and had his cloven foot in his pocket. Why, I vow, now I come to think on't, the candles seemed to burn blue, and I am sure where I sat it smelt tarnally of brimstone.

JESSAMY: Well, Mr. Jonathan, from your account, which I confess is very accurate, you must have been at the play-house.

JONATHAN: Why, I vow, I began to smell a rat. When I came away, I went to the man for my money again; you want your money? says he; yes, says I; for what? says he; why, says I, no man shall jocky me out of money; I paid my money to see sights, and the dogs a bit of a sight have I seen, unless you call listening to people's private business a sight. Why, says he, it is the school of Scandalization. – The School for Scandalization! – Oh! ho! no wonder you New-York folks are so cute at it, when you go to school to learn it; so I jogged off.

In fall 1791 a petition in favor of the legalization of the theatre was presented to the Selectmen of Boston. Hallam and Henry had hoped to bring their company to Boston for some time, and had been repeatedly refused permission. In summer 1792 a group of citizens proceeded to erect a playhouse in Board Alley in defiance of the law. The following account, written by Joseph T. Buckingham and published in 1832, provides a glimpse of that theatre.

33   The New Exhibition Room, Boston, 1792

New England Magazine, 2 (1832), 368–70

In the summer of 1792, induced by a prospect of support from a number of influential individuals, a part of the *American Company*, so called, which was attached to the Philadelphia and New York theatres, visited Boston. A number of gentlemen associated for the purposes of erecting a theatre. The committee who furnished money for the enterprise, were Joseph Russell, Esq. who also acted as treasurer to the association, Dr. Jarvis, Gen. Henry Jackson, Joseph Barrell, and Joseph Russell, Jr. A piece of ground was purchased in Board Alley, now Hawley Street. A building called the "New Exhibition Room," was erected with such rapidity, that it seemed almost the work of magic. It was a theatre in every thing but the name. It had a stage of considerable extent, a pit, one row of boxes, and a gallery, the whole capable of containing about five hundred persons. The boxes formed three sides of a regular square, the stage making the fourth. The scenery was tolerably well executed, and the whole interior was neat and comfortable, both for actors and auditors.

Boston resident Nathaniel Cutting attended a performance in the new Board Alley playhouse shortly after it was opened. He made a short uncomplimentary reference in his diary.

34   Nathaniel Cutting on Board Alley Theatre, Boston, 1792

"Extracts from the diary of Nathaniel Cutting," *Proceedings of the Massachusetts Historical Society,* 12 (1873), 63

September 18, 1792

. . . At evening went to the theatre, as a rough boarded hovel in Board Alley is called, in order to kill an hour or two in gazing at rope-dancing and pantomimics; was particularly invited thereto by an article in the playbill of the day, which announced a piece to be delivered by a "Lady of Cape Ann." The composition may be clever, but the lady who spoke it assassinated both the language and sense.

The theatre built for David Douglass and the American Company in Charleston in 1773 survived the bombardment of the town by the British only to be destroyed in a fire in 1782. The ground-breaking for a new theatre in Charleston to house a company led by Thomas Wade West and John Bignall was reported in a letter to the *New York Magazine.*

35   Description of Charleston Theatre, 1792

New York Magazine September 1792

On Tuesday last the ground was laid off for the new theatre on Savage's Green. The cornerstone of the foundation is to be laid the 20th inst. The dimensions, we are informed, are as follows: 125 feet in length, the width 56 feet, the height 37 feet; with an handsome pediment, stone ornaments, a large flight of stone steps and a court yard palisaded. The front will be in Broad Street and the pit entrance in Middleton Street. The different offices will be calculated so as not to interfere with each other. The stage is to be 56 feet in length, the front circular, with three rows of patent lamps. The boxes will be constructed so that small parties may be accommodated with a single box. To every box there will be a window and a venetian blind.Three tiers of boxes decorated with 32 columns. To each column a glass chandelier with five lights; the lower tier balustraded; the middle and upper boxes paneled; fancy paintings. The ground French white, the moldings and projections silvered; in the ceiling there will be three ventilators. The frontispiece, balconies and stage doors will be similar to those of the opera house, London. The theatre is to be built under the immediate direction of Mr. West. When it is considered that this gentleman has had near thirty years experience in many of the first theatres in England; that he is to be assisted by artists of the first class, Captain Tooner and Mr. Hoban,[1] we may expect a theatre in a style of elegance and novelty. Every attention will be paid to blend beauty with

[1] James Hoban had created the prize-winning designs for the White House.

conveniency, and to render it the first theatre on the continent. The contractors have engaged to complete the building by the tenth of January next.

Boston's Federal Street Theatre was a substantial and elegant brick building. The only known account of the original structure appeared in the *Federal Orrery*. Following a fire in February 1798, which gutted the interior but left the walls standing, the theatre was restored, with a new facade, and reopened in October of the same year. It remained the preeminent theatre in Boston for the next thirty years.

36   Description of Federal Street Theatre, Boston, 1794

Federal Orrery, October 1794

The theatre, in Federal Street, is a lofty and spacious edifice, substantially built of brick, with stone fascias, imposts, etc. It is one hundred and forty feet long, sixty-one feet wide, and forty feet high. As it stands in a conspicuous situation, it has been thought necessary to observe a strict symmetry on the outside. It has the appearance of two stories in height; the lower a basement, with three arches in the front and five on each side, the windows square. The second story is more lofty with large arched windows. The front and rear are decorated with corinthian columns and pilasters; and in front, a projecting arcade gives the conveniences of carriages landing their company under cover.

In the construction of this house, every attention has been paid to keep the entrances to the different parts distinct, and to afford numerous outlets. The doors to the pit and gallery are on each side; that to the boxes is in the front. This entrance is large and commodious. After landing under the cover, the company pass through an open, waiting room to two staircases, which lead to the corridors at the back of the boxes.

The form of the audience part of the theatre is circular, one quarter of the circle being cut off for the stage opening. Four corinthian columns support the ceiling, which is formed of four large elliptic arches. One of these is the opening of the front gallery; two others, those of the side galleries or slips; and the fourth is the proscenium, or opening of the stage.

The columns, which support the ceiling, give the leading divisions of the boxes, etc. The pedestal continued forms the front of the lower side galleries. The second row of boxes is suspended between, without visible support. All the boxes are three seats deep; and it may be affirmed that there are fewer inconvenient seats, than any other form is subject to.

The back walls are painted with a light blue; and the front of the boxes, the columns, etc. are of straw and lilac color. The molding, balustrades, and fret work are gilded. A crimson silk drapery, suspended from the second boxes, and twelve elegant brass chandeliers, of five lights each, complete the decoration.

The stage opening is thirty-one feet wide. It is ornamented, on each side, with two columns; and between them, a stage door and projecting iron balcony. Over the columns, a cornice and balustrade are carried across the opening; and above, is painted a flow of crimson drapery, and the arms of the Union and of the state of Massachusetts, blended with emblems tragic and comic. A ribbon, depending from the arms, bears the motto: "All the world's a stage."

The Haymarket Theatre in Boston for a short time attempted to compete with the Federal Street Theatre. It was a large and crudely constructed building designed to accommodate a large number of spectators. A letter to John Hodgkinson provides the most significant description of eighteenth-century American stagecraft. This letter, written by the playwright John D. Burk, describes the scenic effects of his play *Bunker Hill, or the Death of General Warren*, first performed at the Haymarket Theatre on February 20, 1797.

37   Description of Haymarket Theatre, Boston, 1797
Dunlap, *History of the American Theatre*, I: 313–14

The hill is raised gradually by boards extended from the stage to a bench. Three men should walk abreast of it, and the side where the English march up, should for the most part be turned towards the wings; on our hill there was room for eighteen or twenty men, and they were concealed by a board painted mud color, and having two cannons painted on it – which board was three feet and a half high. The English marched in two divisions from one extremity of the stage, where they ranged, after coming from the wings, when they come to the foot of the hill. The Americans fire – the English fire – six or seven of your men should be taught to fall – the fire should be frequent for some minutes. The English retire to the front of the stage – second line of English advance from the wing near the hill – firing commences – they are again beaten back – windows on the stage should be opened to let out the smoke. All the English make the attack and mount the hill. After a brisk fire, the Americans leave the works and meet them. Here is room for effect, if the scuffle be nicely managed. Sometimes the English falling back, sometimes the Americans – two or three Englishmen rolling down the hill. A square piece about nine feet high and five feet wide, having some houses and a meeting house painted on fire, with flame and smoke issuing from it, should be raised two feet distance from the horizon scene at the back of your stage, the windows and doors cut out for transparencies – in a word it should have the appearance of a town on fire. We had painted smoke suspended – it is raised at each wing, and is intended to represent Charleston, and is on a line with the hill, and where it is lowest. The fire should be played skillfully (this puts one in mind of Bottom playing moonshine) behind this burning town, and the smoke to evaporate. When the curtain rises in the fifth, the appearance of the whole is good – Charleston on fire, the breastwork of wood, the Americans appearing over the works and the muzzles of their guns, the English and the American music, the attack of the hill, the falling of the English troops, Warren's half descending the hill and animating the Americans, the smoke and confusion, all together produce an effect scarce credible. We had a scene of State Street. If you had one it would not be amiss; we used it instead of the scene of Boston Neck. It appears to me you need not be particular, but the hill and Charleston on fire . . . Small cannon should be fired during the battle, which continued with us for twelve or fifteen minutes. I am thus prolix that you may find the less difficulty in getting it up. It is not expensive, and will always be a valuable stock piece . . . We had our hill on the left side of the stage. The painting of Charleston on fire should not be seen till the fifth act.

38   Interior of Chestnut Street Theatre, Philadelphia, 1794

New York Magazine, April 1794; Harvard Theatre Collection

Inside View of the New Theatre, Philadelphia.

This engraving is the best view of the interior of an eighteenth-century playhouse. Modelled after contemporary English theatres, "the stage is known to have been some 71 feet in total depth and approximately 36 feet wide at the apron."[1]

---

[1] Brooks McNamara, *The American Playhouse in the Eighteenth Century* (Cambridge: Harvard University Press, 1969), p. 112.

39   Exterior View of Chestnut Street Theatre, 1804

McNamara, *The American Playhouse*, p. 110.

This view of one of America's most famous theatres is by Gilbert Fox after an 1800 engraving by William Birch. The building was 90 feet wide and 134 feet deep and officially opened on February 17, 1794.

IV. Drama

Prior to the advent of the long run and the starring system, the repertory of eighteenth-century theatres was drawn largely from proven English successes. A surviving list of presentations from the American Company in 1774 (Doc. 42) is representative of this period. After the Revolutionary War there were scattered attempts to create an American drama, but Shakespeare, Sheridan, and John Gay remained cornerstones of most "come any night" resident companies. Pollock records a reference to a performance of Addison's *Cato* on August 22 or 23, 1749, in the diary of a John Smith. (The current location of the manuscript diary from which Pollock obtained his reference is unknown.) Although no newspaper account exists to substantiate this event, the company is thought to have been that of Walter Murray and Thomas Kean, who managed a company in New York from December 1751 to July 1752.

40 *Cato* Performed in Philadelphia, 1749

Pollock, *The Philadelphia Theatre*, p. 6

6 mo. [August] 23.3. Jos: Morris & I happened in at Peacock Biggers, & drank Tea there & his daughter being one of the Company who were going to hear the Tragedy of Cato acted it Occasioned some Conversation in w'ch I Expressed my sorrow that any thing of the kind was encouraged.

Smith's disapproval was shared by many of his contemporaries in Philadelphia as evidenced by the company's eventual dismissal from the city early in 1750. The players moved to New York in February, announcing themselves as a company of comedians from Philadelphia.

A brief review of the 1774 Charleston season concluded with a hopeful promise that the players would return at the end of two years with a greatly augmented troupe. Political events intervened in the actors' plans however and it was not until 1785 that another company of professional actors appeared there.

41   Close of the Charleston Season, 1774

General Gazette. May 27. 1774

CLOSE OF THE CHARLESTON SEASON.

On Friday last the theatre which opened here the 22nd of December was closed. Warmly countenanced and supported by the public, the manager and his company were excited to the most strenuous efforts to render their entertainments worthy of so respectable a patronage.

If it is considered how late it was in the season before the house could be opened, the variety of scenery and decorations necessary to a regular theatre, the number of plays represented and that almost every piece required particular preparations, it must be confessed that the exertions of the American Company have been uncommon and justly entitles them to those marks of public favor, that have for so many years stamped merit in their performances.

The choice of plays hath been allowed to be very judicious, the director having selected from the most approved English poets such pieces as possess in the highest degree the *utile dulce,* and while they entertain, improve the mind by conveying the most useful lessons of morality and virtue.

The Company have separated until the winter when the New York theatre will be opened; Mr. Hallam being embarked for England to engage some recruits for that service. The year after they will perform at Philadelphia, and in the winter following, we may expect them here with a theatrical force hitherto unknown in America. . . .

A list of the plays performed during the American Company's final Colonial season was published in the *South Carolina Gazette.* Only one other such listing is known for this period. The range of plays and afterpieces is impressive, and the additional list of operas suggests a versatile company of exceptional talents.

42   Repertoire of the American Company, 1774

South Carolina Gazette. May 30. 1774

Catalogue of plays that have been performed here this season by the American Company of Comedians, under the direction of Mr. David Douglass:

December 1773:
- 22   *A Word to the Wise* and *High Life Below Stairs*
- 24   *Hamlet* and *Cross Purposes*
- 27   *Suspicious Husband* and *Catherine and Petruchio*
- 30   *Clandestine Marriage* and *Mayor of Garrat*

January 1774:

1   *Earl of Essex* and *Irish Widow*

3   *Love in a Village* and *Lethe*

5   *Gamester* and *High Life Below Stairs*

8   *Stratagem* and *King and Miller*

10 *Constant Couple* and *Catherine and Petruchio*

13 *Mourning Bride* and *Lying Valet*

15 *She Stoops to Conquer* and *Irish Widow*

17 *Jane Shore* and *Cross Purposes*

19 *Busy Body* and *Love a la Mode*

21 *Cymbeline* and *A Wonder!*

25 *Beggar's Opera* and *Love a la Mode*

27 *Romeo and Juliet* and *Miss in Her Teens*

29 *Merchant of Venice* and *Devil to Pay*

31 *Richard III* and *Thomas and Sally*

February:

2   *Tempest* and. . . . .[1]

4   *Love in a Village* and *Love a la Mode*

7   *The Wonder* and *Midas*

10 *Alexander the Great* and *King and Miller*

12 *Tempest* and *Guardian*

14 *George Barnwell* and *Edgar and Emmeline*

17 *Henry IV* and *Thomas and Sally*

19 *Theodosius* and *Citizen*

21 *Bold Stroke for a Wife* and *Mayor of Garrat*

24 *Othello* and *Damon and Phillida*

26 *She Stoops to Conquer* and *Edgar and Emmeline*

28 *Jealous Wife* and *Citizen*

March:

2   *Shipwreck* and *Catherine and Petruchio*

4   *School for Fathers* and *Lethe*

7   *Fashionable Lover* and *Padlock*

10 *Maid of the Mill* and *High Life Below Stairs*

12 *King Lear* and *Irish Widow*

14 *Tempest* and *Padlock*

16 *Cymon* and *Miss in Her Teens*

18 *Recruiting Officer* and *Oracle*

21 *West Indian* and *Devil to Pay*

---

[1] Title is unreadable in the document.

25 *Provoked Husband* and *Lying Valet*
26 *Romeo and Juliet* and *Flora*

April:

4 *School for Fathers* and *Bucks Have At Ye All*
6 *English Merchants* and *Contrivances*
8 *Fair Penitent* and *Cross Purposes*
11 *Roman Father* and *Irish Widow*
13 *Way to Keep Him* and *Contrivances*
15 *Constant Couple* and *Lying Valet*
18 *False Delicacy* and *Witches*
20 *Julius Caesar* (First time in America) and *Register Office*
22 *Macbeth* and *Young American in London*
25 *West Indian* and *Midas*
27 *Tamerlane* and *Catherine and Petruchio*
29 *Cymbeline* and *Love a la Mode*

May:

2 *Bold Stroke for a Wife* and *Neck or Nothing*
4 *Orphan* and *Miss in Her Teens*
7 *Clandestine Marriage* and *Apprentice*
11 *Cato* and *Reprisal*
16 *Douglas* and *Devil to Pay*
19 *King John* and *Guardian*

Of this season's performances twenty were operas, as follows:

1774:
Jan. 3 *Love in a Village* by Arne
24 *Honest Yorkshireman* by Carey
25 *Beggars Opera* by Gay
29 *Devil to Pay* by Coffey

Feb. 4 *Love in a Village* by Arne
7 *Midas* (Ballad-burletta) by O'Hara
17 *Thomas and Sally* by Arne
24 *Damon and Phillida* by Cibber

Mar. 4 *Lionel and Clarissa* by Dibdin
7 *Padlock* by Bickerstaff
10 *Maid of the Mill* by Bickerstaff
14 *Padlock* by Bickerstaff
21 *Devil to Pay* by Coffey
26 *Flora* by Cibber

Apr.   4 *Lionel and Clarissa* by Dibdin
       6 *Contrivances* by Carey
      15 *Contrivances* by Carey
      18 *Witches* by Love
      25 *Midas* by O'Hara

May 16 *Devil to Pay* by Coffey

Mercy Otis Warren, an articulate patriot, author, and supporter of the American Revolution, used dialogue and play form to chastise the British and fan the flames of patriotism. Although there is some controversy about how many plays she wrote, *The Group* is clearly hers. In this excerpt she draws an intriguing parallel between the enslavement of the colonies and the condition of women.

43   Excerpt from *The Group*, 1775

Mercy Otis Warren, *The Group* (Boston, 1775); reprinted Scholars' Facsimiles & Reprints (New York: Delmar, 1980), p. 15

SIMPLE SAPPLING.
  Silvia's good natur'd, and no doubt will yield,
And take the brawny vet'rans to her board,
When she's assur'd 'twill help her husband's fame.
    If she complains or murmurs at the plan,
Let her go out and seek some pitying friend
To give her shelter from the wint'ry blast,
Disperse her children round the neighb'ring cots,
And then — — — —

PUBLICAN.
  — —Then weep thy folly, and her own hard fate!
I pity Silvia, I knew the beauteous maid
E'er she descended to become thy wife:
She silent mourns the weakness of her lord,
For she's too virtuous to approve thy deeds.

HATEALL.
  Pho — —what's a woman's tears,
Or all the whinings of that trifling sex?
I never felt one tender thought towards them.
    When young, indeed, I wedded nut brown Kate,
(Blyth bosom Dowager, the jockey's prey)
But all I wish'd was to secure her dower.
I broke her spirits when I'd won her purse;
For which I'll give a recipe most sure

To ev'ry hen peck'd husband round the board:
If crabbed words or surly looks won't tame
The haughty shrew, nor bend the stubborn mind,
Then the green Hick'ry, or the willow twig,
Will provide a curse for each rebellious dame
Who dare oppose her lord's superior will.

Tyler's *The Contrast*, the first American comedy to be performed by professional actors in New York, owes its form and concept to Sheridan's *The School for Scandal*. Despite this formal debt *The Contrast* contains the earliest stirrings of a nationalistic voice in the American drama. The following review was signed "Candour."

44   Review of *The Contrast*, 1787

New York Daily Advertiser, April 18, 1787

I was present last evening at the representation of *The Contrast*, and was very much entertained with it. It is certainly the production of a man of genius, and nothing can be more praiseworthy than the sentiments of the play throughout. They are the effusions of an honest patriot heart expressed with energy and eloquence. The characters are drawn with spirit, particularly Charlotte's; the dialogue is easy, sprightly, and often witty, but wants the pruning knife very much. The author has made frequent use of soliloquies, but I must own, I think, injudiciously; Maria's song and her reflections after it are pretty, but certainly misplaced. Soliloquies are seldom so conducted as not to wound probability. If we ever talk to ourselves, it is when the mind is much engaged in some very interesting subject, and never to make calm reflections on indifferent things. That part of her speech which respects Dimple, might be retained; she may very well be supposed to talk on so material a subject to her own happiness, even when alone, and her feelings, upon a marriage with a man she has every reason to despise and abhor, are very well painted. Col. Manly's advice to America, though excellent, is yet liable to the same blame, and perhaps greater. A man can never be supposed in conversation with himself, to point out examples of imitation to his countrymen. At the same time the thoughts are so just, that I should be sorry they were left out entirely, and I think they might be introduced with greater propriety, in the conversation with Dimple.

I cannot help wishing the author had given a scene between Dimple and Maria. The affronting coldness of Dimple's manner might have interested us for Maria, and would in some degree have supplied the greatest defect of the play, the want of interest and plot. We might then have been more easily reconciled to the sudden affection and declaration of love between Manly and Maria, which cannot fail, as the play now is, to hurt our opinion of both. The author's great attention to the unity of time, which he has indeed very well preserved, has in some degree produced this sudden attachment.

Jessamy is a closer imitation of his master than is natural, and his language in general is too good for a servant. The character would have produced a better effect if he had been more awkward in his imitation. The satire of the play is in general just, but the ridicule of Lord Chesterfield's letters, should be well considered. If he is sometimes so attentive to his son's person as to mention too trifling things, let us remember that his letters were certainly never meant for the public eye. . . . We may forgive a father's tenderness even when he recommends how to cut the nails, and if we must allow that he appears more solicitous to form his son's manners than his heart (which might arise from thinking him more deficient in the one that the other), let us not overlook his profound knowledge of the world, the excellent sense and most admirable style of his letters.

Jonathan's going to the play, and his account of it, is a very happy thought, and very well drawn.[1] The laughing gamut has much humor, but is dwelt rather too much upon, and sometimes degenerates into farce. To point out the many beauties of the play, though an agreeable, would be an unnecessary task, the unceasing plaudits of the audience did them ample justice, and it cannot fail, if judiciously curtailed, being a great favorite. The play was preceded by a good prologue, which was very well spoken by Wignell, but the effect much spoilt by the unskillfulness of the prompter. It was very well acted. Mrs. Morris gave the sprightly lively coquette with great ease and elegance, and if Wignell had not quite the right pronunciation of Jonathan, he made ample amends by his inimitable humor. Upon the whole the defects of the play are so much overbalanced by its merits, that I have made no scruple of mentioning those which occurred to me, and I have done so the rather, because I think in general they may be easily remedied, and that the piece, particularly when considered as the first performance, does the greatest credit to the author, and must give pleasure to the spectator.

[1] Jonathan's description of his unwitting visit to the playhouse, is thought to reflect Tyler's own first visit to the John Street Theatre for a performance of *The School for Scandal* in March 1787. Wignell appeared as Joseph Surface in that performance. Jonathan's amusing reference to the actor "Darby Wag-all" refers to another of Wignell's popular characters, the rascally Irish soldier, Darby, in O'Keefe's *The Poor Soldier* (1785) which was often presented as an afterpiece to *The School for Scandal*.

Looking back on the drama of the eighteenth century Bernard observed that the manager's repertory was so traditional that companies could perform with a minimum of rehearsal.

45   John Bernard on the Drama, 1887

Bernard, *Retrospectives of America*, pp. 262–63

The modern rage for novelties had as yet to set in. The drama itself was a novelty, which proved quite sufficient. Thus a manager, in those days, was not perplexed for new pieces, or obliged to risk a fortune on those abysses of capital – modern ballet and spectacle. As yet, even a melodrama was unknown to the stage; the nearest approach to it being serious pantomimes, such as *La Perouse* and *Don Juan*; all of which, however, presented a strong human interest, and were as cheaply produced as they were occasionally popular. Shakespeare and O'Keefe were the staple attractions, varied with Farquhar and Cumberland, Goldsmith and Sheridan; and the performances also were only three nights a week, and yet probably averaged as much as our six. Thus he [the manager] had nothing to do at the opening of a season but to put up a cast of the common stock plays – *Hamlet*, *Othello*, the *West Indian*, and the *Rivals*; with the *Padlock*, the *Poor Soldier*, and the *Agreeable Surprise*. The actors were all studied, hardly a rehearsal was needed, and if the fever kept off, the house filled and closed without one jar to his nerves.

William Dunlap, producer, playwright, and historian, recognized the debt that the emerging American drama owed to its English models but he was not entirely comfortable with those models and in assessing the status of the drama near the close of the century he clearly longs for a "moral" theatre as well as a national one.

46   William Dunlap on Drama and Theatre, 1797

Dunlap, *History of the American Theatre*, I: 128–30

When the drama was introduced into this country, the favorites of England were of course the favorites of the colonies. It is a subject for the historian of America, it is the duty of the historian of our literature, to mark the changes from the plays then popular, plays full of wit, but fraught with indelicacies, not to say obscenities, their very plots so entwined with the loose manners and intrigues of the time as to be incapable of pruning so as to leave the wit, the better part, separated from the filth. It is his duty to point out these favorites of former times, and to show that, as our society has improved, these plays have fallen into desuetude, both here and in England. The indecency and immorality of the plays of Charles the Second's time, and a later period, belonged to the state of society, and not to the stage or the writers for it, otherwise than as a part of society. If the wise and the good frequent the theatre, its exhibitions must become schools of wisdom. The lessons taught must be those of patriotism, virtue, morality, religion. These lessons would not be thought misplaced as coming from the stage, if the stage had not been polluted by the licentiousness of its supporters. And when, as it may be, its supporters shall be the moral and the wise, the purest teachings will flow, mingled in the same stream with the delightful waters of Helicon, undefiled by the conduits from which they are received.

If the theatre is abandoned to the uneducated, the idle, and the profligate, mercenary managers will please their visitors by such ribaldry or folly, or worse, as is attractive to such patrons, and productive of profit to themselves.

As Puritanism or bigotry cannot shut the theatre, or even, as in former times in England, fine the actors for repeating the words of the dramatists, or banish the fine arts from society as being too worldly, or stigmatize their professors as ungodly worldlings, or frivolous or vicious men, let those who seek rational amusement and elevating pleasure, and know the value of such amusements in a political point of view upon the mass of the people . . . unite in supporting, and by their presence purifying and directing, the theatre . . . What engine is more powerful than the theatre? No arts can be made more effectual for the promotion of good than the dramatic and histrionic. They unite music, poetry, painting, and eloquence. The engine is powerful for good or ill – it is for society to choose.

But the question arises – "How are the evils flowing from theatrical representations to be banished from them, and the good preserved and secured?" The answer is, make the theatre an object of governmental patronage; take the mighty engine into the hands of the people as represented by their delegates and magistrates. The stream of pure instruction flowing into a city is of more worth than even the purity of the water which is to cleanse it, and afford an aliment to banish the poison of the licensed murderers at every corner and every avenue of our towns. If a state or city government were to direct a theatre, nothing could be represented that was not conformable to patriotism, morality, and religion.

1810–1865

DAVID RINEAR

INTRODUCTION

The changes, conflicts, and tensions evident in the American theatre between 1810 and 1865 reflect the variety of conditions in the rapidly expanding, loosely governed nation. Starting as a small republic stretched along the western shores of the Atlantic Ocean in 1810, the country had become a transcontinental giant by the end of the Civil War in 1865.

In an age unencumbered with rock stars, professional athletes, and media celebrities, the American theatre served as the prime purveyor of the growing country's popular culture heroes. As proud regional and class consciousness became increasingly diverse, certain theatres, actors, plays, and specialty performers profited from that diversity. Professional acting companies increased at least a hundredfold during the period, while the number of cities containing theatres increased proportionally. The conflicts and tensions of laissez-faire capitalism, wild fiscal speculation, class animosity, frontier adventurism, jingoistic manifest destiny, racism, and an emerging sense of a pluralistic national identity are all reflected in the American theatre between 1810 and 1865.

At the end of the War of 1812, the American theatre remained the westernmost extension of the British provincial theatrical circuit. The resident stock companies with their lines of business, frequently changing repertory, and shutter-and-groove system of shabby stock scenery mirrored the typical way of going about the business of the theatre in such English provincial cities as Liverpool, Sheffield, and Manchester. In spite of having won two wars against its former mother country within a quarter century, the United States remained, unabashedly, a cultural colony. However, a changing repertory and the rise of native actors reflect one of the primary tensions of the period, a quest for cultural independence.

As the adolescent nation became proudly convinced of its political independence following the War of 1812, the cry for the development of a truly native drama reflective of both emerging national values and the developing national character rang out frequently from many quarters. But the business of the American theatre impeded the development of a significant and uniquely American dramatic literature. As was the case in England, serious persons of letters wrote for the page, not for the stage. The theatre, a place of mass entertainment more often than not pandering to the lowest common denominator of public taste, remained an impossible venue for the serious thinker. The business of dramatic writing fell to professional theatre folk, and no one in young America made his or her living exclusively from writing plays. Without copyright and royalty protection, the best an aspiring dramatist could hope was that an established actor would purchase a play for a fixed sum plus the traditional author's benefit. Thus, while James Nelson Barker provided Philadelphia theatregoers with several uniquely American plays in the 1820s, he never made a living from those efforts. John Augustus Stone earned more fame than fortune in providing Edwin Forrest with starring vehicles in the 1830s, and the foibles and affectations of New York City's nouveau riche reflected in Mrs. Mowatt's *Fashion* of 1845 earned its author many accolades but few dollars. In spite of these attempts at developing a native drama, the vast number of new plays seen throughout the period arrived on the stages of American theatres from the steamships of London rather than the pens of American dramatists.

Among the native dramas, those written by and for the starring actors, who developed special lines of business from peculiar and unique American character types, number among the most theatrically significant. Ironically, the Englishman Charles Mathews developed the earliest of the indigenous types – the stage Yankee, Jonathan Doubikins. Contemporary actors living in the United States quickly realized the new type as a potentially profitable line of business. James Hackett, George Handel Hill, Danforth Marble, and Joshua Silsbee all developed the stage Yankee and sought dramatic vehicles for their characters. Subtle variations of their Yankee characters reflect an emerging sense of both class and regional identity. Aristocratic Easterners loved Hackett's Yankee, while middle- and lower-class citizens of the same region idolized Hill's. Dan Marble's Yank had the broad twang of the Ohio and Mississippi River Valleys – a daring and opportunistic frontiersman rather than a taciturn "down-easter." In the west, Marble was King. Silsbee, the last of the great Yankee actors, portrayed a type whose time had gone; a historical curiosity and vestigial remnent of an only slightly earlier age. Hackett abandoned the crowded field of "Yankeedom" in the late 30s in favor of both the traditional repertory and another indigenous American type, the coonskin-capped Kentucky frontiersman, Nimrod Wildfire. But both Marble and Hill each eventually developed his own peculiar market with its intensely loyal customers. The imprint of the character on the national character is hard to deny, as it provided the nation what was to become its political cartoon identity, Uncle Sam.

The success of the Yankee actors established a market for both native character types and foreign curiosities on the boards of the nation's theatres. Among the many new American characters developed and played by touring stars, three became especially lucrative and remarkably influential. Forrest's noble American Aborigine, Metamora, served the tragedian well during the early part of his career and spawned many imitators. A wide range of American Indian characters seen in the country's theatres included tragic noble savages, low-comic types, and the white hero's loyal servant and best friend. By 1860, however, the vogue for stage Indians had largely passed.

Thomas D. Rice, a stock actor in F. C. Wemyss's Pittsburgh Theatre in 1833, developed the crippled, black, low-comic character Jim Crow and achieved, within two years, the acclaim and attendant high salary of a touring star. Rice's creation had tremendous impact on the national consciousness in both the short and long term. In the short term, Jim Crow spawned the establishment of whole troupes of white performers in blackface; the variety minstrel shows of the 1840s and later. The long-term result, an extra-theatrical one, indicates the extent to which Rice's popular character became ingrained in the national consciousness. From Reconstruction on, any oppressive legislation victimizing blacks in the United States became known as a Jim Crow law.

Working-class urban whites who developed both a proud identity and political clout as a result of the reforms of Jacksonian Democracy found themselves reflected on the stages of the theatres which they attended. Frank S. Chanfrau modeled his Bowery B'hoy character "Mose" on the members of the pit audience of Mitchell's Olympic Theatre in New York, and established the character as a New York favorite during the late 1840s.

Stage Irishmen had been familiar to American audiences since the closing years of the eighteenth century, most often in the character of Sir Lucius O'Trigger in Sheridan's *The Rivals*. Beginning in the late 1830s, several actors made contemporary Irish characters a low-comic staple in short farces and afterpieces. The most prominent of these actors, Tyrone Power, developed a vogue for the stage Irishman among American audiences during his starring tours. Power was lost at sea on a return trip to England in 1842, but as hundreds of thousands of Irish emigres came to the Eastern cities of the United States between 1845 and 1849, native actors capitalized on the populace's curiosity with the recent arrivals in a steady succession of Irish characters in short comic plays. Some of the most popular actors who played Irish characters, such as John Brougham, were themselves emigres from the Emerald Isle. Others, such as John Nickinson, were native-born Americans. Beginning with the Irish immigration, each large wave of new arrivals from foreign ports was certain to be burlesqued as low-comic characters on the boards of the theatres of the cities in which they disembarked from the old country. The stage Dutchman (German) appeared prior to the Civil War, but the process continued and reached its culmination in the Mulligan Guard series of Harrigan and Hart later in the century.

Other items in the repertory developed, in an odd way, as a result of anti-theatrical forces. Biases against the theatre had existed in American life since the days of John Winthrop's Massachusetts theocracy. During the 1830s and 40s the emerging national double moral standard touched the theatre. Many morally conservative residents of the Eastern cities who would not attend the theatres because of their repertories, liquor saloons, and prostitutes, supported the morally uplifting drama at sanitized theatres: the bastions of "family entertainment" known as gardens and museums. These theatres of another name featured plays developed from the two favorite reform items of the morally conservative agenda – temperance and the abolition of slavery. *The Drunkard, Ten Nights in a Bar-Room, Uncle Tom's Cabin*, and many other plays reflected the political agenda of the righteous and conservative members of the community. *Uncle Tom's Cabin*, first presented as a stage play in 1852, generated enthusiasm at both museums and theatres. The museum audience found it appealing for its abolitionist sentiments, while the "sinners" in the regular theatres thrilled to its sensationally melodramatic elements.

Beginning with George Frederick Cooke's tour of America in 1810, theatrical managers realized that British touring stars could and would do an immensely profitable business, and the lessees of the theatres helped to develop a taste for visiting luminaries so insatiable that empty houses and red ink were the inevitable results of the starless managers throughout most of the period. Two sets of tensions developed as a result of the system they encouraged. The drawing power of the British stars reinforced the position of the United States as a cultural colony. When Forrest and his successors emerged as legitimate competitors to the British luminaries, the native stars' support segmented the American audiences along regional and class lines. Working-class Easterners and Westerners, the beneficiaries of Jacksonian Democracy and good Americans all, paid their money to see the native sons on stage, while the mercantile aristocrats of the Eastern cities continued to look to England for their tastes, goods, and culture heroes. The tensions between the democratic and aristocratic segments of the audience with their respective native and imported culture heroes finally erupted at the Astor Place Theatre in the deadly riot of May 1849.

An economic tension also involved the touring stars. An ever increasing percentage of box-office receipts of the stellar visitors ended up in the pockets of the performers rather than the coffers of management. By the 1840s the exorbitant salary demands of the stars threatened the solvency of many marginal managements during a period of acute national economic depression.

Alternative strategies to dealing with the price-gouging stars began in earnest in the late 1830s. J. W. Wallack's National Theatre in New York, although occasionally relying on the efforts of luminescent visitors, fared well with the efforts of the stock company, tasteful scenery and costumes, and a solid repertory. William Mitchell successfully managed the Olympic Theatre throughout most of the 1840s without either visiting stars or rigid lines of business within his stock company. By relying on a repertory of light, short comic pieces, Mitchell demonstrated that substantial profits could be earned if one simply said no to the stars. William E. Burton employed similar tactics at various theatres in Philadelphia and New York during the 40s and 50s. By the mid-50s, the most successful Eastern managers – Wallack and Laura Keene – profited from their strong stock companies and tasteful stage appointments, not a succession of visiting stars. A logical extension of the reestablishment of the resident company occurred after the Civil War when entire companies and scenery, rather than single stellar performers, took to the road via the recently completed railroad network.

Changes in managerial strategies, including the repertory, had effects on acting during the period. As Americans began to see characters from their daily lives represented on stage, new criteria regarding what constituted good acting developed. Tragedians continued to be evaluated in terms of their intellect, passion, physical presence, and fine voices, while comedians in the traditional repertory relied on their drollery and sense of timing much in the same way their predecessors had. But the new specialty performers were judged by different standards. They were measured against the faithfulness of their creations to the real articles which could be seen walking the streets of most of the cities in which they performed. Thus, beginning in the late 30s and 40s, reviewers discussed the realism of the specialty performer, not in relation to some a priori ideal, but to the extent to which the actors credibly represented the details of the characters from contemporary life which they portrayed. Although the acting of Rice, Chanfrau, Marble, or Barney Williams would no doubt be considered highly artificial by the standards of the present day, their work began to shift the criteria by which acting was judged.

A ruthlessly competitive capitalistic enterprise, the business of the American theatre fostered animosities between rival establishments in the same market. In the lower Mississippi Valley, the firm of Ludlow and Smith pitted itself against James Caldwell for dominance in Mobile and New Orleans during the 1840s. Scrambling to be the first in the field with new plays, competing for the services of touring stars, excoriations in the press, and lawsuits over real estate and contracts characterized the cut-throat competition of the rival managements' quest for a lion's share of the market. Similar tensions between the successive managements of Philadelphia's Walnut Street and Chestnut Street Theatres shaped the history of that city's entertainment industry throughout most of the pre–Civil War period.

Competition in New York was particularly intense and vicious. Ruthless managers may even have contracted arsonists to burn competition out of business during the 1840s; and conflict between Laura Keene and Burton for control of the city's Metropolitan Theatre was particularly intense.

American theatre managers more often than not merely followed norms established in other areas of an unregulated laissez-faire economy. They tended to be no better nor any worse than other businessmen of the period who did whatever was necessary to eliminate competition in a limited market. One must remember that managers were most often just that. Although certain entrepreneurs – Ludlow and Smith, Caldwell, and Burton – had extensive holdings in real estate and owned the theatres which they operated, most theatres tended to be owned by joint-stock companies who leased them to managers and expected between eight and nine percent yearly on their capital investments. Costly leases meant that managers had little operational breathing room if they expected to pay their expenses and make a profit for themselves.

As American society segmented into a number of socioeconomic classes, theatres reflected that segmentation. During the 20s, managers faced the problem of drawing a sufficiently large number of theatregoers of various means in order to maintain profitable operations. Each class had its own section in the theatre's auditorium; the boxes and dress circle for the affluent; the pit for the middle and sometimes lower working class; and the second and third galleries for sailors, prostitutes, and the rougher elements of the community. Prices of admission to the various sections of the auditorium varied, economically segregating the various groups of the community from each other. Many theatres, built on corner lots, contained entrances literally around the corner from the main entrances. These had no connection to the rest of the auditorium and led directly to the highest gallery, reserved especially for black people.

The working-class pride, attendant with the triumph of Jacksonian Democracy, caused animosity on the part of lower-class audience members toward separate, less respectable entrances to theatres. Hostility was frequently expressed toward the management, but only rarely toward the theatre's upper-class patrons.

As the population of the major cities exploded during the 30s and 40s, some theatrical managers found it profitable to concentrate their marketing efforts on a single segment of the community. Thomas Hamblin's Bowery Theatre in New York City, with its sensational melodramas and occasional visits by native stars such as Forrest, developed an almost exclusively working-class audience by 1835. Chanfrau, after becoming an overnight sensation at Mitchell's Olympic Theatre in February of 1848, took the lease on New York's Chatham Theatre and played Mose in a succession of custom-tailored vehicles to the delight of the rough working-class youths who considered the theatre their peculiar province.

As theatres segmented along class lines, they also changed size and shape. The normal capacity of playhouses in large urban centers up through the mid-30s was approximately two thousand, although the St. Charles in New Orleans held well over three thousand. But smaller theatres seating between eight hundred and a thousand began to be constructed in the late 30s and 40s, and most of the museum theatres held fewer spectators than their legitimate counterparts. By the 1850s, theatres in the older Eastern and Southern cities were dividing into first class and popular. But the audience continued to be heterogeneous, and the theatres remarkably varied in size and shape, on the constantly expanding frontier.

Audiences expressed both their approval and disapproval boisterously through much of the nineteenth century. Performances interrupted by both accolades and disorders occurred frequently. The extremely wide range of tolerable audience behavior more closely resembled that of a contemporary sporting event than that of a late twentieth-century theatre. Disturbances requiring police intervention occurred often, and riots resulting in significant damage to furniture and fixtures in the theatres' auditoriums occasionally erupted. Because starring actors served as popular culture heroes to various segments of the audience, those segments sometimes demonstrated open hostility to each other in their support for and detraction of certain performers. The most famous example involved the supporters of Forrest who chased Macready from the stage of the Astor Place Opera House on the first evening of the British tragedian's engagement in May 1849.

The area of theatrical practice least affected during the period from 1810 through 1865 was the spectacular one. Gas lighting became universal in the 30s, and characters drawn from the contemporary scene wore costumes appropriate to their models from life. Yet scenery continued to consist almost exclusively of wings and drops, although box sets seem to have been employed sporadically after the production of *The London Assurance* in 1841.

The documents indicate the general range of practice and change within the American theatre from 1810 through 1865. Brief prefatory remarks accompanying each document indicate its focus and significance. Many pieces were chosen for inclusion because they represent common practice, others because they note new directions.

I.   The Business of Theatre

George Frederick Cooke, the first in a constellation of British stars to tour American theatres in the early nineteenth century, amply demonstrated the tremendous earning power
of English tragedians in the United States, as the following record of his receipts illustrates.

47   George Frederick Cooke's Receipts at Chestnut Street Theatre, Philadelphia, 1811

Wood, *Personal Recollections*, p. 133

25 March–16 April, 1811.

1st	Night, March	25,	as *Richard III* - - - - - - - - - - -	-$1345[1]
2nd	"	"	27,	" " - - - - - - - - - - - - - 1104
3rd	"	"	29,	*Man of the World, Sir Pertinax* - - - 1475
4th	"	"	30,	*Merchant of Venice, Shylock* - - - - - 1160
5th	"	April	1st,	*Richard III* - - - - - - - - - - - - - 1189
6th	"	"	3d,	*Man of the World, Sir Pertinax* - - - 1262
7th	"	"	5th,	*King Lear* - - - - - - - - - - - - - 997
8th	"	"	6th,	*New Way To Pay Old Debts, Sir Giles* 1030
9th	"	"	8th,	*Henry IV, Falstaff* - - - - - - - - - 1020
10th	"	"	10th,	*Merchant of Venice, Shylock* - - - - - 880
11th	"	"	11th,	*Macbeth* - - - - - - - - - - - - - - 780
12th	"	"	13th,	*Douglas, Love A La Mode, Sir Archy* 1196
13th	"	"	15th,	*Every Man In His Humour, Kitely* - - 1356
14th	"	"	17th,	*Lear* - - - - - - - - - - - - - - - - 648

[1] According to a comparative table showing consumer price indexes and wholesale price indexes
from 1800 to 1970 in *Encyclopedia of American Economic History: Studies of Principal Movements and
Ideas*, ed. Glen Porter (New York: Scribner, 1980), I: 235, a 1970 dollar was worth approximately
2.5 times as much in terms of buying power as the 1810 dollar. Inflation has made the 1990 dollar
worth about 2.5 times as much as the 1970 dollar. Thus, multiplying Cooke's receipts by 6 gives an
approximation of their worth in contemporary America.

15th   "   "   19th, *Man of The World, Sir Pertinax* _ _ _ 948
16th   "   "   20th, *Richard III* _ _ _ _ _ _ _ _ _ _ _ _ _ 1000

The following contract for an engagement at the Dock Street Theatre in Charleston is representative of the brevity of contracts between actors and managers in the years immediately following the War of 1812.

48   Actor's Contract, 1817

Ms. contract between Charles Gilfert and C. McCullough; Harvard Theatre Collection

New York, Sept. 1, 1817
I agree to give Mr. C. McCullough thirty dollars per week for fifty-two weeks and a benefit in Charleston the receipt of the whole amount to be divided between management and Mr. McCullough. Mr. McCullough's salary to commence this day. The travelling expenses to be paid by me.

Charles Gilfert

Victor Pepin and John Baptiste Casemere Breschard owned and operated the Olympic Theatre – actually an indoor circus, or equestrian house – at the corner of Ninth and Walnut Streets in Philadelphia during 1811. (The lot on which their unimposing structure stood was to be the future home of the Walnut Street Theatre.) A de facto blockade of Delaware Bay by the British Navy in June of that year caused a severe downturn in the entertainment business. Pepin and Breschard had to mortgage both the lot and its structure to James Clemson, a wealthy flour merchant of the city, in order to continue operations. Note the usurious rate of the loan.

49   Mortgage Document, Olympic Theatre, Philadelphia, 1812

Mortgage document, Olympic Theatre, Philadelphia, dated February 22, 1812; Theatre Arts Collection, Harry Ransom Humanities Research Center, University of Texas at Austin

Whereas the within named Victor Pepin and Jon Baptiste Casemere Breschard by their bond bearing date of the same day and year herewith stand bound unto the within named James Clemson in the sum of twenty thousand dollars, conditioned for the payment of twelve thousand four hundred dollars in the manner therein stipulated and to secure the same have given their mortgage on a lot of ground at the north east corner of Walnut and Ninth Streets, with the building, thereon erected, called the Olympic Theatre.

The equestrian partners defaulted and Clemson obtained the lot and the building through legal action on February 24 1813. Pepin reacquired the theatre in 1818, but then sold it to liquidate his debts. It was renamed the Walnut Street Theatre and owned by a succession of merchants and physicians until it was purchased by Edwin Booth and John Clarke in 1863. When Edmund Kean played the new Walnut Street Theatre during January and February 1822, competition between it, the older Chestnut Street Theatre, and other occasional entertainments was intense. His receipts show greater fluctuation than those of Cooke eleven years earlier when the Chestnut Street was the only theatre.

50 Edmund Kean's Receipts at Walnut Street Theatre, Philadelphia, 1822

Wood, *Personal Recollections*, p. 256

Richard	$1178.00
Othello	837.00
Merchant of Venice	1260.00
Hamlet	718.00
Richard	883.00
Brutus	897.00
First benefit, New Way to Pay Old Debts	1397.00
Macbeth	615.00
King Lear	1351.00
Rule a Wife	699.50
Bertram	650.00
Town and Country	675.00
King Lear	889.00
Second Benefit	1199.00
Merchant of Venice	400.50
Iron Chest	727.50

On Christmas Eve, 1826, Junius Brutus Booth, intending to manage other actors as well as maintain his career as a touring tragedian, wrote the following letter to the English low comedian, George Holland.

51 Letter from J. B. Booth to George Holland, 1826

Montrose J. Moses, *Famous Actor Families in America* (New York: Thomas D. Crowell, 1906), pp. 263–65

Messrs. Wallack and Freeman, a few days since, showed me your letter, with the enclosure sent last winter to you at Sheffield.

It is requisite that I inform you theatricals are not in so flourishing a condition in this country as they were some two years ago. There are four theatres in the city each endeavoring to ruin the others, by foul means as well as fair. The reduction of the prices of admission has proved (as I always anticipated from the first suggestion of such a foolish plan) nearly ruinous to the managers. The public here often witness a performance in every respect equal to what is presented at the Theatres Royal, Drury Lane and Covent Garden for these prices: half a dollar to the boxes and a quarter dollar to the pit and gallery! The Chatham Theatre of which I am the Stage-Manager, at these low prices [earns] one thousand dollars. Acting is sold too cheap to the public and the result will be a general theatrical bankruptcy.[1]

Tragedians are in abundance – MACREADY – CONWAY – HAMBLIN – FORREST (now No. 1) COOPER – WALLACK – MAYWOOD and self with diverse others now invade New York. But it won't do; a diversion to the South must be made – or to jail three-fourths of the great men and managers must go.

Now, sir, I will deal fairly with you. If you will pledge yourself to me for three years, and sacredly promise that no inducement which may be held out by the unprincipled and daring speculators which abound in this country shall cause you to leave me, I will, for ten months in each year, give you thirty dollars per week, and an annual benefit which you shall divide with me. Beyond this sum I would not venture, the privilege of your name for benefits extra to be allowed me. . . . I should expect the terms on which you would be engaged to remain secret from all but ourselves.

Mind this – whether you play in my theatre or elsewhere in the United States, I should look for implicit and faithful performances of your duty toward me or my colleagues. In case I should require you to travel, when in the United States, which is most probable, I will defray all the charges of conveyance for you and your luggage (your living would not be included either by land or water) boarding (three meals a day), and your bedroom, may be had in a very respectable house here, and in Baltimore at from four to six dollars per week. "Lodgings to let" are very scarce and expensive, and the customs of this country in this respect, are essentially different to those of the English. . . .

In the Exeter Theatre last January were two actresses that I should like to engage. Miss P—— (Not the Miss. P. formerly of Drury Lane) and Miss H. If you will inquire after them – I will thank you. To each of these ladies a salary of fifteen dollars a week I can venture offering – 15 dollars are upward of three guineas and benefit annually.

Now sir I have offered to you and these ladies as much as I can in honesty afford to give. Their travelling expenses to and from theatres in the United States (not including board) I should defray as I told you. . . . Your line of business would be exclusively yours. For the ladies I would not make the guarantee. The

---

[1] Typical admissions at Drury Lane and Covent Garden during this period were a shilling for the upper gallery, seven shillings and six pence for the regular boxes, and three to four shillings for the pit. See Marc Baer, *Theatre and Disorder in Late Georgian London* (Oxford: Clarendon Press, 1992).

greatest actress in the world I may say is now in the city (Mrs. D——)[2] and several very talented women. . . . I would endeavour to make such arrangements with Miss P—— and Miss H—— as would not be very repugnant to their ambition.

The reason Mrs. D—— does not go to London is my strenuous advice to her against it. The passages from Europe I should expect repaid to me out of the salaries, by weekly deductions of three dollars each. The captain of the ship would call upon the parties or you might write to them on his visit to you. Everything on board will be furnished that is requisite for comfort, and the expenses I will settle from here previous to starting. Mind the ship you would come over in, is one expressly bargained for, and will bring you here where I shall be (if living) ready to welcome you. Let me recommend you to economy – see what a number of our brethren are reduced to indigence by their obstinate vanity. I have here Mr. D—— who was once in London the rival of ELLISTON, and is now a better actor – approaching the age of sixty, and not a dollar put by for a rainy day – too proud to accept a salary of twenty dollars per week in a regular engagement. He stars and starves. Many have been deceived and misled in their calculations in coming to this country. Some have cut their throats, etc. . . .

If you choose accepting my offer, get me those ladies. SIMS can perhaps tell you where they are, and I will on the first occasion send for you and them, with the articles of agreement to be signed in London and legally ratified on your arrival in America. Recollect this: the passages in summer, owing to the calms are longer in performing, but they are much safer. . . . The Newfoundland Bank is an ugly place to cross in winter, through it is often done, yet still it is a great risk. The "Crises" which left London Docks last January with all her passengers after being out for 68 days, and being spoken to on the banks by another vessel is not yet come nor will she ever. The icebergs no doubt struck her, as they have many – and the last farewell was echoed by the waves.

Write me soon and glean the information I ask for. The letter bag for United States vessels from London is kept at the North American Coffee House near the Bank of England. Yours Truly

Booth

[2] The reference to Mrs. D. is an allusion to Mary Ann Duff, the most highly acclaimed tragedienne in the American theatre prior to Charlotte Cushman. Although she was plagued by a troubled marriage, suffered from an opium habit, and died in poverty, her powers were still strong in the 1830s. See Joseph N. Ireland, *Mrs. Duff* (Boston: James R. Osgood, 1882). See Docs. 72 and 82.

In 1821, a black man known only as Mr. Brown, who had been a steward on the Liverpool Steamships, established the African Gardens, a pleasure resort in which New York's free blacks could purchase treats, walk the promenades, and hear concerts of occasional vocal and instrumental music. The gardens closed about a year later, but a theatre was fitted up there in which a company of black amateurs, led by the talented and historically neglected Jamaican James Hewlett, produced occasional dramas. Under this mulatto tragedian's leadership, the company moved to a building at the corner of Mercer and Bleecker streets in late October 1821, and fitted up a theatre in which a partition was inserted to provide a segregated section at the back of the seating area for white audience members. The companies next move was to be its last, as the following item from the pages of the New York *American* relates.[1]

[1] The best source tracing the history of the African Gardens remains Herbert Marshall and Mildred Stock, *Ira Aldridge, The Negro Tragedian* (Carbondale: Southern Illinois University Press, 1968). See also Samuel A. Hay, *African American Theatre: A Historical and Critical Analysis* (Cambridge and New York, 1994), and Doc. 166.

52   Closing of the African Gardens Theatre, 1822

New York American, January 10, 1822

HUNG BE THE HEAVENS WITH BLACK – SHAKESPEARE

We have heretofore noticed the performances of a black corps dramatique in this city, at their theatre, the corner of Bleecker and Mercer Streets. It appears that the sable managers, not satisfied with a small share of the profit and a great portion of fame, determined to rival the great Park Theatre, belonging to Messrs. Beekman and Astor, and accordingly hired the hotel next door to the theatre, where they announced their performances. The audiences were generally of a riotous character, and amused themselves by throwing crackers on the stage, and cracking jokes with the actors, until danger from fire and civil discord rendered it necessary to break up the establishment. The ebony-colored wags were notified by the police that they must announce their last performance, but they, defying the public authority, went on and acted nightly. It was at length considered necessary to interpose the arm of authority, and on Monday evening a dozen watchmen made part of the audience. The play was *Richard*. The watchmen interrupted the royal Plantagenet in one of his soliloquies with, "Hello, you – there – come along with me."

Richard replied with a real tragic grin, "Fellow begone – I'm not at leisure."

"Not at leisure?" says the watchman. "We'll find time for you, so come along."

Several immediately ascended the stage and arrested His Majesty. "Where am I going?" says he. "To de tower?"

"No, to the watch house," said the Knights of the Lantern.

So forthwith Richard, Richmond, Lady Ann, the dead King Henry, Queen Elizabeth, and the two young princes were escorted in their tinselled robes, to the watch house, into which they marched with royal contempt and defiance. King Richard dropped his character and assumed Macbeth, and, on his entrance, broke out:

"How now you black and secret
Midnight hags – what are you about?"

"Come, come," said the watch, "none of your play-acting airs – into the black hole with you." The sable corps were thrust in one green room together where, for some time, they were loud and theatrical; ever and anon, one would thrust his head through a circular hole to survey the grim visages of the watchmen. Finally they plead so hard in blank verse, and promised never to act Shakespeare again, that the Police Magistrates released them at a very late hour.

Most theatres constructed during the period were owned by joint-stock companies composed of individuals who frequently had little knowledge of theatrical business. They would then lease the buildings to theatre managers. The following minutes from the organization responsible for the construction of New York's first Bowery Theatre are representative.

53   Minutes Regarding Bowery Theatre, 1826
Harvard Theatre Collection

At a meeting of persons called for the purpose of taking into consideration the expediency of erecting a theatre in the upper part of the city Matthew Reed was appointed Chairman and S. L. Gouverners Secretary . . . on 8th April, 1826.

Resolved that a capital be formed of $70,000 to be subscribed if possible by seven persons.

Resolved that a theatre be erected on grounds in the Bowery to be purchased of H. Astor known as the Bully Head, and the building be 75 feet wide, 110 feet deep, and 52 feet high.

Resolved that a committee of four be appointed to superintend the concerns of the theatre association and that Matthew Reed, Thomas S. Smith, George W. Brown, and Samuel L. Gouverners be the committee.

Resolved that Daniel P. Ingraham be appointed Treasurer of the association. Resolved that fifty percent of the stock subscribed for be paid on the first of May to the Treasurer.

Resolved that the Theatre be leased to W. Gilfert for one year at 12 percent on the cost deducting the estimated cost of the stores and cellars, and to be at liberty to take it for 2 years more from 1st May 1827 at a rent to be agreed not more than $10,000.

54   Drop Curtain of First Bowery Theatre, 1826
Harvard Theatre Collection

Like most of the theatres on the Eastern seaboard, the Boston Theatre was owned by a joint-stock company. The following from the treasurer's account book indicates that the season 1830–31 was a profitable one, and the corporation was able to pay its annual dividend to shareholders.

55   Treasurer's Account Book, Boston Theatre, 1831
Treasurer's Account Book, Boston Theatre; Harvard Theatre Collection

Proprietors	No. of Shares	Amount of Dividend (Dollars)	Date 1831
Austin, James T.	1	28	Sept.
Babcock, Samuel M.	2	56	Sept. 1
Blake, George.	3	84	Sept.
Bartlett, Thomas.	2	56	Sept.
Bradlee, Joseph P.	1	28	Sept. 1
Bradbury, Charles.	2	56	Sept. 1
Billings, Samuel.	1	28	Sept. 6
Billings, Wm. G.	1	28	Sept. 6
City of Boston.	1	28	Sept. 1
Collidge, Joseph.	2	56	Sept. 1
Collidge, Thomas B.	1	28	Sept. 1

Clark, Edward D.	I	28	Sept. I
Columbian Ins. Co.	2	56	Sept. I
Dickson, James A.	I	28	Sept.
Dennie, Thomas.	I	28	Sept. 2
Farley, Thomas.	I	28	Sept. I
Howard, Nath'l.	2	56	Sept. 6
Hays, Catherine.	I	28	
Hays, Howey.	I	28	
Hood, Charles.	I	28	Sept. I
Henshaw, Samuel.	I	28	Sept. I
Ingalls, Williams.	I	28	Sept.
Mills, James K.	I	28	Sept. I
Murdock, George.	I	28	Sept. I
Parkman, John.	20	560	Sept. I
Preston, Memember.	I	28	Apr. 13, 1832
Pratt, George. W.	I	28	Sept. I
Pickens, John.	I	28	Sept. 4
Roger, Henry B.	I	28	Dec. 14
Stugins, Russell.	I	28	Sept.
Sigourney, Daniel.	I	28	Nov. 17
Tonro, Rebecca.	I	28	
Thatcher, Thomas.	I	28	Sept. I
	60	1680	

Receipt for dividend of twenty-eight dollars for share, continued August 31, 1831.

Theatrical management could be a perilous enterprise with little profit for the manager. During the Mobile season of 1832, Sol Smith realized only a $25.00 profit at the end of an eight-week campaign.

56   Receipts, Mobile, 1832

Sol Smith, *Theatrical Management in the West and South for Thirty Years* (New York: Harper and Bros., 1868), p. 76

First	Week,	receipts	(4 nights) _ _ _ _ _ _ _ _ _ _ _ _ _ _ _	$320.00
Second	"	"	(6 nights) _ _ _ _ _ _ _ _ _ _ _ _ _ _ _	660.00
Third	"	"	(6 nights) _ _ _ _ _ _ _ _ _ _ _ _ _ _ _	820.00
Fourth	"	"	(5 nights) _ _ _ _ _ _ _ _ _ _ _ _ _ _ _	543.00
Fifth	"	"	(5 nights) _ _ _ _ _ _ _ _ _ _ _ _ _ _ _	505.00
Sixth	"	"	(6 nights) _ _ _ _ _ _ _ _ _ _ _ _ _ _ _	1279.00
Seventh	"	"	(6 nights) _ _ _ _ _ _ _ _ _ _ _ _ _ _ _	764.00
Eighth	"	"	(2 nights) _ _ _ _ _ _ _ _ _ _ _ _ _ _ _	255.00
Total receipts of the season		_ _		$5146.00

My expenses during the eight weeks, including $575 paid to stars and without reckon-
ing travelling expenses to and from Mobile amounted to

$5121.00

Leaving me a profit of -   25.00

The weekly payroll for Francis Courtney Wemyss' Pittsburgh Theatre is representative of
the expenses for operating a typical company. Note that T. D. Rice, soon to earn fame and
fortune as "Jim Crow" is listed as a mere stock actor earning $12.00 per week.

57   Payroll for Pittsburgh Theatre, 1833

Ms. account book, Pittsburgh Theatre; Harvard Theatre Collection

Pittsburgh Theatre salary list for the 1st week of season 9/9/33	am't of saries for the week	Deductions for FC Wemyss[1]	Deductions for cash from office	am't of salaries paid for week
Mr. Wemyss	50.00	"	"	50.00
Mr. J. Sefton	30.00	5.00	5.00	20.00
Mr. W. Sefton	15.00	5.00	"	10.00
Mr. Spencer	15.00	5.00	1.00	9.00
Mr. Parsloe	20.00	"	"	20.00
Mr. L. Cathwell	15.00	8.00	5.00	2.00
Mr. Rice	12.00	"	5.00	7.00
Mr. McDongall (& W ⅔)[2]	10.66	"	5.50	5.16
Mr. Smith & W	25.00	2.00	5.00	18.00
Mr. A. Addams	15.00	5.00	1.00	9.00
Mr. Eberle & W	22.00	5.00	5.00	12.00
Mrs. Turner & Children	20.00	"	7.00	13.00
Mr. Bannister	8.00	"	"	8.00
Mr. Bannister[3]	20.00	"	"	8.00
Mr. Russ (S. S.)	8.00	"	"	8.00

[1] One can only assume that individual members of the company were in debt to Wemyss and that
   he was retiring the debts by withholding amounts from their salaries.
[2] Refers to the performer's wife drawing an additional two-thirds of his base salary.
[3] I assume the repetition of this name is an entry error on Wemyss' part.

The following comparison of expenses and profits at the National and the Park, New
York's two leading theatres during the season of 1838–39, appeared in a London daily
paper. It shows that Wallack's management challenged the venerable supremacy of the
Park strongly until the National burned down on September 28, 1839.

58   Profit Sheets at National and Park Theatres, 1839

Morning Post (London), June 10, 1839; reprinted in *Spirit of the Times*, 9 (July 6, 1839), 216

The weekly expenses of the Park Theatre (Simpson's) are calculated at 1,960 dollars, including everything, excepting "stars" and extras attached to new pieces. The expenses of the National (Wallack's), with the same reservation, are 1,890 dollars, being 70 dollars less than the Park. During the season from the 1st of September, 1838, the average receipts of the Park amounted to 250 dollars per night, making 46,250 dollars for the season, the expenses being for the same period (30 weeks) equal of 58,900 dollars; exhibiting – much to be deplored – a loss of 12,550 dollars, exclusive of "stars." On the other hand, and clearly demonstrating that the fluctuating nature of theatrical property extends across the Atlantic, at the National, from the 1st of September to the 1st of April (185 Nights) the receipts averaging at the rate of 600 per night, made 111,000 dollars for the season. The expenses of this theatre for 30 weeks, at 1,890 per week, would be equal to 56,700 dollars, leaving to pay profits and "stars" 55,300 dollars. The "stars" received at the National . . . [a] total 36,800 dollars. Thus leaving nearly 20,000 dollars profits on the season.

AGGREGATE SUM TOTAL

	Park	National
Expenses per week	1,960	1,890
Receipts for the season	46,250	111,000
Aggregated expenses	48,800	56,700
Stars, etc.	10,000	36,680
Profits		18,620
Loss	12,500	

The following contract is unusual for the 1840s because members of stock companies had their lines of business specified in their annual contracts. Mitchell, manager of the Olympic in New York, was the first to abolish lines of business.

59   Contract between William Mitchell and Mary Taylor, 1843

Ms. *Olympic Contract Book*; Harvard Theatre Collection

I Mary Taylor do hereby engage to render my services as an actress and vocalist in Mr. Mitchell's Company for the ensuing season for a weekly salary of ten dollars.

And I do further agree to be in all things governed by the usual rules of the establishment.

Touring performers contracted for their services in one of two fashions: either a flat fee per evening, with a benefit included during their engagement; or a percentage of the gross receipts for every night on which they appeared. The option to extend the length of the engagement was frequently contained in the contract, as in the following example from the Mobile Theatre under the managment of Ludlow and Smith.

60   Contract between Ludlow and Smith and David Hughes, 1845

Ms. contract between David Hughes and the firm of Ludlow and Smith, January 24, 1845; Harvard Theatre Collection

It is hereby understood that Mr. Hughes and children perform in the Mobile Theatre on Monday evening January 27th 1845 – giving one of their usual concerts – and that Mr. Hughes for the services of himself and children shall receive one-fourth of the entire receipts of the theatre on that night.

It is further understood that after the one night above stated, if Ludlow and Smith shall so determine, Mr. Hughes and children shall give three additional concerts in the theatre or more if so required by Ludlow and Smith, receive the same remuneration as above.

It is likewise understood that if Mr. Hughes and children give more than one concert, or above in the theatre, that then and in that case they are not to give concerts at any other place in the city of Mobile during the present theatrical season of Ludlow and Smith.

Throughout most of the nineteenth century star performers bought new plays outright that would serve them as remunerative performance vehicles. Works from London which were pirated or published were performed without any royalties paid to the playwrights, as no international copyright and royalty agreement was in existence. The following letter to Ludlow and Smith from James Mowatt is an early attempt on the part of a playwright to control royalty payments for performance of a play. *Fashion* had proven phenomenally popular in New York, and Mowatt, the playwright's husband, guarded the manuscript carefully in order to derive additional income from it.

61   Letter from James Mowatt to Ludlow and Smith, 1845

Ms. letter, James Mowatt to Ludlow and Smith, April 7, 1845; Harvard Theatre Collection

Mr. Chippendale has applied to me on your behalf to state the terms for the performance of the new comedy of *Fashion* at New Orleans, Mobile, and St. Louis. As you will see by the papers the comedy has proved the most successful hit the Park has made in a long time, so much so that Mr. Placide who had an engagement at the Park entered into before he went south, has postponed his appearance indefinitely, although he was last week announced to appear on this day. Either he or the Park's management or both have thought it for their mutual interest to keep the comedy running until Mr. Anderson appears . . . on 14th next: a time agreed on in England upon his engagement with Mr. Simpson. These facts speak sufficiently for the merits of the comedy. I have just completed an arrangement for its production at the Walnut St. Theatre in Philadelphia, and have applications from both the Boston theatres. I find that all the theatres prefer an arrangement contingent upon the success of the run of the piece, to paying a definite sum for a given time. I therefore make you an offer on that principle, which leaves you at liberty to represent it one night or more as you may find to your interest. The Park covered all their extra expenditure on the receipts of the first night as I have reason to believe.

The rate I fix upon, is one agreed upon between Mr. Barry of the Park and myself as a fair one for its production at Boston. Considering now that its success is placed beyond a doubt and there was no risk in bringing it out, [it] is this: Fifteen percent of the gross receipts of the house on each of the first three nights of performance, and ten percent on each night the play is performed afterwards. The theatre to have the privilege of announcing the third night as being for the author's benefit. Upon these terms I will send you a copy of the play, and you can perform it as often as you find it to your advantage, exclusively for your use in those cities. Of one thing you may be certain. . . . Should Mrs. Mowatt or any other writer produce two such comedies a year it will effectively put a stop to the foreign stars taking all the profits . . . made by our theatres, and leaving the theatres in a state of bankruptcy.

Mr. Simpson has already offered to engage with me to set aside a given number of nights of the best of the season next fall for the production of a new comedy which Mrs. Mowatt is now engaged upon. Although I am not certain whether it will not be best for my interest to have it first played in London. I merely mention Mr. Simpson's offer to show how effectively a few such pieces would compel the stars to come to more reasonable terms, and good ones can be produced from native talent, if sufficient encouragement is offered by the managers.

The following pay sheet for the Park Theatre's stock company is of interest in that Frank S. Chanfrau, who was to become a major star two years later, was earning $15.00 per week as a stock actor in 1846.

62   Park Theatre Stock Company Pay Sheet, 1846
Harvard Theatre Collection

E. Simpson	$50	D. Anderson	10
T. Barry	50	McDowell	10

C. Pass	35	Sprague, others	10
Mr. & Mrs. Doyett	34	Blake Treasurer	25
George Barrett	30	Hillyard Scene Painter	25
George Andrews	25	Dejone Property Man	15
Mr. & Mrs. Sutherland	25	Chubb Orchestra Leader	25
John Fisher	20	Mrs. Knight	25
Bellamy	18	Mrs. Vernon	20
S. Pearson	16	Mrs. Abbott	18
A. Andrews	15	Miss Kate Horn	12
John Povey	15	Miss Gordon	12
James Stark	15	2 Misses Denin	10
F. S. Chanfrau	15	Miss Julia Mills	6
Jones	14		
Gallot	12		

In the following letter F. C. Wemyss attempts to correct an author's erroneous statements concerning the origins of cash guarantees for starring players.

63   Letter from F. C. Wemyss to McMakin, 1847

Ms. letter, F. C. Wemyss to McMakin, July 3, 1847; Harvard Theatre Collection

A good-natured friend of mine has this morning placed in my hand your book dated July 3, 1847 in which with much glee he pointed out a paragraph signed "One who knows." I should not have thought an anonymous communication worth notice if it had not been followed by an *editorial* remark of a most *insidious* nature. We have known each other many years and you are one among the few whose good opinion I value. The greatest objection urged against the book in question is its *Truth*. It is said to contain too much truth and in the opinion of many, truths which ought not to have been made known. But in all trials where a witness is produced to shake the truth of a statement he has to undergo a severe cross-examination and if proved to be unworthy of credit himself, how much is his evidence worth?

Your correspondent states [that] the practice of giving a certainty[1] for acting commenced with Master Burke (who acted for the first time in Philadelphia on the 14th of December 1830).

Why, in 1828 Mr. Cooper received a certainty of Mr. E. Knight. Miss Povey received $50 a night. In January of 1829 Mr. E. Forrest had received $200 per night. Mr. Wallack in 1828 was engaged to act for a certain sum of money without regard to receipts. Madam Fearon if I am rightly informed was also engaged

---

[1] The practice of a certainty, or minimal cash guarantee, gradually replaced the habitual contractual practice of stars receiving a percentage of the gross receipts for each performance during the 1820s.

for a certainty. Mr. Austin received 10 lbs. sterling per night in 1827 as a certainty. Schiller and wife, Herr Cline, Hamblin and the French Corps de Ballet all received a certain sum per night before Master Burke arrived in the United States!!

These are facts so easily ascertained. . . . Enquire of Mr. W. B. Wood whether the season of 1822–23 or 1824 and 25 he did not pay Mr. Cooper fifty dollars per night as a certainty, instead of sharing after the expenses. . . . Enquire also whether Mr. Cooper ever asked more when he engaged upon a certainty, always excluding the receipts of his benefits. In sharing after the manager's expenses Mr. Cooper demanded *nothing as a certainty* but entered into a speculation upon the thought of the attraction of his name – and a very safe one it was – at that time.

I have perhaps wasted too much of your time upon a subject not worth the ink and paper but I am unwilling *you* should labor under an erroneous conclusion and to your own sense of justice I leave it to remove from your readers' minds the doubts you have raised as to the statements to be found in *Twenty Six Years in The Life of An Actor and Manager* which as a book of statistics can be relied upon in every instance where they are quoted.

P.S. I do not wish you to publish this letter which is written for your own information, but to show you how confident I am of the truth of my statement that Mr. Cooper asked and received only fifty dollars per night when he acted in Philadelphia on a certainty – I will leave it to the decision of Mr. Cooper himself and if you think it worthwhile will address a letter to him on the subject and enclose you his answer.

By the late 1840s many theatrical managers found themselves in an economic dilemma of their own making. Since the day of Cooke they had puffed the stars and developed a taste for stellar performers in their audiences to the point that theatregoers ceased being satisfied with the efforts of a mere stock company. As stars' demands for salaries had risen, managers had complied until they were operating on a perilously thin margin of hoped for profit. The following letter from C. A. Logan to Sol Smith is representative of the manager's problem in the Ohio Valley.

64   Letter from C. A. Logan to Sol Smith, 1848
Smith, *Theatrical Management*, p. 207

My Dear Old Friend – I have just received your friendly letter, and hasten to reply, although there is absolutely no news here, and scarce anything to write about. You, of course, ere this, must be aware that Forrest acted in Louisville, but you *may not* be aware that he received $200 a night for so acting. A melancholy fact:

$200 for each night, and on some nights he *played* to a less sum; one night, at least, the *receipts* were but $150, and he got $200, leaving the manager to pay $50 to the star beyond the gross receipts, besides his own expenses! Blessed system! His whole engagement in Louisville was a failure, and he told me yesterday that the houses were a series of thunderbolts to him – his manner of expressing astonishment at their thinness. He opened here last night to about $700 – a far better house than any he had in Louisville, his benefit there being $514. But he gets his $200 a night here too, and asked me yesterday whether, if successful, there would be a chance of renewal. I suppose he would extend the length indefinitely on the same terms . . . Forrest is evidently angry with you for not offering him an engagement in St. Louis. He told me yesterday (but remember, *this* must not be mentioned as coming from me) that he intended to *pay a visit* in St. Louis. I presume you understand the significance of his *paying a visit.* Some years ago he said to me in Philadelphia, "Logan, I start tomorrow for Charleston." "The devil you do!" I replied. "You told me only yesterday the manager had refused your terms." "True, that's the reason I'm going. When I'm on *that* spot I think I can make him *change his mind!*" *and he did.* I believe you know I am one of your sincerest well wishers, and therefore, if I speak plainly you will not misunderstand me. Your letter contains some justly indignant denunciations of the starring system. Ask yourself if you are not an active *particips criminis in it.* John Bates from the first took a strong stand against this monstrous abuse, and all my influence with him was exerted to confirm him in his resolves to resist these ruinous demands. He has constantly said if you will sustain us in this matter we can break it up in the West. But you always pursued the old course, and (as Bates says) endeavored to force certain stars upon him at exorbitant terms. It seems now that he is tired of refusing terms that all other managers give – tired of hearing the people say, "These performers play in all other cities; why do you not engage them?" Hence Forrest at length has triumphed, and draws from the treasury $200 a night! I rejoice to hear that your Southern season was prosperous. It is quite currently believed that you and the American were in *cahoots.*

It was not long after the discovery of gold at Sutter's Mill that theatres sprang up in California. The inflationary theatrical salaries are noted in the following letter to William Porter, editor of the *Spirit of the Times.*

65   Letter from "Old Pipes" to the *Spirit of the Times,* 1849

Spirit of the Times, 14 (December 15, 1849), 505

Well, here I am, settled. I am driving freight and making money in the auction and commissions business.

This city is growing up rapidly, and vessels are daily coming in, and some, without touching at San Francisco, find quieter and less expensive harbor charges in the principal city of the Sacramento River.

The theatre has opened at San Francisco, and a rich treat, you can imagine, I had in the performance. I send you the bill. . . . The play was the *Bandit, or the Forest Spectre*. It was full of blood and thunder, huge men in winding sheets, representing ghosts, pistols that missed fire, and a very abortive attempt at stage thunder. But the dresses were good and the effect upon the audience startling. The theatre is a beautiful building and is crowded nightly. Only think of it. Boxes $5, Pit $3! And actors(?) getting *four, five and six ounces a night!*[1] . . . Some of them would be glad to get six or eight dollars in the Bowery or Chatham Theatres. Edmund Kean, played once to 17s. 6d., and a man here, who would, perhaps, have been allowed to open his door and tell him he was wanted, or some such menial occupation, gets $50 and $60 a night. Strange country this! I tell you, old fellow, a man who would make a fortune here, sure in twelve months, and do more than any other man I know of in New York, and that is Walcot.[2] If he were out here he would, I think, put 'em through. He and Miss Clarke (of the Olympic) would do capitally.

I am making money and hope to see you, and take a smile once again, ere the clouds of the valley be upon me.

I send you a "gold specimen" and hope you will wear it and think of

"Old Pipes"

[1] Although the price of gold fluctuated wildly during the first year of the rush, the four to six ounces of gold per evening mentioned as a salary would have been worth $300 to $500.

[2] Charles Walcot was a popular New York comic actor who debuted at the Olympic in 1842 and later developed quite a following at Burton's and Wallack's Theatres.

By 1850 the abuses of the star system had become so financially hazardous to managers that some – Mitchell and Burton in New York, and Logan in Louisville – refused to hire stars and ran profitable theatres solely on the strengths of the plays they produced and excellent stock companies. The *Spirit of the Times* published the following article in an effort to show that star salaries had eroded managerial profits to the point of bankruptcy in many instances.

66 Newspaper Article, *Spirit of the Times*, 1850

Spirit of the Times, 20 (May 4, 1850), 128

We have lately come into possession of some statistics connected with the subject, which will be of interest to a portion of our readers. It will be remembered that we made a few remarks, some time ago, on the ruinous effects of the custom of giving a lion's share to a single actor, and these statistics will serve to confirm what we then said. All the managers who have ever submitted to these abuses have been crippled, and many of them have been entirely ruined by their submission. We do not now refer to what is generally known as "the starring system," although that is bad enough, but to the abuse of that system. If theatres are to become permanent establishments – if the drama is worthy of countenance and encouragement – managers should set their forces against these abuses, and the public must bear them out in this plan.

Now the manager of the Louisville Theatre long ago determined to use all his efforts to put an end to this system, and he has persisted in that determination. The result [is] that he is the only manager in all our acquaintance who has been able always to maintain his business relations, and punctually to fulfill his engagements. And there is no other reason for this than his fixed purpose of not allowing actors to control his business. Let us come to the statistics spoken of before, and show that we are not mistaken in this matter.

In 1844 Ole Bull played four nights at the St. Charles Theatre, New Orleans, for the moderate price of two-thirds of the clear receipts, after deducting $100. Now let us work out the sum:

Entire receipts for four nights	$4082.00
Manager's portion	1623.00
Deduct expenses	1200.00
Additions to orchestra	200.00–400.00
Leaving manager's profit	223.00
Ole Bull's profit	2448.00

Macready's first engagement at the St. Charles Theatre was for sixteen nights. The average receipts were $628.42 per night.

Entire receipts	$628.42
Manager's half	314.21
Deduct expenses of theatre	300.00
Manager's profit	14.21
Macready's half	314.21

During the engagement Mr. M performed but four nights per week, which of course injured the other two nights seriously. On this gentleman's return from Mobile he played five nights.

Entire receipts per night	$436.00
Manager's half	218.00
Expenses of theatre	300.00
Manager's loss	82.00
Macready's profit	218.00

In Cincinnati, Mr. Macready played for seven nights to a nightly average of $392.00.

Manager's half_   196.00
Expenses of theatre _   180.00
Manager's profit _   16.00
Macready's profit _   196.00

In 1849, the same gentleman played a farewell engagement at the St. Charles Theatre for twenty-two nights.

Gross receipts _ $15,213.00
Manager's half _   7,606.50
Expenses at 300 per night _   6,600.00
Manager's profit _   1,006.50
Macready's profit _   7,606.50

Macready played gratuitously one night during this engagement. It must be remembered that, after the great actor leaves, the receipts are greatly diminished.

In 1844, Mr. Forrest played in Cincinnati for eleven nights.

Average receipts per night _   269.00
Manager's half_   134.50
Nightly expenses _   180.00
Manager's losses_   46.50
Forrest's profit _   134.50

In 1846 Mr. and Mrs. Kean played at the St. Charles for twenty-six nights.

Average receipts per night _   612.00
Managers half_   306.00
Nightly expenses _   300.00
Managers profit _   6.00
Actor's profit _   306.00

In St. Louis, the same actors played fourteen nights, at an average of $486, of which they received clear half, except on one night.

In 1848, Mr. Forrest performed thirty nights at the American Theatre, New Orleans. The receipts were $15,286.

Manager's half _ $7,643.00
Thirty nights' expenses _   7,500.00
Manager's profit _   143.00
Forrest's profit _   7,643.00

During this engagement Mr. Forrest received an injury which prevented his appearance, and on the sixteenth night the theatre was entirely closed; after which the managers lost, by Mr. Forrest's nonappearance, $1,000. So that the entire engagement resulted in a loss to the management of over $800.00.

We might go on multiplying examples of this kind, but we have already given enough to prove that well-regulated theatres cannot exist under such a method.

These remarks do not refer to the "starring system," but to the course of a few actors who either are really meritorious, or, upon whom a certain class of theatregoers have "thrust greatness." Our own public should greatly support the manager in the firm and truly consistent course he has pursued in this matter; satisfied that even if these "big people" do sometimes pass us by, they will soon weary of proceeding, and be glad in the end to exhibit their attainments, and live and let live.

The public who patronize, must in justice protest, or what will be the finish of the system? A bankrupt treasury or a fraudulent manager, who, when justifying himself to the world, pleads the excuse of having been compelled to engage auxiliaries, and on such terms as precluded the possibility of honesty to his patrons or his actors.

Now the public, whilst entitled to witness all the available talent in the country, will not only carry their point, but correct a selfish abuse, by bearing in mind – "If the mountain will not come to Mahomet, Mahomet must visit the mountain."

II.   *Acting*

The period from 1810 to 1865 is the age of the touring star in the American theatre. While specialty performers and comic actors travelled extensively as stars, the most popular and important of the travelling luminaries were tragedians. Most of them came to America with established English reputations. Some remained here; others returned home. Of the native-born tragedians, the greatest was certainly Edwin Forrest. The following review of his debut indicates that he showed strong promise while still a youth.

67   Review of Edwin Forrest's Debut, 1820

Untitled, undated clipping from a Philadelphia newspaper of 1820, in *Actors and Actresses of Great Britain and the United States: From the Days of David Garrick to the Present Time*, ed. Brander Mathews and Laurence Hutton, 5 vols. (New York: Cassell, 1886), III, pt. 1; Harvard Theatre Collection

We rarely trouble our readers with dramatic news, the pleasures of scenic representation are, however, favorites with us. The tragedy of *Douglas* was presented at the theatre Walnut Street, on Monday, to a very respectable audience, and we understand will be repeated tomorrow evening.

The chief object of attraction was a youth of this city, of about fifteen, of the name of *Forrest*, who made his *debut* in young Norval. The play was well got up throughout, well sustained. . . . Of the performance of young Norval, we must say that it was uncommon in the performance by such a youth, as it was extraordinary in just conception and the exemption from the idea of *artifice*, such as is common in the most practiced players. We mean that the *sentiment* of the character obtained such full possession of the youth, as to take away in appearance every consideration of an audience or a drama, and to give *Norval* as if it were the natural speaking of the shepherd of the Grampian Hills, suddenly revealed by instinct to the son of Douglas. We were much surprised at the excellence of his elocution; his self-possession in speech and gesture; and a voice that, without straining or exertion, was of such volume and fine tenor, as to carry every tone and articulation to the remotest corner of the theatre. We consider this eulogium not more than justice requires. Of faults we had little to say; some occasional stiffness in the still moments of the passive action, and that difficulty of all young performers in the management of the hands. One verbal error only we perceived in the description of the action which led to his introduction; when he says –

> a band of fifty men.

He substituted the word *group* for *band* – slips of this kind are frequent with the very best performers; and we only noted this to prove that our attention was not astray, nor our judgment partial. We trust that this young gentleman will find the patronage to which his extraordinary ripeness of faculty and his modest deportment entitle him.

From October 1826 through spring 1827 Forrest played frequently at the new Bowery Theatre in New York, and rapidly established himself as a star. The following assessment of his abilities indicates, among other things, that the American press and American theatre audiences were hungry to support a native-born tragedian as the young country sought to develop its own cultural identity.

68   Assessment of Edwin Forrest, 1827

New York Mirror, and Ladies Literary Gazette, 4, no. 31 (February 24, 1827), 245

This young gentleman, not yet arrived at the age of twenty-one, as I have learned, from an authority entitled to full belief, has already exhibited a development of powers, a maturity of mind, an adaptation for, and advancement in, the arduous profession he has undertaken, which at once excite the wonder and admiration of all who behold him. Like the enchanted edifices of oriental story, he seems to have sprung into a beautiful existence, without the aid of time; and, while we were complaining that the stage was lighted only by borrowed luminaries of Europe, a star has arisen in our own hemisphere, which promises, ere long, to be hailed as the cynosure of the dramatic horizon.

The person of Mr. Forrest is well formed and commanding; his leg, arm, and hand, in particular, are molded with the most perfect symmetry. His face is handsome and expressive, and flexible to a degree which is seldom surpassed. His eyes are black, and capable of exhibiting, with equal truth, every gradation of feeling, from the meltings of love, to the lightning glances of revenge. His voice is sonorous and sweet, except when exerted for a long time, in giving vent to some demoniac passion; it then becomes somewhat harsh and dissonant, though still powerfully expressive. His attitudes are, in general, easy and graceful; and they invariably seem the result of the impulse of the moment, or of the circumstances of the scene, as they arise. We never see, in him, what so often disgusts us in others, a visible preparation for some particular attitude or start, which is to be ostensibly occasioned by a yet unuttered or unacted part of the drama. To illustrate my meaning, take the play of *Pizarro*, for example. I have seen many persons in the character of Rolla, some of them very good actors, and almost invariably there has been discoverable, to a close observer, a getting ready on the part of the Peruvian to seize the child of Cora, before that mode of rescue could properly suggest itself to his mind. Not so with Mr. Forrest. Let him be inspected every so minutely, and I will venture to say, that no person, unacquainted with the incidents of the story, could possibly foretell, in what a beautifully effective manner the preservation of the infant is to be accomplished. A neglect of propriety, in this respect, is sometimes attended with very laughable circumstances, when the scene, rightly conducted, would have created feelings of the deepest seriousness. . . .

Mr. Forrest has played since his first appearance in this city a variety of characters, and the rapturous applause, which has attended upon every effort, speaks volumes in favor of the ability he has displayed. His Damon, Othello, William Tell, and Sir Edward Mortimer, in particular, have created an impression in the minds of all who beheld him, that will never be effaced. His delineation of these characters, young as he is, displays evidence of a close and discriminating study, of a brilliancy of genius, a depth of feeling, and acquaintance with the working of the human soul; and a grasp of intellect, which, while they already rank him among the greatest, must eventually, if (as is but fair to suppose he will) be increased in mental vigor as he increases in years and experience, place his name upon as proud a summit as has ever been attained by histrionic exertions.

Most of the touring English tragedians prior to 1830 were contracted by Stephen Price to appear at the Park Theatre, and then performed under his auspices on a tour throughout the established cities of the growing country. Not so Junius Brutus Booth, who fled England to escape some complications in his personal life and appeared unheralded and unannounced in Virginia in 1821. Noah Ludlow remembers the effect Booth's playing had on his fellow performers in Petersburg, Virginia when he first appeared there.

69   Noah Ludlow on J. B. Booth, 1821

Noah M. Ludlow, *Dramatic Life as I Found It* (St. Louis: G. J. Jones, 1880), pp. 224–25

When the curtain rose at night all the company were on the alert to see the supposed great actor make his entrance before the audience. When the proper scene opened Mr. Booth walked on the stage, made no recognition of the reception applause, and in an apparently meditative mood began the soliloquy of "Now is the winter of our discontent," which he delivered with seeming indifference, and with little if any point, something after the manner of a school-boy repeating a lesson of which he had learned the words, but was heedless of their meaning; and then made his exit, without receiving any additional applause. I was not where I could ascertain the impression made upon the audience, but on the stage, at the side-scenes, the actors were looking at each other in all kinds of ways, expressive of astonishment and disgust. I was standing near Mr. Benton, an old actor, the King Henry of the evening, and as I turned to go away, he said, "What do you think of him Mr. Ludlow?" "Think," I replied, "why I think, as I thought before, that he is an imposter! What do *you* think of him?" "Why sir," said Benton, "if the remainder of his *Richard* should prove like the beginning, I have never yet, I suppose, seen the character played, for it is unlike any I ever saw; it may be very good, but I don't fancy it." I found that among the company, generally, a like estimate of the great man prevailed, Mr. Russell being the only exception; he, having witnessed Mr. Booth's acting at Richmond, still persisted in saying he was the greatest actor he had ever seen. His scene with Lady Anne, where he encounters and interrupts the funeral procession of King Henry VI, was as tame and pointless as his first soliloquy. I had seen George Frederick Cooke perform Richard III about ten years prior to the time that I saw Mr. Booth first, at which period I was a youth of sixteen years of age, when impressions are vivid and lasting, and I had retained a perfect recollection of the effects Mr. Cooke produced on the audience, myself included; and it seemed to me that no *great actor* would pass through these two scenes with that careless indifference that Mr. Booth evinced. It has ever remained a mystery to me why Mr. Booth *always* slighted the first two acts of *Richard III*, and I can only account for it on the supposition that it was with the view of reserving his powers for the remaining three acts, in which considerable physical as well as mental efforts are required; and yet, when I first met Mr. Booth, he did not appear to be deficient in *physique*. I retained my first impression of Mr. Booth until he came to the fourth act, where, in a scene with Buckingham, he hints at the murder of the young princes. Then I thought I discovered something worthy of a great actor. From that on his acting was unique and wonderful! I had never seen anyone produce such effects, and come so near my ideas of the character; not even Mr. Cooke, who was as far below Mr. Booth in the last two acts as he was above him in the first three. When the curtain fell upon the finishing of the play, there was a burst of applause from audience and actors such as I will venture to say Petersburg never knew before, nor has known since.

One of the greatest sensations to visit America during the 1820s was Edmund Kean. On two separate tours he thrilled audiences with his passionate acting. The following review of his King Lear at the Walnut Street Theatre assesses both strengths and weaknesses.

70   Review of Edmund Kean, 1821

Philadelphia Democratic Press, January 20, 1821; clipping in Harvard Theatre Collection

It has been well remarked, that it is as useless for "presumptious, fat-witted persons," to except against Mr. Kean's style of acting, as it is for "instinctive and ephemeral critics" to praise it, so long as he continues to crowd the theatre with the fashion and intellect of our city. This is the touchstone of merit. This is an indisputable tribute to great powers and attainments. In times like these, no performer other than one of uncommon excellence could fill our theatre. Last night the house was more full than we had before seen it. Do our most intelligent citizens thus pay their money, and consume their time, because they are gratified by the display of Mr. Kean's superior talents, or are they such ... "Self-Punishers," as to crowd the theatre and applaud the performer, for no other motive than a wish to feed the insatiable vanity of "ephemeral critics"?

The Lear of Mr. Kean was a performance worthy of the high reputation he has established. He was a choleric, feeble, old man, his voice and his limbs had all the tremor of passion and the feebleness of age. His madness was of a moody melancholy kind. The darkness of his mind was sometimes lighted up by a gleam of natural and tender feeling. The scenes with Cordelia, when his mind was recovering, and had recovered, its sanity were tenderly affectionate and feelingly apprehensive.

It was in some of those scenes that Mr. Kean used, in his happiest manner, a kind of hysterical sobbing and whimpering, which he, and he alone, has dared to introduce upon the stage. Heretofore all expressions of grief and anguish have been restricted to the shedding of tears, to action, and to words, but Mr. Kean, with a confidence which never exists but in superior minds, has ventured, in order to give a yet more natural expression of sorrow upon wounds which we find it impossible to describe by words, other than by saying they are something in the nature of underhand exclamations of involuntary moans and hysteric sobs. We are frank to confess, that however we may admire the intrepidity of the man who ventures upon an unknown path, we cannot feel that, as he uses those sounds, as to make an epoch in the improvement of the histrionic art, but as it now meets our ear, it is more frequently offensive than admirable.

When Kean returned to this country in 1825, the citizenry was hostile as a result of an affront to audiences in Boston in May 1821 which had produced general condemnation of the actor in the newspapers of the eastern cities and a riot in New York.[1] Feeling that

---

[1] Kean had refused to perform on May 25, 1821, in Boston owing to the almost empty house. He then cancelled the remainder of his engagement and left the city the next morning. The democratically inclined newspapers in Boston, New York, and Philadelphia roundly condemned Kean's behavior as an insult to the emerging national character. The best account of the controversy, with

the national honor had been insulted, playgoers responded negatively to Kean's appearance in all of the Eastern seaboard cities. The broken tragedian tried to make his peace with American audience in several manners. The following "card" (or personal advertisement) is one example of his attempt to regain public favor.

---

reprints of newspaper articles and letters, is in William W. Clapp, Jr., *A Record of the Boston Stage* (Boston: James Monroe, 1853; reprinted New York: Benjamin Blom, 1968), pp. 180–93. See Doc. 115.

71   Edmund Kean "Card" in *New York Enquirer,* 1825

Quoted in Francis Courtney Wemyss, *Twenty-Six Years of the Life of an Actor and Manager* (New York: Burgess, Stringer and Co., 1847), p. 97

Mr. Editor: Sir, With oppressed feelings, heart-rending to my friends, and triumphant to my enemies, I make an appeal to that country famed for hospitality to the stranger, and mercy to the conquered. Allow me to say, sir, whatever are my offenses, I disdain all intention of offering anything in the shape of disrespect towards the inhabitants of New York. They received me from the first with an enthusiasm, grateful, in those hours, to my pride – in the present, to my memory. I cannot recall to my mind any act or thought that did not prompt me to an unfeigned acknowledgment of their favors as a public and profound admiration of the private worth of those circles in which I had the honor of moving.

That I have committed an error appears too evident, from the all decisive voice of the public; but surely it is but justice to the delinquent, whatever may be his enormities, to be allowed to make reparation where the offenses were committed. My misunderstanding took place in Boston – to Boston I shall assuredly go to apologize for my indiscretion. I visit this country now under different feelings and auspices than on a former occasion. Then I was an ambitious man, and the proud representative of Shakespeare's heroes. The spark of ambition is extinct, and I merely ask a shelter in which to close my professional and mortal career. I give the weapon into the hand of my enemies; if they are brave they will not turn it against the defenseless.

While most acknowledge Charlotte Cushman as America's first native tragic actress of the highest magnitude, the immigrant Mary Ann Duff was certainly her most important predecessor. She was an extraordinary actress as the following review suggests. See also Docs. 51 and 82.

72   Review of Mary Ann Duff, 1832

Spirit of the Times, 1 (February 11, 1832), n.p.

Mrs. Duff's Benefit – We attended the benefit of this lady on Monday, and must allow that she even exceeded the high opinion we have ever entertained of her merits. She is justly styled the "Siddons" of the American stage, as all those who have enjoyed the pleasures of seeing her in Jane Shore, Isabella, Belvadire, Lady Macbeth, or Mrs. Haller will acknowledge. She has applied her great and varied accomplishments to improvement in her profession, and her control over the muscular powers of her countenance renders her able to display the conflicts of passion with the greatest verisimilitude to nature. Her enunciation is so clear, so full, so "organ-like," that though she may have possibly an equal, (which we beg to doubt), she certainly has no superior: and none, we boldly affirm, can compare with her in mellowed sweetness and passionate, but harmonious energy in pathetic passages. Her compass of voice is at times startling, and during her present engagement at Richmond Hill, she has in this respect, if we may be allowed the expression, surpassed herself. On Monday she called upon all her thrilling powers, and though the house was crowded, it was in her presence as silent as the tomb. Many a rugged and time-worn worldling, whom the loss of friends and property could not have moved, refused her not the passing tribute of a tear. Although Isabella is not her *chef d'oeuvre*, in her personation of this unfortunate, the effect was *immense*.

Mrs. Duff is an especial favorite withall: her reading being distinguished by an accuracy of phrase and an exceedingly judicious distribution of emphasis in which she particularly excels, which show her to have been a close student, not merely of the words, but the spirit of the author. She has uniformly drawn full houses which we feel gratified to record. It may not be generally known that she has a family depending on her exertions for support, and that as a widow and a mother, despite her unsurpassed talents as an actress, she possesses claims of no ordinary description on the liberal patronage so freely bestowed by the New York community.

Managers were frequently forced to change bills at the last moment owing to the caprice of star performers. Jane Placide, member of a large family of actors during the first half of the nineteenth century, suggested the following last-minute changes to Wemyss, manager of the Chestnut Street Theatre, Philadelphia, during her star engagement of November 1828.

73   Letter from Jane Placide to F. C. Wemyss, 1828

Ms. letter, Jane Placide to F. C. Wemyss, November 26, 1828; Harvard Theatre Collection

Dear Sir,

Tomorrow evening I should like to play Madam Clemant if practicable.

You say it has not been done for some time. Therefore, I think it may prove more attractive than anything else I could do.

On Saturday "Wedding Christy" and "Thuren."

Yours respectfully,

Jane Placide

You had better substitute "Wedding Christy" and "Thuren" for tomorrow evening; "Apostate" on Saturday. I will call as soon as possible.

J. P.

The following letter from Lydia Kelly, a minor star of the 1820s, reflects the conditions that
travelling stars frequently imposed upon theatre managers. It was probably addressed to
Warren and Wood concerning employment at their theatre in Philadelphia or in Baltimore.

74   Letter from Lydia Kelly, 1828

Ms. letter, Lydia Kelly, 1828; Harvard Theatre Collection

Sirs,

I find my letter written yesterday was too late for the post, you will, therefore,
receive it with this. I can commence on Thursday the 8th and play on the Saturday, or commence on the Friday and play on the Saturday. This will give two
nights more and as I make the 1st engagement eight nights and [a] benefit, and
the second six and [a] benefit. We can get the whole over in the one month – this
is the only way I can, or will arrange and I shall look to you for the fulfillment of
the proposals contained in your letters, that is – the option of the second engagement and the agreement and expressions that another star should play on the
alternate nights.

I had written to Boston with a quotation from your letter on the foundation
of which my engagement there was put off. Mr. Simpson was much disarranged
by the contradiction of the terms and yourself. I wait your answer by return.

James Hackett, the first native "Yankee" star, did well in establishing a specialty of his
droll down-easters prior to a tour of England during 1833. But during his absence,
another performer, George Handel "Yankee" Hill, started playing Yankee characters and
began playing a role that Hackett believed was his legal property. Hackett expressed his
outrage to Wemyss.

75   Letter from James Hackett to F. C. Wemyss, 1833

Wemyss, *Twenty-Six Years*, pp. 139–40

My Dear Wemyss:

During my absence in England, *Mr. Hill* has had the impudence, as well as
injustice, to perform, without my permission, my best Yankee character, *Solomon
Swop* (well known as unpublished, and of my own originating) at the Park (some
dozen times) and elsewhere. I have, of course, a remedy *at law* against *him* and

the *managers* who permit it, but a resort to it should be looked upon, perhaps, by the public (who don't understand these matters), as a kind of *ill nature* on my part, and beneath me. . . . Therefore to prevent my property being thus further hackneyed, after being taken down from my mouth, or otherwise surreptitiously obtained, I have notified managers generally of the fact, and shall consider their *permitting* such an infringement of the most inalienable of literary rights (the spinning of one's own brains), an act of open hostility to me, and proceed accordingly. Mr. Hill has characters enough of his own, without carrying on that species of *Yankeeism*; and if I cannot protect myself from having my character made stale by such depredations, I will resort to rigorous measures against both him and the manager, wherever the infringement transpires. Of course, I do not fear *your* permitting or countenancing such *dishonesty*, but I thought I would drop you a line, as you might be ignorant of the *fact* of *Solomon Swop being*, in *every* respect, my own *exclusive property*. I have stopped him in *Boston, New York*, and *here*, but understand he has been trying it in *Albany*; and, though he will not attempt it *again there*, if I can catch him in New York, where I am returning tomorrow, I must clap the "*Grace*"[1] upon him for example's sake.

Wishing you all success, and hoping to have a chance with you next season, I remain

Yours truly,

Jas. H. Hackett

NB I shall esteem it a *personal* mark of friendship, if you will inform me of any attempt at keeping this *Yankee piracy* coming to your knowledge in the course of Mr. Hill's projected peregrinations *in the West, this winter*. J. H. H. What a farrago of nonsense!

[1] To "clap the grace" is an early nineteenth-century equivalent of the contemporary American idiom, to throw the fear of God into someone.

As an established star of the 1830s, Hackett was in a position to dictate his own terms to most managers.

76   Letter from James Hackett to a Theatre Manager, 1834

Ms. letter, James Hackett, August 19, 1834; Harvard Theatre Collection

My Dear Sir

I have read yours of 9th August. I do intend being in Cincinnati the last week in Oct. on my way to Louisville and New Orleans and will endeavor to be with you the week prior to my stay in the first named place if possible. I shall be able to name times in the course of a fortnight and will then name terms and write you.

Mrs. Sharpe is to star for six nights and will probably commence in Cincinnati Monday 29 Sept. If you would like her for three stock nights at 15 percent of receipts and half benefit on the 4th . . . (Monday 15th Sept., Friday 19, Monday 22nd, and benefit Wednesday 24th) write immediately to me at this address. . . . State also whether she would be able to get from Pittsburgh to Cincinnati between 25th and 28th inclusive else she would have to begin with you on Monday 15th Sept and terminate that week. You are aware I suppose that they play no high tragedy and comedy only and some piece of her own – also *Victorine* and *Henriette*.

Many types of specialty performers and theatrical fads waxed and waned during the period. One such was the child prodigy, or infant phenomenon. Small children, frequently under ten years of age, acted adult heroes from the canon of the tragic and comic literature. The following notice of Miss Davenport as Richard III at the National in New York City is typical.

77   Review of Child Prodigy, Miss Davenport, 1836

Spirit of the Times, 13 (May 26, 1836), 113

The most extraordinary personation we ever saw, was the enactment of *Richard* on Monday evening, by Miss Davenport, a child not yet twelve years of age. We abominate quite as much as any one else can do, almost everything we have ever witnessed of "the Roscius"[1] school. We have found them inane, feeble, and disgusting, with the single exception of Burke in his best days. Filled with the greatest possible distaste for such premature exhibitions, we dropped into the National, anticipating another of those parrot-tongued recitations, so frequently puffed up, as indicating the possession of extraordinary powers, and much to our surprise, we saw Richard played in a style of classic elegance that made us readily participate with a delighted audience, in the admiration of the wonderful portraiture. Even in the most difficult and driest portions of the play, when nothing short of the most studied and correct emphasis can convey the subtle point of the reasoning of the philosophic villain, the mere child evidenced a power of comprehension, and the ability to express her conception of the sense, that were marvelous in our eyes. She no longer appeared a child, but rather some fairy being to whom nature had denied the full proportion of manhood, yet had lavished with a bounteous hand, the attributes of a superior and discriminating intellect. It was difficult to believe there was not some optical deception, some lessening operation in the organ of vision, that gave her the appearance of

[1] The earliest and most famous of the child prodigies was Master Betty, frequently billed as the "young Roscius," who flourished in London from 1804 through 1811. Subsequently, the press on both sides of the Atlantic often referred to child prodigies as being of the "Roscius School."

Booth, looked at through the wrong end of a powerfully diminishing opera glass. Nothing, save the tones of her voice, gave token of the reality that we were actually listening to a child, and every now and then, during the exhibition of some fierce passage, the illusion both of the eye and ear was complete, and we saw nothing but the remorseless tyrant concentrating every energy for the achievement of some greater villainy. To all who take delight in witnessing prodigies, we fearlessly commend this instance of the early development of histrionic power, as the most wonderful, and the most effective ever witnessed on our stage.

Although Charlotte Cushman eventually became the leading tragedienne of the American theatre, she served an apprenticeship of nine years and did not achieve star status until after her return from a four-year tour of England in 1849. George Vandenhoff, who acted with her for the first time in 1842, astutely comments on both her weakness and strengths during the early part of her career.

78   George Vandenhoff on Charlotte Cushman, 1860

George Vandenhoff, *Leaves from an Actor's Notebook* (New York: D. Appleton & Co., 1860), pp. 194–96

Charlotte Cushman, whom I met now, for the first time, was by no means, then, the actress which she afterwards became. She displayed at that day, a rude, strong, uncultivated talent; it was not till after she had seen and acted with Mr. Macready – which she did the next season – that she really brought aristocratic study and finish to her performances. At this time, she was frequently careless in the text, and negligent of rehearsals. She played the Queen to me in *Hamlet*, and I recollect her shocking my ear, and very much disturbing my impression of the reality of the situation, by her saying to me in the closet-scene (Act III),

> "What wilt thou do; thou will not *kill* me?"

instead of

> "What wilt thou do; thou will not *murder* me?"

thus substituting a weak word for a strong one, diluting the force, and destroying the rhythm of the verse. She was much annoyed at her error when I told her of it; but confessed that she had always so read the line, unconscious of being wrong.

I played Rolla with her; and she was, even then, the best Elvira I ever saw. The power of her scorn, and the terrible earnestness of her revenge, were immense. Her greatest part, fearfully natural, dreadfully intense, horribly real, was Nancy Sykes in the dramatic version of *Oliver Twist*. It was too true; it was painful, this actual presentation of Dickens' poor abandoned, abused, murdered, outcast of the streets; a tigress, with a touch, and but one, of woman's almost deadened nature, blotted, and trampled underfoot by man's cruelty and sin.

It is in darkly-shadowed, lurid tinged, characters of a low order, like this and Meg Merrilies – half human, half demon, with the savage, animal reality of passion, and the weird fascination of crime, redeemed by fitful flashes of womanly feeling – that she excels. I never admired her Lady Macbeth. It is too animal; it wants intellectual confidence, and relies too much on physical energy. Besides, she bullies Macbeth; she gets him into a corner of the stage, and – as I heard a man with more force than elegance express it – she "pitches into him." In fact, as one sees her large, clenched hand, and muscular arm threatening him, in alarming proximity, one feels that if other arguments fail with her husband, she will have recourse to blows. Meg Merrilies has been her great *fortune-teller* and *fortune-maker*.

The following review of her first American engagement after returning triumphantly from England gives an idea of the extent of her new-found popularity in addition to amplifying Vandenhoff's analysis of her Meg Merrilies, a character from a dramatic adaptation of Scott's *Guy Mannering*.

79   Review of Charlotte Cushman as Meg Merrilies, 1849

Albion, 8 (October 20, 1849), 500

The furor which Miss Cushman's reappearance has created in the playgoing circles of the city is actually without parallel in the stage history of New York for the last twenty-five years. It must indeed be a proud triumph to this gifted and remarkable woman, to receive from her countrymen such a full endorsement of her transatlantic reputation, and to witness nightly from crowded and entranced audiences such a perfect appreciation of her powers. Anxious as we are for the best interest of the drama and reverencing high art without regard to geographical distinctions, we must cordially participate in the general feeling now expressed, that America has produced one of the most thorough and wonderful actresses of the present age. On Tuesday, Miss Cushman gave her first representation of her Meg Merrilies, in which she has capped the climax of her triumphs; for if she has another character, surpassing this in the effects she can produce upon an audience we must resign our critical judgment in despair. . . . We scarcely call it fine acting – for there is really no appearance of acting about it.

Her first appearance from the Gypsy tent was electric – her look, attitude, and almost supernatural air made the most profound sensation upon the audience – testified, after the first impression of her entrance had subsided, by peal upon peal of applause, that actually for some time impeded the action of the play. As the scene progressed, and exhibited the astonishing truthfulness with which she has invested every conceivable minutiae of the character, the effect upon the auditory became more intense. Not only is her unearthly semblance striking as a whole; but the rendering of the part in all its complexity of character is equally new, original, and natural.

Specialty performers became extremely popular during the period. One such peculiar line of business, the stage Yankee, had five major and many more minor practitioners. Hackett, the earliest native stage Yankee, eventually abandoned the line of work. According to Vandenhoff, Hackett lacked a true sense of his strengths as a performer.

80   George Vandenhoff on James Hackett, 1860
Vandenhoff, *Leaves from an Actor's Notebook*, pp. 211–12

Mr. Hackett played alternate nights with me, to indifferent houses; and as his comedies and farces did not draw, he betook himself to tragedy and *Richard III!* This, I need not say, did not mend the matter. Strange, that so excellent an actor in certain character-parts, eccentric and comic, should have deceived himself into the belief that he could shine in tragedy, for which he has not, nor ever had, any qualifications, except good sense and intelligence. When I say that his Kentuckian never ceases to amuse me by its hearty, audacious oddities, that I consider his Solomon Swop the most natural and unexaggerated Yankee I ever saw upon the stage; that I have alternatively smiled and wept at his Rip Van Winkle, one of the most artistic and finished performances that the American theatre ever produced, he will, I know, not take it ill, that I could not discover the merit, or the design, if it had any, of his Richard III. An actor may have great intelligence; a perfect understanding, and even feeling for the author, and yet fall very short in the execution, even of his own concepton. The art and the power that can touch and delight us in the simple pathos of Rip Van Winkle and *Monsieur Mallet,* may be feeble to cope with the frenzy of Lear; and will crack and fall to pieces, in the vain attempt to master and give expression to the complicated agony of his pride, his affection, and his rage; the run of downtrodden royalty, and the wreck of a confiding old father's heart. These are the highest triumphs of the tragic power; it is not wonderful that Mr. Hackett, excellent comedian as he is, should fail to achieve them.

By 1838 T. D. Rice had achieved star status in his phenomenally popular Negro character, Jim Crow. The following letter, written from Charleston, shows him to be an astute observer of the ever widening rift between the North and South.

81   Letter from T. D. Rice to H. E. Johnson, 1838

Ms. letter, T. D. Rice to H. E. Johnson, February 14, 1838; Harvard Theatre Collection

My dear Johnson,

. . . The *South* is much annoyed with the North meddling with their domestic institutions, and seem to say, we must protect ourselves.

Thank God I am finished. "Mawworm" [1] will one day sever this happy union. "One" of them has made an attack upon the Charleston Theatre and the profession at large. A friend of mine has arrived with notes I send you on the "Neptune." Both copies. They are worth perusing. Cotton has taken a rise and the South will flourish as ever. The success of the theatre much depends on the staple of the country, for people will not spend money, when they are not making money.

[1] Mawworm, more often Maw-Worm, is a self-righteous, hypocritical, and meddling character from Isaac Bickerstaff's *The Hypocrite* (1768). Its use here indicates Rice's distaste for the Northern abolitionist and anti-theatrical forces which were beginning to pressure the South during the 1830s.

Mary Ann Duff had fallen on very hard times by late 1835, as the following letter to a creditor shows. See also Docs. 51 and 72.

82   Letter from Mary Ann Duff to C. Page, 1835

Ms. letter, Mary Ann Duff to C. Page, December 10, 1835; Harvard Theatre Collection

Sir,

The bearer of this, Mr. Seaver, will call on you for the purpose of making an arrangement respecting my note which by means of unexpected ill health I cannot make it quite convenient to take up for a little time and must request a renewal of it for such further time as Mr. Seaver may agree with you. The monies which are due me from Mr. J. Jefferson, which you had the collection of, you will please to pay over to Mr. Seaver and his receipt shall be your voucher for the same. It would much please me if it would suit your convenience to purchase the pianoforte and the wardrobe case which you have in your possession and allow me what they are reasonably worth. The price of the piano was $350. The music stool $15 and the green cloth covering $12. The wardrobe case was $65. Making $442 original cost and the articles are none the worse for wear. If you will give me up my note and allow me $150 in money you may have the named articles and conclude the arrangement with Mr. Seaver who is authorized to effect the sale on such terms if better cannot be had. I am going in a few days to play several engagements to the south and shall want all the funds I can command previous to my departure which is the reason of my desiring the arrangements I have proposed. In any event you will be good enough to renew my note as desired and pay over the monies collected from the estate of Mr. Jefferson for me to Mr. Seaver and take his receipt for the same and in a short time I will be able to present you the money to take up my note. . . .

By the time the travelling star system was firmly established as the usual way of doing business in the American theatre, it was being challenged by the reintroduction of solid stock companies who drew remunerative audiences without the aid of touring luminaries. The first, Wallack's company at the National Theatre, flourished from 1836 to 1839, but disbanded when the theatre was destroyed by fire in September 1839. For a decade beginning in 1839, William Mitchell successfully operated the Olympic Theatre with a bill of fare consisting primarily of short comic entertainments and topical burlesques played by a resident company. His success was followed in New York by Burton, Laura Keene, and the return of Wallack as a manager, and in Philadelphia by Mrs. Drew at the Arch Street Theatre. Paul Preston offered the following reasons for the Olympic's success.

83   Newspaper Clipping about Mitchell's Olympic Theatre, after 1849

Paul Preston, "The Olympean Gods and Goddesses," *New York Clipper*, n.d.; clipping in the Harvard Theatre Collection

It was the main merit of the Olympic to rely upon the actual abilities of the company as a congregated mass and not upon the name of a single individual to sustain the popularity of the house.

That the Olympic company was decidedly clever cannot be denied, for the members comprising it were above mediocrity in their talent, yet their efforts, tending to a common end directed by a general supervisory head, gave merited repute to individual artists through success in a concentrated action. None of the Olympic actors or actresses were above the medium grade in professional ability; nevertheless, all were immensely popular through the nicety with which they were dovetailed into mutually sustaining performances.

III.   *Theatre Buildings*

As a result of the disastrous Richmond theatre fire of 1811, anti-theatrical forces had evidence to convince the public that theatres were not only immoral, but dangerous as well. During a holiday pantomime presented on the evening of December 26, the theatre caught fire. Of the 648 persons attending, 77 died, and many more were seriously injured.[1] Thus, theatrical managers went to great lengths to convince their potential patrons that their theatres were both fire-resistant and easy to escape in the unlikely event of a conflagration. The original Chestnut Street Theatre, which had opened in 1794, was destroyed by fire on April 2, 1820. The New Chestnut Street Theatre opened on December 20, 1822, and the following testimonial to its safety contains a great deal of information about the structure of the building.[2]

[1] For a full account of the incident, including reprints of news articles, reports of investigating committees into the fire's cause, and the anti-theatrical articles which the conflagration provoked, see Martin Staples Shockley, *The Richmond Stage, 1784–1812* (Charlottesville: University of Virginia Press, 1977), pp. 360–82. See also Doc. 111.
[2] For an overview of the history of both theatres see Reese Davis James, *Old Drury: A History of the Philadelphia Stage* (Philadelphia: University of Pennsylvania Press, 1932), pp. 1–67. (After the fire, the second building was frequently – but not consistently – referred to as the "New Chestnut Street.")

84   Testimonial to the Safety of New Chestnut Street Theatre, Philadelphia, 1823

Wood, *Personal Recollections*, pp. 151–54

TO THE PUBLIC

The managers of the new theatre beg leave to lay before the public the following circumstances and testimonials to them, that every precaution against accident from fire exists in their establishment. In the original construction and successive improvements of the edifice of the new theatre, the greatest care and attention has been paid by the proprietors and managers, to the protection of the audience from every possible casualty that might happen from fire: three large delivering doors are opened at the back of the stage and communicate with the open street; the three large doors in front for the boxes, pit, and gallery (separately), are so framed that some of them do now, and all will be made to open both outwardly and inwardly, so that the least pressure from within will always force them open. The large Venetian and other windows in front and on the second story, open upon the terrace over the portico into the open air, and a few feet above the ground. In addition to this, one large passage of sixteen feet in width, leading from the eastern lobby through the open arch into Sixth Street, and all the lobbies, as well as the wide and roomy staircases which communicate with them, are entirely unobstructed by doors, and connect fully with each other. Two very large Venetian windows on the western side of the building open upon the ground leading into Chestnut Street, and an additional door hung with counterweights like a sash is now made from the middle of the lobby of the main door. . . . The pit lobbies are supported by massy stone walls of two feet thick, and capable of containing double the number of persons that could possibly occupy the pit; the avenues are no less then four in number to the staircase, which is so capacious that any audience could discharge themselves in three minutes. The columns which support the bases are of wrought iron cased; the girders of the building are ample and bound in with brick, which is twenty inches thick from the basement to the plate of the roof; the house is ventilated by a funnel of six feet in diameter, which runs through to the roof; there are *two fire engines* and *one hose company* within the walls of the theatre.

The subscribers, at the request of the managers of the new theatre, have examined that edifice thoroughly, and report that it is constructed of brick and stone, in the most substantial manner; the roof is of wood, but perfectly secured, supported, and solid; capable of resisting fire for a considerable time. The ventilator is large, and sufficient to throw off any quantity of smoke; the ceilings are plastered with several thick coats of whiting; the scenery is, for the most part, painted on both sides, and therefore not liable to blaze should it take fire. The avenues are large, the doors all open outwards, and the means of egress such, that in the opinion of the subscribers, any audience that the house could contain might walk out in five minutes.

Albany, New York's Green Street Theatre is typical of many such buildings at the turn of the century and an important example of the kind of theatre that was erected in state capitals, producing a season of plays during sessions of the legislature when a large number of people were in town.

85   Interior of Green Street Theatre, Albany, New York, 1811

Harvard Theatre Collection

86   Exterior of Green Street Theatre, 1811

Harvard Theatre Collection

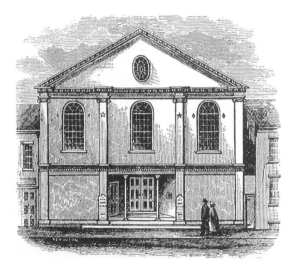

When it opened, the New Chestnut Street Theatre was one of the most elegant in the country. The following description is significant because it contains the theatre's important dimensions.

87   Description of New Chestnut Street Theatre, Philadelphia, 1822

American Magazine, 1834; clipping in the Harvard Theatre Collection

The principal front of the building, a view of which is here presented, is on Chestnut Street, near Sixth Street. It is in the Italian style, and the material marble. Its most prominent features are an arcade, supporting a screen of composite columns, and a plain entablature, and is flanked by two wings. These are decorated with niches, containing statues of tragedy and comedy, which are considered the best productions from the chisel of Rush;[1] and immediately below them are semicircular recesses, with basso relievos, representing the tragic and comic muses.

The approach to the boxes is from Chestnut Street, through an arcade of five entrances, opening into a vestibule fifty-eight feet long by eight feet wide, communicating, at each end, with the box office, and a drawing room. The audience part of the house is described on a semicircle of forty-six feet in diameter, and containing three rows of boxes. The front of the house is such as to place the mass of the audience within thirty-five feet of the stage. The dome is forty-six feet in diameter. The whole building is one hundred and fifty by ninety-two, and will accommodate two thousand people. This theatre combines beauty and convenience, with great security. There are three large doorways, which will discharge a crowded house in a few minutes. It was designed and executed by W. Strickland.[2]

[1] William Rush, prominent sculptor, famous for his statue of George Washington, in Independence Hall, Philadelphia. The statues referred to here (*Tragedy* and *Comedy*) were later housed in the Forrest Home in Philadelphia.

[2] William Strickland was an engraver, engineer, and architect. A native Philadelphian, he studied with and became the protégé of Benjamin H. Latrobe, known for his Greek revivalist architecture. Strickland designed several important buildings in Philadelphia including the Masonic Temple, St. Stephen's Church, the United States Mint, and the United States Customs House.

Noah Ludlow, a pioneer theatrical manager of the Ohio and Mississippi Valleys, wrote an autobiography late in his life in which he recalls the Chapman family's[1] first floating theatre, later called Showboats, on the Ohio River.

[1] For a brief overview of the two generations of the Chapmans and their theatrical peregrinations see James H. Dorman, *Theatre in the Ante Bellum South* (Chapel Hill: University of North Carolina Press, 1967), pp. 111–13.

88   Noah Ludlow on Chapman's Floating Theatre, c. 1832

Ludlow, *Dramatic Life*, pp. 568–69

My first knowledge of the family was, if my recollections be correct, about the year 1831 or 1832, when I beheld a large flat-boat, with a rude kind of house built upon it, having a ridge-roof, above which projected a staff with a flag attached upon which was plainly visible the word "Theatre." This singular object attracted my attention as it was lying tied up at the landing in Cincinnati, and on my making inquiries in regard to it, I learned that it was used for a theatrical company under the management of a Mr. Chapman, "floating down the ribber of de O-Hi ho," as the Negro melody has it. They did not play while there, and I had not time to visit them when I saw the boat; and when I went to the landing for that purpose, they were gone. They were on their "winding way" South to New Orleans, and, as I heard afterwards, stopped at every town or village on the banks of the river where they supposed they could get together a sufficient audience, and gave the entertainment at a small price of admission . . .

Some few years after the commencement of their floating expeditions, the Messrs. Chapman purchased a steamboat, which they fitted up very comfortably, after the fashion of a theatre, and placed on board a pilot, engineers, and deck-hands; they navigated their way at pleasure, down and up the rivers of the West, playing at all towns adjacent.

While new theatres constructed in the established eastern seaboard cities and New Orleans were increasingly large and ornate, the same could not be said for the smaller towns in the Ohio and Mississippi Valley as the following description of a theatre in Mobile suggests.

89   Noah Ludlow on State Street Theatre, Mobile, 1839

Ludlow, *Dramatic Life*, p. 515

Nevertheless the State Street Theatre, under the management of Ludlow and Smith, opened its doors December 31, 1839, with a good comedy and farce, to *seventy-one dollars*. This theatre was about one hundred and ten feet long, forty wide, and about the same in number of feet high. The auditorium was about sixty feet in depth, with seats rising in amphitheater style, on an inclined plane. These were covered with some colored cotton, and the sides and ceiling covered with white cotton, for I could get no plastering done; nearly all good mechanics had left the city, and were afraid to return until frost had killed the yellow fever. The stage part of the building was built of brick, in depth about fifty feet, the other part of the house being wood; and we opened with about four scenes, with three necessary wings, painted by young Joe Cowell, who was sent to me from St. Louis. This house could accommodate about six hundred persons. The price of admission was one dollar for each person, except children, – fifty cents for them.

Ludlow's description of the new theatre built in St. Louis in 1837 indicates both that the robust city was coming of age theatrically, and that the barrooms provided something of a nuisance to those who were primarily interesting in seeing and hearing the plays.

90   Noah Ludlow on St. Louis Theatre, 1837

Ludlow, *Dramatic Life*, p. 478

The inside of the theatre was very conveniently arranged, consisting of three tiers or galleries of seats and a parquet. The first tier, or "dress circle," would seat about three hundred persons; the second tier, or "family circle" about three hundred and fifty; the third tier, or "gallery," about four hundred and fifty, and the parquet about four hundred. The entrance to the first and second tiers and parquet was through a large vestibule twenty feet in depth by forty in width, thence through three large doors into the lobby of the first tier, which was uncommonly wide. Through the center of the first tier was the passage to the parquet, and on each side of the lobby a flight of stairs led to the second tier. The entrance to the gallery was from the outside of the building, to a flight of winding stairs having no connection with the other entrances. The stage was about forty-five feet in depth, from the front of which to the front of the dress circle was about fifty feet. The house being designed for a summer theatre, was constructed with a number of very large windows on each side, and the seats in the first and second tiers surrounded with handsome balustrades, turned of cherry wood, which being highly varnished, looked like mahogany. There was a ladies retiring room on a level with the first tier, furnished with refreshments and conveniences suited to such visitors. On a level with the second floor was a saloon for gentlemen, furnished with refreshments. Both of these saloons were closed before the conclusion of the season; the first, because a very small proportion of the lady auditors ever visited it, a notion having sprung up among some of the leading ladies that their visits to the saloon might be misconstrued, apprehensions that the situation did not necessarily warrant. The gentleman's saloon was closed because it was found to be an annoyance to the occupants, not only of the second, but of the first tier. There were three large doors opening from the saloon to the *auditorium*, and the loud talking that frequently took place there disturbed many persons who came to hear and enjoy the performance on the stage; so we shut that up before the season terminated.

91   Exterior of St. Louis Theatre, 1837

Harvard Theatre Collection

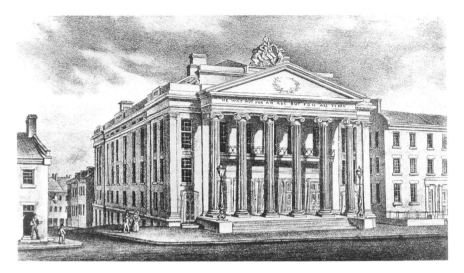

Numerous theatres were built during the late 1830s and early 40s as the populations of the large cities increased dramatically. One which was briefly important was the National Theatre[1] in Philadelphia, originally constructed for William E. Burton. Note the attempts at segregating various classes of the audience.

[1] For an overview of Philadelphia's National Theatre see Arthur Herman Wilson, *A History of the Philadelphia Theatre, 1835–1855* (Philadelphia: University of Pennsylvania Press, 1935), pp. 16–22.

92   Description of National Theatre, Philadelphia, 1840

Spirit of the Times, 10 (June 6, 1840), 168

Burton's new theatre is going up in Philadelphia. It is to be built in the Circus Lot, corner of Chestnut and Ninth Street, and will be opened at the commencement of the next season. We understand he has engaged Richings of the Park as a stage manager. The new building will be of the largest capacity, affording accommodations for three thousand five hundred persons. Three tiers of boxes, at three different prices of admission, with a capacious pit, are to be reached by separate entrances – by this means, the visitors of the third tier cannot be intruded upon the frequenters of the dress circle, and the man of family will be able to secure a box at a moderate price, without being compelled to have his daughters mix in the crowded lobbies with loose females and their rowdy companions.

A range of handsome stores will occupy the front of the building, with five capacious entrances to the various part of the theatre. This will make a material improvement in that part of Chestnut Street, and Mr. Burton, who is the lessee, deserves praise for his public spirit and enterprise. Contrary to the formation of all other institutions, there are no stockholders in connection with the scheme; Mr. Burton, therefore, is untrammelled with the usual crowd of free admissions; and as he has resolved not to dispose of any season tickets, his "free list" must be of a very limited nature.

Mr. Haveland is the architect, and speaks, with much pride, of his plan of the building, which he considers more fortunate in its arrangement than any of the other theatres with which he has been connected.

New York also had a flurry of activity in the construction of new theatres in the late 30s and early 40s. Perhaps the most ambitious was the New National.[1] Note the separate gallery and entrance to it for black people, the installation of single seats in lieu of the traditional benches in the pit, and the sprung stage floor for the safety and effectiveness of dancers.

[1] The New National opened in autumn 1840, and was destroyed by an arsonist on May 29, 1841. See Odell, *Annals of the New York Stage*, IV: 169–70 for details.

93   Description of New National Theatre, 1840

New York Courier and Enquirer, August 11, 1840, n.p.

This splendid establishment, which is now in progress of erection, on the site of the former Italian Opera House and National Theatre, corner of Leonard and Church Streets, is so far as the interior is concerned, nearly completed. It is to be conducted by Alexander M. Wilson, Esq., the well-known tragedian, formerly of the Bowery and Park Theatres. The plans and design of the building were projected by Calvin Pollard, Esq., Architect, and the construction is under the immediate direction of Mr. Edward Black, builder of this city.

The walls, roof, and entire framework of the edifice, are throughout of the most thorough, substantial, and workmanlike description. Indeed, there is not, perhaps, in the city, a public building in the erection of which so much care has been bestowed to insure its permanence and safety.

It is intended, we believe, by the management, to devote the theatre exclusively to the performance of opera, ballet, melodrama, vaudeville, and the lighter order of the drama, for which a powerful, and in every department, effective company has been engaged. It will be completed and in readiness for opening of the first of October next. The style of the building is plain and simple, nearly, if not entirely, in the exterior, on the plan of the former building.

The accommodations for the audience, so far as space and comfort is concerned, have been greatly extended.

There are three full tiers of boxes, with a gallery and over the latter a *semi*, or shilling gallery, for the exclusive use of colored people, the entrance to which is from Leonard Street.

The pit is capacious, well elevated and filled up, with *single* seats, which will preclude the possibility of visitors being annoyed by a crowd, consequent upon an oversale of tickets.

The box seats are well elevated, affording a full view of the stage, each seat comfortably stuffed and backed!

The front of the first tier of boxes presents a plain semicircle, with the customary arrangements. In the second tier, the front of the boxes are each framed into the form of balconies, each projecting over the fronts of the first tier.

Either side of the second tier terminates with four private boxes, separate with the proscenium boxes from the main body of the house. The third and fourth tiers, like the first, extend on either side of the proscenium, and are of the plain circular form.

The stage is constructed with springs, calculated to afford great ease to the dancers, and give additional effect to their performances.

The green-room, dressing rooms, etc. are in a range of galleries on the left or Leonard Street side of the stage, as was the case in the former house. The box, pit, and gallery offices and entrances are located as before.

On the left of, and adjoining the lobby of the first tier of boxes is a spacious salon, 25 by 50 feet in dimension, with, adjoining the same, private drawing, and retiring rooms, for the exclusive use of ladies. This grand salon is to be fitted up in the most costly and magnificent style, with rich draperies, ottomans, divans, couches, attendants, etc., all in the true oriental style – affording an agreeable lounge, wherein to partake of refreshments, or to rest from fatigue during the interval of performance.

The saloons for the second tier are spacious and airy, situated over the front entrance on Church Street.

On the Leonard Street side, on a level with the second tier of boxes is a range or suite of rooms, fitted up with every comfort and convenience, for the residence of the manager, the entrance to which is from Leonard Street, about midway of the building, and is reached by a flight of stairs constructed solely therefore. In the basement is a spacious refectory, some 60 feet in length, with kitchens, out-rooms, and other conveniences. Altogether, the National Theatre will, when completed, be among the most commodious, comfortable, and best appointed of any erected in this country.

From the 1830s down to the Civil War, floating theatres, or showboats, became increasingly important in the inland river valleys. The following description of a floating theatre is unusual in its detail and indicates sophisticated development since the earlier Chapman family efforts.

94   Description of a Floating Theatre, 1845

Boston Times; reprinted in *Spirit of the Times*, 15 (April 12, 1845), 80

It is constructed out of one of the old southern steam packets called the "Virginia," has a 42 feet beam, perfectly flat bottom, 22 feet with a keel of about 26 inches. She is about 385 tons, 90 feet in length, near upon 50 feet high, and draws about 7 feet of water. The entrance is ten feet wide, placed about midship where there is also an engine of about ninety horsepower. The stage, parquette, and boxes are aft. They are formed in the shape of a horseshoe, and have altogether a very neat and chaste appearance.

It has a roomy little stage, four private boxes in the proscenium, one tier of boxes, a pit, and is capable of seating 1,200 persons comfortably. The parquette is 42 feet by 36, the opening of the proscenium 27 feet; the stage is 42 feet wide and 45 feet deep; and the scenery is 16 feet high. The space between the wings is about four feet.

At the back of the stage are two dressing rooms for the ladies; and beneath the stage are the dressing rooms for the male performers, together with dining rooms and bedrooms for the whole company, engineers, etc. In the bow is a large and elegantly furnished saloon, in which all the good things of this life are disposed of, on terms the most reasonable. It is about 36 feet deep, by about 40 wide; in which are two handsomely fitted up bars, well furnished with good eatables and drinkables. The handsome marble-topped tables, the splendid mirrors, and some elegant paintings – the beautiful cut ground glass shades to the lamps, give this part of the vessel a gay and elegant appearance. A brilliant "Drummond light"[1] surmounts the establishment, illuminating the whole neighborhood, and directing the visitors to this floating dramatic temple. The whole establishment is brilliantly illuminated with portable gas, manufactured on board. The whole is so constructed that the north wind can scarce effect it, and she has already buffetted more than one heavy blow. She was moored in the river during the gale of the 12th of December last, and stood it nobly.

[1] The Drummond Light, or limelight – utilizing a filament of lime burning in an oxy-hydrogen flame – was invented by Alexander Drummond in 1826. Macready used one at Covent Garden in 1837–38, and the instrument came into general theatrical usage by the 1850s. For a full account of the development and history of the lighting device, see Gösta M. Bergman, *Lighting in The Theatre* (Totawa, NJ: Rowman and Littlefield, 1977), pp. 273ff.

For over forty years the successive theatres and entertainment centers located at Niblo's Garden in New York City proved significant in the history of the metropolis' amusements.

The first theatre burned in September 1846 and was replaced six years later. The following account describes the 1852 building.

95   Description of Niblo's Garden, 1853

Gleason's Pictorial and Drawing Room Companion, May 14, 1853, p. 308

This celebrated establishment as it now stands, not only holds the first rank among all the places of amusements in New York, but is unequalled by any on the American continent. Indeed it is conceded by many Europeans who have visited all the gay capitals of France, England, Germany, Spain and Italy, that Niblo's Garden, when the whole establishment is taken into consideration, is unsurpassed even in Europe. Containing, as it does, under one roof, a spacious and magnificent opera house, a splendid concert hall, and ballroom, with richly furnished reception parlors, drawing rooms, dressing rooms, and a supper salon sufficiently capacious to accommodate upwards of a thousand guests. . . . On the left of the main lobby are three large, glass, double doors, leading into the interior of the theatre or opera house – one of the most spacious and complete structures of the kind in America. Throughout the whole building, every seat in the parquette, dress boxes, upper circle, and balconies is furnished with spiral steel springs and hair-stuffed cushions, and covered with rich blue damask. The stage is 76 by 64 feet beyond the proscenium, at which point it is 34 feet in width, being modelled after that of the Theatre Royal, Drury Lane, which is acknowledged to be the best in the world. The orchestra is movable, and can by a simple arrangement, be adapted to a band of a hundred performers, or reduced to the most moderate compass. The scenery, machinery, costumes, and other accessories of scenic display in use at Niblo's are of the most costly, complete, and magnificent description.

96   Interior of Niblo's Garden, 1853

Harvard Theatre Collection

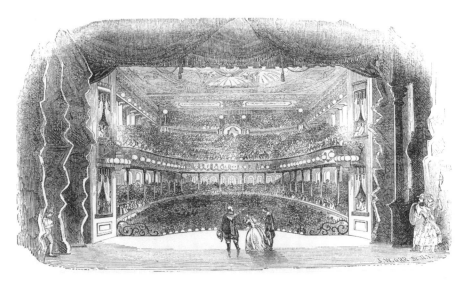

The following is from a souvenir program of the first season of the Boston Theatre.[1] While it may be a bit hyperbolic, its inclusion of dimensions and layout is of interest as typical of a large urban theatre of the 1850s.

[1] It was the city's grandest and most opulent playhouse during the second half of the nineteenth century. For a full account of it see Eugene Tompkins and Quincy Kilby, *The History of the Boston Theatre, 1854–1901* (Boston: Houghton Mifflin Co., 1908; reprinted New York: Benjamin Blom, 1969).

97   Description of Boston Theatre, 1854

Souvenir Programme, Boston Theatre, opening season (1854); Harvard Theatre Collection

In no city in the world, we venture to assert, is there to be found a finer place of amusement than the Boston Theatre, which is by far the most beautiful in America. It is situated on Washington and Mason Streets. The entrance front on the former is a simple three story building, twenty-four feet in width, covered with mastic, and with no attempt at architectural display. On entering, the visitor ascends the incline plane of a spacious and elegant outer vestibule, the walls of which, handsomely ornamented, support a finely-arched ceiling. Here we procure tickets, and enter the inner vestibule; before us is a circular staircase, nine feet in width; ascending, we find it conducts to the first and second circles. Entering the auditorium, we find it to be about ninety feet in diameter, and circular in form, except that it slightly flattens in the direction of the stage; the depth from the curtain to the back of the parquet being eighty-four feet.

The front of the stage projects into the auditorium eighteen feet, and the height of the auditorium is about fifty-four feet. There are three proscenium boxes on either side of the stage, handsomely draped. A space of ten or twelve feet from the parquet wall, and nearly parallel with the front of the first tier, is separated and somewhat raised from the middle portion of the house, the whole parquet floor, however, being constructed in a dishing form, and varying several feet. Around the auditorium above are the first and second tiers, the gallery, and, hanging in front, a little below the first tier or dress circle, is a light balcony, containing two rows of seats.

In the parquet and balcony there are iron-framed chairs, cushioned on the back seat, and arms, and so contrived that the seat rises when not in use; and the first and second tiers are furnished with oaken-framed sofas, covered with crimson plush, and the amphitheater with iron-framed and cushioned settees.

The walls of the auditorium are of a rose tint, the fronts of the balcony and second circle are elaborately and tastefully ornamented, and the frescoed ceiling embraces in its design allegorical representations of the twelve months. Adding to the effect of the painting, the ceiling is decorated with composition ornaments, many of them richly gilded. In front, over the stage, is a splendid clock, with a movable dial.

Returning to the vestibule, we turn to the right, under the arches, and reach the parquet lobby. Passing through this apartment, we reach the saloon and dressing rooms of this story. The parquet corridor is gained by turning to the left, through the arches, until we arrive at the foot of the Grand Oaken Staircase; which is built of solid oak, and separates on a broad landing into two branches, nine feet in width, which terminates in the dress circle lobby. Opposite the staircase are open arches communicating with the grand promenade saloon, which is forty-six feet long, twenty-six feet wide, and tastefully finished with ornamented walls and ceiling and is elegantly furnished. The corridors to the several stories extend entirely round the auditorium. The seating capacity of the house is three thousand four hundred persons, exclusive of orchestra chairs.

The stage side of the theatre is on Mason Street, and the doors and arches breaking the sameness of the brick wall, comprise a passage leading to the carpenter's shop and works, a set of double doors for the introduction of horses, carriages, etc., should such ever be required for the purposes of the stage; a private door for the use of the actors, and an audience entrance at the corner of the building nearest West Street.

The stage is sixty-seven feet deep from the curtain, and, calculated from the extreme front, or footlights, measures eighty-five feet. The curtain opening is about forty-eight feet in width by forty-one in height. There is a depth of some thirty feet below the stage, and the height from the stage to the fly door is sixty-six feet. These distances allow the rising and lowering of scenes without hinges or joints, the use of which soon injures their appearance. There are seven rows of side scenes, or wings, with considerable space beyond the most remote, for perspective. The stage is provided with traps, bridges, and all imaginable contrivances for effect, and is believed to unite more improvements, and to be the best arranged of any structure of the kind in the United States.

Suspended from the center of the dome is a beautiful and massive chandelier, costing seven thousand dollars, with five hundred and twelve burners and two hundred thousand glittering prisms. The light shed by this magnificent work of art is soft and mellow, giving the auditorium a very pleasing appearance.

The green-room on the level of the stage, is a decidedly comfortable looking apartment, thirty-four feet by eighteen feet, neatly finished and tinted, handsomely carpeted, and furnished around the sides with cushioned seats, covered with dark-green enamelled cloth. Adjoining is a small "star" dressing room, appropriately fitted, and nearby is an apartment for the manager, also, a small property room. Above these, are the actors' dressing rooms, handsomely carpeted, furnished with hot and cold water, heating apparatus, and all necessary conveniences; and still higher is the stage wardrobe room.

IV. Technical Production

In 1815, at the beginning of his long career, Noah Ludlow acted as advance man for Samuel Drake's small itinerant company. The following description is of the scenery with which Drake's company toured.

98 Noah Ludlow on Samuel Drake's Company, 1815
Ludlow, *Dramatic Life*, pp. 7–8

About sundown of the day of my departure from Albany, the stagecoach set me down at a hotel door in the small town of Cherry Valley, about forty or fifty miles west of Albany. Early the next day I commenced to seek for a suitable place for our performances, and, with the assistance of the hotel proprietor, had but little trouble in obtaining, through the kindness of the sheriff, the use of the court-house for the purpose. With the aid of a carpenter we very soon had a platform raised, about three feet in height, directly in front of the judge's desk. The sheriff and the landlord helped me in procuring extra seating accommodations and at the close of the second day after my arrival, I had the place ready for the scenery to be put up, which was to come on with Mr. Drake and the company. The stage adjuncts consisted of but six scenes; a wood, a street, parlor, kitchen, palace, and garden. The wings, or side scenes, consisted of three to a side, to be stationary in one sense, but to be so arranged with flaps or aprons as to present, when required, an outdoor view adapted to correspond with garden or street; an indoor view, to suit parlor or palace; with a third to match the kitchen. The proscenium was a painted drapery, made so as to be expanded or contracted to suit the dimensions of the places occupied by our performances. These and a neat drop curtain, and green-baize carpet, constituted our stage facilities. The scenery could be put in place, or taken down and packed, in two or three hours.

During the 1820s, the weekly *New York Mirror* occasionally described scenic effects at New York's theatres in unusual detail. The following account of visual wonders for a production of the nautical melodrama *The Pilot*, adapted by Edward Fitzball from James Fenimore Cooper's novel, at the Park Theatre is significant for its completeness. Note, however, that several scene painters contributed to the production, thus calling into question the overall stylistic unity of the visual effects.

99   Description of *The Pilot*, 1824
New York Mirror, 2, no. 15 (November 6, 1824), 113

The first scene, representing the seashore, and the American vessels, the Ariel, and the Frigate, in the distance painted by Mr. Roberts, had a grand and imposing effect. The gun-deck of the frigate, and Captain Munson's cabin, together with the wreck of the Ariel, painted by Mr. Evers, were the production of genius; but the last scene, painted by Mr. Coyle, was decidedly the best; the stage represented the deck of the American frigate, getting under way, and the English frigate and the headlands, were seen in the distance. They receded as the vessel proceeded, and a heavy fog was seen to rise. The English frigate came along side, and the bowsprit was lashed to the American, when the engagement commenced between the vessels. Captain Munson was shot at the gangway, and the American sailors boarded the English ship – her bowsprit gave way, she fell astern, and the piece concluded with the victory of the pilot. We have never seen anything better managed.

In reviewing a production of *Cherry and Fair Star* by Edward L. Blanchard, an extravaganza which relied heavily on spectacle for its effect, the *Mirror* noted the following inflammatory incident.

100   Review of *Cherry and Fair Star*, 1825
New York Mirror, 2, no. 25 (June 15, 1825), 198

The first scene represented the avis grove, or fairy abode, consisting of a forest, and a waterfall in motion (which, by-the-by, through the carelessness of some persons behind the scene, caught fire, and burnt up; no further damage, however was done. The audience were not at all disconcerted, but sat, with all the composure imaginable, to see a river on fire!).

The cavalier attitude of the audience is to be wondered at, as the Richmond

Theatre Fire,[1] and the destruction of the first Park Theatre[2] by fire were still in the public's mind.

[1] See Doc. 111.

[2] New York's first Park Theatre, which opened in 1798, burnt down in 1820, without loss of life. A new theatre with the same name opened on the identical site in September 1821.

New York's Lafayette Theatre, originally the Lafayette Circus and intended as a show place for equestrian drama and other spectacular para-theatrical entertainment, opened in 1825 as part of a development scheme for an entirely new neighborhood. But the horse-drama failed, and the original structure was modified in 1826 and again in 1827. The circus ring was replaced with a long pit, which was constructed on an inclined plane to connect with the boxes, giving it a rake not unlike modern theatrical auditoriums.[1] The following description of the 1827 renovations is significant in that it indicates the theatre's rigging was quite advanced by the day's standards.

[1] For a full account of the construction and subsequent modifications of the theatre, as well as an overview of the development of the entire neighborhood, see Robert Montilla, "The Building of the Lafayette Theatre," *Theatre Survey*, 15, no. 2 (November 1974), 105–29.

101   Description of Lafayette Theatre, 1827

New York Mirror, 5, no. 13 (October 7, 1827), 102

This building, the largest and most splendid ever erected for theatrical purposes in the United States, is located in a section of the city which has sprung into existence, and arrived at maturity, in so short a period as to astonish even those who were daily witnessing its progress, but which to the occasional visitant, could scarcely be realized.

The stage with its scenery and machinery exceed all former attempts in this country. It is one hundred and twenty feet deep, and in some places one hundred feet wide, being greater than any known in the United States or Great Britain. The machinery is managed above the scenes, and the stage lights are also placed above. This is the greatest improvement of the whole. The light is more natural and imparts an unequalled brilliancy to the production of the artist. It also strips from the stage the lamp ladders, which prevented the wings from being opened beyond a certain width, so that now the width of the stage presented to the audience may be increased at pleasure.

In 1828, Edmund Simpson and Stephen Price, co-managers of the Park Theatre in New York, contemplated selling their property. The following advertisement indicates the physical inventory with which the theatre carried on its business during the 1820s.

102   Inventory of Park Theatre, 1828

Albion, 6 (April 19, 1828), 360

The manager of the Park Theatre, wishing to close his theatrical interest, and circumstances requiring his attendance in England, proposes to dispose of the lease, properties, and fixtures of the theatre to an association of gentlemen, or a joint-stock company, who can have the selection of their own managers or board of control, to whom the entire government of the establishment may be confided.

The lease is for seven years, commencing from the first of September next, at an annual rent of $18,000, which is reduced to $14,000 by the rent of the bars. For the security of the rent the sum of $20,000 is deposited, for which 6 per cent per annum, is allowed.

The scenery, which is the property of the manager, exclusive of that belonging to the proprietors, consists of fifty-nine pair of flats, one hundred and eighty-eight wings, four hundred pieces of set scenery, ten drop scenes, transparencies, etc., etc., etc.; the value of which has been estimated, by competent persons, at $7,626. The total valuation of the scenery, machinery, properties, lamps, chandeliers, wardrobe, music, gas fixtures, etc., etc., have been appraised at $33,387, for which the manager is willing to receive $22,250. It is computed that for the embellishment of the interior of the theatre, and making the necessary arrangements to light the house entirely with gas, the sum of $8,000 will be required, making the sum total required for the purchase of the lease and properties, and refitting of the theatre, and a capital to proceed with, $60,000; of which it must be recollected that $20,000 remains at interest in deposit for the rent, and the actual amount to be applied for the above mentioned is $40,000. . . .

No theatre on the continent has the capacities for bringing out every part of the drama in perfection, equal to the Park; and no theatre in the city possesses so large a share of public patronage. The wardrobe is very extensive and valuable, and the music, for extent and variety, is not to be equalled in any theatre in the country. The principal part of the present company and orchestra are engaged for the next season; and such are the facilities of the Park Theatre, and the reputation it maintains abroad, that performers of eminence can always be engaged, and such always prefer appearing at a theatre which is entitled to the name of Metropolitan.

103   Interior of Second Park Theater, 1822
Harvard Theatre Collection

From the time of Cooke's triumphal tour in 1810 to the rise of the combination company after the Civil War it was usual for stars to tour theatres in the United States. A less frequent occurrence, due no doubt to inadequate transportation systems, was to tour scenery for spectacular productions from one city to another. Nevertheless, the following letter indicates that Thomas Hamblin, manager of the Bowery Theatre in New York, and Francis Wemyss, of the Chestnut Street Theatre in Philadelphia, were interested in working out such an arrangement in 1829.

104   Letter from Thomas Hamblin to F. C. Wemyss, 1829
Ms. letter, Thomas Hamblin to F. C. Wemyss, March 18, 1829; Harvard Theatre Collection

My Dear Wemyss:

On the other side you have a list of property[1] I can send you for the production of Walpole Spectacle. The dunes can be increased if you require it to almost any number you please but think they arch high.[2] As many as necessary 4/8 super numeraries with double and a full company in as many as you want every hand in my theatre double and triple in it.[3] John Scott I cannot send you as he would

[1] The property list was not appended to the letter, and is presumably lost.
[2] I take this to mean that there were cutout scenic elements representing rolling hills or dunes that established the background vista, and that the scenic plot permitted a variable number of these. Hamblin is warning Wemyss that they have a high "trim" in terms of sight lines.
[3] This run-on sentence suggests that with double and triple casting all available personnel the Walpole spectacle can be done with only 4 to 8 extras hired specifically for it, and that the cast required for the crowd scenes is variable, but the larger the number, the greater the effect.

not come to play that alone. The part being nothing he has done. Before the show begins anything else done on the same night except perhaps a one act farce to play them in would damn the whole affair. If you should go into it I should advise your engaging Addis at once for Napoleon as you would get him cheaper and when done you could act your pleasure. The terms I propose are as follows, a clear half of the receipts, taken as follows leaving you the rest of it if it does not draw greatly you shall take the first $50, I the 2nd, you the 3rd, I the fourth, and divide equal afterwards. Anybody can play Napoleon that can look anything like him, and who does *not* with the dress on? The great part is Sergeant Hubert which if he is not altered, it is useless to go into further particulars until I know whether you will give the terms and who your company are as it must be ably acted. . . .

During the 1830s Wemyss managed theatres in Philadelphia and Pittsburgh simultaneously. The following letter indicates that the scene-shop help in the Philadelphia theatre was less than ideal.

105   Letter from A. W. Jackson to F. C. Wemyss, 1831

Ms. letter, A. W. Jackson to F. C. Wemyss, June 15, 1831; Harvard Theatre Collection

My Dear Sir,

According to instructions in your letter I got up *Grace Darling*, painted 4 new flats etc. It drew as much as any drama of the kind could be expected (that was not a striking piece) at this season of the year but bad enough at the best, as we have done a bad business since the fireman's benefit. The piece went well, had there been good houses it would have made a hit as regards applause. The company here [is] steady, regular and well behaved; attentive to business and I have no fault with any one of them. I have not one quarter the trouble I had with some of the members of the Front St.[1] Of course Warren informs you of business here. I move along with him very well. I like his manner of doing business – short and to the point. You close in Pitt. I suppose on the 4th. Is it your desire for me to remain the ensuing fall season? If so let me know, if not, I wish to be advised at once to arrange elsewhere. During Booth's engagement how would it answer to get up a melodrama for the 4th? Maybe new scenery. Your answer by return.

My respects to you,
A. W. Jackson

P.S. Mr. Wilson is a steady good man but not worth a curse as a carpenter and his aide Mr. Piper is no better. Should it be your intention to do any show pieces

---

[1] Refers to a theatre in Baltimore Wemyss also managed and at which Jackson apparently had worked.

next season, that department you will have to reorganize as you know a good man is not to be had in a day. . . . I was not aware they were so damn bad until I took a list of *Grace Darling* and although there was little to do they bungled and made sad work of it. They have not got the brains and there it ends.

By 1830, theatre technicians had developed some effective equivalents of modern fog machines, as the following description of a spectacular production at the Bowery Theatre suggests.

106   Description of Technical Effects at Bowery Theatre, 1831

New York Mirror, 8, no. 49 (June 11, 1831), 390

The spells of the hero, beneath the castle, conjure up volumes of vapor, which at first, float dimly in the air, thicken into a film, and then a mist, till the dark masses of clouds roll over and melt into each other, and the stage is entirely enveloped, like the summit of some sky-clearing mountain. The last scene is, however, by far the most successful. Its magnificence is enhanced by the uncommon depth and height of the stage, flung open to its utmost extent. The shadowy forms of war and ruin, seen confusedly through the gleam of light on the distant battlements – with the bodies of the soldiers hurled from the lofty turrets – the fine masses of dim and gigantic buildings, and the idea of distance and vastness, which the painter has happily produced, afford a very vivid realization of the most interesting descriptions of Ivanhoe, and certain portions of history, the bodily exhibition of which few will have an opportunity of beholding with more striking effect.

Occasionally, the spectacular displays which were becoming increasingly popular during the late 20s and early 30s spilled out from behind the proscenium. Hamblin actually covered the pit and used much of the auditorium for a grand processional in one of his spectacular melodramas at the Bowery Theatre.

107   Review of *Rienza*, 1836

New York Mirror, 8, no. 50 (June 11, 1836), 398

Rienza now is in the full tide of its popularity, and there was not, for an instant, a doubt of its full success; for a better order, or more gorgeous spectacle, the New York stage has never produced, nor one which has met with more unqualified applause. Our eyes are, at present, too much dazzled by the gold and glitter of the pageantry to notice any one particular scene. As a general remark, we may, however, freely say, that they are all costly, and all are good. The grand triumphal *entree* into Rome, over the pit, and out through the center boxes, has never before been attempted in this country, yet it was done with perfect ease. The artist who painted the scenery (Mr. Lehy) deserves unbounded praise; we are happy to hear he is one of our countrymen. For the last three weeks, the average nightly receipts at the Bowery amounted to one thousand two hundred and fifty dollars.

In the age of travelling stars and a standard repertory, not much was spent on scenery. At the Park Theatre in New York stock flats and drops saw decades of service and were frequently shabby according to the following letter to the editor of the *Spirit of the Times*.

108   Description of Park Theatre Scenery, 1840

Spirit of the Times, 9 (February 8, 1840), 558

The scenery of the theatre is in many instances so venerable as to attract little admiration. The same as ten years ago with the exception of marks about the edges, as if handled by the slovenly shifters with greasy hands, and a large quantity of dust spread over the surface. We see in every place the same flower-garden, the same grove, the same castles and towers, and the same individuals managing them; thrusting out their naked arms at the changes, as interludes, to the admiration of the audience.

Again, the furniture and its management have given rise to many complaints: Everything in that line has the appearance of carelessness and indifference on the part of the manager. We see nothing but kitchen chairs in palace scenes; in the banquet of Macbeth, the master of the assembly has placed for his use a similar chair to what may be found in criminal's cells of the Egyptian tombs. How unlike royal pageantry! . . . What enlightened spectator can avoid being disgusted?

Among the more interesting, and perhaps ridiculous, productions to take place in America during the 1840s was the first professional attempt at Greek tragedy. George Vandenhoff, a touring tragedian and astute commentator on the theatre of his day, remembers his experience in *Antigone*.

109   George Vandenhoff on *Antigone*, 1860

Vandenhoff, *Leaves from an Actor's Notebook*, pp. 243–45

Among these miscellaneous leaves, it may not be out of place to state that I was engaged for a fortnight at Palmo's Opera House (afterwards Burton's), in Chambers Street, to produce the English version of Sophocles' ANTIGONE, with Mendelssohn's Music, in the spring of 1845. I did my best with the resources that were at my command; got a presentation of the Old Greek Stage, with its skene and parodoi and altar to Bacchus, built on the stage proper; as good a company and as efficient a CHORUS were collected as could be found. Mr. Geo. Loder directed the Orchestra and the musical arrangements which were fair; Miss Clarendon's youth and classic features harmonized well with the *personnel* of Antigone; I did my best with the part of Creon; and we had the gratification of getting through the first night's performance of this novel and difficult style of play – an upraising of the "buried majesty" of SOPHOCLES, – without a single trip or *faux pas*.

Our efforts were rewarded by great applause, the approval and cordially expressed thanks of artists and scholars, but with indifferent houses! We repeated this *classic disentombment* twelve successive nights, and then "quietly inurned" the mighty Greek, to sleep in undisturbed and unprofaned repose. It was truly a beautiful and highly interesting tragedy, aided by grand music. In Berlin and London it drew crowded audiences; in New York it never paid its expenses.

Our chorus, which amounted to about forty, representing sages of Creon's Court, presented a very grotesque appearance; and one that, at first sight, nearly disturbed my gravity on the first night. Old Allen had made the wigs and beards for these Grecian sages, out of long white and grey *goat's hair*; and, as the whole set were, I presume, contracted for, no great artistic care had been expended upon them. Now, Mendelssohn's music was very difficult; and, on the last rehearsal, Mr. Loder found that his chorus, principally German, could get very well through their work, if they could have the *score* before them, not otherwise. It was therefore arranged that the music should stand open before them: they themselves were to be ranged close to the footlights on the stage, between the second or *raised* stage (the stage of the Greek theatre) and the actual orchestra. Now, some of these gentlemen being shortsighted, had, in order to be able to read their scores distinctly, put on their spectacles; and, I ask you to fancy my horror, mingled with a dreadful *envie de rire*, when I entered, at seeing a parcel of goat-headed, goat-bearded old fellows, in Grecian robes, with spectacles on nose, confronting me, within the proscenium, opening wide their mouths, and baa-a-ing at me, as it were, with all their might. They looked like an assemblage of the ghosts of defunct Welsh bards, summoned to their goat-covered hills by the wand of Merlin; and the spectacles might have been mistaken, by a heated fancy, for the glaring of their spectral eyes!

Luckily, their backs were to the audience; the actors alone were fully conscious of the awful *travestie*.

The following watercolor rendering of the Bowery Theatre's act drop curtain during the early 1850s is significant in that the curtain showed a scene from the adventurous pseudoclassical melodramas for which the Bowery had long been famous.

110   Act Drop Curtain, Bowery Theatre, 1852[1]

Theatre Arts Collection, Harry Ransom Humanities Research Center, University of Texas at Austin

[1] Designed by Harmer.

V. Audiences

One of the great risks to audiences during this period was fire in the theatre. The most disastrous theatre fire in the United States between 1810 and 1865 occurred in Richmond, Virginia on December 26, 1811.[1] The deadly blaze had two immediate effects: it provided the anti-theatrical forces in the community with ammunition for their assaults on all things theatrical as the work of the devil; and it caused safety considerations to be of paramount importance in the construction of new theatres. The following account vividly describes the conflagration.

[1] Refers to a theatre in Baltimore Wemyss also managed and at which Jackson apparently had worked.

111   Description of Richmond Theatre Fire, 1811

Richmond Standard, December 27, 1811; clipping in Harvard Theatre Collection

Last night the playhouse in this city was crowded with an unusual audience. There could not have been less than 600 persons in the house. Just before the conclusion of the play, the scenery caught fire, and in a few minutes the whole building was wrapped in flames. It is already ascertained that sixty-one persons were devoured by that most terrific element. The editor of this paper was in the house when the ever-to-be-remembered deplorable accident occurred. He is informed that the scenery took fire in the back part of the house, by the raising of a chandelier; that the boy who was ordered by some of the players to raise it, stated that if he did so, the scenery would take fire, when he was commanded in a peremptory manner to hoist it. The boy obeyed, and the fire instantly communicated to the scenery. He gave the alarm in the rear of the stage, and requested some of the attendants to cut the cords by which the combustible materials were suspended. The person whose duty it was to perform this became panic-struck, and sought his own safety. This unfortunately happened at a time when one of the performers was playing near the orchestra, and the greatest part of the stage, with its horrid danger, was obscured from the audience by a curtain.

The flames spread with almost the rapidity of lightning; and the fire falling from the ceiling upon the performers was the first notice the audience had of their danger. Even then, many supposed it a part of the play, and were a little time restrained from flight by a cry *from the stage* that there was no danger. The performers and their attendants in vain endeavored to tear down the scenery; the fire flashed in every part of the house with a rapidity horrible and astonishing; and alas! gushing tears and unspeakable anguish deprive me of utterance. No person who was not present can form any idea of this unexampled scene of distress. The editor, having none of his family with him and not being far from the door, was among the first who escaped.

No words can express his horror when, on turning round, he discovered the whole building to be in flames. There was but one door for the greatest part of the audience to pass. Men, women, and children were pressing upon each other, while the flames were seizing upon those behind. The editor went to the different windows, which were very high, and implored his fellow creatures to save their lives by jumping out of them. Those nearest the windows, ignorant of their danger, were afraid to leap down, while those behind were seen catching on fire, and writhing in the greatest agonies of pain and distress. At length those behind urged by the pressing flames, pushed those who were nearest to the window, and people of every description began to fall one upon another, some with their clothes on fire, some half roasted. Oh wretched me! Oh affected people! Would to God I could have died a thousand deaths in any shape could individual suffering have purchased the safety of my friends, my benefactors, those whom I loved! ... The editor, with the assistance of others, caught several of those whom he had begged to leap from the windows. One lady jumped out when all her clothes were on fire. He tore them burning from her, stripped her of her last rags, and, protecting her nakedness with his coat, carried her from the fire. Fathers and mothers were deploring the loss of their children, children the loss of their parents; husbands were heard to lament their lost companions, wives were bemoaning their burnt husbands. The people were seen wringing their hands, beating their heads and breasts; and those that had secured themselves seemed to suffer greater than those enveloped in the flames.

112   Theatre Fire in Richmond, 1811[1]

Harvard Theatre Collection

Engr. by M. Schmitz.   T. Sinclair Lith Philad.
BURNING of the THEATRE in RICHMOND, V.ª 26.Decʳ 1811.

[1] Engraving by M. Schmitz; lithographer T. Sinclair, Philadelphia.

After the War of 1812, egalitarian sentiments began to assert themselves in many areas of American life. By the 1820s, the proud emerging identity of the common man was becoming increasingly vocal, as the following "democratic" broadside complaining of separate entrances for the boxes in the New Chestnut Street Theatre suggests.

113   Broadside Regarding New Chestnut Street Theatre, Philadelphia, c. 1824

Wood, *Personal Recollections*, p. 291

EQUALITY
or the
NEW THEATRE
as it should be.

To the independent citizens, who from a long experience and due appreciation of their rights in the great charter of citizenship, can well understand their relations, and spurn at any indignities in the social compact, the following hints may not be unnecessarily offered:

You, citizens, whose patronage the drama is proud to acknowledge, and whose inclination, taste, or means may lead to the pit or gallery, why subject you to an entrance comparatively less respectable than what has been assigned to those whose assumed superiority has led to distinctions wherein *no* distinctions are at all justifiable?

The national spirit of America has triumphed over the pride of European armies; shall that spirit slumber under the degradation of European distinctions?

The rowdiness of the democratic pit audience in New Orleans during the early 1820s is attested to by the following from Ludlow's autobiography.

114   Noah Ludlow on New Orleans Audience, c. 1821

Ludlow, *Dramatic Life*, p. 238

When the night came I found the pit, or parquette, of the theatre *crowded full* of "river men" – that is, keelboat and flatboat men. There were very few steamboat men. These men were easily known by their linsey-woolsey clothing and blanket coats. As soon as the comedy of the night was over, I dressed myself in a buckskin hunting shirt and leggins, which I had borrowed of a river man, and with *moccasins* on my feet, and an old slouched hat on my head, and a rifle on my shoulder, I presented myself to the audience. I was saluted with loud applause of hands and feet, and a prolonged whoop, or howl, such as Indians give when they are especially pleased. I sang the first verse, and these extraordinary manifestations of delight were louder and longer than before; but when I came to the following lines:

"But Jackson he was wide awake, and wasn't scared with trifles, for well he knew what aim we take with our Kentucky rifles; So he marched us down to 'Cyprus Swamp'; the ground was low and mucky; There stood 'John Bull,' in martial pomp, *but here was old Kentucky*."

As I delivered the last five words, I took my old hat off my head, threw it upon the ground, and brought my rifle to the position of taking aim. At that instant came a shout and an Indian yell from the inmates of the pit, and a tremendous applause from other portions of the house, the whole lasting for nearly a minute, and, as Edmund Kean told his wife, after his first great success in London, "the house rose to me!" The whole pit was standing up and shouting. I had to sing the song three times that night before they would let me off.

When Edmund Kean returned to America in 1825, the incident which had occurred four years earlier (see Doc. 71) had not been totally forgotten, and several demonstrations and minor incidents in New York and Philadelphia theatres marred his performances. But antipathy eventually dissipated and he played to good houses. Similar problems in Baltimore are chronicled by Wemyss, who acted in support of the tragedian there.

115   F. C. Wemyss on Edmund Kean, 1825

Wemyss, *Twenty-Six Years*, pp. 113–14

The Philadelphia Theatre having closed for the season, the company proceeded to Baltimore, where we opened with the play of *The Stranger*. But our season was brought to an abrupt termination by the "Kean Row." From the opening, there was a feverish anxiety to know when Kean's engagement would commence, or whether he intended to visit Baltimore. No sooner did the announcement of his name appear, than it became evident his reception would not be a friendly one, although he hoped, and his friends were sanguine, the result would be the same as in New York and Philadelphia – an expression of public feeling which would subside. He had requested me to play Richmond knowing that so long as it was possible to hold our ground, I should never desert him, although the prospect of being hooted and pelted, was by no means a pleasant one. When he appeared as Richard the Third, the hubbub as usual commenced, but had apparently subsided during the third act, when everything was restored to quiet. . . . I left the theatre to obtain some portion of my dress from the Shakespeare, where I boarded. I was surprised on my return to find the storm raging more furiously than ever. This was owing to the injudicious conduct of Kean's friends, who ruined his cause. During the early part of the evening, they had displayed two placards in front of each stage box, the one bearing the motto, "*Let the Friends of Kean be silent*"; the other "*Kean for ever!*" Had they adhered to their maxim of silence, their triumph would have been complete, but although their tongues were silent, their hands were too active; on the slightest opposition, they seized the aggressor and ejected him from the theatre. Those treated in this unceremonious manner, for what they conceived to be their right, formed a group before the doors of the theatre, recapitulating their wrongs to the already excited populace, waiting only for a leader to commence mischief; a brickbat thrown at the windows of the saloon, was followed by a rush towards the door. The theatre was saved from destruction by the spirited conduct of Mr. Montgomery, the mayor of the city, who interposed his person, assuring the mob, that none could enter that building for the purpose of mischief, except over his body. A pause took place, and that pause, in all probability saved the life of Kean – who was enabled to make his escape from the theatre. Every carriage was searched, and it was not until assured that the object of their vengeance was beyond their reach, that the crowd dispersed, some remaining on the ground until daylight.

And where was the manager during all this riot and confusion? Mr. Wood, fearful of some serious mishap, left the city in the steamboat at five o'clock, on a plea of business thus depriving Kean of the aid of that tongue, which for a long series of years, had guided the taste and quelled the unruly spirits of the theatre. Policy might have dictated his retreat, but justice to those under his control should have held him fast at his post, in the hours of danger. He is a bad pilot who deserts the helm when his vessel is in the neighborhood of breakers.

Of the many British travellers who visited America and wrote of their experiences during the first half of the nineteenth century the most noteworthy was certainly Frances Trollope. Immigrating in the late 1820s, she established a business in Cincinnati which failed. After spending the next two and a half years travelling widely in the United States, she returned to England in 1832, and published her travelogue, *Domestic Manners of the Americans*. It is a generally scathing attack on what she perceived as the vulgar manners and customs which abounded in the country. Americans were furious at what they considered the vicious treatment they had received at her hands, and the appellation "Trollope" came into currency. The following is her assessment of inappropriate dress and behavior of a Cincinnati audience.

116   Frances Trollope on Cincinnati Audiences, 1829

Frances Trollope, *Domestic Manners of the Americans*, ed. by Donald Smalley (New York: Alfred A. Knopf, 1949), pp. 133–34

The theatre was really not a bad one, though the very poor receipts rendered it impossible to keep it in high order; but an annoyance infinitely greater than decorations indifferently clean, was the style and manner of the audience. Men came into the lower tier of boxes without their coats; and I have seen shirt-sleeves tucked up to the shoulder; the spitting was incessant, and the mixed smell of onions and whiskey was enough to make one feel even the Drakes' acting[1] dearly bought by the obligation of enduring its accompaniments. The bearing and attitudes of the men are perfectly indescribable; the heels thrown higher than the head, the entire rear of the person presented to the audience, the whole length supported on the benches, are among the varieties that these exquisite posture-masters exhibit. The noises, too, were perpetual, and of the most unpleasant kind; the applause is expressed by cries and thumping with the feet instead of clapping; and when a patriotic fit seized them, and "Yankee Doodle" was called for, every man seemed to think his reputation as a citizen depended on the noise he made.

[1] The Drakes she refers to are Alexander and his wife, the former Miss Denny. He was the son of Samuel Drake, pioneer showboat entrepreneur.

When New Orleans' St. Charles Theatre opened in 1835, it was the largest and most elegant in the country. Yet the management had little faith in the decorum of the audience, as the following from the bottom of playbills printed during the theatre's inaugural season indicates. Note the different prices of admission for free black persons and slaves.

117   Rules of Audience Conduct, St. Charles Theatre, New Orleans, 1835

Playbill, St. Charles Theatre, New Orleans; Harvard Theatre Collection

No smoking will be allowed in the boxes, lobbies, or salons. Smoking will be confined to the barrooms at the corner of the theatre arcade and at the foot of the gallery stairs.

No auditor can give away his right of admission after having entered the house. Therefore checks transferred will not be received.

Tickets purchased for the night cannot be used afterwards, either in whole or in part.

It is particularly requested that dogs will not be brought to the theatre, as they cannot be admitted.

Peanuts are proscribed.

Prices of Admission

Chairs in the Private Boxes and Parquette	$1.50
Amphitheater, Boxes and Pit	1.00
Free Colored Persons	1.00
Amphitheater of the Gallery	.50
Slaves will not be admitted without exhibiting passes from their Masters: Admittance	.50

Doors will be opened at 6 o'clock and the curtain will rise at 7 o'clock precisely.

The hostility that developed between William Charles Macready and Edwin Forrest which eventually erupted in the Astor Place Riot[1] escalated rapidly after Forrest's hiss of Macready's performance of Hamlet at Edinburgh. In a letter to the editor of *The Times*, the American tragedian defended his actions.

[1] For a full account of the riot and the events leading up to it, see Richard Moody, *The Astor Place Riot* (Bloomington: Indiana University Press, 1958).

118   Letter from Edwin Forrest to *The Times*, 1846

The Times, April 4, 1846

There are two legitimate modes of evincing approbation and disapprobation in the theatre – an expression of approbation, by the clapping of hands, and the other by hisses to mark dissent; and as well-timed and hearty applause is the just meed of an actor who deserves well, so also is hissing, a salutary and wholesome corrective of the abuses of the stage. . . . It was against one of these abuses that *my* dissent was expressed, and not, as was stated, "with a view of expressing his (my) disapproval of the manner in which Mr. Macready gave effect to a particular passage." The truth is, Mr. Macready thought fit to introduce a fancy dance into his performance of *Hamlet*, which I thought, and still think, a desecration of the scene, and at which I evinced that disapprobation, for which the pseudo-critic is pleased to term me an "offender." . . . This was the only time during the performance that I did so, although the writer evidently seeks, in the article alluded to, to convey a different impression. It must be observed also, that I was by no means "solitary" in the expression of opinion.

That a man may manifest his pleasure or displeasure after the recognized mode, according to the best of judgment, actuated by proper motives, and for justifiable ends, is a right, which, until now, I have never once heard questioned. . . . I contend that right extends equally to an actor, in his capacity as spectator, as to any other man; besides, from the nature of his studies, he is much more competent to judge of a theatrical performance than any *soidisant* critic, who has never himself been an actor. The writer of the article in the *Scotsman*, who has most unwarrantably singled me out for public animadversion, has carefully omitted to notice the fact, that I warmly appauded several points of Mr. Macready's performance; and more than once I regretted that the audience did not second me in so doing. As to the pitiful charge of professional jealousy preferred against me, I dismiss it with the contempt it merits, confidently relying upon all those of the profession with whom I have associated, for a refutation of the slander.

In April 1848, F. S. Chanfrau, who had recently leased New York's Chatham Theatre, produced the second play in which he appeared as the Bowery B'hoy "Mose." His new character was extremely popular with the actual Bowery B'hoys of lower Manhattan, and the play's opening night caused pandemonium, but not violence, among the audience.

119   Account of Audience Behavior, Premier of *New York As It Is*, 1848

New York Herald, April 19, 1848

Chatham Theatre: – Never, upon any occasion, did this popular theatre present such a scene as on last evening, in consequence of the vast crowds that flocked forward to witness the performance of the new local extravaganza, entitled *New York As It Is*. In the early part of the evening, every available place of accommodation within the theatre was crowded to excess, long before the commencement of the evening's entertainment. The *Brigand*, which preceded the new and attractive piece, was being performed, when the crowd became so great that those who were in the front seats in the pit were forced to take refuge, for a time, in that part of the theatre allotted for the orchestra. The shouting and confusion here became almost alarming, and no sooner had those who fled there been seated down, when another rush from behind caused them to start on the stage, over the gas lights, and the play was stopped. Soon wave after wave succeeded, and perhaps a more graphic illustration of *New York As It Is* could not be given with better effect. The front of the stage was here immediately filled up, with a motley group, consisting of honest John Tars, and a fair sprinkling of the b'hoys. A humorous looking customer, in the midst of the scene, came forward, and cried out "Who killed Cock Robin?", which caused a vociferous roar of laughter and shouting, from all quarters of the house. Many climbed up to the stage boxes, and all seemed bent on genuine frolic. The police and officers connected with the theatre were rendered powerless.

In the meantime, the outside of the theatre, in Chatham Street, presented a scene of equal confusion. Immense groups were outside, endeavoring to force their way in – while the numbers within, unable to find accommodations, rushed towards the door. . . . Here there was a perfect jam for over half an hour; some rushing in and others rushing out. It was hereupon announced, by one of the company, that the money paid by those who were unable to find accommodation, would be returned to them at the door; and hereupon the rush from all parts of the house made confusion more confounded. Several made their way to the box keeper's office and doors, and were paid back their money. The police and *attaches* of the theatre hereupon commenced to clear the front of the stage, amid the most deafening cheers; and some of the young "b'hoys" were to be seen springing forward on the heads of their different groups of friends, from the stage, whom they soon joined in the pit, amid continued laughter. The humorous character who called out "cock-robin" again made his appearance, which was the signal for a fresh storm of cheering and laughter. After much delay, all was tranquil as the "unruffled surface of the ocean in a calm," and never did a scene of this kind pass off with better humor. We did not learn of a single accident. On inquiry in the proper quarter, it was stated that between those who had left the theatre and those who were unable to get accommodation or make their way in, over one thousand must have left. The interior of the theatre was jam full when the performance was continued. The new local extravaganza was hereupon performed, giving a graphic picture of life in New York.

The Astor Place Riot was certainly the most significant example of, and logical conclusion to, rowdy audience behavior during the first half of the nineteenth century. Macready, victim of the democratically zealous fans of Forrest, reported his impression of the events in his diary.

120   William Charles Macready on Astor Place Riot, 1849

The Diaries of William Charles Macready, ed. William Toynbee, 2 vols. (New York: G. P. Putnam's Sons, 1912), II: 424–28

May 10th. . . . The play began, there was some applause to Mr. Clarke (I write of what I could hear in my room below). I was called, and at my cue went on with full assurance, confidence, and cheerfulness. My reception was very enthusiastic, but I soon discovered that there was opposition, though less numerously manned than on Monday. I went right on when I found it would not instantly be quelled, looking at the wretched creatures in the parquette, who shook their fists violently at me, and called out to me in savage fury. I laughed at them, pointing them out with my truncheon to the police who, I feared were about to repeat the inertness of the previous evening. A blackboard with white letters was leaned against the side of the proscenium: "The friends of order will remain silent." This had some effect in making the rioters more conspicuous.

My first, second, third scenes passed over rapidly and unheard, at the end of the fourth one of the officers gave a signal, the police rushed in at the two sides of the parquette, closed in upon the scoundrels occupying the center seats and furiously vociferating and gesticulating, and seemed to lift them or bundle them in a body out of the center of the house, amid the cheers of the audience. I was in the act of making my exit with Lady Macbeth, and stopped to witness their clever maneuver, which like a *coup de main*, swept the place clear at once. As well as I can remember, the bombardment outside now began. Stones were hurled against the windows in Eighth Street, smashing many; the work of destruction became then more systematic, the volleys of stones flew without intermission, battering and smashing all before them. The gallery and upper gallery still kept up the din within, aided by the crashing of glass and boarding without. The second act passed, the noise and violence without increasing, the contest within becoming feebler. Mr. Povey, as I was going to my raised seat in the banquet scene, came up to me and, in an undertone and much frightened, urged me to cut out some part of the play and bring it to a close. I turned round upon him very sharply and said that "I had consented to do this thing – to place myself here, and whatever the consequences I must go through with it – it must be done, that I could not cut out. The audience had paid for so much, and the law compelled me to give it; they would have cause for riot if all were not properly done." I was angry and spoke very sharply to the above effect.

The banquet scene was partially heard and applauded. I went down to change my dress – the battering at the building doors, and windows growing, like the fiends at the Old Woman of Berkly's burial, louder and louder. Water was running down fast from the ceiling to the floor of my room and making a pool there. . . . The stones hurled in had broken some of the pipes. The fourth act passed, louder and more fierce waxed the furious noises against the building and from without: for whenever a missile did effectual mischief in its discharge it was hailed with shouts outside. Stones came in through the window, and one struck the chandelier, the audience removed for protection behind the walls. The house was considerably thinned, gaps of unoccupied seats appearing in the audience part. The fifth act was heard, and in the very spirit of resistance I flung my whole soul into every word I uttered, acting my very best and exciting the audience to a sympathy even with the glowing words of fiction, whilst these dreadful deeds of real crime and outrage were roaring at intervals in our ears and rising to madness all round us. The death of Macbeth was loudly cheered, and on being lifted up and told that I was called, I went on, and, with action earnestly and most emphatically expressive of my sympathy with them and my feelings of gratefulness to them, I quitted the New York stage amid the acclamations of those before me.

Going to my room I began without loss of time to undress but with no feeling of fear or apprehension. When washed, and half dressed, persons came into my room – consternation on the faces of some; fear, anxiety, and distress on those of others. "The mob were getting stronger. Why were not the military sent for?" "They are here." "Where?" "Why did they not act?" "They were not here, they were drawn up in the Bowery." "Of what use were they there?" Other arrivals. "The military had come upon the ground." "Why did they not disperse the mob then?" These questions and answers, with many others, were passed to and from among the persons round me whilst I was finishing my hasty toilet, I occasionally putting in a question or a remark. Suddenly we heard a volley of musketry: "Hark! What's that?" I asked. "The soldiers have fired." "My God!" I exclaimed. Another volley, and another. The question among those surrounding me (there were, that I remember, Ruggles, Judge Kent, D. Colden, R. Emmett, a friend of his in some official station, Fry, Sefton, Chippendale, and I think the performer who played Malcolm, etc.) which way was I to go out? News came that several were killed, and I was really insensible to the degree of danger in which I stood, and saw at once – there being no avoidance – there was nothing for it but to meet the worst with dignity, and so I stood prepared.

They sent someone to reconnoiter, and urged the necessity of a change in my appearance. I was confident that people did not know my person, and repeated this belief. They overbore all objections, and took the drab surtout of the performer of Malcolm, he taking my black one. They insisted too that I must not wear my hat; I said, "Very well, lend me a cap." Mr. Sefton gave me his, which was cut all up the back to go upon my head. Thus equipped I went out, following Robert Emmett to the stage door, here we were stopped, not being allowed to pass. The "friend" was to follow us as a sort of aide, but we soon lost him. We crossed the stage, descended into the orchestra, got over into the parquette, and passing into the center passage went along with the thin stream of the audience moving out. We went right on, down the flight of stairs and out of the door into Eighth Street. All was clear in front – kept so by two cordons or lines of police at either end of the building stretched right across. We passed the line near Broadway, and went on threading the excited crowd, twice or three times muttering in Emmett's ear, "You are walking too fast." We crossed Broadway, still through a scattered crowd, and walked along Clinton Place till we passed the street leading down to the New York Hotel. I then said "Are you going to your own house?" "Yes." We reached it, and having opened the door with a latchkey, closing it after us, he said, "You are safe here, no one will know anything about you, you shall have a bed in ten minutes or a quarter of an hour, and you may depend upon all in this house."

121   Astor Place Riot, 1849
Harvard Theatre Collection

E. P. Hingston, a travelling companion of Artemus Ward, has left the following account of a visit to the Mormon Theatre in Salt Lake City.

122   E. P. Hingston on Mormon Theatre, Salt Lake City, 1864
E. P. Hingston, *The Genial Showman: Being Reminiscences of the Life of Artemus Ward* (London: John C. Hotten, 1871), pp. 464–74

I left Artemus slumbering before the fire; and in the midst of a heavy snowstorm sought my way to the theatre. I found it on the corner of an adjacent street. In a small office to the left of the entrance was the money-taker, handing out tickets at a window. I found that admission to the dress circle was only a dollar. As I paid the amount in a gold coin bright and fresh from the California mint, I noticed that the money-taker took stock of me. I returned the compliment, and listened to him whistling the air of "The Groves of Blarney"! I was not aware at the time that I was gazing at a bishop!

Internally the theatre presented as incomplete an appearance as the exterior. There was very little attempt at decoration other than that obtainable by the use of white paint and gilding. There was a large pit, or "parquet," as the Americans call it, having a high rake from the orchestra towards the back, thus allowing occupants of seats in the rear to have as good a view of the stage as those in front. I counted the pit, and found that there were about eight hundred people in it. The price of admission was seventy-five cents. Over the dress circle was an upper box tier, the admission to which was fifty cents; and over that again a gallery, to which the charge was twenty-five cents, or about one English shilling.

Some of my cavalry friends undertook to point out the arrangements of the house. They told me that the dress circle was the part which Gentiles frequented, and that the pit was specially reserved for Mormons, with their families. I noticed that nearly every man in it was accompanied by two, three, or more ladies, and that in some instances an entire family occupied a row, there being only one adult male among the number.

On each side of the proscenium was a private box, on the same plane as the dress circle. These boxes were fitted up with green curtains. No other drapery was used for decoration elsewhere in the house.

Under the dress circle to my right, a little more elevated than the floor of the pit, were a series of seats like pews, running parallel with the side walls of the theatre. Occupying them were fifty-nine women and children, all very plainly dressed, and none of them remarkable for good looks.

"That is the Prophet's Pen," said my Gentile informant, "and those are his wives and daughters. There are more of them in those seats of the parquet where you see the large rocking chair."

"Whose is that, and why is it there?" I asked.

"That's where the Prophet sits when he is in the bosom of his family. It's a pretty large bosom," remarked the officer dryly.

"But where is the Prophet himself?"

"That's he. Over in yon proscenium box with the green curtains to it. The lady beside him is his favorite wife – Sister Amelia. Brigham likes to sit up there because he can keep an eye upon his family down below, and see the Gentiles in the dress circle. He's having a look through his opera-glass at the General just now. . . ."

I asked who were the other ladies and gentlemen of the company, and received my reply in nearly the following words:

"They are all Mormons – every one of them. The part of the Baron is being played by Mr. Caine, the stage-manager. Countess Wintersen is Mrs. Clawson, wife of Hiram Clawson, the manager. He has three wives. This lady is No. 2. The part of Peter is being played by Mr. Margetts: he is one of their low comedians, a very good fellow. He has three wives also. All their wives learn to play; so that if one gets ill they can easily send on another for the part."

After the play of *The Stranger* came the farcical piece known as *Paddy Mile's Boy.* The part of Henry, according to the bills, was played by Mr. Sloan. So soon as that gentleman came on the stage I recognized him as being the money-taker to whom I had paid my dollar on entering. . . .

So cold was the evening and so chilly the interior of the theatre, that the Prophet, like everybody else, was well wrapped up. No audience could have behaved better than did the one I saw at Salt Lake. There was no whistling in the gallery; no cries of "Now, the catgut!" No stamping of feet, nor vacating seats before the fall of the curtain. The performers on the stage met with much applause and very deservedly so, for the amateurs were not far behind the professional stars in their knowledge of stage business. Every performer was well dressed for his part. The scenery was good, and there were no mishaps on the part of the stage carpenters. Evidently the rehearsals had been well attended to; there was no laxity of management behind the curtain, and the voice of the prompter was not heard in the land.

Digressing from my narrative of what I saw at the theatre on the evening of my first visit, it may not be out of place to refer to the position of the playhouse among the institutions of Salt Lake. The theatre is essentially a national concern. It enters in the general system of government – social, moral, and religious. Socially, because all classes visit it; morally, because Brigham Young considers it the best substitute for amusement of a less harmless character; and religiously, because its profits go to the support of what is called "The Church." The performances are advertised from the pulpit, and attendance at the playhouse is preached to the people as a portion of their duty. The actresses are for the most part the wives and daughters of church dignitaries. Even the daughters of the Prophet himself occasionally assist in the representations; and Mr. Hiram Clawson, on whom the management devolves, is a son-in-law to Brigham Young. . . .

Brigham Young is as careful of the comfort of his audiences as he is of that of his actors. The theatre was built under his inspection, and he has taken care that visitors shall not be incommoded. In all his arrangements the fact is apparent that he understands what so many managers in London and elsewhere do not comprehend – that the auditorium of a theatre should be attractive simply for its qualifications as a place in which to sit at ease without being cramped, crushed, or annoyed – that it should be the drawing room to retire to after dinner. He understands also – and herein he is ahead of many other managers, and anticipates the theatre of the future – that the playhouse should be a place for paterfamilias, to which without apology he could fearlessly take all his kith and kin, not an institution depending for its success upon ministering to the tastes of fast young men, nor for its patronage on its advantages as an exhibition room for marketable beauty. But a place to which human beings with head and brains can go, and feel that they are not degrading themselves by witnessing senseless trash, nor having their patience tested by listening to uneducated and unqualified performers.

123   Mormon Theatre, Salt Lake City, 1864

Harvard Theatre Collection

VI. Drama

In the late 1820s Edwin Forrest, whose meteoric rise to stardom had established him as the cultural hero of Jacksonian democrats, sought to increase his repertory of star vehicles and further increase his appeal as *the* patriotic and democratic native star by offering prizes to American playwrights who provided him with new material on native themes. The following is the first published announcement of his playwriting prize.

124 Edwin Forrest's Playwriting Prize Announcement, 1828

Critic, November 22, 1828, p. 60

We have received the following note from E. Forrest, Esq. and take great pleasure in communicating his generous proposition to the public, in his own language. It is much to be desired that native genius may be aroused by this offer, from native genius, and that writers, worthy to win, may enter into the laudable competition.

"DEAR SIR – Feeling extremely desirous that dramatic letters should be more cultivated in my native country, and believing that the dearth of writers in that department is rather the result of a want of proper incentive, than of any deficiency of the requisite talents, I should feel greatly obliged to you if you would communicate to the public, in the next number of the *Critic*, the following offer.

To the author of the best tragedy, in five acts, of which the hero, or principal character, shall be an aboriginal of this country, the sum of five hundred dollars, half of the proceeds of the third representation, and my own services *gratis* on that occasion. The award to be made by a committee of literary and theatrical gentlemen. The manuscript to be forwarded to me, 144 North Tenth Street, Philadelphia, before the 1st of October, 1829.

The first play to win the prize was *Metamora, or The Last of the Wampanoags*, by John Augustus Stone. The following reviews its premier production at the Park Theatre in New York. Notice how skillfully the playwright tailored the title role to Forrest's strengths as an actor.

125   Review of *Metamora*, 1829

New York Mirror, 8, no. 24 (December 19, 1829), 190

METAMORA, OR THE LAST OF THE WAMPANOAGS – This Indian tragedy was performed, for the first time, on Tuesday evening last, for the benefit of Mr. Forrest. A considerable interest having been excited, long before the rising of the curtain, the house was completely filled. The prologue, spoken by Mr. Barrett, was received with enthusiastic applause, and every thing indicated, on the part of the audience, a desire to give the piece a favorable reception. The actors, both male and female, were eminently successful in their endeavors to do justice to their several parts, and during the progress of the play, received the most unequivocal proofs of the approbation of their delighted spectators. Independent of the undoubted merits of Metamora, the managers had afforded a gratifying exhibition of scenery, dresses, decorations, etc. We cannot at present particularize respecting the excellence of each actor. . . .

At this period seeds of hostility had been sown between the colonists and the chief of the Wampanoags, Metamora (Mr. Forrest), son of Massasoit, who first received the English pilgrims, and entered into friendly alliance with them. . . . Metamora boldly appears, justifying the description formerly given of him:

> Tow'ring o'er the subject earth he strode, the grandest model of a mighty man.

He manfully and eloquently urges his natural and hereditary rights; reminds them of his father's kindness to the whites in the days of their feebleness, and denies the accusations against him. An Indian is now produced as a witness of his hostile intentions. He is a confidential follower of Metamora, on whom he had heaped benefits. Failing to induce him to retract his words, he stabs him to the heart before the council, asserts his princely power, and utters a prophetic and terrible denunciation on the whole race of whites. They fire upon him but by dexterity he evades the shot and escapes to his home breathing vengeance against his enemies, and rousing his warriors to unite in dealing against them an overwhelming blow.

A scene, terribly illustrative of the horrors of Indian warfare, in which the savages are triumphant, and Metamora gives an extraordinary proof of his magnanimity of soul, terminates the third act. . . . After the most heroic and desperate efforts, Metamora's force is destroyed, his child slain by the victorious whites, and he retreats with Nahmeoke to his last hiding place. A Wampanoag betrays the spot to the allies, who on all sides surround him. To save Nahmeoke from slavery and insult, he slays her with her own consent. The English fire upon him – he meets death fearlessly as he had lived, pronounces a terrible curse upon the whites, and falls to the earth made red with the blood of Nahmeoke, and dies the last of the Wanpanoags.

By the time Dr. Robert Montgomery Bird won a subsequent Forrest prize for *The Gladiator*, some members of the press, and perhaps the public, were treating the prize plays as significant pieces of native dramatic literature, not just performance vehicles for the robust tragedian.

126   Review of *The Gladiator*, 1831
New York Dramatic Mirror, 9, no. 12 (September 25, 1831), 93–94

We have read the manuscript of this tragedy with careful attention, and can therefore speak of its merits confidently, and to the purpose. It is strongly written and well conceived, containing striking scenes, bold characters, and passages of great beauty. The author is evidently one familiar with dramatic literature; most of the dialogue is marked by a Spartan brevity and verve, and even the inferior parts generally are such as talented players need not hesitate to undertake . . . The part of Spartacus abounds with instances of a spirited declamatory style, admirably fit for dramatic effect. . . . The play will undoubtedly become a popular and permanent stock piece. We cannot, however, lay aside the manuscript without complimenting the writer, not only on its actual intrinsic merit, both for the closet and the stage, but on the singular propriety with which it is adapted to the style and powers of the tragedian by whose laudable exertions it was elicited. The character of Spartacus is devised with great art. Its lofty tone of declamation, its bold *gushes* of various passions, are calculated to exhibit those qualities which this fine actor possesses in the highest degree. In a quiet, thoughtful reading part he would find no opportunity for display, and would probably glide through it without much effect; but, when aroused by a mastering interest, and called upon to express the extremes of overwhelming and discordant feelings, thousands have long since borne testimony to his unrivalled powers. *The Gladiator* will undoubtedly add to his well-earned fame, and entitle him to the gratitude of all who interest themselves in the dramatic literature of this country. It will be produced, for the first time, on Monday evening next, at the Park Theatre.

Not all native plays of the period had literary pretensions. Among the most popular type of theatrical entertainments for the working classes during the 1830s and 40s were the Bowery melodramas and their imitators. The following detailed account of one such piece at the American Theatre, Bowery gives an insight into the form's appeal.

127   Description of a Bowery Melodrama, 1833

Spirit of the Times, 2 (May 18, 1833), n.p.

This house has at last produced the long announced *Thalaba the Destroyer*, and with a splendor that does credit to the management, and adds another to the long list of admirable spectacles of which this has long been the Theatre par excellence.

The scenery is entirely new, together with the dresses, decorations, properties, etc. and of the most gorgeous description. The opening scene of the mystic cavern – by James is in admirable taste, nor can we pass over the brilliant effect of his Turkish Chamber. Duke White, a young artist who may perhaps rank as one of the most talented scene painters of the day, has thrown some of his best effects into this piece. His Valley of Dates, Sultan's Palace, and Eastern Garden, are each and all of them, well worthy of the fame he is daily acquiring. There is also a submarine grotto, by the same artist, of the most elaborate workmanship, and poetical conception, and only leaves us to regret that the "spirits of the damned" should possess so exquisite a paradise. James has also added fresh laurels to his well earned reputation as an artist, in the mystic cavern by the moonlight, the Silver Cavern, and brilliant Turkish Chamber.

Demons and evil spirits super-abound, and there is no lack of genies. . . . Thalaba is in possession of a quiver which his foster father had picked up when he discovered him, an infant at the Well of Agra. On this quiver are written certain characters which exactly tally with those on a ruby ring. Suddenly the quiver turns to gold, and the inscription both on the quiver and on the ring changes, and is the same. He is commanded to follow the flight of locusts, to redeem the burning sword in the cavern of silver, and quell the influence of enchanters. The hum of locusts is heard – the swarm appears – he is about to depart but is restrained by the shepherd and his daughter Oneiza. Suddenly a blue cloud appears on the horizon, on which is written "Depart or perish." The command is imperative and he obeys.

To follow Thalaba over mountains and passes of sand – burning deserts, with occasionally a cooling fountain to refresh in – to trace his steps sleeping and waking, pursued by the fiend Abdalda, and as often delivered from his clutches by his good genie Marmina – to recapture the thunder and lightning that are eternally at his beck and call – to enumerate the ghosts – to penetrate the enchanted cavern beneath the waters of Badelmandel with its pillow rock, coral shells, and submarine plants – to introduce the acquatic demons chanting over a cauldron – the galley of Thalaba sinking to the vast abyss; and the prince chained to a rock. . . . On the whole, *Thalaba the Destroyer* may be pronounced one of the most deservedly successful dramas that has ever been produced at the theatre whether we regard the beauty of the scenery, the ingenuity of the

machinery, the splendor of the dresses, decorations, and admirable arrangements of the procession. We are glad to find it played to crowded houses, and
hope the managers will reap a golden benefit from their enterprise.

During most of the nineteenth century American dramatists had no copyright or royalty
protection. The usual way of doing business was for actors or managers to purchase plays
outright and, if they were star vehicles, not to publish them but to retain them for their
own theatrical usage. Occasionally, actors or managers offered prizes for plays. Playwrights who entered competitions and did not win the prize sometimes attempted to sell
their work in the following manner.

128   Advertisement for a New Play, 1836

Spirit of the Times, 9 (May 28, 1836), 119

The author of a comedy in three acts, wishes to dispose of it to some good low
comedian, in order to have it represented in a manner that will be advantageous
to the purchaser as well as himself. The play referred to was written for a prize
comedy, but owing to a misunderstanding between the committee and himself,
it was not read by them. It is now for sale in manuscript with the stage business
arranged for immediate representation. Any person wishing a piece of the low
comedy order, will please address COMICUS at the office of the *Spirit of the Times*,
stating when and where an interview may be had.

Throughout the first half of the nineteenth century, there was little true criticism. Newspapers increased their coverage of theatrical performances by way of reviews, but many
of them were untrustworthy because of personal connections between editors and theatre
managers, or because the members of the press were in some manner favorably rewarded
for positive reviews by the actors. A new weekly founded in New York during 1839 noted
the problems and vowed to take its critical responsibility seriously.

129   Description of Theatrical Criticism, 1839

Paul Pry, 1 (February 9, 1839), 1

Dramatic criticism, as it has been conducted for sometime past, is a mere pastry
system of puffing on the one hand, and personal abuse on the other. Mr. A. or
Mr. B. who attends the theatre for such and such a paper, becomes acquainted
with some third- or fourth-rate actor in one of the establishments, and lauds
him to the skies as a perfect phenomenon. . . . Everything done at the theatre in
which his favorite actor is engaged is admirable, and the performances at any
other house are of course abominable. Suddenly the tables are turned, and all
the critic's eloquence is exhausted in favor of the very establishment he has hith-

erto been decrying. To account for this sudden change, look in the playbills, and you will find that the friend of the critic has transferred his services, and he of course goes with him. But at length we hear no more of the great actor, and why, because, perchance, he has stopped the customary supplies of "cold without," [1] and "half dozens fried or stewed," [2] or else some fresh face has arisen who flatters the critic's vanity, by admiring his "articles" – and the quondam friend is left unheeded.

Another system is to puff in proportion to the pay for advertising. Some editors own stock in certain theatres, and then the way they puff is a caution. Again, some disagreement of a private nature will arise between an actor and a critic, and the latter revenges himself by refusing to notice the offender. Others are paid a certain sum per week to do the theatricals for a daily paper and they sit snugly at home and write flaming accounts of the triumphant success of a new piece. . . . The reader is subsequently surprised to find out that the said piece was not performed on account of the sudden indisposition of a performer. This is fact, not fiction. To be sure, there are two or three papers who have lately shaken off this dull and disagreeable system, and speak candidly, but there are still a great majority, who act as we have described above. These we shall doubtless offend, so be it. . . .

As we have commenced, so shall we continue, independent and impartial. We will not flatter the brightest star, nor abuse nor neglect the poorest super, merely on account of their relative positions. And if the public continue to support us as liberally as they have hitherto done, they shall find us ever striving to deserve success.

---

[1] This refers to a favorite light lunch of the period: cold beef sandwich without condiments or side dishes. The reference is to actors picking up the lunch tab for reviewers.

[2] A favorite after-theatre snack of the period was either a half dozen fried oysters; or a half dozen oysters in a stew – actually a milk-based soup with onions and occasionally potatoes. The reference is to actors treating reviewers after a performance.

Through most of the period, few native plays of significance other than as vehicles for starring performers emerged. Everyone complained of the need for a truly national drama, but few people attempted to write plays on American life requiring a strong cast, rather than the presence of a single star. When *Fashion*, probably the best and certainly the most popular native comedy of the period, debuted at New York's Park Theatre, the *Spirit of the Times* found it ineffective and banal.

130   *Spirit of the Times'* Review of *Fashion*, 1845

Spirit of the Times, 15 (March 29, 1845), 56

Mrs. Mowatt's comedy, *Fashion*, was represented for the first time, on Monday, to a very crowded and indulgent audience. The friends of the fair author did her injustice by previously disseminating opinions in praise of her comedy – its nature and nationality. By thus exciting curiosity the well-wishers of the lady overstripped the mark of propriety, and the people, who were allured to the house by these prejudiced opinions, were very naturally disappointed from the inferior quality of the composition. Mrs. Mowatt possesses few qualifications for dramatic writing, as she lacks the essentials – vigor and ingenuity. Everyone, who has seen a play represented, immediately considers himself able to produce a like work, little reflecting on the difficulty of that task, and here we have a solution for the many failures in dramatic composition. The language of comedy is not the ordinary slipshod conversational stringing together of words, employed in everyday life, and the story of a play cannot be a mere recital of occasional occurrences. Comic writing should be terse, epigrammatic, and nervous, and the plot should comprise a narration of real events, intermixed with others of a decidedly artificial nature. . . . Above all, the action should never be staged in the course of the piece. On the contrary to these rules, the dialogue of *Fashion* is unpolished, spiritless, and disjointed, the satire is dealt out in unconnected items, much after the manner of newspaper squibs. The plot is entirely too light for the dialogue, and the action, although not encumbered by an underplot, is cut up by unnecessary durations. The first act has no earthly connection with the piece, and the third and fourth acts were perfect superfluities. The polka is a bore, and the hiding of Gertrude (the two episodes of the piece) is perfectly unnecessary – inasmuch as it accomplishes nothing save a prolongation of the comedy. A dance may be a very clever wind up to an act of a melodrama, yet in a comedy it is an unmitigated nuisance, and we would contend that the polka is neither national nor theatrical, when danced in the manner the Park Company do it. And mind we do not blame the artists for the style of its execution, as we conceive they were engaged to perform, not to dance. But should they be employed to do both, it is money wasted – for as to the dancing it is a decided swindle. It struck us, however, at first sight that the polka was the feature of the comedy and we did really wonder why it could not be introduced in a play of less compass than five long acts. But we have since been informed that the murder of the dance is an accomplishment among the "upper ten thousand" and had to be brought into a picture of fashionable life. We will not attempt to analyze the plot, because we could not find it, and neither will we attempt to detect the sources of the characters, who, by the way, are almost all the property of earlier dramatists. Mrs. Tiffany is a degenerated Mrs. Malaprop; Adam Trueman, Max Harkaway acclimated; and Snobson's best part was a small imitation of Dick Dashall. To conclude, we may say that the piece, taken as a comedy, is a dreadful failure, and viewed as an exaggerated farce, may be tolerated until the arrival of the steamer. The satire, which bears little connection with the dialogue, is a mere collection of newspaper truisms, . . . while the humor is of a low school unsuited for a dramatic composition of the pretensions of *Fashion*. We would willingly undertake to assist our contemporaries in maintaining the dignity of "Old Drury" and patronize a female writer, but at the same time we have strong conscientious objections against the infection of an indifferent comedy on the public, even if it be for a laudable purpose.

The following review verifies that while critical opinion, such as it was, strongly supported the development of an emerging national drama, opinions varied about the nature of that drama. The *Albion* praised the very qualities of *Fashion* which the *Spirit of the Times* had condemned.

131   *Albion's* Review of *Fashion*, 1845

Albion, 4 (March 29, 1845), 156

It is with no ordinary feelings of satisfaction that we record the triumphant verdict of the public, in favor of Mrs. Mowatt's Comedy of *Fashion* fully sustaining the predictions we ventured to make previous to its representation. It has created a sensation, unexampled in theatricals – and has decisively established the fact, that the time has arrived when a strictly American drama can be called into existence. Mrs. Mowatt herself has but presented us with the "Waverley" of her series.[1]

The satire on modern views and follies, conveyed through the medium of importations from the London stage, fail in their application in this country, from the local character. The "Mirror of Nature" reflects only *English Manners* and peculiarities – the satire is consequently pointless. . . . Change the stage reflector to New York, Boston, Philadelphia, and other large cities, let it faithfully exhibit the "manners living as they rise" in American society, and the drama then assumes its legitimate mission, and we believe it will also regain its original ascendance.

It is contrary to the uniform system pursued in the pages of the *Albion*, to enter into the discussion of the peculiarities of American habits and manners. We must therefore confine our strictures to the comedy, as a work of art, leaving it to our contemporaries to decide the fidelity of the picture it presents of American follies and eccentricities. . . . The language throughout is natural and colloquial, terse and pointed – hence its great charm. Two acts [are] actually nothing but conversation – the action of the play does not progress – and yet the interest of the audience is sustained without flagging. There is not, perhaps, much brilliance in the dialogue, but the absence of this is sufficiently compensated by the

---

[1] A reference to the first of Sir Walter Scott's successful novels. The critic's allusion suggests that he hopes for more quality comedies from the pen of Mrs. Mowatt.

point and solid truths conveyed throughout. The language of Trueman, in particular, is energetic and pointed in the extreme; he is the moralist of the comedy, but he never poses.

Mrs. Tiffany is a modern Mrs. Malaprop in the French tongue with a dash of Lady Deeberley, and the duality is skillfully managed. The dramatic incident of action exhibits, perhaps, the unpracticed hand; the characters talk too much, for modern comedy. We have felt, at times, like the critic on the first representation of *The School for Scandal*, who exclaimed – "Why do not those people leave off talking and let the play go on!" This defect has been materially obviated since the first night, by judicious curtailments of the dialogue. Yet, still more action is desirable. Upon the whole, Mrs. Mowatt may lay claim to having produced the best American comedy in existence, and one that sufficiently indicates her capabilities to write one that shall rank among the first of the age.

The performers exerted themselves in a most praiseworthy manner; it was alike creditable to their standing in the profession, and honorable to the fair author and the public. Chippendale's Adam Trueman has stamped him as an artist of the highest order; his truthful delineation of the noble hearted old farmer, will never be forgotten. Barry played the unthankful part of Tiffany in his very best style. Dyort was judicious and gentlemanly in Col. Howard. We do not exactly coincide with Mr. Crisp's conception of the count; he does not mark distinctly enough the double character. His delineation of the French exquisite is perfect; but it is somewhat tiresome from not being relieved by occasional glimpses of the vulgarity of his national character. Fisher's Snobson is a rich specimen of vulgarity – the character is of itself a necessary, but offensive excrescence in the plot – yet Fisher redeems it by his excellent acting. Skerett is amusing as the "Nigger," but it is a burlesque, not a true portrait. . . . Mr. Bridges as Fogg has not much to do; he is certainly a perfect embodiment of frigid indifference. Mrs. Barry was taxed to the extent of her powers in Mrs. Tiffany, and it is but justice to the lady to say that she proved herself equal to the task. Miss Ellis did ample justice to the gentle Gertrude; and Miss Kate Horn looked lovely and fascinating as Seraphina. We have before noted Mrs. Knight as Prudence; it is a gem! Mrs. Dyort, who has improved amazingly, gave a very lively representation of Millanette, and justly received the warm approbation of the audience.

Mr. Simpson has put the comedy upon the stage, as well as time would permit. The drawing room scene is unexceptionable, but we must object to the ballroom, even in its present improved appearance. If American comedies are to become the rage, the management must remember, that every individual composing the audience, will become critics, of any discrepancies to be detected in the stage arrangements.

The houses are crowded nightly to witness the representation of this novel feature in dramatic annals, and we sincerely congratulate both Mr. Simpson and the authoress on the successful production, which has once more converted "Old Drury" into the Temple of *Fashion*.

Perhaps realizing that its initial condemnatory review of *Fashion* differed radically from both the critical consensus and public reaction, the *Spirit of the Times*, attempting to save critical face, published another article which attributed the play's phenomenal success not to its inherent worth as a piece of dramatic literature, but to the performances.

132   Response to *Albion*'s Review, 1845

Spirit of the Times, 15 (April 5, 1845), 68

The success of the new comedy is attributable to almost any other cause than its literary merits, for against viewing it as a standard piece, its warmest friends would assuredly object. The fate of dramatists had been most marked and emphatic, before the debut of Mrs. Mowatt into this difficult line of comic writing. If by any fortunate chance, or any other unforeseen accident, the playwright managed to elbow his way through the crowd of venal critics and green loungers, who invariably surround the managerial sanctum, if, by show of power, influence, or flattery, the manager is induced to recognize the neophyte's claim, he finds that there is a more powerful cluster of judges, whose whims and inclination are to be consulted – whose dicta are to be implicitly obeyed, and this tribunal is constituted – of actors. To these people mainly is to be attributed the failure of a good piece, and as a reverse, we may say many indifferent writers, (among whom can be classed the author of *Fashion*) are indebted to actors for their notoriety. Although, as in this instance, they have created a piece out of a mere nothing, hitherto they have delighted in crushing the hopes of aspiring comic writers. This remark applies not only to this country, but to England, where actors have shackled talent, nursed animosities, and broken down lofty spirits. They have ruined Jerrold, Kenney, Daniels, and most all writers, not of their own tribe. "To destroy the hope of an author is a matter of small moment to the mimic, to whom *all* feelings are alike," saith Mr. Daniels. "What is his success to *him* even though the decent comforts of a family depend on it? The puffed and pampered player lacks even the small charity of the Fine Gentleman in Garrick's prologue. 'Let the poor devil eat – allow him that!' The poor devil may be damned in a double sense, ere he abate one inch of his dignity – unless to cry quits with some stipendiary hack, some penny-a-line man, or brother buffoon." Again we are rendered joyful, for returning to their sense, they offer amends to the authors by creating a new writer. After murdering some fourscore pieces of standard worth, they absolutely make a comedy of *Fashion* – to the popular eyes, at least. To its neatly turned points of satire one has added a shrug of the shoulders, another a jocose leer, in fine, they have taken Mrs. Mowatt as the one verse text, wherefrom to preach a sermon on mere acting. Without the actors *Fashion* would be intolerable!

Some members of the press consistently argued for a higher quality of theatrical offerings and excoriated both the managers – for their reliance on star performers and pandering to the lowest common denominator of public taste – and the theatregoers, for not demanding the good production of more significant plays. Among the more articulate critics of the general state of theatrical affairs in the 1840s was Walt Whitman, then an editor of the *Brooklyn Eagle*.

133   Walt Whitman on the Theatre, 1847

Brooklyn Eagle, February 8, 1847

Of all "low" places where vulgarity (not only on the stage, but in front of it) is in the ascendant, and bad taste carries the day with hardly a pleasant point to mitigate its coarseness, the New York theatres – except the Park – may be put down (as an Esmeralder might say) at the top of the heap! We don't like to make these sweeping assertions in general – but the habit of such places as the Bowery, Chatham, and the Olympic theatres is really beyond all toleration; and if the New York prints who give dramatic notices, were not the slave of the paid puff system, they surely would sooner or later be "down" on those miserable burlesques of the histrionic art. Yet not one single independent dramatic critic seems to be among the many talented writers for the New York press. Or rather, we should say, not one single upright critic is permitted to utter candidly his opinions of the theatricals of the metropolis; for we would not insult the good taste of the intelligent literary men connected with the press over the river, so much as to suppose that their eyes and ears do not make the same complaint to them as ours make to us in the matter alluded to.

We have excepted the Park Theatre in the charge of vulgarity, because the audiences there are always intelligent, and there is a dash of superiority thrown over the performance. But commendations can go not much further. Indeed it is not a little strange that in a great place like New York, acknowledged as the leading city on the western hemisphere, there should be no absolutely *good* theatre. The Park, once in a great while, gives a fine play, performed by meritorious actors and actresses. The Park is still very far, however, from being what we might reasonably expect in the principal dramatic establishment of the metropolis. It is but a third-rate imitation of the best London theatres. It gives us the castoff dramas, and the unengaged players of Great Britain; and the dramas and players, like garments which come secondhand from gentleman to valet, everything fits awkwardly. Though now and then there is ground for satisfaction the average is such as men of refinement cannot applaud at all. A play arranged to suit an English audience, and to jibe with English localities, feelings, and domestic customs, can rarely be represented in America, without considerable alteration. This destroys its uniformity, and generally deprives it of all life and spirit. One of the curses of the Park, and indeed of nearly all theatres now, is the *star* system. Some actor or actress flits about the country, playing a week here and a week there, bringing as his or her greatest recommendation, that of *novelty* – and very often indeed having no other. In all the intervals between the appearance of these much trumpeted people, the theatre is quite deserted, though the play and playing are often far better than during some star engagements. We have seen fine old English drama, with Miss Cushman, . . . Mrs. Vernon, Placide, Fisher, and several others whose better in their departments could hardly be found, . . . well put upon the stage, and played to a forlorn looking audience, thinly scattered here and there through pit and box – while the next week crowds would crush each other to get a sight of some flippant well-puffed star, of no real merit, and playing a character written (for the play consists of nothing but *one* in such cases) by nobody knows whom – probably an ephemeral manufacturer of literature, with as little talent as his employer.

One of the theatres that Whitman found intolerable, the Olympic, thrived throughout the desperate economic climate of the 1840s by providing its patrons with a steady diet of farce and topical burlesque. Frequented by the apprentices, newsboys, and other young working-class rowdies known collectively as the Bowery B'hoys, it was the site of a phenomenally popular new play in February 1848 with a Bowery B'hoy as the hero: the *Albion* noted both the realism of Chanfrau's *Mose*, and its topicality. See also Doc. 3.

134   Review of F. S. Chanfrau's *Mose*, 1848
Albion, 8 (February 19, 1849), 96

Mr. Baker has shown great tact in preparing these "Olympic peculiarities." He knows how to suit the taste of the "Pit Sovereigns" and is therefore secure with a very influential portion of the audience at this theatre. The present sketch may be called a dramatic version of our police reports, as it exhibits the various modes adapted by the sharpers about town to delude the unwary. A few other incidents are introduced to make up the dramatic personae, the most prominent of which is Mose, a Bowery B'hoy, imitably played by Chanfrau. It is really a character both in the creation by the author and the embodiment by the actor. As may be supposed, it is received with shouts of delight by the thousand originals of the pit.

Among the most popular forms of theatrical entertainment in the nineteenth-century American theatre were the blackfaced minstrel troupes. Appearing for the first time in

1843, they rapidly captured the public's fancy and contributed numerous jokes and songs to American popular culture. Dan Emmett's popular "walkround tune," "Dixie," which became something of a national anthem for the Confederate States of America, was originally written for Bryant's Minstrels as the composer recounts in the following letter to the editor of the *New York Clipper*.

135   Dan Emmett on "Dixie," 1872

New York Clipper, April 6, 1872

Dear Sir. Having received your request for me to forward to you for publication in the *Clipper* a correct statement of the origin of the song known as "Dixie," I will now endeavor to do so in as brief a manner as possible. I have seen several erroneous statements at different times since the close of the war, all of which are wide of the mark; and I never, until now, have taken the trouble to contradict them. One principal reason for my silence was, that I had no further interest in the song, and that its popularity north was among the "things that were." To proceed then, it is necessary for me to state that I have been south of New York but *once since* 1851, and that was on a short trip to Washington with the Bryant's Minstrels some six years since, all other statements to the contrary notwithstanding.

In the spring of 1858, I was playing in New York with the "Bryants"; my particular business was to compose new walkrounds for them as fast as required. Some time in the spring of that year (1858), amongst others, I composed the words and music of a song that I afterwards published by the title of "I wish I was in Dixie's Land," which was afterwards, by universal custom, called "Dixie." It was composed on one rainy Sunday in Elm Street, between Broome and Spring Streets, No. 197, Room No. 1. Previous to that time neither I nor any other person had ever heard anything like it, although "Dixie's Land" is an old phrase applied to the Southern States, at least to that part of it lying south of Mason and Dixon's line. In my travelling days amongst showmen, when we would start for a winter's season south, while speaking of the change, they would invariably ejaculate the stereotyped saying: "I wish I was in Dixie's Land," meaning the southern country; though others have attempted, in vain, to locate it on Staten Island. The song of "Dixie" was never heard south until it was taken there first by the "Buckleys" and the "Newcombs," each of whom purchased a copy of me while they were in New York. It took amazingly south as *something new*! Show people generally, if not always, have a chance to hear every local song as they pass through the different sections of the country, and particularly so with minstrel companies, who are always on the lookout for songs and sayings that will answer for their business; but none had ever heard anything like my song of "Dixie." I did not publish it until it had become common property and then not until it was issued by Mr. P. P. Werling, of New Orleans. He published it in Mr.

Peters' name, at the same time he wrote me a letter offering me *five dollars for the copyright*! Mr. Pond compelled all those who had published my words and music to disfigure their plates of "Dixie" and discontinue its further publication. Every showman and minstrel that was in New York at the time of the dispute about the authorship signed a paper to the effect that they had never heard anything like my song of "Dixie," either north, south, east, or west, until they heard it sung at the Bryant's Minstrels in New York. And now to conclude this short, but correct statement, I will merely say that it was nothing but a plain simple melody, with plantation words, the purport of which is that a negro in the north feels himself out of place and, thinking of his old home in the south, is made to exclaim, in the words of the song: – "I wish I was in Dixie's Land!" This is the first and only statement I ever made.

The Bowery melodramas continued their popularity with working-class audiences throughout the 1830s and early 40s, but by the late 40s the formula had become tiresome, and the plays were in the death throes of their long established appeal, as the following sarcastic notice suggests.

136   Review of *Mines of Riga*, 1848

Spirit of the Times, 18 (August 26, 1848), 324

At the Bowery, a piece entitled the *Mines of Riga* was produced with considerable success, on Monday evening last. Framed in strict accordance with the usual notions governing melodramatic compositions, it teemed with awful combats, insidious speeches, exploded pistols, and hairbreadth escapes. Again we had the cadaverous-countenanced, double-moustached oppressor of female virtue, in drab-colored breeches and dirty-yellow boots, who, for some cause, mysteriously hinted at, seeks to be revenged upon a middle-aged gentleman – a distracted father in purple and gold, by incarceration of his eldest son and a bullying of his youngest daughter. Again did the individual meet with his deserts at the hands of the low comedian, that contemnor of crime and eulogist of virtue, in round hat and Tyrolean waistcoat, who as is his accustomed privilege, performed the almost impossible feat of sending a ball into a villain's body, by levelling his weapon at the North Star. In a word, the *Mines of Riga* was our brother to one half the melodramas in existence, with the addition of a little more villainy, a little more broadsword exercise, and a little more powder.

Among the several reasons for the lack of quality native drama in the first two-thirds of the nineteenth century was the lack of protection for playwrights. No copyright or internal royalty legislation existed.[1] It was, therefore, impossible for dramatists to earn a living from their efforts. Some recognized this as a major impediment to the development of a strong national drama, as the following article indicates.

[1] Of the many available sources dealing with copyright and royalties during the period the best are James J. Barnes, *Authors, Publishers, and Politicians: The Quest for an Anglo-American Copyright Agreement, 1815–1854* (Columbus: Ohio State University Press, 1974) and Aubert J. Clarke, *The Movement for International Copyright in Nineteenth Century America* (Westport, CT: Greenwood Press, 1973).

137   *Spirit of the Times* on Copyright Protection, 1849

Spirit of the Times, 18 (January 20, 1849), 576

The appeals of such an unfortunate class of people as authors rarely meet with anything like sympathy from the grave and reverend seigneurs who direct the affairs of our mighty nation, who, while they project most wise and comprehensive schemes for the protection of those standing in little need of legislation scarce design to cast a smile upon the miserable wretches whose sole wealth lies in the upper story of their earthly tenement – whose revenue is extracted from the brain instead of shining California diet. True, some time ago, a couple of Congressmen delivered their sentiments on the subject of literary proprietorship, and after some hours' reflection, consigned the question of copyright to the lowest depth of senatorial oblivion. It may not be known to our readers, and most especially those who are inclined to support that most chimerical of phatasamagoras – the national drama – that there is in our country no copyright whatever for dramatic production – no protection against the stealing and reproduction of any piece which may emanate from a native brain. It may with justice be said, that as yet we have no dramatic authors, or at least but few who have made any sensation, or coined money in the theatrical world. We are sorry to add, that this is most true, that with the trifling exception of Mr. Howard Payne, no American has up to this time composed a piece which has maintained possession of the stage, and as long as the present state of things continues, we shall present the single spectacle of a nation reputed among the best educated in the world, destitute of a dramatic literature. The meanest community of ancient or modern times has this advantage of us; even the Sandwich Islanders. Undoubtedly we have some MSS. plays, which have flourished on our stage, wherein a bay horse, a red shirt, or a six-barreled pistol, has attracted local or temporary notice, but these pieces have been generally vile concoctions, whose paternity would be repudiated by a respectable bootblack, who had any pretensions to scholastic acquirements. Another, and a more assuming class of dramatists, have manufactured some five-act affairs – *Fashion, Spartacus, Jack Cade* – etc. All these are the property of individuals, who fearing to lose their possession, most properly deprive the printer's devil of the right to soil their dainty pages, for the very instant a play comes off the press, or is even transcribed, any actor or manager who may have the good fortune to buy, beg, or steal a copy, can appropriate it to his own use. The great reputation of a dramatic author, in common with all other writers, depends upon the dissemination of his compositions. Any law, or want of legislation, which deprives him of the right to publish, unless with detriment to his pocket, is an unjustifiable injury to national literature. The other day Mr. Forrest purchased for the sum of $1,000 a five-act, full bloom tragedy, which he will most assuredly produce at some theatre for his own individual benefit – a perfectly proper proceeding on his part, as he has paid what, in his opinion, is the marketable value of the article. Still at the same time, the guarantee of his right deprives the public and the author the pleasure of having it presented to them in good clear type, instead of from the mouth of the great tragedian. Many prefer to escape the infliction too often submitted to by good-natured audiences by perusing a play in the cabinet; and others who are opposed to stage representations, or are too poor in worldly wealth to lend their constant support to theatres yet, being admirers of dramatic works would willingly purchase a copy.

Now that the legislature of our state have incorporated an institution (long since advocated in the columns of the *Spirit*) whereby decayed Roscii and broken down Garricks, can be comfortably provided for, now that the "Dramatic Association" is in successful operation, let the next move be towards insuring of authors' and actors' rights in dramatic compositions by a fair and liberal copyright.

Certainly the most popular dramatic piece during the latter nineteenth century was *Uncle Tom's Cabin* in several different adaptations from Mrs. Stowe's novel. In the case of both abolitionist and temperance drama, special political interest groups supported the theatre – usually in its sanitized museum manifestation – for their political agenda. Some editors and critics saw the abolitionist drama as a danger which fueled the fires of sectional bitterness threatening the union in the 1850s.

138   Review of *Uncle Tom's Cabin*, 1852

New York Herald, September 3, 1852

The practice of dramatizing a popular novel, as soon as it takes a run has become very common. In many instances, and particularly with regard to the highly dramatic and graphic novels of Dickens, these new plays have been very successful, giving pleasure and satisfaction to the public, and putting money into the pockets of the chuckling manager. But in the presentation of *Uncle Tom's Cabin* upon the boards of a popular theatre, we apprehend the manager has committed a serious and mischievous blunder, the tendencies of which he did not comprehend, or did not care to consider, but in relation to which we have a word or two of friendly counsel to submit.

The novel of *Uncle Tom's Cabin* is at present our nine days of literary wonder. It has sold by thousands, and tens, and hundreds of thousands – not, however, on account of any surpassing or wonderful literary merits which it may be supposed to possess, but because of the widely extended sympathy, in all the North, with the pernicious abolition sympathies and "higher law" moral of this ingenious and cunningly devised abolitionist fable. The *furore* which it has thus created, has brought out quite a number of catchpenny imitators, *pro* and *con*, desirous of filling their sails while yet the breeze is blowing, though it does appear to us to be the meanest kind of stealing of a lady's thunder. This is indeed a new epoch and a new field of abolition authorship – a new field of fiction, humbug, and deception, for a more extended agitation of the slavery question – than any that has heretofore imperiled the peace and safety of the Union.

The success of *Uncle Tom's Cabin* as a novel, has naturally suggested its success upon the stage; but the fact has been overlooked, that any such representation must be an insult to the South – an exaggerated mockery of Southern institutions – and calculated, more than any other expedience of agitation, to poison the mind of our youth with the pestilent principles of abolitionism. The play, as performed at the National, is a crude and aggravated affair following the general plot of the story, except in the closing scene where instead of allowing Tom to die under the cruel treatment of his new master in Louisiana, he is brought back to a reunion with Wilmot and his wife – returned runaways – all of whom, with Uncle Tom and Aunt Chloe, are set free, with the privilege of remaining upon the old plantation. . . .

In the progress of these varied scenes, we have the most extravagant exhibition of the imaginary horrors of Southern slavery. The negro traders, with their long whip, cut and slash their poor slaves about the stage for mere pastime, and a gang of poor wretches, handcuffed to a chain which holds them all in marching order, two by two, are thrashed like cattle to quicken their pace. Uncle Tom is scourged by the trader who has bought him, for "whining" at his bad luck. A reward is posted up, offering four hundred dollars for the runaway, Edward Wilmot (who, as well as his wife, is nearly white), the reward to be paid upon "his recovery, or upon proof that he has been killed." But Wilmot shoots down his pursuers in real Christian style, as fast as they come and after many marvelous escapes, and many fine ranting abolition speeches (generally preceding his dead shots), he is liberated as we have described.

This play, and these scenes are nightly received at one of our most popular theatres with repeated rounds of applause. True, the audience appears to be pleased with the novelty without being troubled about the moral of the story, which is mischievous in the extreme.

The institution of Southern slavery is recognized and protected by the federal constitution, upon which this Union was established, and which holds it together. But for the compromises on the slavery question, we should have no constitution and no Union – and would perhaps have been at this day in the condition of the South American republics divided into several military despotisms, constantly warring with each other, and each within itself. The Fugitive Slave law only carried out one of the plain provisions of the constitution. When a Southern slave escapes to us we are in honor bound to return him to his master. And yet, here in this city – which owes its wealth, population, power, and prosperity, to the Union and the constitution, and this same institution of slavery to a greater degree than any other city in the Union – here we have nightly represented at a popular theatre the most exaggerated enormities of Southern slavery playing directly into the hands of the abolitionists and abolition kidnappers of slaves, and doing their work for them. What will our Southern friends think of all our professions of respect for their delicate social institution of slavery when they find that even our amusements are overly drawn caricatures exhibiting our hatred against it and against them? Is this consistent with good faith, honor, or the everyday obligation of hospitality? No, it is not. It is a sad blunder; for when our stage shall become the deliberate agent in the cause of abolitionism, with the sanction of the public and their approbation, the peace and harmony of this Union will soon be ended.

We would from all these considerations, advise all concerned to drop the play of *Uncle Tom's Cabin* at once and for ever. The thing is in bad taste – is not according to good faith to the constitution, or consistent with either of the two Baltimore platforms; and is calculated, if persisted in, to become a firebrand of the most dangerous character to the peace of the whole country.

Throughout the period certain puritanical and moralistic elements in various sections of the country objected to dramatic performances of any kind and would have liked to have had the theatre legislated out of existence. The *New York Home Journal*, in defending the theatre from one such attack, did notice that some theatrical reform seemed to be in order.

139   Article on Reforming the Theatre, 1852

New York Home Journal; reprinted in *Spirit of the Times*, 22 (August 21, 1852), 321

Harper's Magazine revives the old discussion regarding the utility and propriety of dramatic performances. The editor objects to them because life is a very serious affair, and men may find better employment than playing fictitious parts. Perhaps it is *because* life is serious, and because our ordinary pursuits are so absorbing that theatrical diversions are so agreeable, and we may add so proper. We have no intention, however, of pursuing this overwrought topic. Theatres are fixed facts. People like them, and cannot be argued out of their liking. The taste for the drama is as old as the race of men. It is seen in the sports of children when they "play church" and "play school"; and gray-headed age finds enjoyment in the sentimental drama, which reminds him of feelings long extinct in his own bosom. Even in these "declining" days of the drama, the same taste appears in the rage for private theatricals, which at present prevails in most civilized countries.

There is a tendency, nowadays, to rush to the most irrational extremes. If for example, an institution is not altogether what it should be, the cry is not to improve, but to abolish it; if the holder of official station is not faultless, "turn him out," is thought the only recourse; as though there were no conceivable punishment but – decapitation. If the editor of *Harper's Magazine* had devoted his attention to pointing out feasible improvements in our theatres, if he had demonstrated that excellence will "pay" better than trash – as he might – he would have performed a very creditable action. We say he *might*, for the thing is demonstrable. But what he has done will only have the effect – if it have any effect at all – of upholding those utterly frivolous, and we may truly say, demoralizing entertainments, which have sprung into existence and attained their present importance only because of the odium which has been cast upon their dramatic rivals – we need not name those entertainments – they are but too well known.

But the theatre, at present is grievously at fault – we cannot deny it. It does not fulfill, or attempt to fulfill, its proper destiny of being the powerful ally of all that is beautiful and good. As two or three new dramatic enterprises are on foot, at present, in New York, and will soon be ready to march, perhaps we may venture to propose a pet reform or two of our own, for the consideration of the parties concerned. Our first recommendation is, *to do away with afterpieces.* Exhibit one play in the best possible manner, and then drop the curtain in for the night. It is the main piece of the evening that "draws" the audience, and not the afterpiece, which persons of sense seldom stay to see. Send the audience home at an early hour not fatigued and disgusted but inspirited and in good appetite for more. We are persuaded that this reform would save expense and labor, without materially diminishing receipts, and that it would remove one good reason for the repugnance to the theatre which is now cherished by a great many excellent, though we think, inconsiderate persons. Another piece of advice which we would offer is – adopt as the motto of the management the words of Hamlet, "*The play's the thing*" – not the actor, or the scene painter, or the property man, but the play.

1865–1915

DON B. WILMETH

INTRODUCTION

Sandwiched between two major wars and intersected by several national financial crises, the period 1865–1915 was an era of great prosperity in the American theatre, though the theatre as an institution during these five decades was constantly seeking a clear direction, trying to pull away from foreign models and create its own style and identity. Moreover, between 1870 and 1910 the legitimate theatre was challenged from all sides by other forms of live, popular amusement such as minstrel shows and variety acts. Indeed, not until the emergence of film, radio, and then television did live theatre experience such competition again.

As vital as the legitimate theatre was in this fifty-year period, it did not satisfy all patrons of the performing arts. Not all playgoers were eager to see Edwin Booth's Hamlet at the Winter Garden! Many, especially those in more remote areas, found one of the available alternative popular forms, especially the travelling circus and the medicine show, more to their taste. For most rural audiences, who otherwise would have seen no live entertainment, a few occasional showmen did travel to remote areas bringing with them crude and readily accessible shows: one-ring circuses, makeshift med shows, small minstrel troupes. Choices were certainly limited. Even in large urban centers, however, where legitimate theatre was plentiful, people hungered for entertainment of a nonalienating sort, especially during periods when rural migrants and foreign immigrants were moving into major American cities in great numbers. In the larger cities, especially at the end of this period, vaudeville was the most popular of the alternative choices, amusing all classes of Americans. Indeed, by the teens there were more than one thousand theatres playing standard vaudeville acts and in excess of four thousand small-time theatres; at its height, ten people attended a vaudeville show to every one who patronized other forms of entertainment.[1]

During this time, then, more than ever before in American history, there was an identi-

---

[1] See my *Variety Entertainment and Outdoor Amusements* (Westport, CT, and London: Greenwood Press, 1982), pp. 132–33.

fiable split between the elite and the popular in terms of taste, and audiences dictated much of what was seen on American stages and in other assorted amusement venues.

The new middle class in America grew almost eightfold, from 765,000 in 1870 to 5,609,000 in 1910, or from 33 percent of the population in 1870 to 63 per cent in 1910. Between 1830 and 1860 the American population doubled and New York City's population in 1860 exceeded 900,000, more than doubling its 1840 figure.[2] The American theatre was thus faced with a large, diverse, and entertainment-hungry audience, both rural and urban. Travelling stars, so dominant early in this period, could no longer cover the vast network of theatres scattered from coast to coast. Stock companies and repertory theatres were somewhat successful in filling the needs of major population centers, most notably those on the Eastern seaboard. However, by the turn of the century even these proved less than satisfactory and the combination company began to fill the void, taking popular successes to all major American theatres. As the structure of the American theatre shifted, so did the control – from all powerful actor–managers to the iron grip of the individual director or régisseur. Eventually, as theatre became big business and the booking and oversight of a vast network of theatres became virtually uncontrollable (especially outside of New York, now the theatrical hub of the country), a small handful of theatrical barons, mostly businessmen with minimal interest in the art of the theatre, emerged. Indeed as this period ends there were frequent outcries against the Theatrical Syndicate or Trust. Ironically, though the battle cry was "independence," the most visible savior in this regard, the Shubert organization, simply created another monopoly, pointing forward to the need of unions to represent the individual theatre artist, a movement that begins to take shape at the end of this era.

The dilemma of art versus business is significant. The documents chosen for this section, though they do not do justice to all aspects of the American theatre (especially the more popular forms), surely underscore this fact. The period is framed by visionary and ambitious artistic efforts, though largely unsuccessful – those of Edwin Booth and Steele MacKaye at the one end, for instance, and efforts such as the misconceived New Theatre (an abortive notion of a national theater) and the various reactions against the Trust and commercialism (most notably the art and Little Theatre movements and the short-lived civic theatre/pageant movement) at the other end.

With the demise of the stock company and the old tradition of "lines of business," and with the rise of star-makers and directors in the latter part of the nineteenth century (most notably Augustin Daly and David Belasco) theatre artists began to look for ways to improve their talents in a more systematized way. As a result actors began to articulate with some clarity their feelings on their art and approaches to the creation of roles (beginning most notably with Joseph Jefferson's *Autobiography* in 1889) and efforts were made to establish schools of acting. Toward the end of this period academic programs, most notably George Pierce Baker's efforts at Harvard, expanded theatre education to include playwrights and students of the drama.

---

[2] Foster Rhea Dulles, *A History of Recreation*, 2nd ed. (New York: Appleton-Century-Crofts, 1965), pp. 84–168; Shirley Staples, *Male-Female Comedy Teams in American Vaudeville 1865–1932* (Ann Arbor: UMI Research Press, 1984), p. 11.

Some of the major changes of this period occurred in acting style, production structure, and approaches to playwriting. In each category these fifty years can be seen clearly as a time of transition. In acting, for example, there was a shift from Romantic old school acting to a more realistic approach to role playing (a movement roughly parallel with the development of realism in dramaturgy). In the 1860s Edwin Booth was established as the prime example of what good acting should be, especially for cultivated theatre patrons who rallied round his quiet, unassuming, intellectual, and refined style, and rejected the muscular and declamatory style of Edwin Forrest and his disciplines. Others challenged theatrical tradition as well. For instance, parallel with Booth's innovation in serious acting, Joe Jefferson broke with the traditional comedic mold by imbuing his portrayal of Rip Van Winkle with charm, humor, and pathos. His quiet, even casual style *seemed* to most observers free of all staginess, with little forced or unnatural. By the end of this period these styles seemed quite old-fashioned themselves when placed next to the "newer" efforts of actors such as Minnie Maddern Fiske and William Gillette, the latter also a playwright who experimented with a kind of rudimentary Realism, albeit superficial and obvious, but one that enhanced his unique stage presence.

Another influence on performance was the result of a phenomenon especially prevalent throughout the second half of the nineteenth century – the influx of foreign stars, including Jenny Lind, Mlle Rachel, Adelaide Ristori, Mme Janauschek, Helena Modjeska, Sarah Bernhardt, Eleonora Duse, and Tommaso Salvini. These talents not only brought to American playgoers unique theatrical experiences, including many of the important foreign plays of the day, but they exposed American actors to internationally recognized actors whose styles and approaches impacted upon their own.

In production, following a long period in which the central actor largely dominated, the ensemble and the design of the whole takes dominance. Individual actors playing their star vehicles (Frank Mayo, for instance, as Davy Crockett, or later, James O'Neill as the Count of Monte Cristo) were very slowly replaced by a group of actors selected by a manager or even a modern-day director to play roles for which they were best suited. Although star-makers persisted (both Belasco and Charles Frohman carefully groomed actors for stardom) and stars continued to tour with their special roles well into the twentieth century, the trend was away from this nineteenth-century model. From minimum stage management the carefully planned production seemed to require a director or a régisseur and, in time, a producer. Daly, Frohman, A. M. Palmer, Lester Wallack, Belasco, and others began to carve out a new theatrical specialty and literally change the age-old methods of producing plays. Though the director and producer of today may have garnered altogether too much power over production decisions, the roots for such an emphasis were well planted by the 1890s.

As the documents in the design section illustrate, Romanticism in production (see for example the Charles Witham designs) was slowly replaced by a kind of stage Realism – elementary at first – reaching a high point with the productions of Belasco and the dominance of the box set. Elaborate machined theatres appeared, beginning with Booth's in 1869 and reaching a kind of absurd pinnacle with the Hippodrome in 1905 and the New Theater in 1909, both requiring a stage spectacle that dwarfed any meaningful attempt at dramatic excellence. After two major fires (represented by Documents 195–98, 200 on the Iroquois Theatre fire of 1903), safety and lighting control became extremely important. Finally, after a steady movement toward the building of bigger and more elaborately equipped theatres, a somewhat successful reversal took place at the turn of the century. In one of the numerous manifestations of the revolt against commercialism, theatre artists moved away from the bigness trend and created theatre spaces where the emphasis was on seeing the stage rather than seeing the audience. Sightlines were improved, the orchestra pit vanished, the apron was eliminated, and the art of the theatre was given preeminence. Theatre palaces, nonetheless, continued to be built long after this period. Indeed, with the creation of theatre as a national network, a growth stimulated by the transcontinental railroad in 1869, major cities outside of New York constructed large and superb facilities. Still, the anticommercial art theatre beginning in the teens offered a viable alternative to many theatre artists in the United States. It would, however, be misleading not to underscore that after 1895 the kind of theatre seen by most Americans, for the most part a brazenly commercial commodity, was largely dictated by the controlling forces in New York, and that large commercial houses were the common venues for these products.

If American actors, managers and directors, and designers were beginning to gain international reputations, especially in Great Britain, playwrights experienced the greatest identity crisis. Early in the period a small number of playwrights gained reputations by supplying specific actors with appropriate vehicles, often native characters. Still, foreign fare dominated at mid-century. In the 1860s dramatic tastes were changing significantly. Historical costumed dramas were slowly being replaced with sensational melodramas, such as Daly's *Under the Gaslight*, which offered adventure, cliff-hanging danger, and romance. As the century moved toward its apogee, however, playwrights, and especially critics (virtually a new position of this era), pleaded for something different, a theatre form that might be more representative of American ideas and concerns and less indebted to European models, especialy those formula dramas and comedies Americanized by "play makers" such as Augustin Daly and his collaborating brother, Joseph. The problem, of course, was acceptability in the marketplace. The dominant question seemed to be who will determine what is "good" *American* drama? Will it be the critic? the manager? the audience? the playwright? The result of this query was a period of uncertainty and a general hesitancy on the part of most managements to experiment with a "new" American drama for fear that there was not a "new" audience to match. The catastrophic New Theatre experiment is a useful metaphor for the uncertainty at the turn of the century, for here was a project dedicated to all sorts of new ideas but forced to contend with a structure and facility that had little about it that could support the idealism of the venture.

What did seem positive, however, was that journalists and critics – and even writers – were discussing fervently and very seriously the future of the American drama, far more extensively than before the Civil War. There was concern that American playwrights produce a drama that could truly be called "American," that this drama have greater credibility as a forum of ideas and that it move away from Romantic idealism to an American Realism. As early as the 1830s and 1840s in plays showcasing native characters – the Indian, the Yankee, the frontiersman, the Negro – American drama had developed some sense of local identity. With the emergence of city types, first in 1848 with Benjamin Baker's *A Glance at New York* and Mose the fire b'hoy, and expanded by the work of Edward Harrigan and his Mulligan Guard plays, an early foundation was laid for the slow evolution of American Realism between the early 1890s and World War I. The end result was a predictable and formulaic Realistic genre with few major or significant innovations in form. The documents for 1865–1915 clearly reflect these and other issues of the period, including the role of women and their frustrations during the era of the suffragette, the plight of the playwright prior to the first real attempt to make sense out of the Copyright Act of 1909, and the ongoing debate over the state of American drama.

In somewhat simplistic terms the above discussion seems to isolate some of the major characteristics of the period 1865–1915, aspects that are supported by the documents that follow. In addition, however, the following have also been represented with appropriate documents.

In the area of the business of the theatre there are agreements between playwrights and managements, actors and management, and various samples of theatre agreements, rules of management, theatre receipts, touring itineraries, comments on the combination system versus stock, the initial agreement of the Syndicate, and various manifestations of reactions against the Syndicate. Collectively, these documents illustrate several points: (1) the ill-treatment of actor and playwright before copyright clarification and the establishment of Actors' Equity; (2) the somewhat ad hoc and laissez-faire method of doing business during much of this period; and (3) the immediate counterefforts to curtail the rapid expansion of the theatrical trust.

In the acting and directing section there has been an attempt to illustrate how actors and managers visualized their efforts through floor plans and contemporary descriptions and, in several key instances, how early directors such as Daly and Belasco worked. Numerous documents focus on reviews or descriptions of a representative number of important or unique contemporary actors early in this period (Booth, Jefferson, Adah Isaacs Menken, Lydia Thompson, Modjeska). Actors in the latter part of this period have been represented more by what they said about their art, what it was like on the road (especially away from the major population regions), and what suggestions they offered to students of the art of acting.

In addition to the major points already made about theatre buildings, this section illustrates the trend toward greater care in the design of the playhouse and its construction, often for specific purposes. Technical descriptions, floor plans, and a few cross sections are included to provide representative specific data. It is impossible in a limited space to represent important structures throughout the country; however, to suggest that significant efforts were occurring outside of New York or Philadelphia, a description of a typical concert saloon in Wyoming of the 1870s provides an important contrast.

The section on design and technical production attempts to illustrate in more specific terms production practices and developments. Although some of the greatest technical innovations actually occurred at Booth's early in the period, toward the end the movement is toward greater simplicity, often requiring fewer technical wonders and more production finesse and subtleties. As the Belasco documents clearly illustrate, the replacement of gaslighting with electricity as a mainstay of theatrical production provided the designer a greater chance of creating atmosphere and believable environments with fewer stage gimmicks (such as those in *Ben-Hur*). Finally, various inventories illustrate some of the necessities of a stock house, a travelling star, and a representative production of popular fare (G. L. Fox's pantomine, *Humpty Dumpty*).

The final chapter, covering the drama of the period and the increasing influence of criticism and, to some limited extent, an early and developing dramatic theory, offered the greatest difficulty in selection and focus. Many more documents had to be eliminated than were finally included, and because of the transitory nature of the period in American drama lines were often hazy. The final decision was to group together documents that frequently overlap, so that there is no clear division made between criticism, theory, or drama. Ultimately, however, the commentary and examples selected do seem to illustrate the trends indicated earlier in this essay. It is not surprising that Henry James in the 1870s finds drama in America "neither artistic nor fine" and that at the tag end of the period Sheldon Cheney finds American playwrights "pandering" to public taste. The documents chosen here also illustrate the ongoing concerns about native playwriting. Although there are some bright lights and promise along the way, the dominant tone of those writing about the American drama is pessimistic; the perception is clearly one that sees the theatre dominated by a desire to make money; and those writers offering advice (Bronson Howard, Owen Davis) do so from a formulaic point of view. Still, taken as whole, the documents point forward to the possibility of a richer and more uniquely American drama just around the corner.

I. The Business of Theatre

One of three dominant Philadelphia theatres in the nineteenth century (along with the Chestnut Street and Arch Street theatres), the Walnut Street, which opened in 1809, survives as the oldest functioning playhouse in America. Edwin Booth and his brother-in-law John Sleeper Clark comanaged or co-owned a number of theatres, most notably the Winter Garden (1864–67) in New York. As the lease below indicates, the Walnut passed to the ownership of Clarke, where it remained part of his estate until 1919.

140   Lease between Edwin Booth and John S. Clarke, 1870

Hampden-Booth Theatre Library, The Players, New York

This Indenture made the twenty-third day of June one thousand eight-hundred and seventy between *Edwin T. Booth* of the City of New York party of the first part and *John S. Clarke* of the City of Philadelphia State of Pennsylvania party of the second part. *Witnesseth*: . . . that the said party of the second part hath hired and taken from said party of the first part the land, building, and premises known as *the Walnut Street Theatre* situate lying and being at the northeasterly corner of Walnut and Ninth Streets in the City of Philadelphia. . . . *Together* with its appurtenances and the scenery properties and paraphernalia now in said theatre necessary for carrying on its business. . . . *To Have and To Hold* said demised premises to said party of the second part for the term of *Five* (5) years from the first day of August – one thousand eight-hundred and seventy – at the yearly rent or sum of *nine thousand Dollars* ($9000.) to be paid in equal quarter yearly payments, and for which rent said John S. Clarke is to make and deliver to said Edwin T. Booth in advance on the first day of August in each year during the said term, commencing with the first day of August next his said Clarke's four promissory notes for the amount of twenty-two hundred and fifty dollars payable to order of said Edwin T. Booth at the Penn National Bank Philadephia. . . .

And it is agreed by and between the parties hereto that if any of said rent or the

175

notes given therefor shall be due and unpaid or if default shall be made in any of the covenants herein contained on the part of the party of the second part then it shall be lawful for the said party of the first part to reenter the said premises, and the same to have again repossess and enjoy. . . .

And it is further agreed between the parties to these presents, that in case the building or buildings erected on the premises hereby leased shall be partially damaged by fire, the same shall be repaired as speedily as possible at the joint expense of the parties hereto; that in case the damage shall exceed the sum of ten thousand dollars, or be so great as to render the building untenantable, the rent shall cease until such time as the building shall be put in repair, but in case of the total destruction of the premises by fire or otherwise, the rent shall be paid up to the time of such destruction, and then and from thenceforth this lease shall cease and come to an end; *provided however* that such damage or destruction be not caused by the careless negligence or improper conduct of the party of the second part – his agents or servants——

It is further covenanted and agreed by and between the parties hereto that all taxes appurtenant, water rents, and fire insurance premiums upon the premises and the cost of ordinary repairs of the said premises are to be paid and borne by the parties hereto jointly each one half thereof; *and further* that all scenery and properties painted or made in the theatre during the term of the lease shall be the joint-property of the parties hereto, and be left in the theatre at the expiration of the Lease. *But* this clause is not intended to include scenery or properties painted or made outside of and brought into the theatre for temporary use. . . .

And the said party of the *second* part further covenants that he will not assign this lease nor let or underlet the whole or any part of the said premises, nor make any alterations therein, without the written consent of the party of the first part – first had and obtained, under the penalty of forfeiture and damages; and that at the expiration of the said term he the said party of the second party will quit and surrender the premises hereby demised in as good state and condition as reasonable use and wear thereof will permit damages by the elements excepted. . .

Although leading players in the better stock companies made decent livings, especially with the occasional benefit thrown in, most actors existed at the subsistent level. Even in the 1870s when salaries begin to increase, beginners and some utility actors continued to suffer.

As low as some of the salaries are in this document, the reality was even worse. Few actors worked more than 40 weeks in this period, so their per capita income was well below the 1865 average of $779. One actress in the 1880s who earned $20 per week noted that her basic weekly expenses were $16.90, including $10.00 for room and board and $2.00 for lunch.

141   Weekly Salary List, Boston Museum, Mid 1860s

Edward W. Mammen, *The Old Stock Company School of Acting: A Study of the Boston Museum* (Boston: Trustees of the Public Library, 1945), p. 73.

W. Warren	$60	K. Reignolds	$55
W. H. Smith	20	E. Mestayer	28
R. F. McCllannin	24	J. Orton	30
F. Hardenburgh	20	A. Clarke	13
J. Wilson	16	J. R. Vincent	20
J. A. Smith	18	Wheelock	8
J. Wheelock	12	Towle	8
G. F. Ketchum	13	Hunter	6
W. Benn	10	Andrews	6
J. H. Ring	14	Howard	5
Sol Smith, Jr.	12	R. Wood (dancer)	20
Hunter	7	T. Wood "	10
Delano	9	Mason (Ballet)	4
Peakes	6	Wright "	4
H. Woolf	4	Flanders "	4
Pitman	2	Moore "	4
R. Eberle (Prompt)	13	Harrison "	6
L. Szollosy (Ballet Master)	25	Johnson "	4
		C (?) "	4
J. Eichberg (Orch. Leader)	$25	W. H. Lloyd (Property Maker)	18
G. Heister (Scenic Artist)	30	John (Ass't " ")	?
F. W. Mozart (Prin. Machinist)	19	Rutledge (Porter)	7
Marden (Machinist)	12	Kelly (Bill Poster)	11
Horace (Ass't Painter-Flyman)	9	Clarke (Dresser)	2
T. Joyce (Costumer)	33	Two cleaner	7
Frank (Ass't Costumer)	?	Entire orchestra	118
Ladz (?) " "	?		

Income was never secure and depended on many factors, as the following illustrates. These summaries for the New Fifth Avenue Theatre at 728 Broadway have been transcribed and edited. (Augustin Daly had temporarily retired from management in 1877 and Stephen Fiske had reopened it in October 1877.)

142   Contrasting Receipt Summaries for the New Fifth Avenue Theatre, 1877

Hampden-Booth Theatre Library, The Players, New York

5 Season   4 Week   28 Performance
Date, Saturday Night Nov. 10/77
Play, Chimes of Normandy

Weather, Rain & Hail – very bad

Remarks, Good House considering the awful weather. End of the [C. D.] Hess English Opera Company – whatever comes or happens, thank God for that!

	Amount sold	$ cts.	Compts.
Boxes	1	15	
Orchestra chairs	94	141	34
Balcony	40	60	2
Admissions	20	20	
Family Circle Res'd	10	7 .50	
Family Circle Admis	50	25	
Exchanges at $1.00	1		
" " .50	4	2	
" " .25	3	.75	
Orders			36
Bill Boards			25
		$272.25	

Cost, $272.25

Star's Share, $135.37 Paid Parr

6 Season   14 Week   95 Performance

Date, Saturday Matinee Nov. 30 [1878]

Play, Hamlet

Weather, Sunshiny morning; cloudy afternoon.

Remarks, Tremendous Easter[1] matinee at Academy: last matinees of "Our Club" & "Mother & Son" (Nobody there); but Hamlet did the business. Booth pleased.

	Amount sold	$ cts.	Compts.
Boxes			2
Orchestra chairs	436	654	
Dress Circle Chairs	129	193 .50	2
Admissions	102	102	
Family Circle Res'd	93	69 .75	
Family Circle Admis	175	87 .50	
Exchanges at .50	10	5	
" " .25	19	4 .75	
Orders			30
Bill Boards			20
		1116.50	

Cash, $1,116.50

Star's Share, $587.36 Paid by Cheque.

[1] This word is unclear, but the meaning is possibly that attendance was like that for an Easter matinee, traditionally dreadful.

This simple, typed document on a plain sheet of paper, signed only by playwright–director Steele MacKaye, is typical of the lackadaisical approach to rights during much of the nineteenth century. Barrett successfully revived MacKaye's adaptation of Mary Russell Mitford's *Rienzi* in 1887.

143   Memorandum of Agreement between Steele MacKaye and Lawrence Barrett, 1886

Wilmeth Theatre Collection, Providence, RI

Memorandum of agreement made this day the ninth of December 1886, at Washington, D. C., between Steele MacKaye and Lawrence Barrett, which witnesses that the said Steele MacKaye hereby conveys to the said Lawrence Barrett all right and title in the adaptation of Miss Mitford's tragedy of "Rienzi" to the said Lawrence Barrett, agreeing to make no other copy of same for any other person, for the consideration of two hundred dollars, paid in hand, and hereby acknowledged, and a royalty of ten dollars for each and every performance of said play of *Rienzi*, until the sum of said royalties shall reach a total of two thousand dollars. – When said royalties shall cease, and the play with all Mr. MacKaye's rights therein belong to the said Lawrence Barrett without further payments.

Steele MacKaye

The stock companies which sustained the American theatre prior to the combinations and long runs operated according to a strict set of rules.

144   Boston Museum Rules and Regulations, 1880

Mammen, *The Old Stock Company School*, p. 67

The DISCIPLINE that governs every *first class theatre*, will be observed in this establishment, and the cooperation therein of ALL employed is most earnestly solicited.

  1. The Green Room is provided for the quiet and respectable assemblage of the Ladies and Gentlemen of the Company. Previous to the commencement of the performance, three calls will be made at the doors of the dressing rooms, "*half hour*," "*twenty minutes*," and "*orchestra is*." The call for each act will be made in the dressing room corridor, and all subsequent calls for the play will be made in the Green Room only. **TEN MINUTES** will be allowed for change of dress between the acts of the play. **FIFTEEN MINUTES** allowed between pieces when complete "make up," wig, etc., require alteration.

  2. **REHEARSALS MUST BE PROMPTLY ATTENDED.** The calls for same will be put by the Prompter, in the Green and Music Room *before the end of the second act*, on the evening previous to the day for which the call is made. The

Green Room clock is to regulate the time. Ten minutes will be allowed for difference of clocks at beginning of rehearsal. The business for the week will be put up in the Green Room on the preceding Friday of each week. The ladies and gentleman of the Company must keep themselves advised of the calls, and order of business, and inform the prompter of their places of residence. Those who are not in the bills of the day, and expect to be absent from home for any number of hours, will leave notice where they may be found, in the event of unforeseen emergency.

3. Every gentleman engaged in the Museum must provide himself with such hosiery, wigs, feathers, swords, boots, buckles, gloves, cravats, laces, and ornaments, etc., as is of the present period; the whole must be provided by the performer. The ladies of the Company furnish their own dresses in each and every case.

4. During the performance, conversation behind the scenes and in the Green Room must be carried on in very low tones, and **ALL UNNECESSARY NOISE AVOIDED.**

5. **NO SMOKING WILL BE ALLOWED** beyond the limits of the Music Room, which is SET APART FOR THAT PURPOSE for the use of **REGULAR MEMBERS OF THE COMPANY AND ORCHESTRA ONLY**.

6. No one connected wtih the Establishment, in any capacity, will be permitted to introduce friends, relatives, or strangers behind the scenes, into the Green Room, or any of the dressing rooms, without permission of the management.

7. No one will be allowed to enter the auditorium on evenings during which they are concerned in any part of the performance.

8. LOUD TALKING and boisterous laughter at the fall of the drop or curtain, can be heard distinctly by the audience, *and has repeatedly been made the subject of public complaint.* The ladies and gentlemen are requested to remember the proximity of the audience, and leave the stage without noise.

9. The stage manager's and prompter's tables are strictly private. All business will be transacted in the stage manager's office.

10. Each dressing room will be under lock and key, and a key board provided at the back door, where the last person using the room is requested to leave the key.

11. All engagements, for whatever department of the Boston Museum, orchestra, chorus, ballet, mechanical department, etc., except where made by duly signed contract or 'memoranda,' *are by the week*, and may be terminated at any time, with or without the giving of a week's notice, as the management may elect.

By 1880 the phenomenon of the combination company, a touring troupe that carried with it everything needed for a performance (usually originating in a major city, such as

New York, after a successful initial run there), was established: the stock system was declining quickly. By the end of the 1878–79 season only a dozen major stock companies were still in existence.[1]

[1] For useful perspectives on this important shift in theatrical practice, see Levi Damon Phillips, "Arthur McKee Rankin's *The Danites*, 1877–1881: Prime Example of the American Touring Process," *Theatre Survey*, 25 (November 1984), 225–47, and Rosemarie K. Bank, "A Reconsideration of the Death of Nineteenth-Century American Repertory Companies and the Rise of the Combination," *Essays in Theatre*, 5 (November 1986), 61–75.

145   Editorial in Support of the Combination System, 1880

New York [Dramatic] Mirror, January 17, 1880, p. 4; this piece is unsigned

There is very little truth in the oft-reiterated statement that the "combination" system is not conducive to the actor's benefit, that it is the means of severing his family ties and home associations, and that it reduces him, in short, to the level of a genteel tramp.

The actor has been a bird of passage since the earliest days of the acting drama. His existence is migratory; the very name of player is associated distinctively with the wandering habits of a bohemian. Your professional bears the objections of the combination in mind when he accepts the life of a nomad. He does not complain of the detriments which are inseparably connected with the stroller's vocation; he does not lament the stern fact that the figurative berth he has chosen is not a bed of roses, teeming with the delights and comforts of an Arcadia; he knows that the path he has selected is to be the scene of an unflinching, prosaic struggle for bread and butter – a struggle in which a sentimental love of art is generally made subservient to the puzzling questions of unromantic profit or how to make both ends meet.

Application, and sometimes privation, attends advancement and success in any legitimate occupation, and the life of the player is very often accompanied by both of these. Aside from the great amount of travel and the consequent physical wear and tear, the combination system is as beneficial to the actor as it undoubtedly is to the public at large. It has grown to its present importance in this country as in England because the wants of an eager and insatiable public demand that it shall supersede the tottering, fast decaying plan of located stock companies. The entire disappearance of these latter is but a matter of a few months – or years. Already the tocsin that heralds its approaching dissolution is sounding from the places in which the stock system has held long and undisputed sway. The keynote will be taken up and repeated until in every instance the few remaining adherents, already weakening, will have fallen.

Mr. [J. H.] Vicker of Chicago did not relinquish the old method until he was nearly ruined; Manager Gemmill of Philadelphia has dissipated a small fortune in that direction, and is now compelled to announce the Chestnut as a "combination" theatre for next season. The venerable Boston Theatre, the house that has held to the old regime for over twenty years, has also succumbed, and in the Fall will be devoted to playing best travelling attractions. This season it opened with an excellent company, and the exclusive right to several French and American plays, but it was of no use. People had tired of seeing the same old faces appear in a limited number of plays, and the Boston Theatre is compelled to yield to the pressure of public desire. John T. Ford may hold to his present position for a year or so, owing to the fact that he controls three theatres and the Southern Coast circuit, over which he can play his regular companies, but this makes him already more than half a combination manager. Charles Spalding gave way to the innovation only two years ago, but since then he has just doubled his profits annually. . . .

The last season of Mrs. Drew's management of the Arch Street Theatre, Philadelphia, showed a clear loss of $9,000, but when next year she changed the policy of the house and played travelling attractions, her exact profits amounted to $12,000. Figures and facts as strong as these speak for themselves; they are indisputable and conclusive. In the face of these truths who can say that the new order of things is not good? It benefits the public, the manager, and the actor; it has helped to elevate and improve the stage and its surroundings. . . .

The day has passed for a star to draw unless properly supported, well managed, and thoroughly advertised. The combination system has taught the public to demand good entertainments and to be satisfied with nothing else. Things have reached that point that now, when a "queer" organization starts out on the road that is incomplete and unworthy, it receives a dampener at the very first town visited, in the way of unfavorable newspaper comment and bad business. The news is spread among the managers by the dramatic papers, and the consequence is that (if they are wise) they disband, and return to the city as best they can.

So long as such men as [J. H.] Haverly, [A. M.] Palmer, Bartley Campbell, [Augustin] Daly, and the like keep such complete and perfect attractions on the road as they have at present, there will be no need of located stock companies, and the present favor in which the combination system is held will continue indefinitely.

Salaries at Daly's, one the last of the New York resident repertory companies, varied widely depending on one's position in the company. In 1873, for example, Fanny Davenport, a major member of the company, was paid $135 per week; in 1889, John Drew, a leading man, was paid $160 per week; and in 1895, Hobart Bosworth, a player of minor roles, was paid only $40 per week. The standard contract used by Daly, seen here, seems harmless enough; however, the final paragraph, alluding to the Printed Rules, placed control of the actor's life decidedly in Daly's hands.

143   Actor Contract, Daly's Theatre, 1889

Museum of the City of New York

This Agreement, made and entered into this _____ 188_, by and between _____ party of the first part, and _____, party of the second part.

WITNESSETH, That the party of the first part engages the sole and exclusive services of the party of the second part for _____ season, commencing on or about _____ 188_, at a weekly salary of __ Dollars. Also _____ For the season __ commencing _____ at a weekly salary of __ Dollars, _____

It is understood and agreed by both parties, that the number of performances to be given each week shall be according to the custom of the placement of amusement and city at which _____ may be required to appear, and on all legal holidays.

The _____ of the second part engages and binds _____ and engages __ full and exclusive services in every respect unto the party of the first part, for the time, terms and condition stated above; and agrees to aid and assist to the best _____ ability all performances _____ and to act nowhere else in the city of New York from the date of this contract until the termination thereof, and to engage in no other business whatsoever while this contract is in force, without the consent of the party of the first part and to accept two weeks' notification of the termination of this contract as good and sufficient warning of the annulment of the same.

This agreement holding good until it has been faithfully fulfilled by the party of the second part, or cancelled by the party of the first part, as above agreed to, or for infringement of the Printed Rules of the theatre by the party of the second part, which rules are hereby incorporated into this agreement, and so accepted by the party of the second part as part and parcel of the contract.[1]

---

[1] By the 1890s, the following two clauses had been added to the standard Daly contract:

> No performer or other person engaged or employed at this theatre shall be entitled to be paid for any day or days on which the theatre is not opened for theatrical performances on account of any unforeseen calamity or general mourning, or upon any occasion upon which the theatre is closed by law or custom of the country.
>
> The party of the second part agrees that if he shall leave the service of the party of the first part or act at any other place than that designated by the party of the first part before the termination of this contract, he will pay to the party of the first part the sum of _____, hereby agreed upon as liquidated damages for such breach of this contract.

The creation of the Theatrical Syndicate at the end of the century had an enormous impact on theatre practice and business arrangements, creating a virtual monopoly of first-class theatrical production. The final Syndicate agreement expired in 1916.

144   Original Syndicate Agreement, 1896

Transcribed in Monroe Lippman, "The History of the Theatrical Syndicate. Its Effect upon the Theatre in American," unpublished dissertation, University of Michigan (1937), pp. 199–203

THIS AGREEMENT, in triplicate, made and entered into this _____ day of _____, eighteen hundred and ninety-six, between Al Hayman and Charles Frohman, hereinafter designated as parties of the first part; Samuel F. Nirdlinger and J. Fred Zimmerman, trading as Nixon and Zimmerman, hereinafter designated as parties of the second part, and Marc Klaw and Abraham L. Erlanger, hereinafter designated as parties of the third part. WITNESSETH:

WHEREAS, The said several parties hereto of the first, second, and third parts respectively are interested in or own or hold leases of various theatres and places of amusement in the United States, or are in receipt of sundry proceeds from divers theatres for services rendered to such theatres; and

WHEREAS, The theatrical business as at present conducted has resulted in great loss from indiscriminate bookings, in consequence of which similar attractions of the first class repeatedly oppose each other in the same point and thereby injure the other; and

WHEREAS, From the geographical location of the theatres and places of amusement unless tours are arranged in as nearly a direct line as possible needless expense results from railroad fares and hauling theatrical paraphernalia and properties, large companies with equipments being now too often moved forward and backward for the causes mentioned; and

WHEREAS, Under the present system the losses already sustained by managers and owners of theatres and of companies from such indiscriminate bookings as well as from railroad "jumps," so called, have been incalculable; and

WHEREAS, To guard against the repetition of losses of a like character, not only to the parties hereto, but to all persons in the theatrical business who either control companies or own theatres, it is necessary that the defects in the particulars mentioned should be remedied;

NOW, THEREFORE, for the benefit and protection of the parties hereto, and of the premises, and of the sum of one dollar by each part to the other in hand paid, the receipt whereof is hereby acknowledged, and of the mutual promise and covenants hereinafter contained, it is agreed as follows:

FIRST: This agreement shall commence on the 31st day of August, 1896, and continue in full force and effect for the period of five years from last named date.

SECOND: That during the continuance of this agreement all of the following named theatres and places of amusement, to wit, Columbia and Hooley's Theatres, Chicago; Columbia and Montauk Theatres, Brooklyn; Museum, Boston; California and Baldwin Theatres, San Francisco; New Century Theatre, St. Louis; Tabor Grand Opera House, Denver; Walnut Street Theatre, Philadelphia; Coates' Opera House, Kansas City; Euclid Avenue Opera House, Cleveland; Alvin Theatre, Pittsburgh; New Creighton Theatre, Omaha; Talma Theatre, Providence; New Southern and Grand Opera House, Columbus; Valentine Theatre, Toledo; Lyceum Theatre, Cleveland; and Davidson's Theatre, Milwaukee, all of which are controlled by the parties of the first part or in which they are in receipt of income for services rendered; also the Broad Street Theatre, Chestnut Street Theatre, and Chestnut Street Opera House, Philadelphia; Academy of Music, Baltimore; Lyceum Theatre, Baltimore; Lafayette Square Opera House and Columbia Theatre, Washington, D.C.; and Park Theatre, Philadelphia, all of which are controlled by the parties of the second part or in which they are interested or from which they are in receipt of income for services rendered; and also the New Masonic Theatre, Nashville; Grand Opera House, Memphis; Staub's Theatre, Knoxville; St. Charles Theatre and Academy of Music, New Orleans; Walnut Street Theatre, Philadelphia; Coates' Opera House, Kansas City; Euclid Avenue Opera House, Cleveland; Alvin Theatre, Pittsburgh; New Southern and Grand Opera House, Columbus; Valentine Theatre, Toledo; Lyceum Theatre, Cleveland; and Davidson's Theatre, Milwaukee, all of which are controlled by the parties of the third part or in which they are interested or from which they are in receipt of income for services rendered; and all other theatres or places of amusement which may be hereafter (during the continuance of this agreement) acquired by either of the parties of the first, second, or third parts hereto, shall be booked with attractions in conjunction with each other; that is to say, no attraction shall be booked in any of the said theatres or places of amusement (or in any which may be hereafter acquired as aforesaid) which will insist on playing on opposition theatre or place of amusement in any of the cities above named (or any which may hereafter come under this agreement) unless the party hereto having the theatre or place of amusement in said competitive point shall give his or their consent in writing to permit said attraction to play in the opposition theatre or place of amusement.

THIRD: The parties hereto mutually covenant and agree that so far as the attractions owned by them respectively are concerned (or in which they may hereafter, during the continuance of this agreement, become interested) they will play the same in the theatres or places of amusement hereinabove mentioned (or hereinafter to be included), or they will remain out of the cities in which said theatres or places of amusement are respectively located. It is hereby understood and agreed that the respective parties hereto can only play any of their attractions in any opposition theatre or place of amusement if they obtain the written consent of the party hereto having a theatre or place of amusement in said competitive point.

FOURTH: The parties hereto, in consideration aforesaid, also hereby respectively covenant and agree to and with each other to pool the net profits and other income derived from the theatres or places of amusement specifically mentioned in this article, and none other, and to divide the same in the manner hereinafter specified. To the end aforesaid the parties of the first part contribute to the pool the net profits or other income derived from the following theatres or places of amusement, to wit: Century Theatre, St. Louis; Tabor Grand Opera House, Denver; Walnut Street Theatre, Philadelphia; Coates' Opera House, Kansas City; Euclid Avenue Opera House, Cleveland; Alvin Theatre, Pittsburgh; New Creighton Theatre, Omaha; Talma Theatre, Providence; New Southern Theatre and the Grand Opera House, Columbus; Valentine Theatre, Toledo; Lyceum Theatre, Cleveland; and Davidson's Theatre, Milwaukee. The parties of the second part contribute to the pool the net profits or other income derived from the following theatres or places of amusement, to wit: Lyceum Theatre, Baltimore; Lafayette Square Opera House and Columbia Theatre, Washington, D.C.; Park Theatre, Philadelphia. And the third parties contribute to said pool the net profits or other income derived from the following theatres or places of amusement, to wit: Walnut Street Theatre, Philadelphia; Coates' Opera House, Kansas City; Euclid Avenue Opera House and Lyceum Theatre, Cleveland; Alvin Theatre, Pittsburgh; New Creighton Theatre, Omaha; Talma Theatre, Providence; New Southern Theatre and Grand Opera House, Columbus; Valentine Theatre, Toledo; and Davidson's Theatre, Milwaukee. That the net profits or other income accruing or derived from the said above specified parts or shares, or which the parties of the first part shall receive one equal part or share thereof; the parties of the second parts like share; settlements to be made on the first day of July in each year, during the continuance of this agreement.

FIFTH: No theatre or place or amusement shall be admitted under this agreement without the written consent of all the parties hereto.

SIXTH: As regards all other theatres and places of amusement mentioned in Article Fourth hereof and included in said pool, each of the parties hereto bind themselves that they will respectively keep just and true books of account in respect to each of said theatres in which there shall be entered all the receipts from each of the said theatres and places of amusement mentioned, as well as all expenses of every kind and nature which may be incurred in their management, and true vouchers of all and every such expense shall be kept, which books and vouchers shall at all times be accessible to either and all the parties hereto.

SEVENTH: If, during the term of this agreement, any of the theatres or places of amusement herein mentioned (or any hereafter coming under this agreement) shall pass out of the control or interest of the parties now controlling the same respectively, from any cause whatever not the act, negligence or default, either directly, indirectly, or collusively, of said such party or parties, or if said control and interest shall be lost by destruction of said theatres and places of amusement by fire or other casualty, such party or parties so losing such control and interest therein shall not be held accountable or responsible for such loss, but this agreement shall continue to operate upon the remaining theatres and places of amusement herein mentioned.

EIGHTH: It is agreed that Messrs. Klaw and Erlanger, the parties of the third part, shall have charge of all the bookings of the theatres specified in Article Second above, and that Messrs. Hayman and Frohman, the parties of the first part, shall have charge of the finances and of the profits and other income arising from the theatres mentioned in Article Fourth above; and that Messrs. Nixon and Zimmerman, the parties of the second part, shall be the travelling representatives under this agreement. That all and any expense incurred by either of the parties hereto in respect to the duties imposed upon either of them hereunder shall be paid out of the fund to be held by the parties of the first part upon the production of proper statements and vouchers, whenever possible, showing such expenditures; each party to advance the necessary expense which may be incurred by them until the first parties shall become possessed of funds; all such expenses to be included in the general expense account.

NINTH: Finally, it is expressly understood and agreed by all of the parties hereto, that nothing contained herein shall be construed to disturb or change the control which the respective parties hereto now have in the theatres and places of amusement specifically mentioned and described in Article Second hereof, excepting so far as the arrangement herein provided for bookings may be concerned.

IN WITNESS WHEREOF the said parties hereto, and to a triplicate hereof, have hereunto set their respective hands and seals the day and year first above written.

(signed and delivered in the presence of Alfred Rhemshom)

Under the influence of the Syndicate, pioneer play brokers began to bring system to the way plays were brokered or licensed for production, evolving the following early system.

145   Interview with Alice Kauser, 1904[1]

"Alice Kauser: A Chat with the Woman Who Presides over the Largest Play Business in the World." *New York Dramatic Mirror,* December 31, 1904

"What are the principle features of your business?"

"Well, I represent most of the authors and managers of note. I buy, sell, and act as intermediary in the leasing of old and new plays; in fact, I do everything connected with the play business."

"Have you ever discovered an author?" she was asked.

Miss Kauser laughed. "I think I may say I have," she replied; "but you may judge for yourself when I tell you I have brought the following authors and plays before the public. Let me see, now – there was Lorimer Stoddard, with *Tess of the D'Urbervilles*; Paul Kester, with *Eugene Aram* and *Fleur de Lys*; Langdon Mitchell, with *Becky Sharp*; Anne Crawford Flexner, with *Miranda of the Balcony*; George C. Hazelton, with *Mistress Nell*; Mrs. Burton Harrison, with *The Unwelcome Mrs. Hatch*. Is that enough?"

"Yes. And now tell me, Miss Kauser, are you always quite frank with your authors?"

"Too frank, I am afraid, sometimes," she replied, laughing heartily. . . . Not that I consider my judgment infallible. Any man or woman pretending to infallibility is a fool. We can only use our judgment to the best of our ability, but we cannot be sure – the public is too fickle. If it were not so every manager would be a multimillionaire.". . .

"You handle all the big Broadway successes for Mr. Frohman, do you not, Miss Kauser, after they have run their allotted season?"

"Yes, I do; and I am placing a number of good plays for next season. . . ."

"What about the more prominent authors, such as Clyde Fitch, William Gillette, and Augustus Thomas. Do you represent them?"

"Yes, but in this way: Authors of such high standing generally do their business direct with the managers. Clyde Fitch does his business through Elisabeth Marbury,[2] but when his plays become available for stock they are turned over to me, so that I am naturally closely allied with Miss Marbury in the play business. As regards the stock plays, I represent all the well-known authors."

"And about the stock business, Miss Kauser?"

"It is very large indeed, and when you stop to consider for a moment the tremendous number of stock companies throughout the country you will readily understand what a great quantity of material they require, each changing its

---

[1] The earliest prominent broker or licenser of plays to amateur groups was Samuel French who founded his business in the early 1850s. Kauser, pioneer woman play broker, started in the late 1890s.

[2] Author's agent who is credited with having first negotiated a percentage of the box office for playwrights.

bill every week. I furnish the majority of these plays, and at royalties varying from $50 to $1,000 a week.". . .

"Do you lease any play, old as well as new?"

"Certainly. I am in a position to lease any play on the market, old or new, and I have thousands of manuscripts in this office.". . .

"Are not royalties very high, Miss Kauser?"

"Well, the excessive royalties demanded by a number of authors, I am glad to say, have disappeared. A general readjustment of prices has come about and the big play owners are inclined to be liberal. But you cannot dispute the fact that a play at $500 royalty yielding a good margin of profit is better than a $50 play which brings a less profit. In this connection I wish to say that the so-called big stock companies that have gone out of existence, such as the Pike, Cincinnati; the Dearborn, Chicago, and the Auditorium, Kansas City, made a great mistake in producing all the newest plays in quick succession. The most successful stock management's today, such as the Alcazar, San Francisco; the Harry Davis Stock Company, Pittsburgh; Mr. Thanhauser of Milwaukee; Mr. Wiseman, Columbus, and the Castle Square, Boston, show great judgment in the selection of the plays presented. By the revival of some of the good old plays and an occasional Shakespearean production (which, by the way, can usually be made to run more than one week) sandwiched in with the latest metropolitan successes, they keep down the average of their royalties and present an attractive season's bill to their public."

"You must have an enormous stock of manuscripts here, Miss Kauser?"

"Yes, indeed; counting manuscripts of plays and parts, my average stock amounts to over 200,000 copies."

"I suppose your correspondence is also very heavy?"

"Yes. I have a staff of nine people, and we are barely able to cope with the business. We have to deal with some two hundred letters, fifty telegrams, and a countless number of telephone calls daily. . . ."

There were strong opponents and supporters of the Syndicate. Charles Frohman, one of the founders of the trust, was one of the more obvious but persuasive partisans.

149   Charles Frohman's Defense of the Theatrical Syndicate, 1904

"New Phases of Theatre Management," *Harper's Weekly*, 48 (December 31, 1904), 2022–24[1]

. . . Why the bugaboo of "business management" should have become a disturbing question I cannot understand. There is no doubt that the legitimate busi-

---

[1] Charles's brother, Daniel, began this discussion, focusing on the taste of the American public and a preference for "action, movement, and life" in drama: see "A Manager's View of the Stage," *Harper's Weekly*, 48 (December 24, 1904), 1988–89, 1999.

ness management under which theatres are run today is the best that could possibly be devised. It is the business system which obtains with the large business and banking institutions, and is intended for the best interests of actors, playwrights, and employees. But the business of management is misunderstood, so far as the theatres in America are concerned. There is no "concentration" of managers. We managers have not formed an alliance. The public has been misinformed concerning "theatrical syndicates" and the condition of theatrical affairs.

There has been formed in this country a combination for the sole purpose of representing theatres and of facilitating what is known as the "booking" of attractions for these theatres. This combination has nothing to do with the production of plays, or the engagement of actors, or the running of theatres. The members of this combination work separately, except so far as the "booking" of theatres under their control is concerned. . . . For the purpose stated the arrangement was made for five years; it was renewed for five years more, and is now in its seventh year. This indicates the satisfaction which the plan has given. . . .

[The balance of this essay is devoted to Frohman's arguments for the positive effects of the Syndicate on the playwright and the actor.]

The "star system" is one of the developments of theatrical progress, and I have the greatest faith and belief in it. I think the public feels that in getting a play – a good play – with a "star," they are getting additional value . . . the system [the decline of which was being predicted over fifty years ago] is with us today, and it is stronger than ever.

Between 1880 and 1918 Sarah Bernhardt toured the United States nine times. This contract is for the most unusual of her tours, for Mme Bernhardt refused to deal with the Theatrical Syndicate and instead turned to the then smaller Shubert organization. As a result she was forced, especially in the west, to play in tents and other makeshift performance spaces, the novelty virtually insuring the success of the tour.

150   Sarah Bernhardt and Shubert Tour Agreement, 1905[1]

Shubert Archive, New York

AGREEMENT made this 23rd June 1905 BETWEEN MONSIEUR LEE SHUBERT of New York, Theatrical Manager in the United States of America and Canada of the one part and MADAME SARAH BERNHARDT, Veuve Damala Manag-

---

[1] Stephen M. Archer, "Bernhardt's 1905–1906 Farewell Tour," in *The American Stage*, ed. Ron Engle and Tice L. Miller (Cambridge and New York: Cambridge University Press, 1993), pp. 159–74, provides a detailed analysis of this season.

eress of the Theatre Sarah Bernhardt of Paris, France, residing at 56 Boulevard Pereire, of the other part,

IT HAS BEEN RESOLVED UPON AND AGREED as follows:

1. Madame Sarah Bernhardt undertakes by this agreement to be ready to embark for the United States of America in the first fortnight of the month of November 1905 by the vessel which she shall herself choose with her Company, which is to consist of about forty persons amongst artistes, costumiers, accessoiriste, hairdresser, and other employees in order to appear personally in the representations which she shall give with the said Company in the French language in the United States of America and in Canada under the management of Mr. Shubert. The repertoire of Madame Sarah Bernhardt shall consist of the following pieces:

Angelo of Victor Hugo
La Sorciere of M. Victorien Sardou
La Tosca   "   "   "   "
Adrienne Lecouvreur of Madame Sarah Bernhardt
La Dame aux Camelias of Alexandre Dumas fils
Magda of H. Suderman (translation of M. Remond)
Sapho of A. Daudet
La Femme de Claude, of A. Dumas fils
L'Aiglon of Edmond Rostand

and besides those pieces Madame Sarah Bernhardt shall have the right of adding to the repertoire works which she shall think fit to add to it in the common interest. The order in which the pieces shall be represented shall be fixed by Madame Sarah Bernhardt after agreement with Mr. Lee Shubert.

The duration of this agreement is fixed at twenty weeks to commence from the first performance which is to take place at New York on the next day or at latest two days after the arrival of Madame Sarah Bernhardt and her Company, that is to say, that Mr. Lee Shubert undertakes to cause to be given by Madame Sarah Bernhardt at least one hundred and forty performances at the rate of seven a week in the period of twenty consecutive weeks in the United States of America and Canada, and that Madame Sarah Bernhardt agrees to appear in all those performances which are to be given in first-class theatres.

Madame Sarah Bernhardt is prohibited formally during the whole period of this engagement from playing any part other than in theatres managed or hired by Mr. Lee Shubert.

2. Madame Sarah Bernhardt undertakes to supply without any remuneration the costumes and special accessories for all the pieces of her repertoire, as well as such scenery as she shall consider indispensable to bring from Paris, but it is agreed that Madame Sarah Bernhardt shall lend this material in the state in

which it shall be found and that it shall be returned to her in the same state. The cost of mounting, dismounting, and repairs of the scenery or accessories belonging to Madame Sarah Bernhardt shall be defrayed by Mr. Lee Shubert who likewise undertakes to insure this material.

3. The travelling expenses of Madame Sarah Bernhardt and of her company and the transport of the baggage and material from the departure from Paris until the return to Paris shall be paid by Mr. Lee Shubert. All steamship journeys shall be made by the steamship lines chosen by Madame Sarah Bernhardt from leaving Paris until the return to Paris.

Mr. Lee Shubert undertakes to have reserved for Madame Sarah Bernhardt for every steamship voyage a cabin de luxe. The persons who shall accompany her shall travel partly first class and partly second class according to the direction of Madame Sarah Bernhardt as well by boat as by railway.

Madame Sarah Bernhardt shall have always at her disposal for herself and her suite at the cost of Mr. Lee Shubert a Pullman car, the most comfortable possible, composed of saloon, bedrooms, dining room, etc. For every arrival and departure in each town Madame Sarah Bernhardt shall have at her disposal a carriage for herself and her baggage at the cost of Mr. Lee Shubert. Mr. Lee Shubert undertakes to convey Madame Sarah Bernhardt and her Company from the town where the last performance shall take place to Paris on the conditions above specified.

4. Mr. Lee Shubert undertakes to pay to Madame Sarah Bernhardt for herself and her company, of which she shall be the sole Manageress for every performance.

1. A minimum sum of $900 (nine hundred United States dollars) whatever may be the total amount of the receipts.

2. Thirty percent (30%) out of every sum exceeding $1,800 (eighteen hundred dollars) of receipts for each performance.

The sums payable to Madame Sarah Bernhardt for the guaranteed minimum of $900, and the 30% of the receipts after deduction of $1,800 shall be settled and paid to her before the end of each performance, one performance not being entered into account with another.

At the time of the settlement of accounts, Mr. Lee Shubert or his representative shall hand to the representative of Madame Sarah Bernhardt a detailed note of the receipts allowing her to check the seats occupied. The representative of Madame Sarah Bernhardt shall also have the right of checking as well at the entrance doors as at the offices for sale of tickets, and that in the hall. No free seats shall be given except to the authorities and to the press without common agreement.

5. Mr. Lee Shubert undertakes to pay to Madame Sarah Bernhardt the sum of $200 (two hundred dollars) per week for her personal hotel expenses.

6. Mr. Lee Shubert undertakes to pay Madame Sarah Bernhardt in advance the sum of Fcs. 75,000 (seventy-five thousand francs). That sum shall be paid in the following manner:

1. Fcs. 25000 (twenty-five thousand francs) on the signing of the present contract against receipt.

2. Fcs. 50,000 (fifty-thousand francs) one month before the date fixed for the departure for America at the place and to the person whom Madame Sarah Bernhardt shall appoint and who shall give a discharge for it.

In default of a single payment, whether as advances, or as a daily payment, the sums already paid shall remain the property of Madame Sarah Bernhardt, and the present agreement be cancelled, without prejudice to the damages which Madame Sarah Bernhardt may claim from Mr. Lee Shubert. Madame Sarah Bernhardt shall refund to Mr. Lee Shubert the said sum of Fcs. 75,000 at the rate of one thousand francs for each performance to commence from the 66th (sixty-sixth) performance and during 75 performances until complete payment.

7. Mr. Lee Shubert undertakes to enter into an arrangement with the Society of Authors and Composers of Paris for the rights of authors to pay for the pieces which have not become public property. The author's rights according to the contract which he shall have procured shall be deducted from the receipts after the eighteen hundred dollars provided in Article 4, and before the distribution of the thirty percent out of the surplus due to Madame Sarah Bernhardt.

As to the author's rights for *Adrienne Lecouvreur* written by Madame Sarah Bernhardt, Mr. Shubert undertakes to pay to her direct the sum of fifty dollars ($50) for each performance.

8. Mr. Lee Shubert shall have the right if he thinks it beneficial to announce the visit as the farewell visit of Madame Sarah Bernhardt in America.

9. The present agreement being contracted between Mr. Shubert and Madame Sarah Bernhardt, Mr. Lee Shubert is prohibited from assigning it to a third party without the consent of Madame Sarah Bernhardt.

10. A forfeit fixed at the sum of Fcs. 125,000 (one hundred and twenty-five thousand francs) is stipulated between the two parties. That sum of one and twenty-five thousand francs shall be due by whichever of the parties shall fail wholly or partly in the execution of this contract to the other party, and it is understood that if it was Madame Sarah Bernhardt who failed she must repay the sums received by way of advances.

11. All questions arising or giving cause for proceedings shall be brought before the jurisdiction of the Department of the Seine France.

Done in duplicate and in good faith at London 23rd June 1905.

(signed and sealed)

ADDITIONAL ARTICLES

1. In case Madame Sarah Bernhardt shall decide to return with her Company direct from Buenos Aires to New York, Mr. Lee Shubert agrees to remit to Madame Sarah Bernhardt one month before the date appointed for the departure, the amount of the cost which he would have had to bear for the journey from Paris to New York and for the transport of the material and baggage according to the account which shall be provided by Madame Sarah Bernhardt according to the tariff of the French Transatlantic Company, provided that Mr. Shubert should not have any other cost for the journeys of the Company to New York. In that case the date of the first performance of the tour shall take place on the 30th October 1905.

2. Excepting Madame Sarah Bernhardt undertakes to give in the course of the tour performances in the town of La Havana.

The actress-manager Minnie Maddern Fiske also opposed the monopoly of the Syndicate and negotiated numerous contracts through her critic–producer husband, Harrison Grey Fiske.

151   Play Agreements for Minnie Maddern Fiske, 1899, 1908

Harvard Theatre Collection

BECKY SHARP

Agreement with Langdon E. Mitchell, Feb. 10, 1899. Exclusive rights in the United States and Canada in perpetuity. 100 performances, guaranteed during five years following first season of play. English rights for five years from first performance, Sept. 4, 1899, which will be Sept. 4, 1901.[1] English performances are restricted to Mrs. Fiske. Same rights for same period for Australia, but optional as to Mrs. Fiske's appearance there. Mitchell has right to publish play after December 1, 1907, protecting stage rights.

Terms: 5% first $5,000; 7½% next $1,000; 10% on all exceeding $6,000 weekly gross. For broken weeks 5%.

SALVATION NELL

Agreement with Edward Brewster Sheldon, of Chicago, made on Jan. 20, 1908. Author grants exclusive right to play for the United States and Canada until Jan.

---

[1] *Becky Sharp*, based on Thackeray's *Vanity Fair*, actually opened September 12, 1899, at the Fifth Avenue Theatre (formerly the New Fifth Avenue Theatre) and ran for an initial 116 performances. It was one of Minnie Maddern Fiske's most successful roles and stayed in her repertoire for a number of years.

1, 1918. Upon signing of contract party of second part to pay the sum of $150 as an advance of royalty. Play to be produced on or before Jan. 1, 1909.[2] If not produced on or before Jan. 1, 1909, by payment of $250 as a further advance of royalty – to party of first part, party of second part secures right to extend date of first production to Oct. 15, 1909.

Terms: If Mrs Fiske appears in title part: 5% of the first $10,000 and 10% on all over $10,000. When Mrs. Fiske does not appear: 5% of first $6,000; 7½% of the next $2,000; 10% on all over $8,000.

---

[2] *Salvation Nell* opened at the Hackett Theatre, New York, November 17, 1908, and ran for 71 performances. For a photograph of the production, see Doc. 229.

By 1906, the Theatrical Syndicate was beginning to come under attack from various sources, including the Shubert organization which was itself becoming a strong power in the American theatrical landscape and would ultimately usurp much of the control previously held by the Syndicate. The following documents illustrate some of the signs of discontent.

152   Cartoon by Halladay Illustrating Independent Theatre Movement, 1906[1]

Providence Sunday Journal, July 29, 1906, p. 1; used by permission of the Rhode Island Historical Society

[1] For an analysis of the movement for independence in Providence, see Stephen B. Pollock and Don B. Wilmeth, "The Shuberts and the Syndicate: The Independent Theatre Comes to Providence," *Rhode Island History,* 45 (August 1986), 95–106.

153   Newspaper Article on Colonel Felix Wendelschaefer, 1907

Providence Journal, May 2, 1907, p. 1

In the amicable adjustment of business differences recently entered into by the Klaw-Erlanger and the independent interests in the theatrical world, Col. Felix R. Wendelschaefer sees a promise of a very material benefit for Providence theatergoers, to accrue not only from the wider range of attractions now open to the local house, but also from a considerable extension of the season.

While laying great stress on the fact that the Providence Opera House does not in any respect sacrifice its recognized and highly valued independence, through the working agreement formed, he declared yesterday in an interview that the arrangement would mean a much longer season here, and, with the broader field from which to select shows, a distinct improvement as a whole in the character of the attractions offered. . . .

Col. Wendelschaefer is now a member of the Independent Managers' Association, having joined about two weeks ago, being one of the first theatrical managers to associate himself with that organization outside of New York.

He believes that the alliance just announced will prove of great benefit to the independents. Hitherto the booking of independent shows have been restricted to certain territories. Now, under the agreement, the bars are down and no such restrictions obtain. . . .

154   Announcement of Shubert Theatre in Minneapolis, 1910[1]

Dedicatory Program, August 29, 1910; Shubert Archive, New York

In honor of the late

SAM S. SHUBERT

the founder of the
INDEPENDENT THEATRE MOVEMENT
IN AMERICA

MESSRS LEE AND J. J. SHUBERT of the Shubert enterprises have given his name to this theatre which is dedicated to the public as a home of the drama that will in its management perpetuate the progressive and broad-minded policies for the independence of the American stage which, first inaugurated by him and fearlessly championed throughout his life, are inseparably associated with the memory of Sam S. Shubert.

This is one of a number of the Sam S. Shubert Theatres which are being erected in the principal cities of the United States and Canada in addition to the already long list of playhouses owned and controlled by the Messrs. Shubert.

[1] Sam S. Shubert died in a train wreck in 1905. Soon after his death the remaining two brothers, Lee and Jacob J., increased their efforts to add to their ownership of theatre buildings, which began in 1898 with the Bastable Theatre in Syracuse. The earliest Sam S. Shubert Memorial Theatre was most likely in Kansas City. By 1916 the Shuberts had broken the Syndicate monopoly and, in addition to many major New York City theatres, they ultimately owned or operated 100 theatres throughout the country and booked attractions for more than 1,000 others. See Brooks McNamara, *The Shuberts of Broadway* (New York: Oxford University Press, 1990), pp. 5–7.

155   Letter from Open Door Publishing Company[1] to Chicago Managers, 1909

Typescript, June 22, 1909; Shubert Archive, New York

Harry Sommers, an employee of the Theatrical Syndicate, otherwise known as the Klaw and Erlanger Booking Agency, is visiting managers throughout this section in an effort to persuade them to sign an exclusive booking contract with Klaw and Erlanger. The statements he is making are absolutely and unequivocally untrue.

The independent managers have over one hundred and fifty attractions, more than twice as many as the Syndicate controls. Charles Frohman, Henry W. Savage, Wm. A. Brady, Henry B. Harris and other managers, who are considered allies of the syndicate, are on record that they will not be excluded by Klaw and Erlanger from this territory or from the house of any manager upon whom Klaw and Erlanger seek to make reprisals.

The Open Door movement means exactly what it indicates. It does not seek to exclude the attractions of Klaw and Erlanger or any other producer, believing that the true interests of the one-night-stand manager lie in a policy that admits the booking of any and all attractions that may seem profitable to him.

There is no reason for any manager to pay booking fees to any booking agency. It is a form of robbery pure and simple, and is not to be tolerated.

Why should Klaw and Erlanger attempt to exclude the productions of any manager from your house because they happen to have a personal difference with him. The principals of the Chamberlain and Harrington circuit will tell you that their loyalty to the syndicate cost them $100,000 in the last fight between the Shuberts and Klaw and Erlanger.

The disintegration of the blackmailing system that has so long controlled the theatrical business is only a matter of weeks. You cannot afford to close your house to the Independent attractions if you want your season to be a great financial success. Work this next season for your OWN interests and not for the interests of a New York Booking Agency which has overreached itself, and whose club has fallen helplessly and feebly to the ground.

[1] Aka the Shuberts.

Actors' Equity Association was founded in December 1912; its constitution and bylaws were approved on May 26, 1913. It was not, however, until the actors' strike of 1919 that any appreciable progress was accomplished.

156   Minutes of Actors' Equity Association Steering Committee and Letter, 1913

Performing Arts Collection, Robert F. Wagner Labor Archives of the Tamiment Institution Library, New York University

PLAYERS CLUB
New York City

January 18th, 1913 – 5:30 P.M.

Meeting called to order by Chairman Frank Gilmore, at 5.40. Present, besides the Chairman, Messrs. William Harcourt, Arthur Byron, Grant Stuart, and Charles Coburn.

Mr. Coburn was appointed Secretary pro tem.

Minutes of the previous meeting of January 13th were read and accepted. The letter which was formulated at the previous meeting to be presented to Mr. [Francis] Wilson[1] for approval was read with the amendments and additions suggested by Mr. Wilson. Two additional clauses were added by him, one relative to "women's wardrobe," the other "signing of contracts with corporations," both of which were approved and accepted by the committee. It was moved and seconded that a vote of thanks be tended Mr. Wilson, through Mr. Harcourt, and that Mr. Harcourt request Mr. Wilson to defer the date for the meeting with Messrs. Frohman, Grismer, and Thomas for two weeks, (until Tuesday, February 4th) to allow the present committee to augment its membership, thereby giving a better representation of the Actors Committee in discussing the problems to be presented to the gentlemen above mentioned, who are asked to give us their counsel in aid of this movement. In lieu of this, it was moved and seconded that our chairman invite the following gentlemen to become members of this committee: Messrs Wilton Lackaye, Robert Edeson, Bruce MacRae, Cyril Scott, and Fritz Williams, to meet with the present members of this committee on Tuesday, January 21st, at 3 P.M. at the Players Club and from that time on, become regular members and be informed of the business transacted by this committee up to date.

The letter as amended by Mr. Wilson and accepted by the committee follows:

January 24th, 1913

Dear Sir:

In pursuance of our duty, we, the undersigned, having been appointed a temporary committee by a meeting of actors held on December 22nd, 1912 feel that

---

[1] The actor Francis Wilson was elected the first president of Equity, a position he held until 1921. The original 1913 constitution and bylaws are not in the Equity Archives, although AEA began publishing them in booklet form in the early 1920s. A 1926 edition, the earliest one in the Archives, has been amended and is thus not identical to the initial documents. The basic details of the actors' struggle to establish a union can be found in Alfred Harding, *The Revolt of the Actors* (New York: W. Morrow & Co., 1929).

it would be an inestimable advantage if you would give us the benefit of your counsel as to the need and practicability of forming an organization for:

(A) Correcting the abuses that have crept into the profession, and

(B) Deciding upon a uniform form of contract that would be acceptable alike to the fair-minded manager and the fair-minded actor.

To illustrate what is meant by "the abuses that have crept in," we cite a few flagrant instances:

1. Actors have repeatedly, recently, rehearsed for five weeks or even longer and have received only three days pay, indeed in one or two cases nothing at all, for their services.

2. Companies playing in one night stands have had to lose a Saturday night – and its pay – in order to jump to a Sunday night performance for which they received no remuneration.

3. Certain forms of contract now employed by some managers exact six weeks work at half salary during the season, to wit: two weeks before election, two weeks before Christmas, and two weeks before Easter.

4. Certain forms of contract contain a clause that obliges the manager to provide transportation only from "the point of opening to the point of closing," instead of from New York to New York.

5. Actresses have been required of late to pay out large sums for gowns, etc., which in case of a play's failure are a serious loss.

6. Contracts with a corporation – without the signature of an individual fixing personal responsibility – are used as loopholes through which the contracts are shirked.

Our movement is in no sense a crusade; what we seek is a reestablishment of the best form of contract previously prevailing under the best managers; a renaissance, not a revolution. It is an endeavor to uphold and advance the dignity of our calling.

Mr. Francis Wilson, having met us in committee, has expressed his sympathy with our views and has kindly offered us his house for our next meeting.

We herewith extend to you a most cordial invitation to meet us at Mr. Francis Wilson's house, 24 Gramercy Park, on Tuesday, February 4th, 1913, at four o'clock.

An invitation similar to this has been sent to Messrs. Daniel Frohman, Augustus Thomas, and Joseph R. Grismer.

II.   Acting and Directing

Edwin Booth, who played Hamlet from 1853 to 1891, was involved in two *Hamlet* productions of special note – the first in 1864 (the "100" night *Hamlet*) and then his definitive production in 1870 at his own theatre.

157   Review of Edwin Booth's Hamlet, 1870

New York Times, January 7, 1870[1]

Mr. Edwin Booth is undoubtedly the best Hamlet seen in this country, by the present generation, and perhaps the best America has produced. We wish, in saying this, that it signified more. It is, however, undeniable that satisfactory representatives of this arduous character have been very few among us, and that for some years past the niche has hardly been filled at all. This is, in some respects, fortunate for Mr. Booth. If he had such rivals as either of the great Hamlets of the stage – Betterton, Garrick, Kemble, Charles Young, Edmund Kean, or Macready – and if the present generation were accustomed to see such players, the success that he has gained would be a triumph indeed. . . .

. . . Physically and in temperament Mr. Booth is capitally adapted to the usually received ideal of Hamlet. His spare and almost attenuated frame, his thoughtful, and, indeed, habitually mournful expression; his hollow, low-pitched voice; his splendid dark eye; his jetty, disheveled locks, and a certain morbidness that is suggested by his whole look and bearing, carry conviction to the mass of beholders that in him they see as near an approach as possible to the Hamlet of Shakespeare. . . .

Mr. Booth's Hamlet is in truth a remarkably well-studied and harmonious piece of acting. It is the product of much patient thought, and of a rigid determination to achieve in the character the utmost that nature and art will permit. . . .

---

[1] Charles H. Shattuck, the authority on Booth's most famous and successful role, considers this the most balanced of the reviews of Hamlet. Shattuck's *The Hamlet of Edwin Booth* (Urbana and London: University of Illinois Press, 1969) provides a detailed reconstruction of this role.

Most of Mr. Booth's readings are traditional – that is to say, others have adopted them before him. He makes the "Into my grave," in answer to Polonius' question if he will walk out of the air, an ironic inquiry instead of affirmation, transposes the "bitter" before "day" and puts it before "business" in the speech that ends the play scene, and points his sword neither towards the Ghost nor his friends, but holds it up as a cross toward the apparition, as if to exorcise a possible fiend. These and some other slight changes we have not seen before on our stage, and they are for the most part judicious and effective. As regards the "business," it is almost universally altered and sometimes not for the better. The rule seems to have been to repeat nothing that is old, which secures the advantage of novelty, but not always that of propriety. The free use of seats from which to deliver the soliloquys and long speeches gives variety to the scene, and is therefore commendable. Mr. Booth's temperateness in the matter of vocal display is, in general, most praiseworthy. It verges, at times, upon austerity, and in some instances causes disappointment by falling short of the expected passion of the situation. As the reaction from "robustiousness" is one of the secrets of Mr. Booth's rise, and as this reticence of his is productive of much-needed good results, it seems ungracious to object to it. Yet is is undeniable that, whether it is to be attributed to this or other causes, there is a want of fire and *electricity* in the great test scenes of Mr. Booth's Hamlet which is inconsistent with the requirements of the part and with the artist's own reputation. We would except from this criticism the "nunnery" passage, and the scenes with the Ghost, the last of which, in particular, is most tenderly and beautifully rendered. In passages of violent declamation Mr. Booth appears to lack power, and he is, as a consequence, uniformly more successful in subtle and complicated indications of character than in heroic or oratorical ones. In the latter, too, his action is rather against him. He is languid rather than easy, his gesticulation is angular, and, for a man of so much suppleness and so keen an eye to effect, he falls into enormously ungraceful attitudes. He has, moreover, an unpleasant habit of sinking the head between the shoulders, of crouching as it were, which better comports with the idiosyncrasies of the snake-like Richard than with those of the highly-bred Prince of Denmark, "the glass of fashion and the mould of form." . . . His mouth, the sole defect of an otherwise singularly fine face, has, naturally, not the best of expressions. The upper lip is flat and sinister. Now, he exaggerates the effect of this by his fashion of keeping it, when speaking, almost immovable, using the lower lip and showing the under teeth almost exclusively. This may tend to produce the occasional sibiliant effect in his enunciation, and to intensify an air of virulent ferocity, that, being apparently uncalled for by the text, sometimes disfigures his manner. These are matters of detail, but are not unworthy of attention, especially in a performance in which such immense pains have been taken with minutiae.

In spite of these faults, and his disposition at intervals to fall into a mechanical manner, Mr. Booth's Hamlet is a very interesting and a very fine performance. If it fails to excite our enthusiasm by the force of unquestionable genius, it commands our respect by its fidelity, its self-restraint, its obvious reverance for art and the admirable influence of its example. To see Mr. Booth's Hamlet is not, as the critic said Kean's was, like reading Shakespeare by flashes of lightning, but it is like reading him by a steady light which illumes the beauties of his magnificent poetry, and reveals the intricacies of his teeming imagination with an equable and instructive ray. The appreciative closeness of Mr. Booth's study of his text is shown in a hundred gratifying instances – such as in the covert but exquisitely marked allusion to Ophelia in the last scene of the first act after the Ghost's departure – and this conscientiousness and discernment deserve hearty praise. Even higher encomiums are due for the liberality and dignity with which Mr. Booth has placed the sublime tragedy on the stage of his theatre. Such work in behalf of the art that charms and soothes, and elevates and instructs is more ennobling than the laurels of a conqueror; and it is the more creditable to Mr. Booth, inasmuch as no precedent existed to suggest that such toil and expenditure might be looked for at his hands. For this, and independently of his high claims as an actor, he merits, and, we rejoice to say, he receives, the honor and gratitude of the community.

M. Isabella Stone, a theatregoer from Framingtham, Massachusetts, saw Booth as Hamlet a half dozen times in New York and Boston (1879–84) and noted her impressions of his performances,[1] one example of which is transcribed (as it appears in her notebooks) here.

[1] See Daniel J. Watermeier, ed., *Edwin Booth's Performances: The Mary Isabella Stone Commentaries* (Ann Arbor: UMI Research Press, 1990).

158   Description of Edwin Booth's "To Be or Not to Be," 1880s

M. Isabella Stone manuscript, Harvard Theatre Collection

In Booth's soliloquies there is none of the raving of insanity, – it is preposterous to suppose him crazy. It is marvellous, even miraculous, with what freshness & force & originality, Booth delivers this famous but hackneyed soliloquy, – or rather thinks it out loud. You can see the thoughts slowly rise, as for the first time in his mind, so vividly are they painted on his speaking countenance, portrayed in his walk & attitudes; his whole bearing shows him utterly absorbed in deepest meditation & profound melancholy, so that he realizes not *his* own body, whether he sits or stands, sees or hears, but does all this mechanically. His very voice is lower & deeper than usual, sometimes sounding sort of muffled.

At first he is discovered in the door-way at "left", holding on to the curtain, apparently leaning against it. There he stands some time, motionless & silent, brooding on thoughts too great for utterance. His dress conveys the impression of being somewhat disordered, though in what respect is not definable. . . . The man's *soul* is what attracts your whole attention. He walks slowly into the room with eyes fastened upon floor & head bent. Like drops from the deep ocean of infinite thought, – like an approaching culmination to some previous train of thought, & yet a link between a past of thought unknown to us & a future perhaps never to be fathomed by himself – "a sound between two silences" – the words "To be, or not to be, – that is the question:" fall from his lips unconsciously, slowly, in a low voice [at the end of the first line]. Then absently he sinks down upon one of those quaint chairs at "left-back" of stage, resting his right arm upon arm of chair, with hand hanging from its end. [On "Devoutly to be wished] Lifting his eyes to heaven. [On "To Sleep!"] Then slowly like the flushing dawn there rises in his face & radiates from his dilating eyes the thought of what that future life may be, – & The wonder & the awe-fulness of it seems to draw him up on to his feet.

[At "Ay, there the rub] Stepping quickly forward with uplifted finger. Booth stands still most of the time, & uses less gesticulation than usual, which is suitable. The varying expressions of his face are everything; & these seem not voluntary contortions for a purpose, but – like the alternating gray shadows & gleams of light, the hollows & the swelling billows, that sweep like emotions over the face of the ocean, as the sun & wind command. . . .

The following letter from Booth to a young physician who had announced his intention of becoming an actor is illuminating about the actor and his profession.

159   Letter from Edwin Booth, 1884

Unidentified newspaper clipping; Seymour-Davenport Papers, Princeton Theatre Collection

I was, indeed, startled and, I must confess, pained by the letter announcing your determination to abandon your profession for that of the stage, and in sincere frankness I beg you to reconsider the matter, for I really have no hope for a satisfactory result from such a change. The feelings which prompt you to take the step (I mean your love, enthusiasm, and natural inclination) do not imply an ability for the art.

There are hundreds of disappointed lives wasting on the stage where they felt as you did that a brilliant destiny awaited them. You may be able to recite in private with perfect ease and propriety, even with excellence, and yet have no other qualifications for the highest forms of dramatic expression. It is a life of wearisome drudgery, and requires years of toil and bitter disappointment to achieve a position worth having.

You can form no idea of the many who solicit my influence every season – professionals and amateurs, friends and strangers, of all qualities, male and female – and it is very seldom that I can serve them, for managers prefer to judge for themselves and as my support, no matter how capable it may be, has been abused by the [original unclear: possibly papers?] many years past, and will always be until the end of my career, my recommendation is not regarded by managers, whose judgments are quickly influenced by what the critics say.

I have known many who, like you, gave up home, friends, and respectable positions for the glitter of the actor's calling, who are now fixed for life in subordinate positions unworthy [of] their breeding, education, and natural refinement.

I beg you, as your friend and well-wisher, to abandon the mistaken resolve, and enjoy the drama as a spectator, which pleasure as an actor you would never know, and retain the family, friends, and happy home that are now yours. Had nature fitted me for any other calling I should never have chosen the stage.

Were I able to employ my thoughts and labor in any other field, I would gladly turn my back upon the theatre forever. An art whose professors and followers should be of the very highest culture, is the mere makeshift of every speculator and boor that can hire a theatre or get hold of some sensational rubbish to gull the public.

I am not very much in love with my calling as it is now is and, I fear, will ever be. Therefore, you can see how loath I am to encourage anyone to adopt it. I think you will take my advice as it is meant, in kindness, and believe that my only wish is to spare you a sorrow that must follow the course you will pursue.

Booth's contemporary Joseph Jefferson III, the most popular and respected comic actor of his day, was best known for his portrayal of Rip Van Winkle. In his autobiography he has left the following insights on playing the role.[1]

[1] A useful modern reconstruction of this famous role is Stephen Johnson's "Joseph Jefferson's *Rip Van Winkle* (1865)," *Drama Review*, 26 (Spring 1982), 3–20, and see *Nineteenth Century Theatre*, 20 (Winter 1992) for a sequel to his reconstruction.

160   Joseph Jefferson III on Acting Rip Van Winkle, 1895

Joseph Jefferson, Introduction, *Rip Van Winkle as Played by Joseph Jefferson* (New York: Dodd, Mead and Co., 1903), pp. 16–19

In acting the part of Rip, I have always found that what to do was simple enough, but what not to do was the important and difficult point to determine. The earlier scenes of the play being a natural and domestic character, I had only to draw upon my experience for their effect. But from the moment Rip meets the spirits of Hendrick Hudson and his crew, I felt that the colloquial speech and lazy and commonplace actions of Rip should cease. After he meets the elves, in the third act, the play drifts from realism into idealism, and becomes poetical. After this, it is a fairy tale, and the prosaic elements of the character should be eliminated.

Rip's sympathy with nature is always very keen, and he talks to the trees and his dog as if they were human. . . . If the sleep of twenty years were merely incongruous, there would be room for argument pro and con; but being an impossibility, the mind accepts it, not because it is an impossibility, but from curiosity to know the psychological result if such an event could happen. And it is this strange and original attitude of the characters that has kept my interest in it alive for so many years.

I have never "staged" Rip with the realism in fashion of later years, though I have had various suggestions made to me for elaborating the spectacular and scenic effects of the play. . . .

So unreal a theme could not have been interwoven with all this realism without marring the play.

For this reason, when a lady once asked me, "Why don't you have a dog in the play?" I replied that I disliked realism in art; and realism alive, with a tail to wag at the wrong time, would be abominable. . . . We must not be natural, but appear to be so."

So, too, I have never felt that the dialect was an important element in the presentation of the character. I do not make it so prominent or so consistent as they would do in a variety show. If I were to do that, I would destroy the larger element. . . .

The following are rare onstage photographs of Jefferson's production of *Rip Van Winkle.*

161   Photographs of Joseph Jefferson as Rip, 1873

Harvard Theatre Collection

The top photograph is Act IV, scene 3, the return of Rip into town, and the townspeople deriding him. The bottom is later in the same scene when Rip encounters his wife Gretchen and his nemesis Derrick, who has been married to her for fifteen years. Derrick has mistreated her badly and here orders her to stop crying and to pretend happiness for the sake of appearances. The photographs are by Bachrach, Boston photography firm.

The reputation of Adah Isaacs Menken rests almost totally on her role of Mazeppa in an equestrian drama based on Byron's poem of the same name in which she first appeared in 1861. Though not a great talent, the risque nature of her performance became one of the great popular attractions of the day, receiving a vivid review from the young Mark Twain in the Virginia City, Nevada *Territorial Enterprise*, a paper he wrote for in the early 1860s.

162   Mark Twain's Review of *Mazeppa*, 1863

Territorial Enterprise, September 13, 1863; reprinted in *Mark Twain of the "Enterprise,"* ed. Henry Nash Smith (Berkeley: University of California Press, 1957), pp. 78–80

When I arrived in San Francisco, I found there was no one in town – at least there was no body in town but "the Menken" – or rather, that no one was being talked about except that manly young female. I went to see her play *Mazeppa*, of course. They said she was dressed from head to foot in flesh-colored "tights," but I had no opera glass, and I couldn't see it, to use the language of the inelegant rabble. She appeared to me to have but one garment on – a thin tight white linen one, of unimportant dimensions. I forget the name of the article, but it is indispensable to infants of tender age – I suppose any young mother can tell you what it is, if you have the moral courage to ask the question. With the exception of this superfluous rag, the Menken dresses like the Greek slave; but some of her postures are not so modest as the suggestive attitude of the latter. She is a finely formed woman down to her knees; if she could be herself that far, and Mrs. H. A. Perry [an actress in Menken's company] the rest of the way, she would pass for an unexceptionable Venus. Here every tongue sings the praises of her matchless grace, her supple gestures, her charming attitudes. Well, possibly, these tongues are right. In the first act, she rushes on the stage, and goes cavorting around after Olinska; she bends herself back like a bow; she pitches headforemost at the atmosphere like a battering ram; she works her arms, and her legs, and her whole body like a dancing-jack: her every movement is as quick as thought; in a word, without any apparent reason for it, she carries on like a lunatic from the beginning of the act to the end of it. . . . After a while they proceed to strip her, and the high chief Pole calls for the "fiery untamed steed"; a subordinate Pole brings in the fierce brute, stirring him up occasionally to make him run away, and then hanging to him like death to keep him from doing it. The monster looks round pensively upon the brilliant audience in the theatre, and seems very willing to stand still – but a lot of those Poles grab him and hold onto him, so as to be prepared for him in case he changes his mind. They are posted as to his fiery untamed nature, you know, and they give him no chance to get loose and eat up the orchestra. They strap Mazeppa on his back, fore and aft, and face uppermost, and the horse goes cantering upstairs over the painted mountains, through tinted clouds of theatrical mist, in a brisk exciting way, with the wretched victim he bears unconsciously digging her heels unto his hams, in the agony of his sufferings, to make him go faster. Then a tempest of applause bursts forth, and the curtain falls.

The fierce old circus horse carries his prisoner around through the back part of the theatre, behind the scenery, and although assailed at every step by the savage wolves of the desert, he makes his way at last to his dear old home in Tartary down by the footlights, and beholds once more, O, gods! the familiar faces of the fiddlers in the orchestra. The noble old steed is happy, then, but poor old Mazeppa is insensible – "ginned out" by his trip, as it were. Before the act closes, however, he is restored to consciousness and his doting old father, the king of Tartary; and the next day, without taking time to dress – without even borrowing a shirt, or stealing a fresh horse – he starts off on the fiery untamed, at the head of the Tartar nation, to exterminate the Poles, and carry off his own sweet Olinska from the Polish court. He succeeds, and the curtain falls upon a bloody combat, in which the Tartars are victorious. *Mazeppa* proved a great card for Maguire [Tom Maguire's Opera House where it ran for sixty nights] here; he put it on the boards in first-class style, and crowded houses went every night it was played . . .

The success of the landmark production of the musical extravaganza *The Black Crook*[1] in 1866 at Niblo's Garden in New York led to other managements' attempts to climb on the bandwagon. One such effort was that of the talented actress and performer Lydia Thompson, whose series of burlesque musicals helped to create a rage for this form of popular theatre.[2]

---

[1] Documents on *The Black Crook* are quite plentiful and readily available, for example Leigh George Odom, "*The Black Crook* at Niblo's Garden," *Drama Review*, 26 (Spring 1982), 21–40; Laurilyn J. Harris, "Extravaganza at Niblo's Garden: The Black Crook," *Nineteenth Century Theatre Research*, 13 (Summer 1985), 1–15; and Robert C. Allen, *Horrible Prettiness: Burlesque and American Culture* (Chapel Hill: University of North Carolina Press, 1991).

[2] The most frequently reproduced review of Thompson's troupe (at Niblo's Garden) is Richard Grant White, "The Age of Burlesque," *Galaxy*, 8 (August 1869), 200–202. See *The American Theatre as Seen by Its Critics, 1752–1934*, ed. Montrose J. Moses and John Mason Brown (New York: Norton, 1934), pp. 78–82 and Barnard Hewitt, *Theatre U.S.A., 1668 to 1957* (New York: McGraw-Hill Book Co., 1959), pp. 209–12. For a brief overview of Thompson's career, see Marlie Moses, "Lydia Thompson and the 'British Blondes,'" in *Women in American Theatre*, ed. Helen Krich Chinoy and Linda Walsh Jenkins (New York: Crown Publishers, 1981), pp. 88–92.

163   Newspaper Account of the "British Blondes," 1868

Unidentified essay from New York *Clipper*; Theatre Collection, Museum of the City of New York

The skirmishes of the British Blonde Brigade made Wood's Museum [New York City, Broadway below 30th Street], this city, their first American outpost, opening on Sept. 28 in *Ixion*, a burlesque. . . .

To adopt a well-worn phrase that has no literal meaning except to a Frenchman, the success of the three blondes [Thompson, Pauline Markham, and Lisa Weber] was pronounced. Half the callow youths of the town shed their coats, and nightly in choice seats at Wood's the graybeards of the metropolis renewed in fancy the days of their prime. As the ocean wafted fresher burlesquers to our shores, there was a merry Hades in these United States. Duplicate blondes troupes were organized. . . . Half the playwrights in the country forswore "American comedies" and turned their pens towards parodies upon the charming fictions of paganism. Harry Murdoch wrote a burlesque for the Thompson Troupe, and even John Brougham caught the fever in a modified form. . . .

[Olive Logan, the actress–playwright, was partially driven to the cause of women's rights as a result of the visit of the British Blondes, and spoke the following at Steinway Hall:]

"I cannot advise any woman to go upon the stage, with the demoralizing influences which seem there to prevail more and more every day, when its greatest rewards are won by brazen-faced, stained, yellow-haired, padded-limbed creatures . . . while actresses of the old school, well trained, well qualified, decent, cannot earn a living."

Having been misconstrued, as she thought, she subsequently "rose to explanation" through the public press:

"I referred the other night to decent young women, who are not celebrities – merely honest, modest girls, whose parents had left them the not very desirable heritage of the stage, and who find it difficult to obtain any other employment, being uneducated for any other. When these go into a theatre to apply for a situation now, they find that the requirements of managers are expressed in the following questions:

"'1. Is your hair dyed yellow? 2. Are your legs, arms, and bosom symmetrically formed, and are you willing to expose them? 3. Can you sing brassy songs, and dance the cancan, and wink at men, and give utterance to disgusting half-words which mean whole actions? 4. Are you acquainted with any rich men who will throw you flowers and send you presents, and keep afloat dubious rumors concerning your chastity? 5. Are you willing to appear tonight, and every other night, amid the glare of gaslights, and before the gaze of thousands of men, in this pair of satin-breeches ten inches long, without a vestige of drapery on your person? 6. If you can answer these questions affirmatively, we will give you a situation. If not, there's the door.' "[1]

[1] Logan wrote passionately against the "leg business" frequently, especially in her books *Before the Footlights and Behind the Scenes* (Philadelphia: Parmelee, 1870) and *Apropos of Women and the Theatre* (1896).

A large number of international stars appeared on the American stage in the latter half of the century. The Polish-born actress Helena Modjeska, for example, fled to the U.S. for political asylum, settling in California and making her American debut at the California Theatre in San Francisco on August 20, 1877 as Adrienne Lecouvreur. Later, she played Thora (Nora) in an early production of Ibsen's *A Doll's House* (it had a happy ending) with little success. She performed in English, though imperfectly at first, throughout her American career.[1]

[1] The review from the *Louisville Courier-Journal*, December 8, 1883, is reprinted in Moses and Brown, *The American Theatre*, pp. 101–3. For additional documents on her American performances, see William C. Young, *Famous Actors and Actresses on the American Stage: Documents of American Theater History* (New York: R. R. Bowker, 1975), 11: 804–10.

164   Review of Helena Modjeska's U.S. Debut Performance, 1877

Peter Robertson, "Life on the Stage," *Pacific Life*, August 25, 1877

The fifth act of *Adrienne Lecouvreur* . . . is one which tests an actress, and when we say that Miss Helena Modjeska, rising above all defects of pronunciation and accent, made it an emphatic success, it is enough to stamp her as considerably better than most of the strange stars we have hitherto met in this western boundary of the continent. It is not that this scene, in its madness of agony and death, is any great example of dramatic power; but the actress who can put so much into facial expression and bodily contortion must have the power to adapt herself to pure dramatic situation, and it is more in showing what Miss Modjeska is capable of than what she has done, that she deserves the encomiums being passed upon her. We admit a firm belief that no actress who is dealing with a foreign language can ever give a thoroughly satisfactory performance, and Miss Modjeska has to thank a particularly kindly audience for giving her every encouragement to strive through three more or less tedious acts, and to work up to the climax in the last. . . . We are glad that fortune and friends so favored the lady that she was able in the last act to give us a piece of acting which we have not seen equalled for a long time. She is a pleasing actress in every way, with an eminently sympathetic voice, and charming and engaging in movement and action. What her voice lacks in force, it makes up for in a sweetness and delicate modulation which, when she acts in her own language, must be doubly effective. . . . It is in little points . . . that Miss Modjeska establishes her claim to be a great actress; and even where the effort to give effect to the English lines is evident, the acting, if it sometimes does not exactly suit the words, suits the passion and meaning of the scene perfectly. There is but one fault in her voice, and that is, she does not seem always to have it under control. We should recommend our emotional actresses to study Miss Modjeska's very graceful way of falling on the stage, although about her last pose there was something not unnatural, but almost unpleasant.

In 1821 the fledgling African Company had presented *Richard III*, which received insulting commentary in the *National Advocate* and other papers.[1] Shortly thereafter, with pressure from the manager Stephen Price and harassment by white spectators, this pioneer company was forced to give up playing Shakespeare. By 1884 the situation had not improved dramatically. A production at Ford's Opera House in Washington, D.C., on May 7, 1884, with scenes from *Macbeth*, *Richard III*, and Lovell's *Ingomar* and featuring the outstanding black actress Henrietta Vinton Davis, supported by other black actors, amateurs, and students, received a similar reception from some white audience members, although both blacks and whites were in attendance.[2]

[1] See Doc. 52.
[2] In contrast, the black press was quite positive about this evening's entertainment, sensing the history and irony of a black performance in the theatre where Lincoln had been assassinated.

165   Review of Henrietta Vinton Davis Co., 1884

Washington Post, May 8, 1884; quoted in Errol Hill, *Shakespeare in Sable: A History of Black Shakespearean Actors* (Amherst: University of Massachusetts Press, 1984), p. 69

There were many white people in the house who seemed disposed to turn to comedy the tragic efforts of the actors. In this they were not wholly successful, for the earnestness and intelligence of several of the leading performers were such as to command the respect of those most disposed to find cause for laughter in everything that was said or done. . . . The scene from *Macbeth* went credibly, all things considered, Miss Davis and Mr. [Powhatan] Beaty showing a knowledge of the requirements of the parts which they essayed which, it is safe to say, surprised those in the audience competent to judge. The most enjoyable thing of the evening was *Richard III*. Here the "guying" disposition of the audience found ample opportunity to vent itself, although the title role was not badly filled by Mr. W. R. Davis, while Mr. W. H. H. Hart's Richmond was a most credible performance for an amateur. . . . The combat between Richard and Richmond waked the most derisive plaudits from the auditors, and "Time" was repeatedly called by particularly irreverent individuals.

Theatre flourished in "the provinces" during this period, although playing on the road was almost always difficult. The next three descriptions suggest what it was like acting in various parts of the country away from major theatre centers.

166   Frederick Warde on Touring in the Southwestern U.S., 1879–80

Frederick Warde, *Fifty Years of Make-Believe* (New York: International Press Syndicate, 1920), pp. 188–92, 224–26

It was my first visit to the Lone Star State. . . . The theatres were not elaborate; in fact, many of them were simply halls, with wooden backed benches and very little scenery; but they served the purpose and our audiences came to see the acting of the plays and were not influenced by the environment.

In Galveston we found the Tremont Theatre very well equipped; but in Dallas we played in a long room over a newly built store on the main street. It was approached by a steep stairway on the side. Two dry-goods cases had been improvised on the curb for a box office, and there Jake Moniger, a humpbacked billposter, sold the tickets . . .

There were no dressing rooms in the Opera House. We dressed in our rooms in the Windsor Hotel, across on a diagonal covered bridge to the Exchange Hotel on the opposite side of the street in the rear, entered a back room, climbed out of a window, crossed a roof, and entered the Opera House by another window that opened on the back of the stage. When a change of dress was necessary we had to make a return round trip by the same route. . . .

One of the most interesting cities in Texas was San Antonio. . . . At the time of which I write we played an entire week in the Casino, a large hall built by a German Society, on the banks of the river. It was fairly well equipped with scenery, accommodated a large audience and we taxed its capacity at every performance . . .

. . . In Austin, I played Iago to the Othello of Mr. McCullough. The following morning I was informed that I had had a narrow escape from being shot during the performance. . . . I append in part the account as it appeared in the newspaper.

"On Friday night when McCullough was playing Othello at the Opera House in this city, a countryman became terribly excited at the villainy of Iago, as portrayed by Mr. F. B. Warde. Towards the close of the play he drew his six-shooter and declared he would kill the d—n scoundrel. On being told that the actor was only impersonating a character, he remarked, 'He must be a damned villain, anyhow, or he couldn't act it so well, and if he didn't stop abusing that woman (Emelia) he would shoot him, anyhow.' . . ."

[Several years later] We were touring New Mexico. There had been trouble with the Apache Indians and a rising was feared. The citizens throughout the territory – it was not then a State – were all armed in anticipation of raids, and the towns and their approaches were patrolled.

In Silver City, I played Virginius in a newly built store. The male portion of the audience came armed with rifles, revolvers, and belts of cartridges to be in readiness if an alarm should be sounded. No interruption occurred, but at the close of the performance the citizens insisted on providing an armed guard to escort the company to the hotel.

We continued on the Santa Fe railroad to Arizona. In Tucson, the Opera House was built of adobe. It had a stage and some scenery, but no seats. The box sheet was marked like a checker board, space was sold in squares and the audience brought their seats with them or sent them in advance. The effect was unique. Every kind of chair and stool was brought into requisition, from an upholstered rocker to a school bench, and as the time for the performance approached, groups of people might be seen coming from different directions carrying stools or chairs as if it were a general moving day.

Pigeons in large number had made their home in the loft above the stage. . . . when the audience applauded, the flapping and rustling of hundreds of wings above our heads by the frightened birds sounded like rushing water. The effect was somewhat disconcerting to the actors, but we became used to it and the play proceeded successfully to its conclusion and the birds were left in peace.

167   Luke Cosgrave on Playing in Kansas City, 1892

Luke Cosgrave, *Theater Tonight* (Hollywood: House-Warven, 1952), pp. 98–100

Out here [in rural Kansas] the people were the same "covered wagon" people I had known and liked on my previous trek through the state in '86 and '87. Although it was January, the weather was very pleasant.

Those were the times of many revival meetings and medicine shows. I thought they seemed to go together, giving the pioneers an opportunity to help their bodies or their souls. However, they offered little opposition to our small show. . . .

At Kansas City, my brother Joe was at the station to meet us. . . . The next day I walked down to the Ninth Street Theater and got a job as stage manager from Captain Peabody, the owner. This was a museum and specialty house . . .

The Theater occupied the second floor of a three-story structure. Downstairs, Captain Peabody had his Wild Animal Show, including cougars, a family of badgers, two eagles, rattlesnakes, and a fine assortment of lizards and horned toads. There were three or four different kinds of owls, a panther, two big gray wolves from New Mexico, parrots, a white cockatoo, and a nice den of monkeys. At one end of the room was a small stage where the Captain gave short nature lectures. Admission was ten cents.

On the top floor were the freaks. There were the Trocci Twins, the Tall Man, over eight feet high, dressed as an Austrian Hussar; the Strong Man; a Barrel Kicker named Barrelmus; the Transparent Turk – you could see through him. This was done by means of a cylinder and mirrors. On the side he ate tacks and nails, and swallowed swords. On the stage the Turk also did black art. Admission to the Freak Show was ten cents. These freaks travelled, staying a week and then going on.

This company had a band which played in front of the theater every night before the show. . . .

Captain Jack Crawford, called the Poet-Scout of the world, was . . . a particular friend of Captain Peabody . . . Sunday night we were to open with a Western piece. . . . During the rehearsal of a breath-taking scene in the play, I . . . persuaded Captain Jack to take at look at it. He caught the spirit, and when I told him to go as far as he liked, he agreed.

. . . At the scene we had selected, [the heroine and hero] were about to be slowly burned by the Indians, who were whooping around the two fires raging brightly on either side of the stage. Captain Jack could no longer contain himself. He sprang to the stage and laid low the Indians. Nine redskins bit the dust! The curtain came down as if to close off the disastrous scene. Captain Jack came out, panting and exhausted, as if waking from a trance. . . .

168 William Brady on Touring the West in the 1880s–90s

William A. Brady, *Showman* (New York: E. P. Dutton, 1937), pp. 46–53, 60–64

. . . the lowest I sank was playing with the melodrama company at the worst saloon-theater joint in Portland, Oregon. At that period Portland was just two streets on the Columbia River, pretty wide open and tough. . . . I arrived in town as a member of a fairly respectable company touring with Irish plays. But business was so bad that, two days after we hit town, the manager jumped the show, taking the cash box along after the immemorial custom of managers, and left his company as flat as a tenderfoot after one of the local gambling hells was finished with him. . . .

. . . on the Coast . . . we played in anything – theaters with full equipment of scenery were relatively rare and we had to carry our own. A platform of wide boards on trestles in one end of a schoolhouse, with candles or kerosene lamps set along the edge for footlights, was plenty good enough. Or, lacking a school-house, the local eating-house dining room would serve. Our portable scenery was painted on canvas which would fold up to travel in trunks, then taken out and tacked up on walls or strung across the stage on ropes, like the week's wash. And, if the scenery we found in a third-rate theater was so worn you couldn't tell whether it represented a swamp or a desert, we tacked our own over the worn paint on the theater's flats. It was wonderful what you could pack away in a trunk . . .

In the process of playing everything from farce to *Hamlet*, we paid very little attention to copyright and royalties. Back then nobody bothered with such details, except the flossiest theaters in the largest towns where performances were conspicuous and a checkup easy. The bootleg playbroker flourished in the land. . . . If the author could hunt out an illicit performance in Tombstone or Ashtabula or Pierre, he could sue. But hunting them out was expensive and ten to one you couldn't collect from a barnstorming manager even if you got a verdict, so there was very little point in resistance.

Many actors did not tour but remained members of specific stock companies. William Warren, Jr., son of the Philadelphia manager, spent virtually all of his career with the Boston Museum stock company (1847–83), reportedly having given 13,345 performances of 577 characters. No actor of this period was identified so thoroughly with a single theatre; his versatility as a comic actor was virtually limitless, although he excelled with eccentric types such as Dogberry, Sir Peter Teazle, Polonius, and Touchstone.[1]

[1] For a good contemporary overview of Warren's career see Evelyn Greenleaf Sutherland, "William Warren," pp. 178–93, in *Famous American Actors of To-Day*, ed. Frederic E. McKay and Charles E. L. Wingate (New York, 1896).

169   Henry Austin Clapp on William Warren, Jr., 1902

Henry Austin Clapp, *The Reminiscences of a Dramatic Critic* (Boston: Houghton Mifflin Co., 1902), pp. 53–71; excerpts reprinted in *The American Theatre*, ed. Moses and Brown, pp. 82–83 and Young, *Famous Actors and Actresses on the American Stage*, 11: 1146–47

. . . Of the modern mode of histrionic vagabondage [William Warren] had no experience, – no experience, of course, of the mercenary "star" system, which binds the artist to very numerous repetitions of a very few plays. . . . As I look back upon Mr. Warren and his playing, the lives of all his rivals seem narrow, monotonous, and unfruitful. His art touched life, as life is presented in the drama, at ten thousand points. His plays were in every mode and mood of the Comic Muse, and ranged in quality from the best of Shakespeare to the worst of Dr. [Joseph Stevens] Jones. In old-fashioned farces, with their strong, sometimes vulgar, often noisy, usually vital fun; in tawdry patriotic or emotional melodramas; in standard old English comedies; in cheap local pieces, narrow and petty in their appeal; in delicate French comediettas, whose colors are laid on with a brush like Meissonier's; in English versions of the best Parisian dramas, subtle, sophisticated, exigent of *finesse* and *adresse* in the player, – in each and all of these Mr. Warren was easily chief among many good actors; to the demands of each and all he was amply adequate. The one fault of this style was a slight excess in the use of stentorian tones, – the result, I suspect, of his early immersion in farce, – and his gift of pathetic suggestion, though generally sure, did not always have the deepest penetrative power. Otherwise, it may be said, with sober scruple for the exact truth, that Mr. Warren was nearly faultless. His acting seemed the fine flower of careful culture, as well as the free outcome of large intelligence and native genius. . . . So Mr. Warren was a school and conservatory of acting in himself. . . .

Acting in a stock company was a demanding task, especially under the eye of an actress–manager like Louisa Lane Drew.[1]

[1] For this aspect of the Arch Street's history and function, see Rosemarie K. Bank, "Louisa Lane Drew at the Arch Street Theatre: Repertory and Actor Training in Nineteenth Century Philadelphia," *Theatre Studies*, 24/25 (1977–79), 37–46.

170   Memoirs of the Arch Street Theatre, Philadelphia, 1905

A. Frank Stull, "Where Famous Actors Learned Their Art," *Lippincott's Monthly*, 75 (March 1905), 372–79

Nearly every member of the company was constantly in apprehension of the Duchess [Louisa Lane Drew]. She used to sit in a box and watch the performance with a hawk's eye that nothing escaped . . .

Mrs. Drew had a way of putting up for a long time with things that she felt should be remedied; but, little by little, as her patience ebbed, her silence would become more pronounced, like the lull before the storm; then, some day, upon arriving at the theatre, she would walk into the box office and don a certain red Paisley shawl which . . . fittingly reflected her mood. So long as that shawl was in evidence, all the people of the Arch, from stage carpenter to leading man, realized that perfection in the performance of duty was the smallest return they could give for their salaries . . .

The season at the Arch lasted from the first Saturday in September until the Fourth of July. For the first thirteen nights Mrs. Drew appeared in some role for which she was famous. . . . She had an erudite trick of hunting up old comedies and dramas that made new members of the company memory-sore and heartsick.

. . . An actor who did not happen to know [these old plays] had to learn and be able to reel off his part perfectly, with a change for every night.

After the thirteen introductory performances a star usually descended from somewhere out of nowhere, about every two weeks, and we were expected to support him. It was quite customary to put on three and four pieces a night. . . . I expected, usually, to break the back of a new part in an afternoon, and it was a giant of a role that the average actor of the old stock company could not conquer within forty-eight hours.

Actor–managers like Mrs. Drew eventually evolved into "directors" like Augustin Daly who is generally recognized as America's first régisseur. The following two excerpts suggest Daly's working methods from the viewpoint of actresses in the company.

171   Dora Knowlton on Augustin Daly, 1910

Dora Knowlton, *Diary of a Daly Debutante* (New York: Duffield, 1910; reprinted New York: Benjamin Blom, 1977), pp. 6, 130–31

. . . for some time I watched the principals in a little one-act play called *Love's Young Dream*, which is to precede *Newport*.[1] All the company was present, some on the stage, others sitting at the side, and a few persons were out in the auditorium. Mr. Daly sat on an old wooden chair on the stage with his back to the footlights, so close to them I thought he would surely topple over; old Mr. [John] Moore held the book of the play, and the actors moved slowly about the stage with manuscript copies of their *roles* in their hands and read their lines aloud. Mr. Daly would often bounce up to rush to some actor, twisting and turning him about, waving his long arms, and going through the funniest motions showing him how to do things; then he would return to the kitchen chair, push that hat a little farther to the back of his head, and watch the action until he felt called upon to bounce up again. . . .

We rehearse almost all day long. . . . He is a wonderful teacher of acting; I believe he could teach a broomstick to act; he shows everyone just how to move, to speak, to look; he seems to know instinctively just how everything should go to get the best effect. . . .

Mr. Daly usually sits in one of the orchestra chairs during rehearsals, about five rows back, with folded arms, hat on the back of his head, watching everything with those keen blue eyes; suddenly he will stop someone in the midst of a speech and request that person to repeat the lines or perform some bit of business in a different manner. Then, if the change does not suit him, he springs to his feet and rushes up on the stage, striding over the backs of the chairs and along a plank laid from the orchestra railings across the footlights. He darts about the stage, with his coattails fairly flying, while he talks fast, gesticulates emphatically, and assumes the most peculiar attitudes to illustrate his meaning, winding up with "Now do you see?" Then he strides over the chairs again, sits down and the rehearsal goes on.

[1] *Love's Young Dream* and *Newport; or, The Swimmer, the Singer, and the Cypher*, the latter by Olive Logan (Sykes), were presented to open the 1879 season as the first productions in the new Daly's Theatre.

172   Clara Morris on Daly, 1870s

Clara Morris, *Life on the Stage* (New York: McCure, Phillips & Co., 1901), pp. 326–32

Before I came under the management of Mr. Daly, I may say I never really knew what stage management meant. . . .

. . . he had the entire play before his "mind's eye," and when he told me to do a thing, I should have done it, even had I not understood why he wished it done. But he always gave a reason for things, and that made it easy to work under him.

His attention to tiny details amazed me. . . . One of my early experiences of his way of directing a rehearsal made a deep impression upon me. In the play of *Jezebel* I had the title part. There were a number of characters on in the scene, and Mr. Daly wanted to get me across the stage, so that I should be out of hearing distance of two of the gentlemen. Now, in the old days, the stage director would simply have said: "Cross to the Right," and you would have crossed because he told you to; but in Mr. Daly's day you had to have a *reason* for crossing the drawing room, and so getting out of the two gentlemen's way – and a reason could not be found.

Here are a few of the many rejected ideas: There was no guest for me to cross to in welcoming pantomime; no piano on that side of the room for me to cross to and play on softly; ah, the fireplace! and the pretty warming of one foot? But no, it was summertime, that would not do. The ancient fancywork, perhaps? No, she was a human panther, utterly incapable of so domestic an occupation. The fan forgotten on the mantelpiece? Ah, yes, that was it! you cross the room for that – and then suddenly I reminded Mr. Daly that he had, but a moment before, made a point of having me strike a gentleman sharply on the cheek with my fan.

"Oh, confound it, yes!" he answered, "and that's got to stand – that blow is good!"

The old, old device of attendance upon the lamp was suggested; but the hour of the day was plainly given by one of the characters as three o'clock in the afternoon.

These six are but few of the many rejected reasons for that one cross of the stage; still Mr. Daly would not permit a motiveless action, and we came to a momentary standstill. Very doubtfully, I remarked: "I suppose a smelling bottle would not be important enough to cross the room for?"

He brightened quickly – clouded over even more quickly: "Y-e-e-s! N-o-o! at least, not if it had never appeared before. But let me see – Miss Morris, you must carry that smelling bottle in the preceding scene, and – and, yes, I'll just put in a line in your part, making you ask some one to hand it to you – that will nail attention to it, see! Then in this scene, when you leave these people and cross the room to get your smelling bottle from the mantel, it will be a perfectly natural action on your part, and will give the men their chance of explanation and warning." And at last we were free to move on to other other things.[1]

[1] Morris joined Daly in 1871, first gaining attention in *Article 47* in 1872, and left in 1873, after a disagreement and a better offer from Lester Wallack. *Jezebel*, adapted by Boucicault from a French play by Lessière, was presented in the spring of 1871.

The stock company operated on a "lines of business" concept which was the subject of this 1888 survey.

173   Survey of Actors According to Lines of Business, 1888[1]

Harrison Grey Fiske, ed., *The New York Mirror Annual* (New York, 1888), pp. 161–86; reproduced in Benjamin McArthur, *Actors and American Culture, 1880–1920* (Philadelphia: Temple University Press, 1984), pp. 13–14

Actors	No.	%	Actresses	No.	%
Line					
Stars	68	4.7	Stars	73	77
Leading Men	138	9.5	Leading ladies	151	16.0
Heavy leads	7	.5	Heavy leads	2	.2
Leading heavies	47	3.3	Leading heavies	17	1.8
Heavies	100	6.9	Heavies	16	1.7
Character actors	222	15.4	Characters	47	5.0
Leading old men	8	.6	Leading old women	4	.4
Old men	108	7.5	Old women	82	8.7
Character old men	17	1.2	Character old women	7	.7
Eccentric old men	2	.1	Eccentric old women	4	.4
Leading juveniles	48	3.3	Singing old women	2	.2
Juveniles	162	11.2	Leading juveniles	47	5.0
Singing juveniles	1	.1	Juveniles	128	13.5
Leading comedians	19	1.3	Singing juveniles	3	.3
Comedians	251	17.4	Leading comediennes	7	.7
Singing comedians	40	2.8	Comediennes	18	1.9
Light comedians	34	2.4	Eccentric comediennes	12	1.3
Low comedians	11	.8	Light comediennes	3	.3
Eccentric comedians	47	3.3	Singing comediennes	2	.2
Character comedians	7	.5	Ingenues	24	2.5
Walking gentlemen	22	1.5	Leading soubrettes	4	.4
Singing walking			Singing soubrettes	65	6.9
gentlemen	1	.07	Soubrettes	138	14.6

[1] For a study of this phenomenon, see James C. Burge, *Lines of Business: Casting Practice and Policy in the American Theatre 1752–1899* (New York: Peter Lang, 1986).

Responsible	16	1.1	Boy's parts	6	.6
Utility	60	4.1	Singing chambermaid	1	.1
Total	1,436	99.6	Chambermaid	1	.1
			Walking ladies	24	2.5
			Responsible utility	10	1.0
			Utility	22	2.3
			Children's parts	25	2.6
			Total	945	99.6

"Lines of business" began to be eliminated during the 1870s to 90s. James A. Herne, actor–playwright, compares the old-school actor of the 1860s with those of the 1890s.

174   James A. Herne on Lines of Business, 1899

"Forty Years before the Foot-Lights," *Coming Age*, 2 (August 1899), 121–29;[1] portions in Young, *Famous Actors and Actresses on the American Stage*, 1: 508–10

Q. Tell us something about the old stock company [of the 1860s and earlier].

A. It differed totally from the modern company. . . . It possessed some points of advantage over the present order, but there were also many disadvantages. In its very nature it was static rather than dynamic, – a machine with grooves in which the different actors were to take their respective places, and from this stationary vantage ground act all the parts belonging to their line, regardless of the eternal fitness of things. Thus, for example, the part of the leading lady might call for a slender, willowy figure, but the first lady might be as stout and rubicund as one of the Merry Wives of Windsor. I have seen leading roles, which called for a man tall and of graceful carriage, enacted by a veritable Falstaff in build; and this was one of the least objections. Men and women who were temperamentally unfit even to grasp the sentiments to be portrayed, and were in every way immeasurably inferior to some other members of the company for the impersonation of certain roles, demanded these parts because, according to precedent, the leading man or lady, or the first juvenile, or the heavy man had had the role when the play had been first produced.

The members of the old stock company were, as a rule, hired for a season of forty-two weeks. The company was made up as follows:

Leading Man.	Respectable Utility.
1st Juvenile Man.	General Utility.
2d Juvenile Man.	Leading Lady.
1st Heavy Man.	Juvenile Lady.

[1] This lengthy interview includes fascinating anecdotes of older actors, especially Edwin Forrest, John McCullough, and McKean Buchanan, Herne's earliest stage experiences (including benefits), and his real beginnings in California.

2d Heavy Man.

1st Walking Gent.

2d Walking Gent.

1st Singing Walking Gent.

2d Singing Walking Gent.

1st Old Man.

2d Old Man.

1st Comedian.

2d Comedian.

1st Walking Lady

2d Walking Lady.

1st Heavy Woman.

2d Heavy Woman.

1st Old Woman.

2d Old Woman.

1st Singing Chambermaid.

2d Singing Chambermaid.

Utility.

Ballet.

Now, every season in the principal cities some of the really great actors appeared for a short time and were supported by the stock company, just as during one season in the eighties Booth appeared at the Boston Museum supported by the stock company of that theater. . . . It was the most liberal education the ordinary actor received to witness nightly men like Forrest, for example.

Q. Do you think the old actors were as great as those of our time?

A. Oh, yes; greater, much greater, when all things are considered. . . .

Now, the old stock not unfrequently took these idiotic parts [in old, artificial plays] and made them live for the time, – made the audience actually forget their impossibility and absurdity. . . . If they were alive now they would be greater than men occupying the same relative positions on the stage today. There were some very great people on the stage in those days, more relatively than there are today, and the cause of their being so great lies, I think, in the fact that there was no incentive for a man or woman to go on the stage. They were ostracized from society; the salary was small and very uncertain, so that only those people gravitated to the stage who were impelled by an inherent love of the art to go there. Now all this is changed. Today it is an easy way of earning a living. Salaries are good; the world has taken them up; cheap magazines have become largely picture galleries for popular actors and actresses, – so that it is not strange that all sorts of people go on the stage. . . .

Q. How did the performances in those days compare with those of the present time?

A. . . . They were less complete from an artistic point of view, because everyone went on his own idea of things. There was no director or manager working for a consistent whole and directing and coaching the various actors. What you did on the stage then was your own. That was where you showed whether you were a genius or not. How much of the scene you could dominate and carry away from the other fellows – that showed what you could do. . . .

Q. Do you not believe that the stage will more and more become a practical educator along lines of real progress?

A. I certainly do. As I have said before . . . I believe the tendency of the stage is onward and upward, and I believe it is going to become more and more an ethical, economic, and sociological educator, – a real factor in forwarding the many-sided revolution or evolution which marks our present transition period.

With the breakup of the stock company system a need arose for a proper method of training young actors. Schools of acting appeared, as well as essays by performers on the technique and art of their profession. The following three documents are representative.

175   Essay on Schools of Acting, 1907

Algernon Tassin, "The American Dramatic Schools," *Bookman*, 25 (April 1907), 151–65

In 1884 Mr. Franklin Sargent . . . established his school [at the Lyceum Theatre]. . . . The venture marked the first attempt to place the teaching of acting on the same footing as the teaching of anything else, and to give a school of acting the same status and method as any other educational institution. . . .

Other schools followed in the steps of the pioneers. . . . Mr. F. F. Mackay and Mrs. Stanhope-Wheatcroft, who conduct the two other leading dramatic schools, retired from successful careers to devote themselves to teaching. . . .

Besides these schools, of course, there have always been sterling actors and actresses who give up some part of their time to pupils, pursuing thus the individual method of the [Paris] Conservatoire. . . . But not every teacher can find means to teach her fledgling the use of her wings on the actual stage itself, and the three schools above mentioned have solved the problem by bringing the stage to their pupils in public matinees at New York theatres. . . .

[The middle portion of the essay describes classes in makeup, voice, physical exercise and pantomime, and stage rehearsals.]

Thus through an entirely occupied day of six hours or more the student goes. Besides his regular classes and rehearsals, he must put in some time at lectures on the theory and science of his art; or its pictorial side, costuming, color, and decoration; on its historical and literary side, and on its psychological and spiritual side – all aiming to develop his intellectual appreciation and his imagination. . . .

. . . The cost of the six months' course ranges from $300 to $400. . . .

[Details follow on productions by the American Academy, noting that this school presented the first Maeterlinck, Ibsen, and Greek tragedy in New York.]

When the schools were first started, they met, strangely enough, with much opposition from the profession itself, and though they have made their way, even nowadays actors speak contemptuously of them. . . .

One sees nightly on our stage prominent actors by the score who are sadly in need of the technical skill they claim must be picked up at random on the boards themselves, and which, despite long and successful careers, they have not picked up. . . .

That there are plenty of "fake" schools . . . Acting is a profession which is in all its branches particularly at the mercy of bunco and blatancy. . . . All the big cities are full of such extemporized academies, devised at first to fill the intervals in a bad season or to eke out the summer vacation, and kept up afterward, as often as not, because it is found more profitable to be a teacher than a poor actor. . . .

The schools are training the rank and file. Not many, perhaps, out of each year's batch of theatrical beginners come from the schools or in any state of preparedness, but a little leaven has before this leavened many a lump. Even the most careless student cannot fail to learn much which many successful ones of his profession are in easy ignorance of, and an alert student can take away enough to revolutionize the little area he is allotted each year to inhabit. . . .

176   Pamphlet for Steele MacKaye's Conservatory, 1877[1]

Excerpts reproduced in Percy MacKaye, *Epoch – The Life of Steele MacKaye, Genius of the Theatre* (New York: Boni & Liveright, 1927), I: 267–69

The glory of dramatic art lies in its power to move the heart of the common mass to sympathy with the exceptional few, in their battle with vulgarity and selfishness, and in their struggle to attain to higher forms of manhood. So also its glory lies in its capacity to expose to the super-refined, the wealthy, the fortunate, and hypercultured, that divine spark which slumbers with latent power within the breast of the rudest and most untutored man.

Dramatic art – true to its highest destiny – would convert the theatre into an unsectarian temple, where both light and low would be brought into sympathetic rapport; where the most opposite classes might learn to understand each other better, and to love and respect each other more. But the theatre, in order to exert this influence, must be able to command the services of a corps of artists who can, by the perfection of their art, make the finest dramatic literature fascinating to those promiscuous masses of society upon whose support the existence of the theatre depends. . . .

The public has two distinct sides by which it may be won – its senses and its soul. The theatre appeals to the senses through the spectacular art of the scene painter and the sensational effects of the mechanician; it appeals to the soul through the emotional art of its actors. . . . The limited number of earnest, intelligent, disciplined actors, renders the emotional effects of a play far less certain

---

[1] MacKaye was not successful with this effort to establish a "Conservatoire Aesthetique, or School of Expression"; however, in 1885, at his innovative Lyceum Theatre on 4th Avenue, which he had built, he began an acting school that ultimately became the American Academy of Dramatic Arts.

of realization than its mechanical effects [scenography, says MacKaye, is far ahead of the art of the actor].

. . . [M]ore and more dangerous prominence [is being given] to the merely spectacular portion of theatric art. . . . the purely material side of the art threatens to outstrip the ideal and aesthetic side, and to end in dedicating the theatre to mere sensation and frivolity. . . .

Every aspirant to the stage should realize [the need to master his/her instrument], and hasten to acquire the same command of expression in his body that a good violinist possesses in his violin. . . . In the scenic art *behind* the actor, and in the musical art in *front* of him, preparatory training is essential to excellence and position. Why should the actor's art, which is the *center* and *core* to which the others are merely accessory, be an exception to this rule?

Genius may accomplish all things, but genius requires work to perfect its powers, and work often develops a genius latent and unsuspected. – *Genius is the power in the individual spontaneously to express the universal experiences of the race. It unmasks man to himself. It implies two distinct faculties: to feel, to express.*

The system of training used by Mr. MacKaye develops the student's faculty to feel by a scientific exposition of the natural facts and laws governing the manifestations of human emotions. It develops his faculty to express by thorough discipline in practical pantomime, stage business, and vocal gymnastics. *Thus it aims to equalize and increase the activity of these complementary faculties, ultimately rendering their cooperation so complete and instinctive as to endow the art of the actor with the crowning characteristic of genius, – spontaneity.* . . . It is to be hoped that his school may prove the germ from which there may be developed, at last, a permanent and national institution for aesthetic training in all its branches.

177   Speech, "Illusion of the First Time in Acting," by William Gillette, 1913[1]

Published in 1915, with an introduction by actor George Arliss, in "Papers on Acting" series for the Dramatic Museum of Columbia University (pp. 37–48); reprinted in *Papers on Acting*, ed. Brander Matthews (New York: Hill and Wang, 1958) and excerpted in Young, *Famous Actors and Actresses on the American Stage*, I: 427–30 and in *Actors on Acting*, ed. Toby Cole and Helen Krich Chinoy (New York: Crown, 1954), pp. 564–65

. . . the closeness to Life which now prevails has made audiences sensitive to thousands of minor things that would not formerly have affected them. To illustrate my meaning, I am going to speak to two classes of these defects. . . . There are plenty more where these two came from. . . . One I shall call, to distinguish it, "The Neglect of the Illusion of the First Time"; the other, "The Disillusion of Doing it Correctly." There is an interesting lot of them which might be assembled

---

[1] Gillette, an actor and playwright, delivered the speech in November 1913 at the fifth joint session of the American Academy of Arts and Letters and the National Institute of Arts and Letters in Chicago.

under the heading of "The Illusion of Unconsciousness of What Could Not Be Known" – but there will not be time to talk about it. All these groups, however, are closely related, and the First Time one is fairly representative. . . . I have separated a couple of these poisons so that you may see how they work, and incidentally how great little things now are.

Unfortunately for an actor [or an actress] . . . he knows or is supposed to know his part. He is fully aware – especially after several performances – of what he is going to say. The character he is representing, however, does *not* know what he is going to say; but, if he is a human being, various thoughts occur to him one by one, and he puts such of those thoughts as he decides to into such speech as he happens to be able to command at the time. Now it is a very difficult thing – and even now rather an uncommon thing – for an actor who knows exactly what he is going to say to behave exactly as though he didn't; to let his thoughts (apparently) occur to him as he goes along, even though they are there in his mind already; and (apparently) to search for and find the words by which to express those thoughts, even though these words are at this tongue's very end . . . Living and breathing creatures do not carry their words in that part of their systems; they have to find them and send them there – with more or less rapidity according to their facility in that respect – as occasion arises. . . .

This menace of death from neglect of the Illusion of the First Time is not confined to matters and methods of speech and mentality, but extends to every part of the presentation, from the most climactic and important action or emotion to the most insignificant item of behavior – a glance of the eye at some unexpected occurrence, the careless picking up of some small object which (supposedly) has not been seen or handled before. Take the simple matter of entering a room to which, according to the plot or story, the character coming in is supposed to be a stranger; unless there is vigilance the actor will waft himself blithely across the threshold, conveying the impression that he has at least been born in the house – finding it quite unnecessary to look where he is going and not in the least worthwhile to watch out for thoughtless pieces of furniture that may, in their ignorance of his approach, have established themselves in his path. . . . [Other examples follow.]

The foregoing are a few only of the numberless parts or items in drama presentation which must conform to the Illusion of the First Time. . . . there yet remains the spirit of the presentation as a whole. Each successive audience before which it is given must feel – not think or reason about, but *feel* – that it is witnessing, not one of a thousand weary repetitions, but a life episode that is being lived just across the magic barrier of the footlights. That is to say, the whole must have that indescribable life-spirit or effect which produces the Illusion of Happening for the First Time. Worth his weight in something extremely valuable is the stage director who can conjure up this rare and precious spirit!

The dangers to dramatic life and limb from the Disillusion of Doing It Correctly are scarcely less than those in the First Time class, but not so difficult to detect and eliminate. Speaking, breathing, walking, sitting, rising, standing, gesturing – in short behaving correctly, when the character under representation would not naturally or customarily do so – will either kill that character outright or make it very sick indeed. Drama can make its appeal only in the form of simulated life as it is lived – not as various authorities on grammar, pronunciation, etiquette, and elocution happen to announce at that particular time that it ought to be lived.

. . . To use every possible means and device for giving drama that which makes it drama – life-simulation – must be the aim of the modern play constructor and producer. And not alone ordinary errors, but numberless individual habits, traits, peculiarities are of the utmost value for this purpose.

Among these elements of life and vitality, but greatly surpassing all others in importance, is the human characteristic or essential quality which passes under the execrated name of personality . . . cheap or otherwise, inartistic or otherwise, and whatever it really is or is not, it is the most singularly important factor for infusing the life-illusion into modern stage creations that is known to man. Indeed, it is something a great deal more than important, for in these days of drama's close approximation to life, it is essential. . . .

The actors of recent times who have been universally acknowledged to be great have invariably been so because of their successful use of their own strong and compelling personalities in the roles which they made famous. . . . [As examples, he mentions Salvini's Othello, Booth's Hamlet, Jefferson's Rip, and lists others, including Irving, Terry, Modjeska, Fanny Janauschek, and Mary Anderson.]

. . . I am only too well aware that the foregoing view . . . is sadly at variance with what we are told is the highest form of the actor's art. According to the deep thinkers and writers on matters of the theatre, the really great actor is not one who represents with marvelous power and truth to life the characters within the limited scope of his personality, but the performer who is able to assume an unlimited number of totally divergent roles. . . . This . . . brings it down to a question of pure stage gymnastics. Watch the actor who can balance the largest number of roles in the air without allowing any of them to spill over. . . . In another art it would be: "Do not consider this man's paintings, even though masterpieces, for he is only a landscape artist. Find the chap who can paint forty different kinds." I have an idea the theatregoing public is to be congratulated that none of the great stage performers, at any rate of modern times, has entered for any such competition.

After the death of Daly in 1899, David Belasco was the most influential and powerful director–régisseur in the American theatre during the early 1900s.

178   David Belasco on Play Production, 1919

David Belasco, *The Theatre through Its Stage Door* (New York: Harper Brothers, 1919), pp. 53–89

. . . My first step in the practical work of production is to study out the scenes, which must be constructed as carefully as the play itself, for a skillfully devised scene is always of vital assistance to an episode. In this preliminary work I seldom follow the stage directions on the printed page. . . . I prefer to plan the scenes myself with reference to stage values.

. . . The feeling of the scene is always a great factor in determining its arrangement, for symbolism to a certain extent enters the production of every play. . . .

. . . as I become more familiar with the lines and episodes the scenes gradually form themselves. Then I make a rough sketch, taking into account the necessary arrangement of furniture or other properties and considering how the characters can be maneuvered to best advantage.

When I have settled these matters approximately, I send for my scenic artist. . . . I take the empty stage and, as far as possible, try to act the whole play, making every entrance and exit and indicating my ideas of the groupings of the characters and their surroundings. This process . . . will consume perhaps four or five evenings. . . .

. . . the scenic artist proceeds to make a drawing of the scenes . . . and thus we reach a definite starting point. In due course of time – it may be a week or a month – the scenic artist will have constructed the actual scene models which are set up in the perfectly equipped miniature theatre of my studio. But changes are always suggesting themselves and often these models . . . have to be taken apart and reconstructed several times.

It is time now to begin to consider what to me is the all-important factor in a dramatic production – the lighting of the scenes. With my electrician I again go over the play in detail. . . . When he has thoroughly grasped my ideas and become quite familiar with the play itself, we begin our experiments, using the miniature theatre and evolving our colors by transmitting white light through gelatin or silk of various hues. Night after night we experiment together to obtain color or atmospheric effects, aiming always to make them aid the interpretation of the scenes. . . .

. . . The greatest part of my success in the theatre I attribute to my feelings for colors, translated into effects of light. . . .

The scene models having been approved . . . it is time now to begin the building of the actual scenes. I turn my carpenters over to my scenic artist, who furnishes to them the plans. They then construct the scenery in my own shops. . . . I will allow nothing to be built out of canvas stretched on frames. Everything must be real. . . .

Meanwhile, if the play has a musical accompaniment, I read it to the composer

I have engaged, indicating its moods and feeling. He must interpret every scene and speech as if he were writing the score for a song. . . .

I generally prefer to leave the costuming until after the first week of rehearsals, when I am reasonably sure of my actors, unless it happens to be a costume play which I am producing. If it demands other than modern clothes, I write a full description for the characters, deciding whether their hair shall be smooth or shaggy and whether they shall or shall not wear beards, and then call a costume-designer into consultation. . . .

While all these various details of the production are moving along [except for the costuming] . . . I am hunting everywhere for my cast. In fact, I have been on the lookout for actors and actresses suitable to the various characters from the moment I made up my mind to accept the play. Applicants for parts come to my office in swarms. . . . I ransack the varieties and the cheap stock companies, and I both go to see the people and have them come to see me. . . . I would much prefer to have an actor resemble the character he is to represent than have him depend upon disguise and the assumption of manners, for my motto as a producer has been to keep as close to nature as possible. . . .

. . . [in casting actors with contrasting vocal qualities the] small details . . . are not ordinarily noticed by audiences; nevertheless, they are unconsciously felt, and consequently they become of utmost importance in every artistic production of a drama.

. . . In due course of time – I usually allot about six weeks to rehearsals of a play which does not offer unusual difficulties – notices are sent out for the people to assemble. . . . I introduce them to one another and treat them as guests in my drawing room, rather than as employees on my stage. . . .

As the following excerpts illustrate, knowledge of theatrical traditions from other parts of the world by American critics was slight. While frequently complimentary about acting, attitudes about other aspects of production (especially the final section here on the Chinese) were sometimes deprecatory and condescending.

179   Essays on the Foreign Stage in New York, 1900

Hutchins Hapgood, "The Foreign Stage in New York: I. The Yiddish Theatre," *Bookman*, 11 (June 1900), 348–58; Norman Hapgood, II. "The German Theatre," *Bookman*, 11 (July 1900), 452–58; Hutchins Hapgood, III. "The Italian Theatre," *Bookman*, 11 (August 1900), 545–53; Edward W. Townsend, IV. "The Chinese Theatre," *Bookman*, 11 (September 1900), 39–42.[1]

The Yiddish actors take themselves with peculiar seriousness, justified by the enthusiasm, almost worship, with which they are regarded by the people. Many

---

[1] This series of articles considers all aspects of these four ethnic theatres in New York; space prevents the inclusion of the full texts. The rich tradition of most non-English speaking theatre in the United States has been given considerable coverage in *Ethnic Theatre in the United States*, ed. Maxine Schwartz Seller (Westport, CT, and London: Greenwood Press, 1983).

a poor Jew, man or girl, who makes no more than $10 a week in the sweatshop, will spend $5 of it on the theatre, which is practically the only amusement of the ghetto Jew . . .

The actor responds to this popular enthusiasm with sovereign contempt. He struts about in the cafés on Canal and Grand Streets, conscious of his greatness. He refers to the crowd as "Moses" with superior condescension or humorous vituperation. Like thieves, the actors have a jargon of their own, which is esoteric and jealously guarded . . .

The Yiddish actor is so supreme that until recently a regular system of hazing playwrights was in vogue . . . When a new writer came to the theatre with a manuscript, various were the pranks the actors would play . . .

The managers and actors of the three theatres [the People's, the Windsor, and the Thalia] criticize one another indeed with charming directness, and they all have their followers in the ghetto and their special cafés on Grand or Canal Streets, where their particular prejudices are sympathetically expressed. The actors and lessees of the People's are proud of their fine theatre, proud that no babies go there. There is a great dispute between the supporters of this theatre and those of the Thalia as to which is the stronger company and which produces the most realistic plays. The manager of the Thalia maintains that the People's is sensational, and that his theatre alone represents true realism; while the supporter of the People's points scornfully to the larger number of operas produced at the Thalia. They both unite in condemning the Windsor as producing no new plays and as hopelessly behind the times.

. . . what makes the little house on Irving Place [the principal German theatre] so notable is something thoroughly familiar and intimate to the minds of cultivated Americans. It is merely that the drama, as we know it, is on a higher plan than it is in any other theatre in this city – on a very much higher plane than it was at Daly's during the lifetime of Mr. Daly . . .

For this superiority two causes are easily discovered. One is the audience. Germans come to this country with traditions connecting the playhouse with education and the life of the intelligence . . . Only part of the difference is the audience. Another point is that it is almost impossible to think of a cast that would play it [Max Halbe's *Jugend*] as well as did the members of Mr. [Heinrich] Conried's company . . .

In trying to tell how the actors at this theatre are superior to our American players one is met with the difficulties which always exist in describing solid, mature excellence. Let one quality stick out, and it is rather easy to give an eloquent picture of it; but the superiority of Mr. Conried's company consists in objectivity, in harmonious work together, and in versatility. The actors play farce, on the whole, perhaps, neither better nor worse . . . than our own superior farce companies, but these same actors can play the highest poetic dramas; they know how to recite verse, and they know the meaning of poetry. This is a prime requisite, if we are ever to have in English anything corresponding in quality to what we have in German ... From September 30 last, sixty-five dramas were played in Irving Place, and this number is smaller than it should have been [several productions had to be abandoned] ... On the list are plays by Schiller, Goethe, Lessing, Sudermann, Hauptmann, Freytag, and Shakespeare ... This is the kind of theatre that we need in English ...

On Spring Street, within a few blocks of the Bowery, the heart of the Italian quarter is laid open to the stranger [including one theatre proper and a puppet-show] ...

... of realism in the ordinary sense the Italian understands nothing. He has no respect for exact fact, and sees more compelling interest in these brilliant and noisy puppets than in the most intellectual and convincing comedy of manners or problem play ...

The regular theatre also satisfied the romantic and fiery Italian heart. The grace of the race ... and the spontaneous characters of its farce are manifested in a company of actors not particularly endowed with histrionic power, but possessing to the full the natural spirit and honest directness in passion and in fun of the people. Their farce is allied to their serious play in one important respect: it is pure fun, never approaches the comedy of manners, as it lacks entirely the intellectual and critical element; just as the serious play is pure passion and sentiment, without the reflective or philosophic element, which distinguishes the tragedy of the Anglo-Saxon, the German, and the Jew ... the actors make no pretence of knowing their lines. But the audience, simple and at the same time sensitive to what is fundamentally dramatic, do not mind in the least. Quick to respond to the emotional situation, they do not need realistic setting and devices to make them feel the illusion of the stage. That they ignore what are really trivial incongruities points to feeling and imagination, and in aesthetic competencey puts them far ahead of those *blasé* rounders on Broadway who watch closely the mechanics of the scene.

... The company [at the Teatro Italiano] has not, as a whole, much histrionic resource, and the subordinate parts are usually played without intelligence, except in the specifically Southern or Neapolitan play abounding in poverty, passion, and death ...

In comedy, too, the same quality as in the serious drama is predominant ... The excellence of the acting here also rests in the naturalness with which the unsophisticated characteristics of the race are rendered. They never play the hard, metallic, mechanical farce so popular at the uptown theatre – the same play may be given, but by the Italians it is softened, made more natural and more simply enjoyable ...

... The audience, the actors, are just the same as they might be in a little theatre in southern Italy, and the plays are imported, written by men in Italy. In this respect . . . there is a marked contrast between the Italian and the Yiddish stage in New York. On the latter there is much which portrays the life of the Jews in New York, an original and local element in the plays, for the making of which there are a number of Yiddish playwrights. The reason, no doubt, is that the Yiddish community have become once and for all identified with New York and are undergoing changes and modifications incident to a genuine life here; but the Italians remain Italians, dreaming of sunny Naples . . .

. . . Numerous visits to Chinese theatres in half a dozen American cities have never discovered a "bad house," a "frost," nor any of the ills which plague the drama in other theatres. The reason for this may be that the plays are given in installments serially, and this begets at once a suspended interest, for which all dramatists strive with damp, corrugated brows; and it also suspends judgment . . .

. . . the Chinese school of acting is impressionistic; and the Chinese knew all about impressionism thousands of years before we discovered the word and fondled it to death . . .

The little musty-brown entrance [on Mott Street] suggests that your guide is conveying you to a moonshine distillery or an unlicensed prizefight, it is so meagerly lighted, unobtrusive, narrow; shrinking away from the thoroughfare and reluctantly admitting to a snuffy hall, one of whose walls is portholed for a ticket seller, who, grave and unblinking, charges anywhere from five to ten times the usual price of admission, because a lounging Chinaman on the sidewalk, whose low, plaintive cry you noted, had thereby signalled that your guide had in charge a party of white devils whose dress denoted the propriety of charging five, six, ten prices, as it may be.

. . . The play is on; the stage is filled with characters; the orchestra is shrieking and clashing descriptive music; a tall man with a face made up to resemble those on china garden pots, in which flowers never grow, is incanting; and a number of stagehands are moving about in full sight, picking up properties used in a previous scene. The old gargoyle roars, pulls his moustaches, which reach to his breast, stamps his thick-soled shoes, and talks and talks and talks. When he gets tired of standing still he stalks in long strides across the stage and talks some more, and raps the floor with the butt of a handsome bamboo lance. All the while he talked, but as he talked one was forced by some power no school of acting can teach to watch the silent, motionless figure of the actor, richly dressed, evidently playing the part of the princess in distress. "She" had scarcely moved for minutes; certainly not more than the slow raising of eyelids, the nervous trembling of dainty finger tips . . . the actor seemed to know that the art of paramount value in acting is the art of – repose?

III. *Theatre Buildings*

Opening on February 3, 1869, with a production of *Romeo and Juliet*, Edwin Booth's "Temple of Art" was designed by the distinguished architect James Renwick, Jr. Although the configuration of the stage and auditorium were traditionally nineteenth century, there were numerous technical innovations (described in the documents). Booth's control of his theatre, due to poor financial management, lasted only four years. After numerous managements Booth's was rebuilt as a department store in 1883; the structure was razed in the 1960s.

180 Description of Booth's Theatre, 1869

Harper's Weekly, 13 (January 9, 1869), 21–22

This new theatre . . . has its frontage on Twenty-third Street. Mr. Booth designs that it shall become . . . the best theatre in this country, both as an edifice and on account of its stage representations.

The building is in the Renaissance style of architecture, and stands 70 feet high from the sidewalk to the main cornice, above which is a Mansard roof of 24 feet.[1]

That part of the building occupied as the theatre proper extends 149 feet along Twenty-third Street, and is divided into three parts, so combined as to form a superb ensemble, with arched entrances as either extremity on the side for the admission of the public, and on the other for the use of the actors and others employed in the house. Directly in the center of this frontage are three other

---

[1] Contemporary sources do not agree on the various dimensions of Booth's Theatre. See, for example, an even more detailed description in the New York *Tribune*, November 18, 1868 (written two months before the Theatre opened); transcribed in William C. Young, *Famous American Playhouses: Documents of American Theater History* (Chicago: American Library Association, 1973), I: 195 ff. A later description of interest is William Winter's in *Life and Art of Edwin Booth* (New York: MacMillan Co., 1893), pp. 46–52. Some of the contradictions are resolved in Loren Hufstetler, "A Physical Description of Booth's Theatre, New York, 1869–1883," *Theatre Design and Technology*, 43 (Winter 1976), 8–18.

doors, devised for the purpose of securing the most rapid egress of a crowded audience in case of fire or any other sudden emergency. . . . Between these entrance doors, and on either side, are spacious and lofty windows, while above them, and forming a part of the second story, are roomy niches, surrounded by coupled columns resting on finely sculptured pedestals. Between these columns, at the depths of the recesses, are neat pilasters, sustaining the elliptic arches that will serve to crown and span the niches, the latter to be occupied by statues of the great dramatic authors and interpreters of every age and country. The main niche in the center is flanked on either side by curiously-contrived blank windows. This entire façade, as well as that on Sixth Avenue, is built of the finest Concord granite, from the best quarries in New Hampshire.

The interior is subdivided . . . into four heights, the first and lowermost embracing the parquette, circle, and orchestra seats, capable of accommodating eight hundred persons. The second tier is thrown into the dress circle; the third is the family circle, and the fourth constitutes the gallery or amphitheatre. The stage is 55 feet in breadth, and 75 feet in depth, by 50 feet in total height, and . . . is set in a beautiful ornamental framework. . . . On either side of the stage the boxes are tastefully arranged on a novel style of substantial comfort and elegant adornments. Immediately opposite, on the other side of the building and in a line with the stage, are the scene rooms, and above them the painting saloon. Parallel with the range the green room, general dressing rooms, and managers' offices. This part of the building is five stories in height, so distributed as to contain the apartments necessary for the actors, coryphers of *ballet*, and the corps of assistants of all grades connected with the theatre. . . .

181   **Interior of Booth's Theatre, 1869. Watercolor by Charles W. Witham, Showing the First-Act Setting for *Romeo and Juliet***

Theatre Collection, Museum of the City of New York

182   O. B. Bunce's Backstage Description of Booth's Theatre, 1870

O. B. Bunce, "Behind, Below, and Above the Scenes," *Appletons' Journal*, 3 (May 28, 1870), 589–94

. . . We are first led, not beneath the stage at all, but to the spacious excavations under the sidewalks, where we find the carpenters' shop and a great array of timber, and, to our surprise, large boilers, and an engine pursuing its noiseless task. This engine in the daytime . . . gives motive power to the machinery in the carpenters' busy quarter, elevates the Croton to the huge water tanks at the top of the building by which the hydraulic rams, hereafter to be mentioned, are worked, and at night sets a huge fan in motion under the auditorium, which in summertime fills the theatre with cool, and in the winter with warm air. We may note that the rise of each seat in parquet and circle is pierced with numerous circular holes, through which constant ventilation is secured for every rapt listener above. . . . Descending numerous steps, we emerge beneath the stage. . . . The great hydraulic rams . . . lie beneath this spot; they act as the power that thrusts up and lets down the scenes.

Usually in theatres the scenes are principally on the stage, set in grooves, and run in by hand from the sides to meet in a common center. In some instances scenes are hung on large rollers, and let down or wound up by ropes adjusted for the purpose. But at Booth's Theatre is the first instance we have of scenes worked altogether by machinery, which are lifted from below, by means so carefully and accurately adjusted that the scene almost noiselessly, and with perfect precision, glides upward into its place. This is effected by hydraulic rams. . . . To the auditor, comfortably seated in the theatre, the scene rises like magic, often transporting him with its beauty. . . . We also note . . . a series of platforms; these are under the traps on the stage, from which mounts the ghostly or other visitor, or upon which descend the disappearing genii. These platforms, called bridges, are lifted and moved by the rams.

We may now ascend to the level of the stage. . . . The visitor at Booth's has doubtless noted that the stage is not dressed after the old style. The side wings, that in other theatres stand at right angles to the spectator, are abolished, and instead there is an arrangement by which the scene apparently extends to the right and the left, as well as to the rear. When seated at the side of the theatre, you do not look between the wings, but your vision is confronted, if the scene is a room, by enclosed walls; if an exterior, by rocks, or trees, or plains, that recede, and carry the eye off into imaginary space. . . .

Now let us leave the level of the stage and ascend. We wind up a circular stairway that seems almost endless, and arrive at what is called the "fly-gallery." . . . We here see the flies – the top scenes that are let down from above, to meet and unite with those that are sent up from below. They hang in a long array, and are moved by manual force, aided by countless ropes and pulleys – a very wilderness of ropes. . . . At this point we are sixty-five feet above the level of the stage, and ninety-five feet above the rams hidden darkly away in the depths far below the stage . . .

Above the fly-galleries, and crowning all, is the great, gloomy, spacious "rigging-loft." This is directly under the roof, and above the pendant flies . . .

. . . the scene-painter's room . . . is situated on the right side of the stage, as you face it, in a portion of the building formed by an L. It is admirably arranged for its purpose, the scenes being adjusted against the walls, and movable up and down at the painter's will, through openings in the floor . . .

. . . The "property room" gathers within its fold a marvellous curiosity-shop . . . a multitude of things, in fact, more numerous than can readily be catalogued. The "armory," if not a collection of such strange things, is interesting, and looks as if we were wandering through some ancient tower or castle rather than "behind the scenes" at a theatre.

183   Illustration from Bunce, Beneath the Stage – Traps and Platforms, 1870

184   Bunce, Rigging Lofts, Showing Upper Portion of Act-Drop, 1870

185   Bunce, Working Fly-Gallery, 1870

The concert saloon, especially popular on the American frontier in mining-camp towns, was roughly parallel to the British song and supper rooms.[1] Whereas that venue is considered one of the predecessors of the music hall, the concert saloon was a forerunner of the later and more respectable vaudeville house. In these basic playhouse facilities, vivid contrast to the elaborate urban theatre complexes represented in this chapter, enterprising saloon owners found a way to cater to the lower elements of the burgeoning urban population with an entertainment atmosphere overtly masculine, rough, and bawdy.

[1] Concert saloons were certainly not limited to smaller frontier towns. By the late 1850s and early 1860s such venues were well established in New York, where there were over 300 such establishments (mainly around Broadway and on the Bowery), and in other major Eastern cities.

186   Description of a Concert Saloon in Cheyenne, Wyoming, 1877

"Across the Continent," *Frank Leslie's Illustrated Newspaper,* October 13, 1877, pp. 85–86

For two or three blocks the main street of Cheyenne keeps up a character of solid respectability . . . but it soon drops such mimicry of the "effete East," and relapses into a bold disregard of architectural forms and proprieties. The oddest examples of this are in the two theatres, owned and "run" by an enterprising citizen, who also keeps one of the largest gambling establishments in town. . . . The larger of the theatres – "variety shows" in the fullest sense of the term – connects with the gambling rooms and bar, in a long, low brick building, which hangs out numerous flaming red signs under the moonlight. Entering the bar-room, the curious visitor is confronted by a glittering show of chandeliers, fresh paint, cheap gilding and mirrors, and some extraordinary frescoes, supposedly of Yosemite views, which blaze in every conceivable gradation of color over the bar itself. Turning to the right, we enter a passage leading to the parquette, or pit, of the theatre; a narrow flight of stairs passes up to what, in the East, would be the dress circle; but in the Cheyenne house is a single tier of small boxes, open at the back upon a brightly lighted passageway. At the head of the stairs is another and smaller bar, from which the waitresses procure strong drinks, to be served to order in the boxes aforesaid; and over the staircase is posted a gentle hint, couched in the words: "Gents, Be Liberal" – a hint not likely to be ignored in Cheyenne, we fancy.

From these little boxes, gay with tawdry paintings and lace hangings, we look down upon as odd a scene as ever met critical New York eyes. The auditorium departs from the conventional horseshoe pattern, and is shaped rather like a funnel, expanding at the mouth to the width of the stage. It is so narrow that we, leaning out of one box, could almost shake hands with our opposite neighbors. The trapeze, through which the wonderful Mlle. Somebody is flying and frisking like a bird, are all swung from the stage to the back of the house, so that her silken tights and spangles whisk past within a hand's-breadth of the admiring audience, who can exchange civilities, or even confidences, with her in her aerial flight. Below, the floor is dotted with round tables and darkened with a sea of hats; a dense fog of cigar smoke floats above them, and the clink of glasses rings a cheerful accompaniment to the orchestra, as the admiring patrons of the variety business quaff brandy and "slings," and cheer on the performers with liberal enthusiasm. The house, for all its cheap finery of decoration, its barbaric red and yellow splashes of paint, and *bizarre* Venuses and Psyches posing on the walls, is wonderfully well-ordered and marvelously clean; the audience, wholly masculine, is unconventional (let us put it courteously), but not riotous. As for the performance, it is by no means bad, and the trapeze feats are indeed excep-

tionally startling and well executed. The hours of the entertainment are from
8 p.m. until 2 a.m., while the doors of the connecting gambling saloons are
never closed.

187   Interior of Cheyenne Concert Saloon, 1877

"Across the Continent," *Frank Leslie's Illustrated Newspaper*

As gutted and redesigned by the visionary Steele MacKaye in 1879, the Madison Square
Theatre, previously Daly's first Fifth Avenue Theatre (structure built in 1862), became one
of the more advanced theatres in America, boasting a double stage, its most famous feature, a somewhat crude air-conditioning system, his invention of the folding chair, the
orchestra placed above the stage, and experiments in atmospheric stage lighting. When
MacKaye's most famous play was staged there, *Hazel Kirke*, the program underscored the
time saved between acts (between Acts I and II, forty-five seconds; between Acts II and
III, eight minutes; and between Acts III and IV, two minutes). The theatre was also noted
for its simple elegance. With a capacity of only 700, it was compared by some to a drawing
room. The theatre was razed in 1908.

188   Cross-Section Drawing of the Elevator Stage at Madison Square Theatre, 1879

Scientific American, 50 (April 5, 1884), 207

189   Description of the Elevator Stage at Madison Square Theatre, 1884

A condensed version of a longer description from *Scientific American* (p. 208) in Albert A. Hopkins, *Magic: Stage Illusion and Scientific Diversion* (New York: Munn, 1897), p. 271[1]

. . . The first movable stage is probably that which the late Steele Mackaye patented in 1869. The details of Mackaye's patent were not completely worked out,

---

[1] The *Scientific American* text (excerpts) is reproduced in Hewitt, *Theatre U.S.A.*, pp. 236–37. Hopkins
also includes in his book descriptions of the inventions for MacKaye's ill-fated "Spectatorium,"
planned for the Chicago World's Fair in 1893. For studies of this visionary project see Tim Fort's
essays "Steele MacKaye's Lighting Visions for *The World Finder*," *Nineteenth Century Theatre*, 18
(1990), 35–51, and "Three Voyages of Discovery: The Columbus Productions of Imre Kiralfy, E. E.
Rice, and Steele MacKaye," *Journal of American Drama and Theatre*, 5 (Spring 1993), 5–30.

but this was done by Mr. Nelson Waldrop, the stage machinist, who elaborated the system and obtained a patent on it. The stage . . . is moved up and down in the same manner as an elevator car, and is operated so that either of its divisions can be easily and quickly brought to the proper level in front of the auditorium. This enables the stagehands to get one scene ready while the other one is in view of the audience. The shaft through which the hugh elevator moves up and down measures one hundred and fourteen feet from the roof to the bottom. The stages are moved up and down in a compact, two-floored structure of timber strapped with iron, and knitted together with truss beams above and below, and substantially bound by tie and tension rods. The whole construction is fifty-five feet high and twenty-two feet wide and thirty-one feet deep, and weighs about forty-eight tons. A vertical movement of the structure or car is twenty-five feet two inches at each change. The car is suspended at each corner by two steel cables, each of which would be capable of supporting the entire structure. These cables pass upward over sheaves or pulleys set at different angles, and thence downward to a saddle to which they are all connected. Secured to this saddle is a hoisting cable attached to a hoisting drum, by the rotation of which the stage is raised or lowered. Only about forty seconds are required to raise or lower the stage into position, and the entire structure is moved by four men at the winch. The movement is effected without sound, jar, or vibration, owing to the balancing of the stage and its weight with counterweights, which are suspended from the saddle to which the cables supporting the stage are attached.

The borders and border lights are supplied to each of the movable stages, and each stage has its own trap floor, with traps and guides and windlasses for raising the traps. The space for operating the windlass under the top stage is about six feet . . . while the play is proceeding before the audience, the stagehands [set] the scene on the stage above.

190   Steele MacKaye's Patent Drawings for the Elevator Stage at Madison Square Theatre, 1879

Percy MacKaye, *Epoch*, II: xli.
Figure 1: a front view of stage and orchestra; figure 2: a vertical section of the stages at line xx of figure 3; figure 3: a plan or top view of the same with the casing removed.

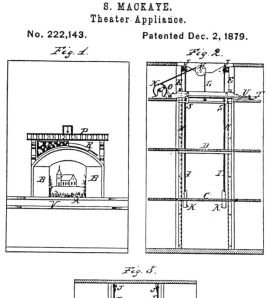

S. MACKAYE.
Theater Appliance.
No. 222,143.   Patented Dec. 2, 1879.

Fig. 1.   *Fig. 2.*

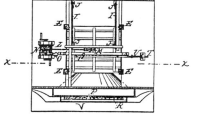

Fig. 3.

Witnesses   Inventor.
John W. Bipley   Steele MacKaye
Boyd Eliot   by S. J. Gordon
                                his Atty.

191   Madison Square Theatre Program Cover, 1880

Wilmeth Theatre Collection, Providence, RI

With a trend toward bigger and more complex theatres, offering variety as well as legitimate theatre, Oscar Hammerstein opened on November 30, 1895, his pleasure palace on Broadway between 44th and 45th Streets. It featured two theatres, a concert hall, a roof garden, bowling alleys, restaurants, and other amusement venues. Unfortunately, like most of Hammerstein's projects, this one ultimately failed. In 1899 the two theatres became the New York and Criterion Theatres. The roof garden in 1907 introduced what became the prototype of Follies-type revues; after several other mutations, the theatres were razed in 1935.

192   Main Floor Plan of Oscar Hammerstein's Olympia, 1895

William H. Birkmire, *The Planning and Construction of American Theatres* (New York: John Wiley and Sons, 1901), p. 43

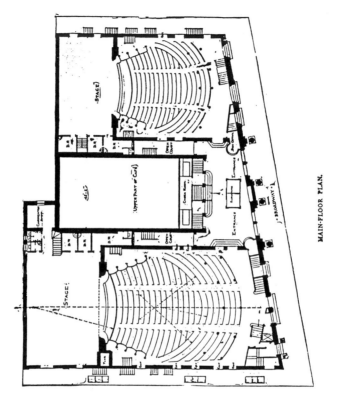

193   Dimensions of Oscar Hammerstein's Theatres, 1895

Birkmire, *The Planning and Construction of American Theatres*, pp. 41–47

The building has a frontage of 203 feet on Broadway, 156 feet on Forty-fifth Street, and a little less on Forty-fourth Street. The greatest height of the building is 96 feet at the center of the Broadway side . . .

The dimensions of the music hall are: auditorium, 70 x 100 feet; stage, 43 x 70 feet; proscenium opening, 36 x 36 feet; height to rigging-loft, 80 feet; height to fly-gallery, 30 feet . . .

Ample provision has been made for seating in the music hall. There are six tiers of boxes and five tiers of mezzanine boxes, making a total of 124, the largest number known of any single place of amusement . . . The concert hall is 85 feet long, 43 feet wide, and 45 feet in height. It is in the center between the music hall and theatre, separated by courtyards, and is on a level with the first balcony tiers . . .

The theatre, situated at the south end, has a seating capacity less than the music hall, although it contains eighty-four boxes.

. . . The dimensions of the theatre are as follows: auditorium, 60 x 68; proscenium opening, 32 x 32 feet; stage, 31 x 60 feet; height to rigging-loft, 80 feet; height to fly-gallery, 30 feet . . .

The music hall has a seating capacity of about 1,625, in seats arranged as follows: first floor, 576 chairs, 16 boxes; first box-tier, 32 boxes, 160 people; second box-tier, 32 boxes, being similar to the first box-tier; balcony, 210 chairs, 40 boxes, 410 people; gallery, 165 chairs, 12 boxes, 225 people. In addition to the above there is 934 square feet of standing room . . .

The seating capacity of the theatre is about 1,000, in seats as follows: first floor, 371 chairs, 6 boxes, 401 people; first and second box-tiers, 22 boxes each, 110 people each; balcony, 106 chairs, 28 boxes, 248 people; gallery, 77 chairs, 8 boxes, 117 people. In addition there is about 900 square feet of standing room. The steppings of the different tiers are about 2 feet 8 inches wide.[1]

[1] Birkmire provides description of decorations as well. Young, *Famous American Playhouses*, I: 243–44, includes another descriptive document from the New York *Dramatic Mirror*, November 30, 1895. Data on this and other New York theatres can be found in Mary C. Henderson, *The City and the Theatre: New York Playhouses from Bowling Green to Times Square* (Clifton, NJ: James T. White, 1973), and in her entries for the *Cambridge Guide to American Theatre* (1993). Birkmire, an important source of documents, also includes useful details on Proctor's Pleasure Palace, Castle Square Theatre (Boston), Fifth Avenue Theatre (the fourth of that name), American Theatre (1893), B. F. Keith's Gaiety Theatre (Boston, 1894), Abbey Theatre (New York, 1893), and Empire Theatre (1893).

Even though electricity was quickly replacing gas (the cause of numerous fires after 1815), the concern with theatre safety grew during the latter half of the nineteenth century. The following document, which also includes various entries on safety exits, building materials, fireproof curtains and scenery, and even skylights over the stage that could open instantly causing an updraft, is indicative of the concerns. These strictures, however, as succeeding documents will illustrate, overlooked key safety elements.

194   Excerpt from Section 500 of the New York Building Law Relating to Theatres, 1890s

Birkmire, *The Planning and Construction of American Theatres*, pp. 101–17

Every portion of the building devoted to the uses or accommodation of the public, also all outlets leading to the streets, and including the open courts and corridors, shall be well and properly lighted during every performance, and the hall shall be lighted until the entire audience has left the premises.

At least two or more oil-lamps on each side of the auditorium in each tier shall be provided on fixed brackets not less than seven feet above the floor. Said lamps shall be filled with whale- or lard-oil, and shall be kept lighted during each performance, or in place of said lamps candles shall be provided.

All gas or electric lights in the halls, corridors, lobby, or any other part of said buildings used by the audience, except the auditorium, must be controlled only in that particular place.

Gas mains supplying the building shall have independent connections for the auditorium and the stage, and provision shall be made for shutting off the gas from the outside of the building.

When interior gaslights are not lighted by electricity, other suitable appliances, to be approved by the superintendent of buildings, shall be provided.

All suspended or bracket lights surrounded by glass in the auditorium or in any part of the building devoted to the public shall be provided with proper wire netting underneath.

No gas or electric light shall be inserted in the walls, woodwork, ceilings, or in any part of the building unless protected by fireproof materials.

All lights in passages and corridors in said buildings, and wherever deemed necessary by the superintendent of buildings, shall be protected with proper wire network.

The footlights, in addition to the wire network, shall be protected with a strong wire guard not less than two feet distant from said footlights, and the trough containing said footlights shall be formed of and surrounded by fire-proof materials.

All border-lights shall be constructed according to the best known methods, and subject to the approval of the commissioners of the fire department, and shall be suspended for ten feet by wire rope.

All ducts or shafts used for conducting heating air from the main chandelier, or from any other light or lights, shall be constructed of metal and made double with an air space between.

All stage lights shall have strong metal-wire guards or screens, not less than ten inches in diameter, so constructed that any material in contact therewith shall be out of reach of the flames of said stage lights, and must be soldered to the fixtures in all cases.

The standpipes, gas-pipes, electric wires, hose, footlights, and all apparatus for the extinguishing of fire or guarding against the same . . . shall be in charge and under control of the department of buildings. . . .

During the fifty-year period explored in this section, two of the three most costly theatre fires in the history of America occurred. In 1876, 295 individuals died in a fire at Mrs.

Conway's Theatre in Brooklyn. Although this fire led to a demand for better fire and safety ordinances, it was the Iroquois fire (during which 602 perished in only 8 minutes) on December 30, 1903, during a performance of *Mr. Bluebeard*, starring Eddie Foy, that resulted in more effective regulations and proper enforcement.

195   Ground Plan of Iroquois Theatre, Chicago, 1903

John R. Freeman, *On the Safeguarding of Life in Theaters* (New York: American Society of Mechanical Engineers, 1906), p. 19

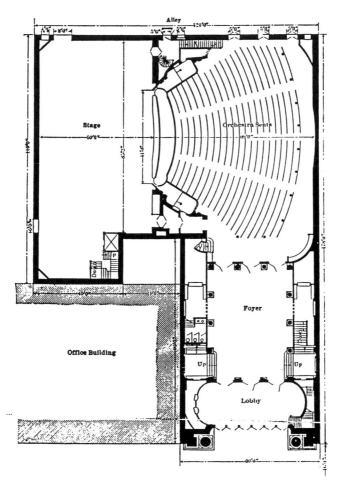

196   Verdict of Coroner's Inquest, Iroquois Theatre, 1904

Quoted in Edwin O. Sachs, *The Fire at the Iroquois Theatre, Chicago. 30th December, 1903* (London: Batsford, 1904), p. 37.

City laws were not complied with relating to building ordinances, regulating fire alarm boxes, fire apparatus, dampers, or flues on and over the stage and fly galleries. We also find a distinct violation of ordinance governing fireproofing of scenery and all woodwork on or about the stage. Asbestos curtain totally destroyed, wholly inadequate considering the highly inflammable nature of all stage fittings, and owing to the fact that the same was hung on wooden battens.

197   Assessment of Emergency Exits, Iroquois Theatre, 1905

"The Perfect Theatre," *Architectural Record*, 17 (January–June 1905), 105

The only exits on the right hand or north of Chicago's Iroquois Theatre, seating 1,900 people, were three emergency fire escapes. The manager had told his employees never to open them except on his personal orders. Consequently when needed to save life they were not ready for the emergency, and when forced open, were found, but too late, to be utterly inadequate.

198   Extract from Eddie Foy's Eye-Witness Account, Iroquois Theatre, 1928

Eddie Foy and Alvin F. Harlow, *Clowning through Life* (New York: E. P. Dutton, 1928), pp. 276–86

[After the fire had been burning for some minutes and the asbestos curtain had not been lowered,] I stood perfectly still, and when addressing the audience spoke slowly, knowing that these signs of self-possession have a calming effect on a crowd. Those on the lower floor heard me and seemed to be reassured a little, but up above and especially in the gallery, self-possession had fled; they had gone mad.

Down came the curtain slowly, two-thirds of the way – and stopped, one end higher than the other . . . Then the strong draught coming through the back doors by which the company were fleeing, bellied the slack of it in a wide arc out into the auditorium, letting the draft and flame through at its sides. "Lower it! Cut the wire!" I yelled. "Don't be frightened, folks! Go slow! . . . No danger! Play, Dillea!" Below me, Dillea [the orchestra conductor] was still swinging his baton and that brave, fat little German was still fiddling alone and furiously, but no man could hear him now, for the roar of the flames was added to the roar of the mob. In the upper tiers they were in a mad, animal-like stampede – their screams, groans, and snarls, the scuffle of thousands of feet and of bodies grinding against bodies merging into a crescendo half-wail, half-roar, the most dreadful sound that ever assailed human ears. . . .

[After the so-called fire curtain disintegrated and a "cyclonic blast of fire from the stage" flew into the auditorium, Foy left the stage but noted:] The horror in the auditorium was beyond all description. There were thirty exits [although only three led directly out to the street from the auditorium], but few of them were marked by lights, some even had heavy portieres over the door, and some of the doors were locked or fastened with levers which no one knew how to work . . .

199   Note on Fire Safety at Proctor's 23rd Street Theatre, 1904

Program for February 1, 1904; Wilmeth Theatre Collection, Providence, RI

Mr. F. F. Proctor, realizing that the recent unfortunate occurrence in Chicago has engendered a feeling of uncertainty everywhere, desires to assure his patrons that in all the theatres under his management every care has been exercised to avoid such a happening, and he points to his record of twenty-five years as a manager, **without having had a single fire in any of the theatres under his control**. The house employees, both upon the stage and in the auditorium, have been **carefully drilled in fire and panic tactics to meet any emergency, and the house is officered by a larger force of men than is employed in any other theatre in the city**. Ample provision of fire hose has been made throughout the auditorium, both on and under the stage, and throughout the entire house.

The accumulation of inflammable material has always been strictly prohibited, materially reducing the risk of an extended conflagration, and rendering easy the inspection of electric lights, wires, and other sources of danger. Moreover, the stage force have instructions to put the fire hose in use at the slightest evidence of a blaze, turning on the water, with no regard for possible damage to scenery.

Another point to which Mr. Proctor desires to call attention is the constant patrol of the theatres at night and day. Immediately after the performance the stage is taken in charge of by the carpenters and scene painters, and there is practically not an hour of the twenty-four when the house is not under the supervision of from fifteen to twenty employees, occupied in various tasks about the building. This, and the extra large staff required for the conduct of a continuous performance theatre, gives the audience assurance that **any emergency will be promptly dealt with. The "Proctor Plan"** is intended to appeal particularly to women and children, offering them commodious and comfortable theatres, at which the matinee performances are precisely the same as given at night, and the presence of so many unescorted ladies and children alone would induce Mr. Proctor's especial care in providing for their safety as well as comfort. The theatres bearing his name are **all of modern construction, provided with absolutely fireproof asbestos curtains, as thoroughly fireproof as it is possible to make them, generously provided with exits from every floor, and patrolled at all times by a force of ushers and superinten-**

dents, who are ready, at the slightest sign of danger, to clear the house quietly and without confusion. **Mr. Proctor** would also call attention to the fact that after an extended and systematic inspection of all his theatres by the new Fire Commissioner, **few changes have been suggested** by that official. Mr. Proctor has endeavored at all times to keep strictly within the spirit, as well as the letter, of the fire regulations, and in many respects has exceeded the caution mentioned in those regulations. In conclusion, Mr. Proctor desires to assure his patrons that this care will be exercised at all times, irrespective of the conditions, such as at present exist, and that, both in the matter of safety and comfort, **the interest of his patrons will be absolutely protected**.

200   Summarized Findings of the Iroquois Theatre Fire, 1906[1]

Freeman, *On the Safeguarding of Life in Theaters*, foreword

1. It is not a difficult matter to provide safeguards such that a theater or other hall of public assembly may be made reasonably safe.

2. In the great theater fires of history the loss of life has commonly resulted from the rapid spread of flame on a stage covered with scenery, followed within two or three minutes by an outpouring of suffocating smoke through the proscenium arch into the top of the auditorium, before those in the galleries could escape. Death has come chiefly to those in the balconies, and often within less than five minutes of the first flame.

[Freeman recommended the following safeguards:]

1. The providing of ample, automatic, quick-opening smoke vents over the stage.

2. The thorough equipment of the stage with automatic sprinklers by means of which the action of the heat will promptly release, over the burning scenery, a rainfall tenfold heavier than the heaviest thundershower, drenching the scenery and extinguishing the flames.

3. The providing of especially ample exits and stairways from the gallery.

[1] This was from an independent study presented at the annual meeting of the American Society of Mechanical Engineers.

Conceived of by the same entrepreneurs who created Coney Island's Luna Amusement Park, Frederic W. Thompson and Elmer S. Dundy, the Hippodrome Theatre on Sixth Avenue between 43rd and 44th Streets was billed as the world's largest theatre and designed to satisfy the growing public hunger for spectacle. Lavish scenery, enormous casts, and the use of every technical device then conceivable, including a movable stage and the capacity for an enormous tank of water in front of the more conventional proscenium stage, were commonplace. Ultimately costs were prohibitive and the theatre was razed in 1939.

201   Sectional Drawing of Hippodrome Stage, 1905

Scientific American, 92 (March 25, 1905)

202   Technical Description of Hippodrome, 1905

Scientific American, 92 (March 25, 1905), 242[1]

. . . the total seating capacity . . . is 5,300, which may be compared with the Metropolitan Opera House, 3,400; the Academy of Music, 3,000; and the Broadway Theatre, 1,800. The building is lighted by 25,000 electric lights, and the sunburst in the center of the ceiling alone contains 5,000 electric lights.

. . . [The stage] may be divided for purposes of description into two portions: that which is behind, and that which is in front of the proscenium arch. This arch, by the way, is the largest in the world, having a total width of 96 feet and a clear height of 40 feet, and its fire curtain is the biggest piece of asbestos ever woven. The depth of the stage from the extreme front to the back wall is 110 feet, or 50 feet from the back wall to the proscenium arch, and 60 feet from the arch to the extreme front of the stage. The main stage at the rear of the arch measures 50 feet in depth, by 200 feet in width between the side walls. Of this area, the central portion immediately back of the arch, measuring 50 feet in depth by 100 feet in width, is carried on four 12-inch hydraulic rams, and is capable of a vertical movement of 8 feet. The weight of this platform, which is virtually nothing more nor less than a huge elevator, is carried upon four deep plate girders, with the plungers placed at the four intersecting points. This rear stage and the mov-

[1] See Milton Epstein, *The New York Hippodrome: A Complete Chronology of Performances, From 1905 to 1939*, volumes 17–18 of *Performing Arts Resources* (New York: Theatre Library Association, 1993).

able apron with their fittings weigh about 230 tons, and the rear stage can be raised from the normal level to a height of 8 feet.

The movable stage is provided with massive counterweights, one line of which will be noticed in the accompanying photograph, showing the underside of the stage and one of the hydraulic plungers. The stage is guided in its vertical movement by steel columns, at the top of which are carried the sheaves for the counterweight cables. Attached to the underside of the stage are vertical guides, which slide within the steel columns. These glides are provided with slots, which are attached to massive dogs that slide horizontally in the steel columns, and serve to lock the stage at any desired elevation. The dogs are operated in unison by means of lines of countershafting, which are driven by a single electric motor. At each column the countershafting carries a small pinion, which engages a rack on the upper side of the dogs, and when the motor is started, the dogs are thus simultaneously moved into the locking position. The plungers which lift the stage are made to travel at one and the same speed by means of . . . automatic equalizing valves . . . In the movable stage itself there are seven "traps" provided, each capable of independent operation.

That portion of the stage, 60 feet in depth, which lies forward of the proscenium arch, is known as the apron. It is generally elliptical in form, and measures 48 feet in depth and 92 feet in width. Like the main stage, it is carried on 12-inch hydraulic plungers, with, in this case, a vertical travel of 14 feet . . . It is large enough to contain two circus rings, each 42 feet in diameter. Beneath the apron is built a huge steel and concrete tank, over 14 feet in depth, and large enough for the whole apron to sink within it . . . Two circular inclined runways lead on each side of the main stage, down to the basement to the animal stalls, and adjacent to the main runway is a narrow runway for the wild beasts. As the runways communicate on a common level, it is possible for processions to make the circuit through the basement and across the stage . . .

. . . The scenery, in place of being dropped and lifted, is carried, by means of traveling electric hoists, on four separate lines of overhead tracks, which are attached to the gridiron, and curve in concentric semicircles above the stage, and extend into deep side wings known as scene pockets, each of which is of sufficient depth to enable the whole of the one-half of the scenery to be moved within it, clear of the stage . . . There are four double electric hoists and two single hoists. Each . . . has a capacity of from two to three tons.

When the Stuyvesant Theatre opened on October 16, 1907, it marked a landmark for innovations designed to cater to producer–director–playwright Belasco's ideas of stage production; it also represented a trend at the turn of the century away from enormous auditoriums and an encouragement of more "naturalistic" staging. The Belasco Theatre, as it was known after 1910, was especially well equipped on stage and backstage, with the most sophisticated lighting system then known, a large elevator stage, and studios for developing scenic and lighting effects.

203   Description of Stuyvesant Theatre, 1907

From the column "The Matinee Girl," New York *Dramatic Mirror*, August 10, 1907[1]

Passing the new Stuyvesant Theatre on Forty-fourth Street, near Broadway, one has a dull eye and a duller fancy if in this new playhouse, built by David Belasco, one sees not the resemblance of the house to the builder.

Its scant, two-storied height reminds one of the somewhat less than medium stature of the playwright–manager. Its plain façade, unbroken by needless excrescence of false adornment, is as plain as his own priestlike attire. No Greek temple ever had severer lines. A glance at the exterior of this newest playhouse and there comes drifting back into memory the Belasco declaration:

"I am a simple fellow. I like simple things. I prefer simple people. My choice is the simple play, played simply."

In the exterior of the theatre, which will be opened soon by David Warfield,[2] there is the keynote of simplicity. Within there mounts high the wave of theatrical reform. Curiously wide in proportion to its depths is the Stuyvesant. David Belasco has heard the muttered objurgation of the man who sits far back under the balcony, seeing naught and hearing less. In pity for this man he has built a theatre with only fifteen rows of seats in the orchestra. Even the man on the farthest side of the fifteenth row is in direct line of vision and hearing with the stage. The auditorium will be of colorings so soft and of a note so confidential that it will seem rather a drawing room.

But the innovations will be found chiefly on the other side of the footlights, and are addressed to the comfort and well being of the actor. He will not be in jeopardy of life and limb by "props" lurking unyielding in the darkness of the wings. All "props" will be hurried upon an elevator in the middle of the stage and lowered to their place beneath it. And the gridiron, fifteen feet higher than any gridiron in the city, will dispose of whatever properties have not been banished by the elevator. And in each dressing room a shower bath! This not for the purpose of pampering his players, but of fostering their health and preserving their lives. Having been an actor himself Mr. Belasco knows well how many a player has caught a fatal cold because at fever heat from some last scene in a play he has gone out after hurried dressing into the bitter cold of a midnight in midwinter.

---

[1] A more technical description of the theatre appeared in the New York *Tribune*, October 13, 1907; reproduced in Young, *Famous American Playhouses*, II: 13–14.

[2] Belasco's favorite leading actor who was most famous for his role in *The Return of Peter Grimm* (1911).

At the turn of the century one of the great debates of the modern American theatre began to take shape – the efficacy of an endowed national art theatre, aping to some extent European models, versus independent commercial ventures, the latter the norm early in the twentieth century. The discussions that ensued demonstrated tensions between supporters on both sides of the issue; likewise, the majority of advocates for such an endowed national theatre focused on New York as the logical location, as the producer Joseph Papp did in our own time.

The end result of a decade of deliberation was the building of the New Theatre on Central Park West between 62nd and 63rd Streets, dedicated on November 6, 1909. Under the supervision of Heinrich Conried, director of the Metropolitan Opera, funds were subscribed by thirty wealthy opera patrons and Winthrop Ames, director of Boston's Castle Square Theatre, was appointed director. From the beginning the venture, which instead of making good theatre available to all citizens quickly became an elitist institution, was unsuccessful, in part because of the size of the facility (2,500 seats) and, according to some, the extremely poor acoustics. After two seasons the idea of an art theatre devoted to opera and plays was scrapped, the theatre, later acquired by the Shubert brothers, had its name changed to the Century and became a conventional Broadway house devoted to musicals and spectacle, such as Max Reinhardt's *The Miracle* (1924). The art theatre movement sought new directions, choosing in time intimate theatres and often semiprofessional production.

204   Orchestra Level Floor Plan of the New Theatre, 1909

Program for *Merry Wives of Windsor*; Wilmeth Theatre Collection, Providence, RI

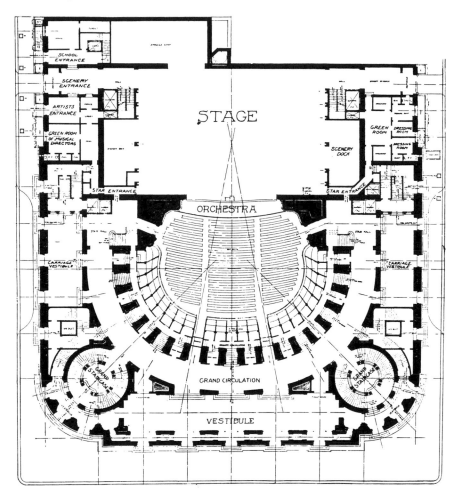

205   Description of the New Theatre's Revolving Stage, 1910

New York *Tribune*, January 6, 1910

The revolving stage at the New Theatre is said to be the most intricate and yet, in its operation, the most simple device of its kind in the world. It is sixty-four feet in diameter and revolves in one minute. It is made up of eight transverse sections and four segments, weighing altogether 56,000 pounds. There are more than one million pounds of steel in the stage machinery alone, and it requires

700 horsepower to put it in full operation. The cost of the stage machinery alone was over $250,000. The device was the invention of Claude L. Hagen, technical director of the New Theatre.

[Hagen explained that] . . . "The stage of the New Theatre is a distinct type, inasmuch as it revolves, moves backward and forwards, or transversely and up and down, as a whole or in parts. It also permits sections of the transverse stage to be dropped, and the rest of the sections to be opened so as to form sinks or cuts through which to lower whole sections.

"The main or underlying stage consists of eight members, each 7 by 48 feet. Each one of these members is operated by a vertical screw at each end so arranged as to engage with or be disengaged from a trackway on each side of the stage. Each one of these members is supplied with its own motor power, pneumatic drops, switches, and telltales, for the purpose of safety and registering their positions. On the top of the transverse sections are 360 radial rollers, and pointing to the exact center of the revolving stage floor.

"The revolving stage floor consists of eight sections, 7 by 48 feet each. These sections, when not used as a revolving floor, form the top floor of the transverse sections. At each side of the square formed by these eight sections is the segment, which, when locked together with the eight transverse sections, forms a circular slab 64 feet in diameter and 4 1/2 inches in thickness. Two scenes may be built upon this stage – one facing the audience and one facing the back wall. When the first scene is through, the stage can be revolved, bringing the second scene to face the audience, after which the first scene can then be taken from its place and the third scene set . . ."

206   Clayton Hamilton's Impressions of the New Theatre, 1910

"The New Theatre and Contemporary Plays," *Bookman*, 3 (January 1910), 456–64

. . . [Granville Barker, who was offered the position as director of the New Theatre] said that the theatre was altogether too large for the effective presentation of modern plays. This prognostication . . . has been borne out by the issue. The immensity of the auditorium has been a great handicap to both actors and producers in the case of all the plays that have thus far been presented . . . the main difficulty is not the matter of acoustics. Now that the theatre is finished in all details, it is not noticeably hard to hear in it . . . [On the other hand] from the topmost gallery it is impossible to see the back wall of the set; and the actors therefore appear divorced from their setting. . . . From the sides of the largest and most important balcony the view of the stage is so restricted that the spectator again is robbed of all sense of a relation between the actors and the setting. But by far the most serious defect of the edifice inheres in the fact that from all parts of the house, excepting only the first dozen rows of the orchestra, it is impossible to perceive any alteration in the facial expression of the actors . . . the sense of acting can be derived only from their gesture and the handling of their voices. And furthermore, the spectator is left conscious always that he *is* a spectator, and is not brought into any feeling of intimacy with the people on the stage.

. . . In one word, the New Theatre, considered as an edifice, is an anachronism. It offers an ideal stage for Forrest's performance of *Metamora*, but a very unfortunate stage for contemporary plays acted in the modern manner.

207   Claude L. Hagen's Explanation for the New Theatre's Failure, 1912[1]

Robert Grau, *The Stage in the Twentieth Century* (New York: Broadway Publishing Co., 1912), pp. xxii–xxiv

. . . the enormous size of the theatre was not considered when its director selected its repertoire of plays and its actors. Wonderful scenic effects were produced every few days, ranging from opera to sketches. Premier performances of Shakespearean plays were given after matinee performances of other heavy scenic plays. The most remarkable schedule was carried out without a single postponement. The productions were praised without stint, yet after two seasons of experiment by its directors, they had to hang up the sign "FAILURE." This magnificent temple of art, seating nearly 3,000 persons, planned and molded into exquisite form and color by experts, was blamed for the failure. It had no acoustic properties. . . . Its late director is engaged in directing a theatre [Little Theatre] seating 300 persons, because he knows now he must have his audience intimate with his actors.

. . . for opera, it was ideal. Yet it was dedicated to the drama. After the building was nearly complete, the commission for the stage machinery appurtenances and illuminating effects for the stage were awarded with the result that when the theatre opened they were not finished [with the exception of the revolving stage] . . . The illumination of the stage was the direct system under perfect control of an operator located under the stage in front of the musical director. The combined use of all the illumination provided did not light the scenes and characters properly. The stage house contained more than three quarters of a million cubic feet of space. Some idea may be gleaned of the size of the auditorium by the fact that the back of the gallery was 191 feet from the back of the stage, 112 feet horizontally from the curtain line, and 70 feet above the stage floor.

---

[1] Hagen designed the stage for the New Theatre and was its technical director. For a more objective explanation, see Walter Prichard Eaton, *At the New Theatre and Others* (Boston: Small, Maynard, 1910), pp. 13–19.

IV. Design and Technical Production

According to Edwin Booth's bankruptcy papers, January 26, 1874, prepared by James P. Deuel, the following is illustrative of the personal wardrobe required of a leading actor in the nineteenth century.

208   Inventory of Edwin Booth's Costumes, 1874

The original is in Washington National Records Center; a copy can be found in the Hampden-Booth Theatre Library, The Players, New York. This list, including corrected punctuation, is based on the transcription by Richard Stoddard, "A Costume Inventory in Booth's Bankruptcy Papers," *Theatre Survey*, 16 (November 1975), 186–88[1]

INVENTORY OF PERSONAL THEATRICAL PROPERTY,
LATELY OWNED AND USED BY EDWIN T. BOOTH.

Richard III.

Yellow tunic, much worn and frayed, lavender and green velvet cloak, cap to match, silk skull cap, stained and faded. Long gold cloth shirt, ornamented purple belt, purple velvet robe, embroidered velvet skull cap – in tolerably good condition. Leather armor, tin helmet, embroidered velvet surcoat, crimson robe, blue velvet cap with coronet – used 4 years. Plush surcoat. Boots, 2 pair shoes, wig, all worse for wear. Crown, collar, dagger and sceptre, with other stage-jewelry of little value and no use to any but a performer of Richard 3d.

Hamlet.

Black and blue merino tunic, with an extra skirt; long robe of same, short ditto, black fur robe, black tights and shoes. In pretty good order.

---

[1] See Stoddard's commentary for additional details.

Richelieu.

Black cloth soutan, red poplin ditto, large robe of same, yellow satin morning gown trimmed with dark fur, dark brocade ditto, 2 pair shoes, 2 skull caps, and square ditto. Worn 7 years. Grey wig.

Othello.

Long white merino shirt with green satin vest and sleeves (slightly soiled). Bournous of striped cloth, blue and white cloth ditto, dark woolen ditto, green silk sash, "Roman" woolen and silk ditto, white goat's-hair ditto; white serge tunic. Long gown (made of striped silk shawls). Long white serge gown (worn seven years). These dress [sic] in very good condition.

Iago.

Elizabethan grey velvet jacket and trunks, puffed with cherry satin (somewhat soiled), long cloak, white and black striped plush – 1 pair shoes, old black velvet hat.

Macbeth.

Chain armor shirt and head piece, red cloth tunic (much stained), green cloth ditto, brown reps [sic] ditto. Long green cloth shirt, large brown cloth robe, small red cloth ditto, brass and jewelled belt and collar, gold cloth band (or crown), 2 steel ditto, brass sceptre, 2 pair shoes. In tolerable condition. Wig.

Shylock.

Long green stuff shirt, large brown gaberdine lined with green flannel, black and red silk sash, yellow flannel cap, shoes, wig and beard. Of very little account.

Julius Caesar.

Brutus. White merino tunic, white crape toga, brass Roman armor, shield, spear, helmet; scarlet cloak, brass wristlets; 1 pair sandals with fur tops.
Cassius. Gilt leather armor, wig; the rest, same dress as worn for Brutus.
Antony. Short white crape tunic, light wig, scarlet cloth tops to sandals; the rest, same as worn for Brutus.

Tarquin Brutus.

Claret colored tunic, black sandals (rather worn), the rest same as worn for *Julius C.* Brutus.

Lear.

Yellow serge gown, lavender serge robe, wig and beard.

Fool's Revenge.

Parti-colored fool's dress, cap and bells, made of serge (partially worn out). Long brown gown, black cloak and cap of serge, red wig (of no account except for this part, because of its arrangement for hump and other deformities).

Apostate.

Crimson velvet tunic. Black wig.

Iron Chest.

Elizabethan black velvet jacket, trunks and cloak.

New Way to Pay Old Debts.

Brown arm hole cloak (velvet cotton), Elizabethan embroidered velvet jacket, trunks and cloak (much worn). Grey wig.

Stranger.

Black cloth breeches, brown cloth coat and vest, boots, high black felt hat. Worn seven years.

Lady of Lyons.

Grey serge jacket and breeches, crimson serge vest, worsted leggins [sic], shoes, felt hat. Black velvet coat lined with cherry satin, black velvet breeches. "Chapeau bras" of same, lavender satin vest striped with green velvet, black shoes, red heels. Long buckskin breeches, blue cloth military cloak, buff cloth vest, long blue cloth cloak lined with crimson, red white and blue sash, bearer chapeau, boots, gloves.

Much Ado about Nothing.

Drab cloth tunic, blue cloth vest, hat to match, green velvet cloak, trimmed with gold braid and lavender satin, hat to match, boots, shoes, mauve serge domino.

Petruchio.

Brown satin cloth tunic, trimmed with dark fur. Leather jerkin, delaine cloth trunks, old hat, one boot, one shoe.

Don Caesar.

Ragged dress (indescribable, worth 3 cents a lb.), striped white and green satin jacket and trunks (much soiled), crimson velvet shoulder cloak, felt hat. Light wig.

All these dresses more or less "shabby" having been in pretty constant use for the last seven years.

Charles W. Witham, a leading designer of the second half of the century, was employed by Booth, Daly, and Edward Harrigan. Designs reproduced include those for Booth's production of *Richelieu* and for Harrigan's comedy *The Leather Patch* (Act II, scene 1, "Grand view of Baxter Street").[1] (Poorly reproduced in Richard Moody's *Ned Harrigan: From Corlear's Hook to Herald Square* [Chicago: Nelson-Hall, 1980] are additional designs for Harrigan, including sketches for *McSorley's Inflation* and *Squatter Sovereignty.*)

[1] For additional documents on Harrigan, see Docs. 232 and 235. The only useful overview of Witham's art and career is Thomas F. Marshall, "Charles W. Witham: Scenic Artist to the Nineteenth-Century American Stage," in *Anatomy of an Illusion: Studies in Nineteenth-Century Scene Design* (Amsterdam: Scheltema & Holkema, 1969), pp. 26–30.

209   Charles Witham's *Richelieu*, Booth's Theatre, 1870

Theatre Collection, Museum of the City of New York[1]

[1] There are some forty Witham drawings in this collection; only a few have been available for reproduction. In addition, there are ten designs for Booth's *Hamlet* in the Harvard Theatre Collection, reproduced and described in Shattuck's *The Hamlet of Edwin Booth*. The only other extant Witham drawings are in the hands of a distant relative, consisting of twenty-one sketchbooks containing a few theatrical drawings and a dozen or more watercolors.

210   Charles Witham's Sketch for *The Leather Patch*, 1886

Theatre Collection, Museum of the City of New York

Until the last quarter of the nineteenth century most scenery was painted by individual artists either in their own scene-painting studios or in studios attached to specific theatre establishments. Itinerant artists filled the needs of many provincial playhouses; stock scenery was commonplace in all but the most sophisticated and successful houses. The East Coast and Chicago were the first to see a "studio system" emerge; with the expansion of the railroad these commercial studios could be found in most major cities, creating scenery to fit all needs in an efficient, factory environment.

211   Paint Room of a New York Theatre, c. 1880; Watercolor by Charles Witham

Theatre Collection, Museum of the City of New York

212   Photograph of Twin City Scenic Studio, Minneapolis, c. 1915[1]

W. R. Brown and the Twin City Scenic Collection–Performing Arts Archive of the University of Minnesota

[1] The studio operated 1896–1980. An exhibit of the Twin City Scenic Collection was mounted at the University of Minnesota, April–June 1987; subsequently it was seen throughout the country. The catalog (compiled under the direction of guest curator C. Lance Brockman) published for the exhibit (University Art Museum, 1987), not only includes colored and black-and-white reproductions of designs, but essays comprising the most complete history of this phenomenon to date.

The following four documents provide a sense of the technical requirements for the American version of pantomime at mid-century as practiced by George L. Fox in his production of *Humpty Dumpty* at the Olympic Theatre.

213   Review of George L. Fox's *Humpty Dumpty*, 1868[1]

New York *Tribune*, March 11, 1868; reprinted in Hewitt, *Theatre U.S.A.*, pp. 206–7[2]

The Olympic games have commenced. All the rosy gods of mirth presided at that theatre last night. *Humpty Dumpty* was acted for the first time. The house was

[1] The only full length study of Fox and the American version of pantomime is Laurence Senelick's *The Age and Stage of George L. Fox* (Hanover, NH: University Press of New England, 1988). A recommended essay by Senelick is "George L. Fox and American Pantomime," *Nineteenth Century Theatre Research*, 7 (Spring 1979), 1–26.

[2] Although Fox excelled in pantomime, he was also a competent straight actor and appeared in several burlesques, most notably in a travesty of Edwin Booth in T. C. De Leon's arrangement of *Hamlet* in 1870. See Laurence Hutton, *Curiosities of the American Stage* (New York: Harper & Brothers, 1891), pp. 182–91, and Yvonne Shafer, "George L. Fox and the *Hamlet* Travesty," *Theatre Studies*, 24/25 (1977–79), 79–93.

full in every part. On the stage almost everything was delightful, and in the audience everybody was apparently delighted. Under ordinary circumstances this would be the language of enthusiasm. Under the jovial circumstances that prevailed, it is the calm language of rational praise. To all lovers of fun *Humpty Dumpty* furnishes a delicious treat. It is a new work – the author being Mr. George L. Fox, the comedian – and so far as a pantomime can be original, that deals with the old familiar passages of that art, it is an original work. In a description necessarily rapid we can get but a faint idea of the extent, the character, the novelty, and the scenic luster of the piece. *Humpty Dumpty* introduces nearly 60 personages, beside a *corps de ballet*, and presents 17 entirely new scenes. Caricatures by Mr. Thomas Nast are included in some of the scenes and contribute to their comic effect. . . . It were long to tell – and we will not essay to tell it now – what mazes of merriment were traversed by Mr. G. L. Fox as Clown (in which character is *facile princeps* and altogether admirable) and Emilie Rigle as Columbine, Mr. C. K. Fox as Pantaloon and Mr. Lacy as Harlequin. The pathway of their adventure was, of course, the familiar one. . . . But, while the well-worn track was followed, many a gem of novel sport was found by the wayside. Local hits abounded. The true atmosphere of mirth brooded softly over all. And the pantomime was received with . . . hearty and happy laughter. At the outset, indeed, the gallery portion of the audience was somewhat boisterous in its demonstration; but this turbulence soon died away, and after that the applause was indicative of genuine . . . and continually increasing interest. A parody of the *cancan* dance in the burlesque-opening, particularly inspired it, and it became most deafening when Mr. Fox made his comic entrance, driving a white donkey [see woodcut below]. Of this actor's extraordinary play of comic expression, and of the delightful apparent unconsciousness with which he perpetrates all sorts of mischief, we have often . . . had occasion to speak. He was all himself last night, and, accordingly saw before him a sea of laughter-lighted faces. . . . It would be idle to recount his tricks. . . . One of the best scenes, for pantomine trickery, was that of the billiard room, terminated with a caged view of the "performing foxes." The candy-eating boy, who grew from little to more, like the poet in Hood's ballad, created a good deal of merriment, and the skating carnival was cordially greeted.

214   Advertising Woodcut for George L. Fox's *Humpty Dumpty*, 1875[1]

Specimens of Theatrical Cuts (Philadelphia: Ledger Job Printing Office, 1875)

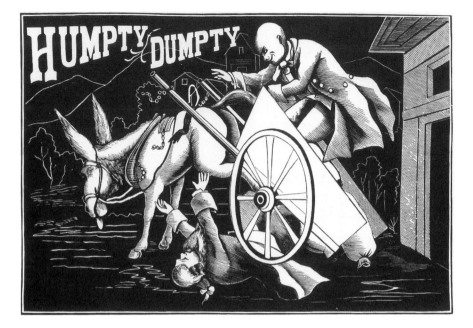

[1] This illustration was selected because it represents the typical advertising woodcut as sold by a commercial printer. There are extant photos and a wonderful lithograph poster, c. 1880, with Fox demonstrating various facial expressions around a civilian portrait of the actor. The artist Thomas Nast, mentioned in the review, drew a number of studies from the pantomime for the 1868 souvenir program, reproduced in Senelick, *Age and Stage*.

215   Scenic Effect Plot for George L. Fox's *Humpty Dumpty*, 1872

Transcribed and edited from William Seymour Theatre Collection (The McCaddon Collection), Princeton University

Act I, scene 1: [Icy Regions]. Moonlight.
    Scene 2: [Village Scene] Village drop. Set pcs. to work up at cue. Set collage to fly on at change. L.3.E. upper window prac. Lower door prac. Steps behind for window. Ladder to work up from under stage at signal, & lower at same. Set pig sty to fly on R.3.E. at change. Steps behind to mount wall. C. Trap used to work up cobbler's bench & flip & lower at signal. All to work up at cue and discover.
    Scene 3: Grotto.
    Scene 4: [Inn & Post Office] Panorama flats to work at cue. Village inn on first. Blk Bckg. Doors right and left to flip at cue. Figure head to flip.

Scene 5: Dry Goods Store & Trick Door. Doors right and left used blk backg. Trick doors to work at cue. Trick boot to work at cue.

Scene 6: Snow flats. House & sled to work on at cue. Act Drop.

Act II, scene 1: Humpty Dumpty Palace. Backed by H. D. small drop. Act Drop.

Act III, scene 1: Library. Fireplace c. with vampire backg. Leap used in flat. Star Trap R. used. working pictures on parallels to work at cue. Trick chairs right and left to work at cue. Opening in flat for album. Small platform behind flat for alubum to rest on.

Scene 2: Candy Store & Trick Shutters. Leap in flat. Opening in flat, left. Door left used black backg.

Scene 3: Moonlight Street (Fire Scene). Working balcony right. Window in flat right. Platform & steps behind. Leap in flat under balcony. Upper door in flat left & trick steps to work at cue. Lower door in flat left. Set trick lamp post to work at cue by balcony.

Scene 4: Moonlight Street.

Scene 5: Hall of Statuary. To be explained. Working bridges, platforms, etc.

Curtain

This elaborate plot, including a live pig, is indicative of the visual and spectacular nature of Fox's pantomimes.

216 Property Plot for George L. Fox's *Humpty Dumpty,* c. 1872

Transcribed and edited from William Seymour Theatre Collection (The McCaddon Collection), Princeton University

Act I
Scene 1: Icy Regions
Dress etc. for Ice King
Staff for Ice King
Wand for Sun Spirit

Scene 2: Village Scene
3 bundles straw
Pair shoes for Tommy Tucker
Trick Bee Hive with Nose
Donkey & Cart with Bags, one bag
    filled with sawdust
Fishing net against cottage
Stuffed sticks ready by Hive
2 Chairs discovered

Scene 2 continued:
Apply for Humpty
Stuffed log ready
Egg basket ready
Discovered: Saw
        Saw Buck
        Axe
        2 Sticks Wood
Table and Ironing material

Scene 2 continued:
Furnace and Irons ready in Cottage
Discovered:
Lager beer keg and spiggot on stand
Stone Pitcher by keg
Table ready for Doctor
Advertising banner for Super
Trombone for Black Servant
Box for Doctor containing Tooth,
    pistol loaded, packages, etc.
Working bee ready in hive
2 Brooms back of cottage
Glass of water, in wings
Glass of wine, in wings
Stuffed bricks ready behind pig sty

Scene 3: Grotto
Miscellaneous

Scene 4: Inn and Post Office
Trick Trap box ready
Large letter ready back of flat
Newspaper soldier hats for boys
Drum and sticks for boy
Wooden guns for soldiers
Waiter with Chicken, bread, etc.
Policeman's club for officer

Scene 6: Snow Scene
Snow balls
Snow man in ball discovered: arms,
    head, legs, etc.
Trick sleigh chair with dummy
Man to work X and cut in two
Stretching house and sled
Whip for driver
Small sled ready in wing
Wilson's carpet in wing
3 legged stool ready in wing
Gong and stick in wing
Uhlan Lances and flags in wing

Act II
Scene 1: [Humpty Dumpty's palace]
Folly sticks for ballet
Wilson's carpet ready in wing

Scene 2 continued:
Flute ready in wings for Dandy
Tin Horn ready back of cottage
Tin Horn ready by pig sty
Crow to work over wall
Stretching pig ready in wings
Trick cobblers bench ready to work
Cobbler tools – Gold shoes on bench
Iacapodium used under stage when
    cobblers bench works
Rough Staff & Gown for Fairy Queen
Live pig ready in sty
Harlequin's bat for Fairy
Head & Apron for Gnome cobbler
Saws head to work in pig sty

Scene 5: Dry Goods & Shoemaker
False arms coat for super
Dummy female figure ready behind
    flat
Dummy bundles back of flat
Lobster & basket ready in wing
Bag-hook & cat for rag picker in wing
Girl of the period & trick hair
Giant policeman

Scene I continued:
2 paper balloon hoops ready in wing
All the Iron shields–wooden shields
All the large lances, small spears
Red poles to support steps
Garlands for ballet
Blow up elephant back stage?
Wilson's table in wing
6 Tamborines (3 right and 3 left in wings)

Act III

Scene 1: Library
Turkey tables
Trick table cloth in table
Trick table cloths on flat
Large knife & fork on table
Trick bottle by table right
Turkey dress for boy
Trick bookcase
Album in flat
Stool
Bricks ready in Chimney
Stretching Harlequin up chimney

Scene 2: Candy Store & Shutters
Stick candy ready for boy
Candy boys heads ready
2 chairs ready back of flat
Trick bakers basket ready with bread
Basket chips for boy in wing
Boy with marbles in wing
Profile board to break in wing
Pail & Squirter [later cut]
Behind opening have bed for boys to
    fall on

Scene 3: Fire Scene
Trick table for boys
Trick hot corn pail for Negrowoman
    on table
Trick umbrella for man in wing
Bundles in sheets back of flat
Baby with bladder back of flat
Red fire back of flat
Trick elephant on stage

Scene 4: [Moonlit Street; orginally
    indicated as Seminary & Fireworks]
[Props crossed out]

Scene 5: Hall of Statuary
All the statue props

Russell Smith, a designer and painter, has left a vivid account of scenic practice during the third quarter of the century.

217   Memoirs of Russell Smith, 1884[1]

Excerpted from the unpublished holograph "Autobiographical Recollections of Russell Smith," 1884; courtesy of Vose Galleries, Boston

. . . I ever strove [to avoid] all false color, glitter, and exaggerations of every kind, whilst striving to represent the most beautiful features of nature, I could see, and with reverential love of truth. The material, canvas, and color I used, were also as genuine as that of the best oil pictures; and as I painted in my own painting room, out of town, I was freed from the injudicious dictation of prompters, stage managers, etc. who care little for real good art and are justly blamed for the shortcomings of the stage, but who always justify themselves by saying: "the business must pay, and therefore, it is our duty to give the public just what they want to see." . . .

. . . An idea prevails in the theatres (and somewhat out of them), and more unfortunately with the stage managers, that a scene that is quickly painted has a better effect than one that is more carefully wrought up. And as the exigencies of the stage often call for much new scenery in a very short space of time, they thrust upon the painter far more than can be well done . . . If he be good-natured and obliging, he will give the manager a good quantity of bad work. But if he should be independent, and desirous of doing himself and the public justice, there is continual trouble between him and the manager. I always was esteemed a fast painter; for, besides being temperate and energetic in my habits, and ambitious to excel, I liked the pursuit. It offered such opportunities for the exercise of the imagination and invention; and where one uses the best material and has sufficient time, there is nothing to prevent his making good work.

After the refreshment of sleep I would lie an hour and plan in my mind my days, – contrive the composition, dispose of the masses of light and shade and color, and go over it more than once. In fact, think it out; so that when I came before the canvas after breakfast, I never hesitated, or lost time rubbing out; but went straight forward . . . By night, there would often be a finished scene. Some of the other prominent scene painters . . . would express their surprise at the directness and the speed with which I pushed forward. They knew not the cause.

[1] Smith began his career as scene painter in 1833 and continued this work throughout the eastern United States until the 1870s. Although most of his work for the Boston Museum, the National Theatre in Philadelphia, the American Academy of Music in Baltimore, and especially the Philadelphia Academy of Music, among others, was accomplished by 1865, his painted scenery was in use throughout the second half of the century. I am grateful to Orville Larson for calling my attention to the Smith manuscript. A colored reproduction of an oil on canvas backdrop of the Nile River by Smith can be found in Henderson's *Theater in America*, p. 195.

But even that speed would not satisfy some stage managers, and I have been induced to paint three entire scenes in forty-two consecutive hours, and they were not simple scenes, like a calm sea and sky, or a quiet lake and distant hills, but represented an encampment, fortifications, and a city, for *Edward the Black Prince*.

Unfortunately for me and other scene painters, such an effort was taken as a criterion of what might be done, at any time! And when sufficient time might have been had by giving the order for work sooner, it was delayed with the conviction that the scenery could be got ready in almost no time. In my own painting room, I could have time, and the numerous drop curtains, I painted for other city theatres, I was determined, let them be good or bad, they should be all my own. Another practice I doggedly pursued throughout my career, was, that I would not use a fictitious style of color, although many respectable people think that scene painting should be gaudy, – done for show alone . . . This opinion prevails so much with scene painters, that I have seen them paint rocks with blue verditer, and shade them with rose-pink, another make all his lights with chrome yellow, no matter what was the local color of the object represented; and still another, gild every thing with Dutch metal, – rocks, green leaves, bark, and all else, – and their work would be applauded! We cannot reach the beauty of Nature in the splendor of her choice effects with even the best ability and color, but to be striving after it with Dutch and Rose Pink and red lead and chrome yellow for everything, is an outrage. At the same time, I would not have any one suppose that I would have scenes either dull or commonplace. I knew a painter who painted nearly everything he represented with Vandyke brown and whiting, another must have Indigo in all he did, and a French artist I observed mixed nearly all his tints from Dutch and Rose Pink, and Paris green; and it was surprising to see what a wide reach of capability he had with them. But his work looked like French wall paper, it wanted depth and tone, besides the look of Nature. I labored under one great disadvantage in painting for the [Philadelphia] Academy [of Music]. I seldom painted a scene especially for one single Opera, it must be "generalized" so that it might be used in many. The stockholders could not afford to do better with their income, but it deprived me of the opportunity to give the scenes that individuality of character and local truth which I should have liked. . . .

The climatic effect in Daly's melodrama *Under the Gaslight* (Act III, scene 3), 1867, was one of the most sensational thus far produced in the American theatre. The following three documents reconstruct the famous railroad station scene at Shrewsbury Bend.[1]

---

[1] For additional Daly plays and a lengthy introduction to his production methods and careers, see Don B. Wilmeth and Rosemary Cullen, eds., *Plays by Augustin Daly* (Cambridge and New York: Cambridge University Press, 1984).

214   Description and Final Dialogue from Augustin Daly's *Under the Gaslight*, 1867

Under the Gaslight (New York: Printed for the author, 1867), pp. 40–43

Scene: Railroad Station at Shrewsbury Bend. Up R. the Station shed R.H. Platform around it, and door at side, window in front. At L.1.E. clump of shrubs and tree. The Railroad track runs from L.4.E. to R.4.E. View of Shrewsbury River in perspective. Night. Moonlight. The switch, with a red lantern and Signalman's coat hanging on it L.C. The Signal lamp and post beside it.

[At the conclusion of the scene Laura Courtland, who has been locked in a signalman's shed awaiting the train, forces her way out in order to rescue her friend Joe Snorkey. The following dialogue ensues:]

Snorkey. Who's that?
Laura. It is I. Do you not know my voice?
Snorkey. That I do; but I almost thought I was dead, and it was an angel's. Where are you?
Laura. In the station.
Snorkey. I can't see you, but I can hear you. Listen to me, Miss, for I've got only a few minutes to live.
Laura (Shaking door). God help me? and I cannot aid you.
Snorkey. Never mind me, Miss. I might as well die now, here, as at any other time. I'm not afraid. I've seen death in almost every shape, and none of them scare me; but, for the sake of those you love, I would live. Do you hear me?
Laura. Yes! yes!
Snorkey. They are on the way to your cottage – BYKE and JUDAS [the villains] – to rob and murder.
Laura (In agony). O, I must get out! (*Shakes window bars.*) What shall I do?
Snorkey. Can't you burst the door?
Laura. It is locked fast.
Snorkey. Is there nothing in there? – no hammer? – no crowbar?
Laura. Nothing! (*Faint steam whistle heard in the distance.*) O, Heavens! The train! (*Paralysed for an instant.*) The axe!!
Snorkey. Cut the woodwork! Don't mind the lock – cut round it! How my neck tingles! (*A blow at door is heard.*) Courage! (*Another.*) Courage! (*The steam whistle heard again – nearer, and rumble of train on track. Another blow.*) That's a true woman! Courage! (*Noise of locomotive heard – with whistle. A last blow; the door swings open, mutilated – the lock hanging – and LAURA appears, axe in hand.*)
Snorkey. Here – quick! (*She runs and unfastens him. The locomotive lights glare on*

scene.) Victory! Saved! Hooray! (LAURA *leans exhausted against switch.*) And these are the women who ain't to have a vote!

(*As* LAURA *takes his head from the track, the train of cars rushes past with roar and whistle from L. to R.H.*)

Until full stage photographs became common (starting in 1883), scenes from popular plays were most frequently depicted in woodcuts used for program and billboard advertisement. Although such stock illustrations are of some use, they are idealized representations and somewhat misleading.

219   Advertising Woodcut for Augustin Daly's *Under the Gaslight*, 1867

Specimens of Theatrical Cuts (Philadelphia: Ledger Job Printing Office, 1876); reproduced in *Scenes from the Nineteenth-Century Stage in Woodcuts*, ed. Stanley Appelbaum (New York: Dover, 1977)

220   Explanation of Train Effect by Joseph Daly, 1917

Joseph F. Daly, *The Life of Augustin Daly* (New York: Macmillan, 1917), pp. 74–76

. . . With regards to this new play, the effect was wrought by moral agencies which were potent without the climax of the visible railroad train.

On the first night the audience was breathless. . . . The intensely wrought feelings of the spectators found vent in almost hysterical laughter when the "railroad train" parted in the middle and disclosed the flying legs of the human motor who was propelling the first half of the express. Had the effect of the scene depended not upon the suspense and emotion created by the whole situation, but upon the machinery, the piece had been irretrievably lost; but the real sensation was beyond chance of accident. . . .

221   Photograph of *A Russian Honeymoon*, 1883.

Theatre Collection, Museum of the City of New York

This is the first onstage photograph of a theatrical production in the United States: *A Russian Honeymoon*, photographed by Benjamin Joseph Falk, May 1, 1883, on the stage of the Madison Square Theatre. Prior to this date, publicity photos and photographic records of a production were limited to the studio, thus lessening the importance of the historical record of a theatre production and limiting design details to easily transportable properties.[1]

[1] For details on this and other photographs of historically important New York productions, see Stanley Appelbaum, ed., *The New York Stage: Famous Productions in Photographs* (New York: Dover, 1976). For general background on American theatrical photographs of this period, see Mary C. Henderson, *Broadway Ballyhoo* (New York: Abrams, 1989).

A Russian Honeymoon, by Mrs. Burton N. Harrison, was an adaptation of a play by Scribe, Mélesville, and Carmouche, produced by Daniel Frohman, directed by Franklin H. Sargent and David Belasco, with settings by Mazzanovich and W. H. Lippincott. The production opened on April 9, 1883, and ran through June 2. This scene is the closing tableau of Act II.

Arthur Edwin Krows in *Play Production in America* (New York: Henry Holt, 1916) explained the early process of stage photographs:

> Dispatch is necessary, mainly because the stage hands, waiting for the photographer to complete his work before "striking" the scene, are being paid for all time on duty, whether active or not.

> At conclusion of each act, the photographer, with a couple of assistants, erects his heavy tripod in the auditorium at about the middle of the eighth or tenth row of the orchestra, so as to give his camera proper range for comprehension of the entire stage. Then, in swift succession, by instructions from the producer or stage director, the actors arrange themselves in poses from the preceding action. (p. 311)

These photographs by Joseph Byron of scenes from the stage version of *Ben-Hur*, 1899–1900, demonstrate the climax of stage spectacle of the nineteenth century. The original play version based on Lew Wallace's novel had a prologue and six acts (plus seventeen tableaux). In the first act alone there were fourteen scenes; the production required twenty-two speaking principals, eighty chorus members, and over a hundred supernumeraries. As the photographs suggest, the scene painter was all important in this and similar productions, and the quick succession of scenes approximate a method that soon would be accomplished more successfully by films. Only a few scenes in the stage production were successful. Compare the greater verisimilitude of the galley scene as contrasted to the chariot race scene in the arena (where, despite the use of real horses and a treadmill, there was movement but no action).[1]

[1] For a backstage account of the production, see William W. Ellsworth, "Behind the Scenes at 'Ben Hur,'" *Critic*, 36 (March 1900), 245–49; quoted in Hewitt *Theatre U.S.A.*, pp. 273–78. The production's relationship to its screen treatment is discussed in A. Nicholas Vardac, *Stage to Screen: Theatrical Origins of Early Film: David Garrick to D. W. Griffith* (Cambridge, MA: Harvard University Press, 1949; reprint New York, 1987), pp. 79–82 ff.

222   Galley Scene from *Ben-Hur*, 1900

Souvenir Album: Scenes of the Play Ben-Hur (1900), Wilmeth Theatre Collection, Providence, RI

223   Race Scene from *Ben-Hur*, 1900

Souvenir Album: Scenes of the Play Ben-Hur (1900), Wilmeth Theatre Collection, Providence, RI

This photograph by Joseph Byron shows the first-act saloon scene in *The Girl of the Golden West* (1905), written and directed by Belasco with scenery by Ernest Gros and costumes by Mme. E. S. Freisinger. Lise-Lone Marker in *David Belasco: Naturalism in the American Theatre* (Princeton: Princeton University Press, 1975), says this frontier drama "represented a peak in Belasco's endeavors to present a suggestively picturesque as well as strikingly 'real' stage milieu" (p. 139).[1]

[1] Marker provides a detailed reconstruction of this production, as well as Belasco's productions of *Sweet Kitty Bellairs* (1903), *The Easiest Way* (1909), and *The Merchant of Venice* (1922).

224   Photograph of *The Girl of the Golden West*, 1905

Theatre Collection, Museum of the City of New York

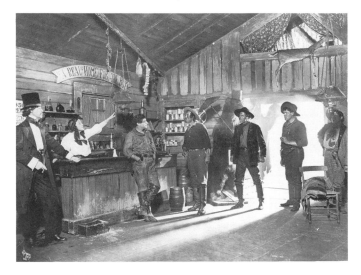

Belasco's pictorial realism depended not only on scenic exactitude but on electric lighting to help create mood. Louis Hartmann, who was his lighting designer from 1901 until c. 1925, has provided a description of lighting effects for *Madame Butterfly* (1900).

225   Lighting Effects for David Belasco's *Madame Butterfly*, 1900

Louis Hartmann, *Theatre Lighting* (New York: D. Appleton, 1930), pp. 16–18

For a diffusing medium . . . we used either frost gelatine or colored silks; and these media spread the light and softened it. . . . David Belasco used these silks . . . [for a scene representing] the interior of a Japanese house, where, at the back of the room, were the shoji windows. In Japanese houses these windows are made of paper. The stage windows were made of tracing cloth, a semitransparent linen.

During the action . . . an interval of twelve hours was supposed to elapse. Cho

Cho San was seated at the closed window through which she watched for the approach of her American lover, Lieutenant Pinkerton. . . . She began her vigil in the early evening, and it lasted throughout the night and into the following morning. The interval of time was denoted by the changing light that was projected on the windows through the medium of these aforementioned colored silks.

The several colors of silk were in long strips. These strips were attached to tin rollers; the rollers were set into bearings fastened to a wooden frame that slid into the color groove of the lamp. The turning of the rollers passed the colors in front of the light and they were projected on the windows in a series of soft blends. As the orange deepened into blue, floor lanterns were brought on the scene and lighted; as the pink of the morning light was seen the lanterns flickered out one by one. The light changes were accompanied by special music. Music and lights were perfectly timed and the entire change consumed less than three minutes.

Belascan effects, often obtained through trial and error, and frequently at great initial cost, sometimes developed in surprising ways, as Belasco's description of one moment in his and John Luther Long's *The Darling of the Gods* (1902) illustrates.

226   David Belasco's Description of Lighting *The Darling of the Gods*, 1902

Belasco, *The Theatre through Its Stage Door*, pp. 58–60

In my production . . . it was comparatively easy to indicate by lights the tragic feeling of the scene in which the band of Samurai commit suicide by hari-kari. I set the stage in the picture of a gaunt bamboo forest, behind which was a great blood-red setting sun to symbolize ebbing life. In the shadows Kara's followers could be faintly seen and the audience could hear the clatter of their lacquered armor as they went to their self-inflicted deaths.

But when it came to the scene of the River of Souls, in which the dead were to swim to the lower depths, or purgatory, in preparation to entering the celestial hereafter, a most troublesome problem arose. I had built the translucent scene of the river at a cost of $6,500 and had devised a kind of harness in which fifteen girl were suspended to represent the passage of the souls. When I tested the scene with manikins in my miniature theatre, it invariably worked perfectly; but when I tried it on the regular stage something was sure to go wrong. Some of the girls swam well, while others swam badly, and almost always one or two got tangled in their harness. Such accidents in a performance before an audience would have caused laughter, which would have been fatal to a production that had cost $80,000.

For two days and two nights, barring short recesses, we worked over that stubborn scene, and at last I decided to give it up. . . . The opening performance had already been twice postponed, but reluctantly I made up my mind to put it off again.

I ordered the scene "struck," and my carpenters hoisted all the opaque setting which had been made at great cost, leaving a single gauze curtain suspended in irregular folds at the front of the stage. Just at this moment one of the workmen happened to pass between the curtain and a light at the back. Seen through the folds of the curtain his movements were almost ghostly. I saw at once that the effect for which I had been striving had come to me ready-made. Each of the fifteen girls was told to count ten and then cross the stage, using her arms to suggest a kind of swimming motion. The effect was remarkable, for the number of figures seemed increased a thousandfold. Having already thrown away $6,500, I built the scene in a day for $90 and it is being imitated yet.

227   Chart and Floor Plan for David Belasco's *The Rose of the Rancho*, 1906

Hartmann, *Theatre Lighting*, pp. 68–69

"THE ROSE OF THE RANCHO" ACT I

EQUIPMENT USED

On the fly-gallery Right there are hung two light bridges. The lower one is 22 feet from the stage, and the upper one 30 feet above the stage.

On the upper bridge there are ten 25-amp lenses.

On the lower bridge there are eleven 25-amp lenses.

On the Left of stage and suspended from the fly-gallery is a light bridge 25 feet from the stage. On this bridge are eleven 25-amp lenses.

Under the back of the fountain there are two 250-watt baby lenses.

On a platform, Backstage Right is one 25-amp lens.

Back of wall Right two olivettes to light drop.

Back of wall Left two olivettes to light drop.

Back of second foliage border are hung two flaming arcs in a special housing with color slide. The slide is worked from the second light bridge Right with an endless line.

Two baby lenses on stands in the first entrance Right and Left for chasers.

4 border lights, three circuits, amber, orange, and blue.

For setting of lenses see diagram.

For light changes and cues see following light plot:

RIGHT BRIDGES

1 and 2 cover fountain.

3 and 4 cover area back of fountain.

5 and 6 cover orange tree (full spread).

7 on rose bush (full spread).

8 and 9 cover floor back of gate (full spread).

10 and 11 strike thickness of wall at gate, throwing shadow of gate on thickness piece.

12, 13, and 14 strike front of arbor, sharp focus to throw shadow of leaves on floor.

15 strikes on flowers in center of fountain, sharp focus.

16 covers vines in front of porch, sharp focus.

17 and 18 on roses at gate, each lens focused sharp to cover a single rose.

19 and 20 on vines over porch, sharp focus.

21 on vines on top of wall Left, sharp focus.

22 shoots through back of trellis on porch, to throw shadow on leaves on Padre's face as he sleeps in chair.

23 and 24 baby lenses set under fountain to strike gate to kill shadow of foots on faces

LEFT BRIDGES

(All lenses on the left bridges have frosted gelatines.)

1 and 2 on flowers and wall of house Downstage Right.

3 and 4 cover area in front of fountain.

5 covers area in front of porch.

6 on orange tree.

7 covers wall and flowers left.

8 and 9 cover area back of gate.

Chaser babies Right and Left First entrance follow Miss Starr throughout act.

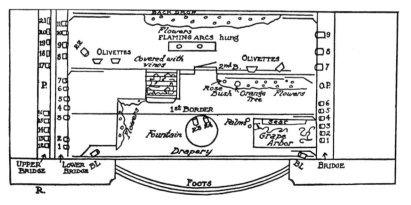

The setting represents a California mission garden. At Right is the Padre's house with a vine-covered porch. The back drop shows the mission with its bell tower. It is a hot day and the scene is flooded with sunshine.

At the turn of the century Owen Davis was the most successful American writer of popular melodrama ("ten, twent', thirt'" cent seats). Davis admitted that he wrote for the eye rather than the ear, catering to an audience heavily populated with imigrants who had little understanding of the words and playing out "each emotion in action" while saving dialogue for the "noble sentiments so dear to audiences of that class." With over 200 titles to his credit, he invariably ended each act (and there were usually four) with "a moment of perilous suspense or terrifying danger," more often than not built around a mechanical effect. (See Doc. 238.)

228   Stage Directions for On-stage Electrocution in *At the World's Mercy*, 1906[1]

Playscript in the Billy Rose Theatre Collection, New York Public Library at Lincoln Center

JACOB: Go away! Go away! I do it. (*Doctor exits as the storm breaks – clouds of dust blow in from left; Flashes of lightning through storm clouds at back – thunder, etc.*) Dey vill come! De bridge! I must be quick! (*He picks up Job's axe from center and cuts loose rope off trunk of tree – then runs up cliff to bridge and cuts away one of the supports with axe – ties rope to end of plank and descends to stage, taking one end of rope with him. Effects of thunder and lightning and storm clouds. He stands under tree up left and puts his foot on an iron plate on stage. Both of the heels of his shoes are shod with iron and a wire runs up his trouser legs and meets on a small iron button on his chest.*) Now! Ven dey gets on bridge, I pulls on rope – Ah – (*Bud and Grace seem to come on cliff toward bridge. Electric lamps start toward effect on back drop – trees, rocks in wind, dust, etc., plenty of thunder – stage almost dark, excepting for flashes of lightning. Bud and Grace go out on bridge. Jacob grabs rope and jumps from behind tree.*) Now I kill! (*He puts his other foot on second charged plate on stage, the electric current goes up wires and there is a flash of flame from his chest. Loud report of thunder, at the same time an electric bomb comes down from the flies and explodes on limb of tree. Limb breaks away and falls. Jacob falls on stage dead. Bud draws Grace off bridge and clings to bushes on cliff as bridge falls. Lamps climax the storm effect. Thunder – lightning – waterspout effect – big tree falls with crash – brick wall at right falls and lights out for dark change. Curtain.*)

[1] This occurs in Act IV, scene 1. The production was at Star Theatre, New York, in February 1906.

Salvation Nell by Edward Sheldon was directed by Harrison Grey Fiske and Minnie Maddern Fiske (seen at center as Nell Sanders) in 1908 (November 17) with this setting for
Acts I and II designed by D. Frank Dodge and costumes by Mme. E. S. Freisinger. An
example of Belascan-style realism, this production utilized actual furnishings (such as the
mahogany and brass bar seen here) bought at auction.[1]

[1] For a review of this production, see *Theatre Magazine*, January 1908, reprinted in Hewitt, *Theatre
U.S.A.*, pp. 300–301. Orville K. Larson in *Scene Design in the American Theatre from 1915 to 1960*
(Fayetteville: University of Arkansas Press, 1989) reproduces this photograph and the Byron photo
of the realistic slum street corner in Act III (p. 24).

229   Photograph of *Salvation Nell*, 1908

Theatre Collection, Museum of the City of New York

V. Drama

Henry James wrote frequently about the sad state of America drama at mid-century. The following remarks are extracted from a review of *The School for Scandal* at the Boston Museum.

230 Henry James on American Drama, 1874

Henry James, "The School for Scandal at Boston" (unsigned), *Atlantic Monthly,* December 1874; reprinted in *The Scenic Art,* ed. Allan Wade (1949; New York, 1957), pp. 13–20.

. . . The drama at large in America, just now, is certainly neither artistic nor fine; but this is a reason for caring with some tenderness for what it may be in particular cases. . . . When a play is barbarous both in form and rendering, and ignoble in sentiment, there is little doubt but that it can do no one any good. Often, however, one is struck with the high – the oppressively high – moral tone of dramas replete with aesthetic depravity; and we are thinking just now of pieces in which sentiment is maintained at a reasonable level, but machinery, using the term broadly, comes out with especial strength. Does it really much matter . . . whether such machinery is made to produce vulgar effects or charming ones? Is there any very tangible relation between the working consciousness and the playgoing consciousness of people in general? . . . People go thither to be amused, and tacitly assume that amusement is one thing and workaday life another, and that the world exhibited in plays is a purely fictive and artificial world, with a logic quite distinct from that of the dusky world of umbrellas and streetcars, into which they hustle back when the play is over. If plays are artificial, so, in a minor degree, are pictures and novels; part of the machinery of that pleasure which is indeed in some degree tributary, as rest and relief, to the business of life, but not harmoniously interfused with it and animated by the same energies. We are inclined to think, in spite of the evidence, that this view of the case is exaggerated, and that it does seriously matter whether even uncultivated minds are entertained in good taste or in bad. Our point would be simply that it matters rather less than many of the people interested in the moral mission of art are inclined to admit. We are by no means sure that art is very intimately connected with a moral mission; and a picture that one dislikes, or a novel that one cannot read, or a play that one cannot sit out, is therefore to our sense a less melancholy phenomenon than to that of more rigid philosophers. . . .

At mid-century and for almost the next half century native plays were largely limited to those with characters identified with the American scene – the Yankee, the Negro, the Indian, City types, and the frontiersman – regardless of their verisimilitude and more frequently than not the quality of the text. It would be some years before themes and contemporary topics would supersede these more superficial efforts. *Davy Crockett* by Frank Murdoch, though superior to many in its treatment of the theme of Western strength and inherent goodness triumphant over Eastern weakness and corruption, as Hewitt suggests, is representative of a "native" play of the time; it is also typical in that it made the actor in the titular role of the uneducated frontiersman with an arm-of-iron and a heart-of-gold a star.

231   Review of Frank Mayo's Performance as Davy Crockett, 1874

Spirit of the Times, March 14, 1874; reprinted in Hewitt, *Theatre U.S.A.*, pp. 223–26

. . . The play is not sensational, and depends upon no claptrap effects for favor. It fairly brims over with humanity, and appeals strongly to the hearts of all classes. Stories of the affections are ever popular with theatregoers. Whether it be the love of the helmeted knight or the love of the rough but honest backwoodsman, like Davy Crockett, the interest is the same if the playwright has skillfully performed his work. . . . The element which gives to *Davy Crockett* its claims to success is a simple story of pure love that runs through the play like a thread of gold. . . . The play opens with an exterior view of Davy Crockett's home in the backwoods, and the arrival of a party of travellers, consisting of Major Hector Royston . . . , who has accidentally sprained his ankle, Eleanor Vaughn . . . , and her betrothed, Neil Crampton. . . . Eleanor recognizes in Davy Crockett a friend of her childhood. She is young, refined, and beautiful, and the sight of her inspires in his heart a sudden love. She has received a letter from a lawyer, who has something to do with an estate she is heir to, warning her of the uncle of her lover, and when Oscar Crampton . . . comes upon the scene, and seems to exercise some mysterious power over Royston, her guardian, she wishes for some friend to guard and protect her. Crockett offers himself, and seems intuitively to recognize in Crampton an enemy of Eleanor. The party presently depart, and the act closes with Davy Crockett following to protect the young girl from the machinations of her foe. The second and third acts are laid in Davy Crockett's hunting lodge; a fearful snowstorm rages without and Davy is discovered musing over the recollection of the beautiful girl whose voice awakened in his heart a new life. . . . A faint cry is heard and Neil Crampton stumbles in, and after telling Davy that Eleanor is without, lost and freezing in the snow, falls exhausted. Davy rushed into the storm, and returns bearing the lifeless form in his arms. He cares for her tenderly, and to warm the rude log hut throws upon the fire the wooden bar which secures the door. Eleanor revives and discovers her preserver. She sees in a moment that the backwoodsman loves her. Her romantic rescue, coupled with this knowledge, kindles the spark in her heart. . . .

They are interrupted by the howling of the wolves that soon surround the hut, seeking whom they may devour. Davy rushes to the door to bar it. The bar has been burnt up, and he supplies its place with his strong arm, while the ravenous brutes are howling without and striving to force an entrance. The third act opens with Davy still at his post, and the wolves still howling and snapping without . . . Major Royston and Oscar Crampton come to the rescue. Davy's arm is extricated, swollen and bleeding, after a little delay, and then, maimed as he is, he starts off to the settlement ten miles away for help. Act Four opens in a drawing room in Major Royston's house. We learn that Oscar Crampton holds several notes forged by Royston in an hour of financial distress. Hence his power over him. He forces Royston to betroth his ward Eleanor to his nephew that he may control her fortune. . . . Enter Davy Crockett, to take a last farewell of the woman he loves. She approaches and he conceals himself behind a picture, and learns that the coming ceremony is as distasteful as the attentions of Neil Crampton. Once more she calls aloud for a friend. Davy once more appears. Eleanor confesses that she loves him, and he promises to save her. . . . [He carries her off, marries her, Eleanor agrees to pay the notes, and] The curtain falls on a very pretty domestic picture. . . .

Mr. Mayo earned the laurels. . . . [His] conception is correct, and his delineation of the backwoodsman never overdone. The light and shade of the character are portrayed very artistically, and a degree of sympathy is created by his acting that provoked many expressions of satisfaction. If we were to suggest anything that would give the characterization a more perfect and rounded out appearance, we would suggest a little more roughness, a little less refinement; otherwise it was perfect. . . .

Playwrights of the decade prior to the turn of the century, though generally complacent, were aware of some of the weaknesses of native drama and the changes beginning to take place in their genre, as evidenced from the following forum.

232   Major American Playwrights on American Drama, 1889

Excerpted from "American Playwrights on the American Drama," *Harper's Weekly,* 33 (February 2, 1889), 97–100[1]

Augustin Daly

I do not consider that there is any such thing as an American school, or an American drama. The drama is one and the same thing wherever it is written. . . . It is merely a matter of the individuality of the author. A play can be American in the sense that it portrays American characters and American life. In that sense we have an American drama, and beyond any question the distinctive work of that kind that has been done is Mr. Harrigan's. . . . [2]

. . . The dramatists of America have made a good showing of work in the past, considering the youth of our country, and certainly there seems to be every prospect of their doing good work and plenty of it in the future. . . .

As for the prospects for the American dramatist today, there are always chances for the artist who does good work, and the rewards for the dramatist who succeeds are very great. . . .

It seems to me that the future of the drama in America is exceedingly bright. The status of the theatre was never as good as it is at present; and it is a remark that I have made before, that attacks upon the theatre nowadays are attacks upon the patrons rather than upon the players. Certainly the very best people we have in American society patronize the theatre today, and it is to gratify their tastes that the theatre is made what it is. If, then, the theatre is attacked, the critics are animadverting on the tastes of the best society.

Not only is the drama pure and the theatre respectable, but the morale of actors in this country is unsurpassed by that of any other country or age. With these conditions, and the constant competitive efforts of a small army of dramatic writers to produce the best work, there is no reason to have any misgivings about the future.

Edward Harrigan

. . . Though I use types and never individuals, I try to be as realistic as possible. Not only must the costuming and accessories be correct, but the speech or dia-

---

[1] By necessity, these statements have been drastically edited, especially that of Gillette, who writes extensively of changes in pictorial realism over the previous twenty years. Excluded from this abridgment are statements by John Grosvenor Wilson (pleading for a romantic American drama), Bronson Howard, and the critic William Winter.

[2] Daly's own plays, mostly adapted and "Americanized" from French or German originals, were written in collaboration with his brother, Judge Joseph Daly. He defended collaboration in an important essay, "The American Dramatist," *North American Review,* 142 (May 1886), 485–92. For details on this process and an introduction to Daly's prolific career as a playwright (and régisseur), see *Plays by Augustin Daly,* ed. Wilmeth and Cullen.

lect, the personal "makeup," the vices and virtues, habits and customs, must be equally accurate in their similarity to the facts. Each drama is a series of photographs of life today in the Empire City. As examples, the barroom in one of the Mulligan series was copied from a saloon in Roosevelt Street, the opium den in *Investigation* from a "joint" in Pell Street, and the "dive" in *Waddy Googan* from an establishment in the neighborhood of the Bowery.

If I have given undue prominence to the Irish and Negro, it is because they form about the most salient features of Gotham humanity, and also because they are the two races who care the most for song and dance. There are at least three hundred organizations in New York like the Mulligan Guards, and probably fifty like the Full Moons.

In constructing a plot, I use one that is simple and natural. . . . While doing my best to obtain realism in the plot, I try to avoid that whose sole value is local or temporary, and construct something that will interest and amuse ten or even twenty years hence. With the plot fixed or started, and with the types and places in my mind, it is easy to construct the characters and write the piece. . . . The next stage is "smoothing and brightening the raw material." Here I elaborate what situations I have sketched out and create new ones, arrange antitheses between the characters and between the different scenes, increase the wit and humor of the dialogue and the fun or nonsense of the climaxes. The third stage sees it cast and rehearsed. . . . The first stage is the shortest, and the third the longest of the three. . . .

It may be that I have struck a new idea in confining my work to the daily life of the common people . . . Their trials and troubles, hopes and fears, joys and sorrows, are more varied and more numerous than those of the Upper Ten. . . .

In the realism which I endeavor to employ I believe in being truthful to the laws which govern society as well as to the types of which it is composed. A playwright drops to a low level when he tries being a moralist, but to a much lower level when he gilds vice and sin and glorifies immorality. All of these are parts of life, and as such are entitled to be represented in the drama. The true realist will depict them as they are. . . .

William Gillette

. . . In the development of the American drama a promising feature is the tendency toward realism as opposed to conventionalism. By realism should be inferred not actualism, but the artistic representation of reality. This proposition verges on very debatable ground. Every recent essay toward putting the actual upon the boards has met with unbounded applause from the galleries and a portion of the parquet. The success of live horses and a real steam fire-engine in one play, of a fiery steed in *Mazeppa* and numerous so-called border dramas, of a long assorted lot of water tanks in aquiferous spectacles, and of a large healthy cow in a new comedy, seem for the moment indisputable evidence to the contrary. Yet the success of these will not be permanent if we are to judge from the past. . . .

It is impossible to exactly reproduce nature upon the stage as upon the easel. Art must have recourse to the principle of suggestiveness. . . .

Steele MacKaye

The most pleasing feature of the American drama of today is the ever-increasing attention paid to stage setting. This is true in a popular as well as in a technical sense. Never before has so much money and thought been directed toward those details on which artistic success depends.

Yet we are far from not only where we ought to be, but from the proud position occupied by the European stage. This is not due to any lack of public spirit, nor to false economy, but partly to the intellectual carelessness of the American public and partly to the absence of the artistic spirit in the general management of theatres. . . .

There are scores of magnificent playhouses which are worthy settings of the noblest dramas of the race. But they are desecrated by being the scene of the dramatic imbecility, the serio-comic absurdity, and the meaningless spectacles of the present day. In one respect the manager is not to be blamed. Human nature does pursue the flying dollar, and doubtless will forever. . . . [The manager] . . . is to blame for not realizing that the highest art, when properly presented, is in the long run most remunerative. . . .

. . . with the development of breeding on the boards there is going on a corresponding art development through every branch of the profession . . . theatregoers are now patronizing that class of theatres which present the dramas suited to their individual tastes. Thus, ere many years have gone by, there will be a wide demarcation between the great temples of amusement devoted to art and culture and numberless small and cheap playhouses devoted to the inartistic and commonplace recreations of the unthinking.

The tension between entertainment and art heightened in the 1890s and led to a number of articles and opinions about the state of the drama.

233   Requirements for Successful Plays in the 1890s

Alfred Hennequin, "Characteristics of the American Drama," *Arena,* 1 (May 1890), 700–709

. . . theatrical performances are still placed, as they were in the period of dominant Puritanic influence, on a par with bear-baiting and rope walking, actors are still rated in some quarters but a degree above vagrants and sturdy beggars. . . . The American audience will consent to be amused by its drama or to be moved to fictitious sorrow, but it will not patiently permit itself to be instructed . . . it will not listen to the discussion of a serious social problem. The amusement must be laughable, but nothing more.

Nor will it suffer itself to be instructed or amused in what it calls an immoral way. It likes to see virtue rewarded and vice sent to the penitentiary. . . .

This shrinking from the immoral precludes the discussion of what are known as delicate questions. . . . Adultery may, indeed, be hinted at in American plays, as it may even form an important element of the plot, but it must not be seriously discussed or even presented as a problem. The dramatist must let us see his opinion, and that opinion must be openly, definitely, unhesitating condemnatory. In fact, the subject must not be presented as question at all, but as a sin . . .

[As a result, because of the influence of French melodrama and comédie, or what the author calls comedy of incidents or comedy of manners,] we may arrive at the following characteristics as being *in the main* those most likely to prove successful in American plays:

    1. Strong melodramatic situations.
    2. Farcical scenes and incidents.
    3. Horseplay, song, and dance, etc.
    4. Poetic justice.

    . . . Does not the hope of the future drama lie in the possibility that some dramatist will break away from the French traditions and either return to the earlier source of inspiration, or else find here on native soil the spring whose waters fill us with immortal thirst?

234   Dion Boucicault on the Future of American Drama, 1890

Excerpts from Dion Boucicault, "The Future American Drama," *Arena*, 2 (November 1890), 641–52.

There is not, and there never has been, a literary institution, which could be called the American Drama. We have produced no dramatists essentially American to rival such workers as Fenimore Cooper, Bret Harte, Hawthorne, Mrs. Harriet Beecher Stowe, and others of worldwide reputation in the realms of narrative fiction . . . Within the last two or three years our homemade plays have asserted their value: partly because our playwrights have improved and advanced in their craft, but mainly because the French and English dramatic authors are played out, and so we are thrown upon our own resources. . . .

[Boucicault attacks at length the growing Naturalistic/Realistic movement in Europe, including the work of Zola and Ibsen, and suggests that writers should study the public more carefully] . . . when gathered into a theatre, they are free from every prejudice, they present an assembly of human beings, with open hearts, and ready sympathies unembarrassed and unbound . . . Public opinion is the highest and sole court of jurisdiction in literary and artistic matters. . . . And what is success? It is simply the consensus of those wretched creatures whose opinions we are bound to despise; it is the fiat of the people. . . .

. . . the Future Drama of America is with our people, and with their voice, the press . . . the public verdict is supreme and final. The jury is composed here, as it was composed in Greece, of the people, and the drama is, therefore, made by the collaboration of the people and the poet. And this is as it should be. . . .

. . . The prominent features of the theatre are burlesque operetta, and the kind of farce we used to call extravaganza. The money changers have displaced the priests in the temple. The burlesque operetta is a hybrid, produced by a mixture of the old English burlesque, the French opera bouffe, and Negro minstrelsy. . . . This piece of nonsense is offered for the serious appreciation of our public as the important subject and feature of our drama!

In the United States there are but four theatres devoted legitimately to the cultivation of the drama; of which three are in New York and one in Boston. And these theatres are the smallest in the cities. . . . Elsewhere and throughout this great country the Drama is a tramp. The theatres regard her as a transient guest . . . or a bag man who brings on show samples of goods. Thus it is in New York, where its principal theatres let lodgings by the week to stars, and managers are merely janitors.

. . . American cities are provincial, and even in the few small theatres that entertain fixed companies, one depends on the German stage [Daly], another relies on English plays [Wallack] in preference to risking the production of American works, which have pushed themselves into notice in the theatres of less pretension, at the risk perhaps of the authors, or of some actors desirous of obtaining a "pedestal" play. He uses New York as a fence on which to post his bills and reap the profits of this advertisement in the provincial towns.

. . . The public has changed in this generation, and are eager now to recognize and support a native American drama. The managers fail to recognize this revolution, but they must come to it.

. . . the drama of modern life, the reflex of the period, will prevail over every other kind of entertainment. This drama will present a character or a group of characters, not a complicated or sensational action, affording a physiological study by way of illustration, not by way of description. . . .

William Dean Howells, one of the foremost literary figures of the time, was a champion of Realism in fiction and drama, although his own efforts in the latter were generally failures. Of his three dozen plays, only a couple were commercially successful.

235   William Dean Howells on Edward Harrigan, 1886

William Dean Howells, "The Editor's Study," *Harper's New Monthly Magazine*, 73 (July 1886), 315–16; portions reprinted in Hewitt, *Theatre U.S.A.*, pp. 248–49 and *The American Theatre*, ed. Moses and Brown, pp. 132–35

. . . The outlook is not hopeless . . . we have still no drama. Yet we have the prospect of something of the kind . . . we have the plays of Mr. Edward Harrigan . . . It is the work of a man in whom the instincts of the author combat the theatre's traditions, and the actor's experience censures the author's literary vanity.

Mr. Harrigan writes, stages, and plays his pieces; he is his own playwright, manager, and comedian. He has his own theatre, and can risk his own plays in it, simply and cheaply, in contempt of the carpenter and upholsterer. . . . Mr. Harrigan accurately realizes in his scenes what he realizes in his persons; that is, the actual life of this city. He cannot give it all; he can only give phrases of it; and he has preferred to give its Irish-American and Teutonic phases. It is what we call low life, though whether it is essentially lower than fashionable life is another question. But what it is, it is; and it remains for others, if they can to present other sides of our manifold life with equal perfection . . . In his own province we think he cannot be surpassed. The art that sets before us all sorts and conditions of New York Irishmen, from the laborers in the street to the most powerful of the ward politicians and the genteelest of the ladies of that interesting race, is the art of [Carlo] Goldoni – the joyous yet conscientious art of the true dramatist in all times who loves the life he observes . . . Mr. Harrigan shows us the street cleaners and contractors, the grocery men, the shysters, the politicians, the washerwomen, the servant girls, the truckmen, the policemen, the risen Irishman and Irish woman, of contemporary New York . . . Mr. Harrigan instinctively repeats the same personages in his Mulligan series.[1] Within his range the New Yorker is not less admirable than the Venetian. In fact, nothing could be better than the neatness, the fineness, with which the shades of character are given in Mr. Mulligan's Irish people; and this literary conscientiousness is supplemented by acting which is worthy of it. . . .

All the Irish aspects of life are treated affectionately by this artist, as we might

---

[1] There were six full-length Mulligan plays between 1878 and 1881 and two additional plays that continued the saga of the Mulligan family, both in 1884 (*Cordelia's Aspirations* and *Dan's Tribulations*). Although the Mulligan plays were more popular than Harrigan's more serious efforts and he never quite fulfilled Howells's implied prediction, Harrigan's city plays were important forerunners of more realistic city plays after the turn of the century. For an excellent introduction to the Mulligan plays, see Richard Moody's introduction to *The Mulligan Guard Ball*, in *Dramas From the American Theatre 1762–1909* (Cleveland, OH: World Publishing Company, 1966); also recommended is Moody's *Ned Harrigan: From Corlear's Hook to Herald Square*, and Alicia Kae Koger's "An Edward Harrigan Bibliography," *Nineteenth Century Theatre*, 19 (Summer 1991), 29–44 and (Winter 1991), 105–29.

expect from one of his name; but the colored aspects do not fare so well under his touch. Not all the Irish are good Irish, but all the colored people are bad colored people. They are of the gloomy, razor-bearing variety; full of shortsighted lies and prompt dishonesties, amusing always, but truculent and tricky; and the sunny sweetness which we all know in Negro character is not there. We do not wholly object to the one-sided picture; it has its historical value; and so has the contemptuous prejudice of both Irish and Negroes for the Italians which comes out in the *Leather Patch*; that marks an epoch and characterizes a condition.

. . . The error of the dramatist [in *Leather Patch*] has been that he has at times not known how to hold his hand; he has given us the whole truth where part of it would have been enough; he might have spared us some shocking suggestions of the undertaking business. At other times he quite forgets his realism. . . .

In spite of such lapses, however, we recognize in Mr. Harrigan's work the spring of a true American comedy, the beginning of things which may be great things. We have more than intimated its limitation; let us say whatever its offenses, it is never, so far as we have seen it, indecent. . . .

. . . we cannot do less than cordially welcome reality as we find it in Mr. Harrigan's comedies. Consciously or unconsciously, he is part of the great tendency toward the faithful representation of life which is now animating fiction.

Playwright–actor James A. Herne's essay on art versus commercialism in playwriting is one of the most articulate statements on the subject.

236   James A. Herne on "Art for Truth's Sake in the Drama," 1897

James A. Herne, "Art for Truth's Sake in the Drama," *Arena*, 17 (February 1897), 361–70

. . . "Art for art's sake" seems to me to concern itself principally with delicacy of touch, with skill. It is aesthetic. It emphasizes beauty. It aims to be attractive. It must always be beautiful. It must contain no distasteful quality. It never offends. It is highbred, so to speak. It holds that truth is ugly, or at least is not always beautiful. The compensation of the artist is the joy of having produced it.

"Art for truth's sake," on the other hand, emphasizes humanity. It is not sufficient that the subject be attractive or beautiful, or that it does not offend. It must first of all express some *large* truth. That is to say, it must always be representative. Truth is not always beautiful, but in art for truth's sake it is indispensable.

Art for art's sake may be likened to the exquisite decoration of some noble building; while art for truth's sake might be the building itself.

Art for truth's sake is serious. Its highest purpose has ever been to perpetuate the life of its time. The higher the form of expression the greater the art. . . . But in expressing a truth through art, it should be borne in mind that *selection* is an important principle. If a disagreeable truth is not also an essential, it should not be used in art. . . . Truth is an essential of all art. I do not well see how there can be art without some truth. I hold it to be the duty of the true artist to state his truth as subtly as may be. In other words: if he has a truth to manifest and he can present it without giving offense and still retain its power, he should so present it, but if he must choose between giving offense and receding from his position, he should stand by his principle and state his truth fearlessly.

In all art, ancient and modern, that which is in touch with contemporaneous life adheres closest to truth, because it is produced through some peculiar social condition. . . .

[For several pages Herne reviews nineteenth-century drama and his own work, crediting the influence of Dickens and noting the dramatic treatment by Boucicault of Irish peasant life; his own plays are used as examples of how persistent a force truth can be, and "how it compels the unconscious medium to express it."]

. . . I did not set myself the task of writing *Shore Acres* as it now stands; it grew, and I grew with it; and while I did not realize all its spirituality until its stage presentation set that spirituality free, still it must have had possession of me while writing, or I could not so have written.

When I sat down to write *Hearts of Oak*, I did not say to myself, "I'm going to write a play in which there shall be neither the traditional stage hero nor the stage villain." They are not true and therefore did not assert themselves, did not persist – that's all. Such characters do not exist in life, nor do they appear in any of my plays.

Art is a personal expression of life. The finer the form and color and the larger the truth, the higher the art.

. . . Art is universal. It can be claimed by no man, creed, race, or time; and all *art* is good. It serves its time and place, and fertilizes the art to come. The artist of today is the medium for the expression of the art of today, fertilized by race memories of past ages of art – more perfect by reason of the struggles, the failures, the inferiority, and the sublimity of ages of art.

"Art for art's sake" and "Art for truth's sake," in the last analysis, it seems to me, are identical.

"Art for truth's sake" is the higher art, because it contains a larger degree of the vital principles of fertilization. Its race quality is its supreme quality, and therefore it will better serve the race and the art to come. . . .

. . . I stand for art for truth's sake because it perpetuates the everyday life of its time, because it develops the latent beauty of the so-called commonplaces of life, because it dignifies labor and reveals the divinity of the common man.

It is generally held that the province of the drama is to amuse. I claim that it has a higher purpose – that its mission is to interest and to instruct. It should not *preach* objectively, but it should teach subjectly; and so I stand for truth in the drama, because it is elemental, it gets to the bottom of a question. It strikes at unequal standards and unjust systems. It is as unyielding as it is honest. It is as tender as it is inflexible. It has supreme faith in man. It believes that that which was good in the beginning cannot be bad at the end. It sets forth clearly that the concern of one is the concern of all. It stands for the higher development and thus the individual liberty of the human race.

Playwright Bronson Howard, often termed "the dean of American drama" and a champion for playwright's rights, was known for the involved plotting of his plays, as demonstrated in the following suggestions for judging the construction of a play.

237   Bronson Howard on Play Construction, 1900

Bronson Howard, New York *Dramatic Mirror*, 1900; reprinted in Howard's *The Autobiography of a Play* (New York: Columbia University, 1914), pp. 51–52,[1] and in *Papers on Playmaking*, ed. Brander Matthews (New York: Hill and Wang, 1957), p. 285

So much is written in critical notices of plays, about their "construction," that I should like to suggest a few of the considerations which that term involves. It is possible that some of the beginners, who are to become the future dramatists of America, will see the necessity of thinking twice before using the term at all. Some of the more general considerations to be kept in view, when a careful and properly educated critic feels justified in using the word "construction," may be jotted down as follows:

I. The actual strength of the main incident of a play.

II. Relative strength of the main incident, in reference to the importance of the subject; and also to the length of the play.

III. Adequacy of the story in relation to the importance and dignity of the main incident and of the subject.

IV. Adequacy of the original motives on which the rest of the play depends.

V. Logical sequence of events by which the main incident is reached.

VI. Logical results of the story after the main incident is passed.

VII. The choice of the characters by which the sequence of events is developed.

VIII. Logical, otherwise natural, use of motives in these particular characters, in leading from one incident to another.

IX. The use of such human emotions and passions as are universally recognized as true, without those special explanations which belong to general fiction and not to the stage.

---

[1] Howard's famous essay on the writing of his successful play *The Banker's Daughter* (1878) was first delivered as a lecture to the Shakespeare Club at Harvard in 1886, later to the Goethe Club, and in 1889 to the Nineteenth Century Club in New York.

X. The relation of the story and incidents to the sympathies of the audience as a collection of human beings.

XI. The relation of the story and incidents to the sympathies of the particular audience for which the play is written; to its knowledge and ignorance; its views of life; its social customs; and to its political institutions, so far as they may modify its social views, as in the case of a democracy or an aristocracy.

Minor matters – such as the use of comic relief, the relation of dialogue to action, the proper use of superfluous characters to prevent an appearance of artificiality in the treatment, and a thousand other details belonging to the constructive side of a play – must also be within the critic's view; but a list of them here would be too long for the space available. When the young critic has made a careful study of the standard English drama, with a special view to the proper considerations above indicated, his opinion on the "construction" of a play will be of more or less value to American dramatic literature.

According to Owen Davis, author of scores of sensational popular plays written from 1899 to 1913, melodrama followed a successful "formula." Later he changed his style to a more Realistic approach, including his Pulitzer prizewinning play, *Icebound* (1922). His melodramas included titles such as *Convict 999, Nellie, the Beautiful Cloak Model, Drive from Home*, and *Edna, the Pretty Typewriter*. (For a typical effect, see Doc. 228.)

238   Owen Davis's Formula for Melodrama, 1914

Owen Davis, "Why I Quit Writing Melodrama," *American Magazine*, 78 (September 1914), 28–31, 77–80[1]

. . . In designing my plays, I have never taken my characters from real life. They have all been born of the hazy, indefinite pictures that chanced to come into my mind. In drawing up the events that followed these characters I have never depended upon the actual truth as I saw it. To me the stage, even in a modern play, should be colored with some tinge of romance and these events should properly be a little more highly colored and a little more frequent in their happenings than the events of real life. I have a great respect for the drama of the commonplace, but what talents I have are adapted to the description of the unusual rather than to the happenings of everyday life.

My usual time for writing a melodrama was about a month. Not that I spent that much time on the actual writing of it, since in addition to keeping up the literary end of the job I had to select the players, design the scenery and lithographs, and stage direct. An itemized account of the time spent per month would be about three days thinking out general outline of play, three days on the first

---

[1] Davis expands on some of these ideas in his book, *I'd Like to Do It Again* (New York: Farrar & Rinehart, 1931).

act, about two days on each of the three succeeding acts, and about two weeks to the general business of production. . . .

The plays that we produced were written largely by rule. In fact the actual writing of one of these sensational melodramas I had reduced to a formula, about as follows:

TITLE (at least fifty percent of success)

PLOT: Brief story of the play.

CAST: *Leading Man*, very (even painfully) virtuous.

> *Leading Woman*, in love with him.
>
> *Comedy Man*, always faithful friend of *Hero*.
>
> *Soubrette*, very worthy person (poor but honest) and always in love with *Comedian*.
>
> *Heavy Man*, a villain, not for any special reason, but, like "Topsy," "born bad."
>
> *Heavy Woman*, – here I had a wider choice, this lady being allowed to fasten her affections upon either *Hero* or *Villain* (sometimes both) but never happily.
>
> *Father* (or *Mother*), to provide sentiment.

Fill in as desired with character parts.

ACT I – Start the trouble.

ACT II – Here things look bad. The lady having left home, is quite at the mercy of *Villain*.

ACT III – The lady is saved by the help of the stage carpenter. (The big scenic and mechanical effects were always in Act III.)

ACT IV – The lovers are united and the villains are punished.

I suppose that I have been responsible for as many executions as the Queen in *Alice in Wonderland*. I am honest enough to admit my cold-blooded attitude; but apply this chart to many plays of authors who consider their work inspired, and see if it fits.

These plays depended very greatly upon scenic effect, sensational dramatic title, and enormously melodramatic pictorial display on the bill boards. I think we touched upon every theme known to man, and every location. We limited ourselves, however, to American subjects. We always had a clear and dominant love interest, which we crossed with an element of danger, usually furnished by a rather impossible villain or adventuress. The themes of some of these plays were absolutely legitimate and the stories in many cases, with different dressing, would have done for a Broadway theatre of the present day. But we had to, or fancied we had to, have such an overabundance of climactic material that our plays resulted in an undigested mass of unprepared situations. Where one carefully prepared and well-developed episode would really have been of far greater dramatic value, we made a rule of dividing our plays into no less than fifteen scenes, the end of each being a moment of perilous suspense or terrifying danger. This gave the playwright rather less than seven minutes to instruct his audience, to prepare his climaxes, to plant the seed for the next scene, and to *reach* his climaxes, which of course was absurdly impossible and resulted, I feel sure, in a form of entertainment which was only too ready to yield to the encroachment of the cheap vaudeville and moving pictures. . . .

During the teens women playwrights began to gain some limited recognition, though only Rachel Crothers had some degree of commercial success, while attempting to articulate the case for woman's freedom.[1] Dealing with equal responsibility between the sexes, *A Man's World* (1910), a modest success, provoked a male chauvinistic response from Augustus Thomas in *As a Man Thinks* (1911). Nonetheless, playwrights both male and female were beginning to discuss with some candor the problems of being female in a male-oriented society, though solutions were still very tentative. Some writers, like Mary Shaw, failed to gain acceptance, in large measure because of her more cerebral approach to the suffrage issues.[2] The following documents illustrate some of perceptions and concerns of women playwrights during the early teens.

[1] An interesting, though overly optimistic, contemporary overview of women playwrights is Lucy France Pierce, "Women Who Write Plays," *World Today,* 15 (1908), 725–31; she stated that of one-hundred recognized American playwrights of her day, thirty were women. For suffrage plays, see *On to Victory,* ed. Bettina Friedl (Boston: Northeastern University Press, 1987).

[2] One of the most outspoken women with a diversified career in the theatre: see Rose Young, "Suffrage as Seen by Mary Shaw," *Harper's Weekly,* 60 (May 8, 1915), 456.

239   Interview with Rachel Crothers, 1910

Ada Patterson, "Woman Must Live Out Her Destiny," *Theatre Magazine,* May 1910, pp. 134–35, xxiv

"I have convictions, but I am not a reformer." Rachel Crothers . . . smiled a serious little half smile. It was pleasant flashlight, but did not thoroughly illumine the proposition.

"I have convictions," she went on. "I believe every playwright has, or no play could be written. But try to reform the world, to reform men" – her slim hand waved away the possibility. It was an eloquent gesture, showing the helplessness and hopelessness of such effort.

"Do you yourself believe the principle which Frank Ware stands for in *A Man's World,* that a man should have the same standard of morals as a woman?"

"I believe it with all my soul, but I am not trying to force that opinion upon the world. The playwright's province is not reform. If a conviction of the playwright can be clothed in a dramatic story and make an entertaining play, very good. But it was never my intention to preach. . . .

"Given a certain character, she must live out her destiny. What she does is the logical outcome of her character. That is not always the theatre, but it is always life.

"Frank Ware [in *A Man's World*] couldn't do other than send her lover away – being Frank Ware. She wanted to keep him. She had many lonely hours because she did send him away. She said, 'I want to forgive you.' But her reason dominated, and she gave him up. She lived out her destiny."

"And so showed herself the modern woman, who thinks as well as feels, and who in crises is ruled by reason."

Miss Crothers nodded.

"Then you don't believe that women are illogical?"

She smiled a sideglance with mirth in it.

"They are logical. Their logic has been repressed by man's biased view of life. Women have always had logic. It is their logic that has kept the family from going to pieces. O, the 'reason' that has made women hold the ship of the home steady! Their tact! Their patience! It is their logic that has made them live out their destiny. . . .

"Women should write plays. . . . They have dramatic instinct. That is the indispensable thing. Construction comes afterward. . . . I think the best plays are written in the middle of a career. The crudities of the beginnings have worn off. Feeling is at its flood tide. And construction has not taken the place of what is more vital. Every playwright is an actor in embryo."

Crothers's *Young Wisdom*, produced on January 5, 1914 at the Criterion Theatre, New York, ran for fifty-six performances. It dealt with the premise that a woman should live with a man before marriage. Ultimately the play has a traditional romantic ending with two young couples going off to get married after a number of misadventures. However, in Act I, Victoria, the ingenue of the piece, has the following exchange with her husband to be.

240   Dialogue from Rachel Crothers's *Young Wisdom*, 1914

Manuscript in Burnside–Frohman Collection (Billy Rose Theatre Collection), New York Public Library at Lincoln Center

VICTORIA: Don't you understand, Chris dear? *You* have your work. I want mine. Things I want to make my lifework.

CHRISTOPHER: What is it you want to make your lifework?

VICTORIA: It's – it's – to – free women.

CHRISTOPHER: Let her vote, you mean?

VICTORIA: Oh no – no – no! That is only a piffling, little stop in their development. The real thing – I – I – mean – she mustn't marry for the sake of marrying – but only when she has found the man who can complete her nature – her destiny.

241   Essay on Women's Movement and American Plays, 1914

Excerpts from Florence Kiper, "Some American Plays: From the Feminist Viewpoint," *Forum*, 51 (1914), 921–31

Every play produced on the American stage, with perhaps a few negligible exceptions, has its say on the feminist question. Until sex ceases to be the main preoccupation of drama, this must necessarily be so. . . .

. . . it is by the unconscious rather than the conscious method that the American dramatists are revealing themselves in regard to the woman movement . . . Few among our playwrights are attempting to interpret to us the meaning of the growing divorce "evil," of the suffrage agitation, of women in the professions, of young girls in industry, of the sudden awakening of the sheltered woman to a knowledge of prostitution and venereal diseases. Almost none among our clever writers for the stage are bringing to these vital themes a conscious philosophy or an informed understanding. Yet the woman movement is undoubtedly, if perhaps the class consciousness in the labor struggle be excepted, the one most important tendency of the century. . . .

It is the enviable privilege of the dramatist "to popularize the pressing questions of the time." That is, he must be an interpreter to the people of what they have heretofore vaguely sensed, of what is already implicit in the public mind, but through him is realized with vividness. The drama . . . develops correlatively with the developing social and artistic consciousness of a people. . . .

. . . America is really beginning to take its drama seriously . . . Until the American audience ceases to demand only cant and provincialism, prudishness and sentimentality, America can produce no dramatists of import – minds that are conscious of large issues and that have the ability to fuse at white heat into one, thesis, plot, characterization.

To many it appears that even now the time is ripe for a new birth and that there are the stirrings of parturition. . . . While we are awaiting our big American playwrights . . . it is of interest to the feminist to hear what the present writers of the theatre have to say about American women.

Mr. Augustus Thomas . . . has chosen the double standard of sex morality as one of the themes in his play, *As a Man Thinks* [1911]. . . .

This play from the standpoint of feminism is an interesting study, because it represents a sex ethics that is more or less typical. That the author did not see bigger than his story and is innocent of satirical intention, does not invalidate the play as a fair enough picture of that American home in which the function of the wife is to be the ornamental symbol of her husband's prosperity. . . .

The explanation of the double standard of morals – a necessity, Mr. Thomas states, inherent in the biological nature of things – is somewhat reminiscent of Henry Arthur Jones and the unfortunate lady in *Mrs. Dane's Defense* [1900]. Both Mr. Jones and Mr. Thomas regret kindly and urbanely as humanitarians that the woman alone must bear the social penalty of sex indiscretion, even though that penalty be visited on the appearance of sin and not its actuality, but – with a faint sigh! – what can one do about it? So the matter has been, so will it be always. . . .

A young Chicago playwright, Mr. Joseph Medill Patterson, has given us [Ibsen's] *Ghosts* in the terms of modern Chicago, in a thoroughly sincere and workmanlike drama [*Rebellion*]. . . . The public was said to have found it gloomy, depressing. Either this was so, or its arraignment of the Catholic Church spelled its failure. This arraignment was not a one-sided or distorted propaganda, but grew inevitably from the situation. In fact, the depiction of the Catholic priest was so sympathetic that one truly regretted one's intellectual disagreement with him. When he calls to the conscience of the deserting wife in the terms of a duty that seeks not the individual happiness, one is thrilled with the fervor of all those moralists, in church or not, who are adjuring us of the present day to be mindful of the sacred and high responsibilities of marriage. But it is precisely because we are so mindful that we are insisting on the dissolution of those marriages not inherently sacred. Divorce may be – often is – a religious act also. That it is not infrequently sought with light-minded and licentious motives is true enough, doubtless – but the miseries of light-mindedness and licentiousness within marriage, who shall recount them!

Georgia Conner, under the influence of the priest, returns to her reformed drunkard. To him she bears a child, a weakling who before birth has been tainted with his father's alcoholism. The baby is born doomed and the little life flickers out to the accompaniment of the mother's anguish. At this moment the father is brought in from the street, a beast with drunkenness. He falls from the chair in which they have propped him, and, standing above his sprawling body, the wife bursts into hysterical laughter.

There is the answer to your preachment of duty! Both Mrs. Alving of Norway and Georgia Conner of Chicago learn too late the first responsibility of physical motherhood – the choice of a mate clean physically. But the spiritual injustices done those children who are the victims of dull and bitter, and of quarrelsome marriages, this also is the stuff of drama. . . .

The High Road [1912] by Edward Sheldon and Rachel Crothers's A Man's World . . . are two plays that deal with the modern woman who has attained self-support in the occupation of her choice and is thereby enabled to make her own terms with men. . . . Here at last we have an American playwright [Sheldon] who recognizes that the woman of 1912 [in the character of Mary Page] is not the woman of 1880, or even of 1900. Miss Page at thirty-eight is capable, keen, resourceful, a woman who is filling in an important way an important position. No one would think for a moment of patronizing or pitying her because she is nearing forty without a husband and children. . . .

Miss Crothers's play is also of a mature woman, younger than Mary Page – a woman who has made a place for herself as a writer . . . a type of the modern feminist. And the conflict of the drama is waged not so much without as within her own nature, a conflict between individual emotion and social conviction. . . . There is no sentimentalism, no attempt to gloss over the situation with the pet American dramatic platitude that love makes right all things. A Man's World is honest, well-built drama, interesting to feminists not only because of its exposi-tion of a modern sex-problem, but also because it is written by a woman – one who does not attempt to imitate the masculine viewpoint, but who sees the femi-nine experience through feminine temperament. . . .

. . . There will be an increasing number of women playwrights in America as the doors of occupational and educational opportunity are thrown wider. It is to be hoped that they will feel impelled – they and their brother-writers – to set forth sincerely and honestly, yet with vital passion, those problems in the devel-opment and freedom of women that the modern age has termed the problems of feminism.

The American pageant movement represents an important and often underestimated phase of the development of American drama. After its initial period (historical topics in general were used at first), it was based on native themes and subjects, and more signifi-cantly involved the community in dramatic presentations that attempted to move away from commercialism toward more artistic conceptualization. From 1909 through 1917, over 240 pageants were presented in order to celebrate the history and accomplishments of various towns or regions, primarily in the Eastern United States. Ultimately, this move-ment was eclipsed by the Little Theatre movement and community theatres. However, during its heyday, thousands of amateur performers and professional pageant creators were involved in these productions. The following remarks indicate the preeminence of the visual over the spoken word, although there was some dialogue and vocal music in most pageants.

242   Description of Percy MacKaye's *The Gloucester Pageant*, 1909[1]

Ms. letter, Susan E. Tracey, historian of the Boston stage, to [Mary] Caroline Crawford; Brown University Library.

. . . The setting was fine except that it included *no sea*. It did seem a pity with that splendid harbor and eastern point that the sea should be entirely ignored. The great rocks were fine and the necessary background and all required screens were formed by artificial rock. It was far more of a *stage* production than *Joan of Arc* [an adaptation of Schiller's *The Maid of Orleans* presented in the Harvard Stadium in 1909 with Maude Adams]. It was really all acted on a stage [unlike most subsequent pageants that utilized a panoramic sweep of the natural topography]. This stage was of grass and presented this outline, which remained practically unchanged throughout the play.

There was much of great beauty but some striking incongruities. The audience was *vast* [the *Gloucester Daily Times*, August 5, estimated 20,000 spectators]. I never felt the simple pressure of numbers as I did there even in the open air. We waited about two and a half hours for it to open. We were well seated but the time seemed interminable. My first disturbed feeling was caused by a big bunch of yellow *bananas* which hung from the porch of the old Tabard Inn [scene of Act I]. Surely no old Canterbury Pilgrim ever saw a banana! The color was good on the quaint little brown inn but it did seem far from consistent. The old white goat tethered at the bottom of the stairs was in far better keeping and would have done credit to Harlem. Why could they not have substituted game or other early English suggestion for the bananas? A few movable screens were used made of wire covered with branches of trees. Before the play opened they carried an enormous pair of angel's wings up to the highest pinnacle of rock and set one of these screens before them. The screen not being large enough to quite conceal them we were painfully conscious of an angelic presence all through the piece and it also made an ugly square center.

Now let me tell some of the beautiful things. First the robing of many of the characters among the rocks. In the waning light we watched gray, black, and white nuns, here and there a glorious red cardinal; there was one splendid burnt orange robe. Lovely! After a time a long, long procession of many hundred children wound down the grassy slope; these were in many and beautiful shades, simple little pilgrim robes. I took down these colors for you. At first apple and darker greens, so many! Pink (not a good shade, but used sparingly), yellow, two shades, with white, royal purple, and pale lavender – the purples were beautiful. An unusual and fine combination was dark blue with a very greeny turquoise. Black and white, red and white, brown and blue, brown and green, dark reds

---

[1] At Gloucester, Massachusetts, on August 4, 1909.

and blue and green. To my great disgust none of these children were seen on the stage; not even for the ensembles . . . , for it was a most straggling windup. People didn't know whether to go home or not. They tried to have a final procession, some nuns came in chanting a fine ecclesiastical chant accompanied by a flight of sky rockets!!! There was a strange mixture of municipal fireworks and "whooping up Taft" [the President attended the performance] with Chaucer and his contemporaries. The character of the "wife of Bath" was the only one which stood out very well. She was consistent and vigorous throughout the piece, if not elegant. Old English coarseness certainly dominated but I felt that it was not more than might be found then, but why make all this great beauty and its possibilities so subservient to the commonplace? For true dignity the thing could not touch the Maude Adams production [of *Joan of Arc*]. It might as well have been indoors as out except for the large numbers. The children were simply to constitute a chorus which was extremely feeble. But such a glorious opportunity for fine pictures! An opportunity largely missed. How I wish that you might have seen it with me. I could hear your voice saying "A lack of organization" at my very elbow. . . .

243   Explanation of the Value of Pageantry, 1914

Mary Porter Beegle, "The Fundamentals of Successful Pageantry," *Bulletin of the American Pageant Association*, no. 7 (September 15, 1914)

. . . so far as the public can see, the commercial pageant apparently fulfills the superficial aspects of the true pageant, and it is only through education and publicity that the many individuals composing the public may be made to realize the significance of pageantry as a new and possible art for the people, of which the final aim is social service . . . [, meaning to bring] to the people the opportunity to organize, cooperate, and unite in a form of art production readily accessible to them all.

The social value of the pageant is chiefly dependent upon the ideals of the pageant master or director, and his ability to impress them upon the community. . . . He must serve the community by teaching the participants to develop their minds through self-expression – and not merely to absorb his ideas. His skillful guidance will end in their creating the pageant for themselves. To do this successfully the pageant master must be able to recognize creative ability among his fellow workers and direct it so that the performance may be a real artistic production.

It is not right to assume that the highest social value of the pageant may only be gained from a spirit of loyal cooperation. If the pageant is lacking either in artistic or dramatic qualities it is a failure, for the reason that such a pageant does not establish a true standard. . . . It may be simple; but it must be well done, or it cheats not only the audience but the performer.

Last of all, the pageant master must leave with his people a definite sense of something new in their lives. Some definite awakening and response to this new form of art, that stimulates the community or the individual with a desire for a more intimate expression of an art form. It may be the beautifying of the town, the formation of a local orchestra, classes in dancing, organization for serious dramatic study. . . .

The question, it would seem, is after all one of purpose; if the purpose is to bring into the lives of the people a new form of recreation that awakens a sense of beauty and pride in the community, it is necessary that we have a clear idea of what we mean that new art to be called.

244   Graphic chart of a pageant organization scheme, 1914[1]

Supplement to the *Bulletin of the American Pageant Association*, no. 11 (1914)

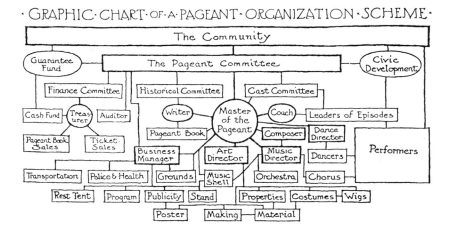

· GRAPHIC · CHART · OF · A · PAGEANT · ORGANIZATION · SCHEME ·

[1]   The caption under the chart states:

> This chart is only of value in assisting to indicate the best *general* lines of division of a pageant organization. Local conditions, or individual peculiarities in various pageant schemes, may modify details. The pageant master may also be writer of the pageant book; or perform the duties of coach, or art director, or business manager in small pageants – while several directors are often concerned in the same item.

> For histories and analyses of U.S. pageantry, see Naima Prevots, *American Pageantry: A Movement of Art and Democracy* (Ann Arbor: UMI Research Press, 1990) and David Glassberg, *American Historical Pageantry: The Uses of Tradition in the Early Twentieth Century* (Chapel Hill: University of North Carolina Press, 1990).

W. E. B. Du Bois believed that the pageant format was ideal for the mass education of African-American people who had been excluded from much traditional theatre in the nineteenth century. In 1913 as part of a fifty-year celebration of emancipation Du Bois wrote and produced a panoramic account of African people called *The Star of Ethiopia* which dramatized significant historical moments and paraded the contributions of African-American men and women. After three episodes which depict prehistoric times (discovery of iron) and flourishing civilizations in Central Africa, the scene shifts to the United States where the brutality of slavery is contrasted with the revolutionary fervor of Nat Turner, John Brown, and others. In the finale contributions since emancipation are highlighted with a huge parade symbolizing African-American achievement. *The Star of Ethiopia* cost $6,000 and featured over three hundred performers. It opened in New York on October 25 and subsequently was performed in Philadelphia and Washington, D.C.

245   Synopsis of *The Star of Ethiopia*, 1913

Crisis, 7 (November 1913), 339–41; reprinted in Leonard C. Archer, *Black Images in the American Theatre* (Brooklyn: Pageant-Poseidon Press, 1973), p. 109[1]

PRELUDE

The lights of the Court of Freedom blaze. A trumpet blast is heard and four heralds, black and of gigantic stature, appear with silver trumpets and standing at the four corners of the Temple of Beauty cry:

"Hear ye, hear ye! Men of all the Americas, and listen to the tale of the eldest and strongest of the races of mankind, whose faces be black. Hear ye, hear ye of the gifts of the black men in this world . . ."

First Episode: The Gift of Iron

Second Episode: The Gift of the Nile

Third Episode: The Gift of Struggle Toward Freedom

Fourth Episode: The Gift of Faith

Fifth Episode: The Gift of Humiliation

Sixth Episode: The Gift of Freedom for the World

EPILOGUE

A single voice sings "O Freedom." A soprano chorus takes it up. The Boy Scouts march in. Full brasses take up "O Freedom." Little Children enter and among them the symbolic figures of the Laborer, the Artisan, the Servant of Men, the Merchant, the Inventor, the Musician, the Actor, the Teacher, Law, Medicine and the Ministry, the All-Mother, formerly the Veiled Woman, now unveiled in her chariot with her dancing brood, and the bust of Lincoln at her side. With burst of music and blast of trumpets, the pageant ends and the heralds sing.

[1] See also Hay, *African American Theatre* and Glassberg, *American Historical Pageantry* for additional information on *The Star of Ethiopia*.

Dissatisfaction with the commercialism of the professional theatre led to a largely amateur theatre movement (the Little Theatre movement)[1] seeking the promotion of drama
on a higher plane. Dating as a conscious effort at least from the founding of the Hull-
House Players in Chicago in 1897 by Jane Addams and Mrs. Laura Dainty Pelham, it
experienced its greatest surge in the teens, spurred on by the founding of the Drama
League in 1909, the visit of the Irish Players in 1911, and Percy MacKaye's plea for greater
efforts in this direction in his book *The Civic Theatre* (1912). Other influences include the
art theatre movement and the new stagecraft in Europe, and the early efforts in academic
institutions, in particular George Pierce Baker's Workshop '47 at Harvard (1912), to pro-
mote better theatre and drama.

   Addams founded Hull-House in 1889 on the west side of Chicago. This settlement from
the beginning confronted poverty, poor housing, disease, and all the ills that existed in an
industrial city. One of its early aims was to make the arts part of the life of the community;
indeed, the result was a kind of cultural renaissance in Chicago. Almost from the beginning there was drama at Hull-House, for Addams and others realized the power of theatre
as an educational institution and an agent for immigrant assimilation.

   (The Little Theatre movement is not limited to the time period of this section. Indeed,
many of the more notable efforts took place after 1915; by 1920 there were more than
fifty groups across the country. Today there are more than five thousand amateur groups
which grew out of this movement.)

[1] An early and useful overview of early groups, including several mentioned in this section as well
as the more notable groups founded c. 1915, is Constance D'Arcy Mackay's *The Little Theatre in the
United States* (New York: H. Holt and Co., 1917). A source with greater perspective is Kenneth
Macgowan's *Footlights across America* (New York: Harcourt, Brace & Co., 1929). See also Adele
Heller and Lois Rudnick, *1915, The Cultural Moment* (New Brunswick, NJ: Rutgers University
Press, 1991).

246   Jane Addams on Hull-House, 1910

Jane Addams, *Twenty Years at Hull-House* (New York: Macmillan, 1910), pp. 382–95[1]

... One of the conspicuous features of our neighborhood, as of all industrial
quarters, is the persistency with which the entire population attends the theater
... young people looked upon an afternoon a week in the gallery of a Halstead
Street theatre as their one opportunity to see life. The sort of melodrama they
see there has recently been described as "the ten commandments written in red
fire." ...

   ... The theater, such as it was, appeared to be the one agency which freed the
boys and girls from that destructive isolation of those who drag themselves up
to maturity by themselves, and it gave them a glimpse of that order and beauty

[1] A useful collection of essays on the Hull-House experience is *Eighty Years at Hull-House*, ed. Allen
F. Davis and Mary Lynn McCree (Chicago: Quadrangle Books, 1969). For a vivid account of the
Hull-House Players' tour of Ireland in 1913, see Elsie F. Weil, "The Hull-House Players," *Theatre
Magazine*, September 1913, pp. xix–xxii.

into which even the poorest drama endeavors to restore the bewildering facts of life. . . .

. . . we would have been dull indeed if we had not availed ourselves of the use of the play at Hull-House, not only as an agent of recreation and education, but as a vehicle of self-expression for the teeming young life all about us.

Long before the Hull-House theatre was built we had many plays, first in the drawing room and later in the gymnasium. The young people's clubs never tired of rehearsing and preparing for these dramatic occasions, and we also discovered that older people were almost equally ready and talented. . . .

The immigrants in the neighborhood of Hull-House have utilized our little stage in an endeavor to reproduce the past of their own nations through those immortal dramas which have escaped from the restraining bond of one country into the land of the universal.

A large colony of Greeks near Hull-House, who often feel that their history and classic background are completely ignored by Americans, and that they are easily confused with the more ignorant immigrants from other parts of south-eastern Europe, welcome an occasion to present Greek plays in the ancient text. With expert help in the difficulties of staging and rehearsing a classic play, they reproduced the *Ajax* of Sophocles upon the Hull-House stage. It was a genuine triumph to the actors who felt that they were "showing forth the glory of Greece" to "ignorant Americans." . . . The Lithuanians, the Poles, and other Russian subjects often use the Hull-House stage to present plays in their own tongue, which shall at one and the same time keep alive their sense of participation in the great Russian revolution and relieve their feelings in regard to it. There is something still more appealing in the yearning efforts the immigrants sometimes make to formulate their situation in America. I recall a play written by an Italian playwright of our neighborhood, which depicted the insolent break between Americanized sons and old country parents, so touchingly that it moved to tears all the older Italians in the audience. Did the tears of each express relief in finding that others had had the same experience as himself, and did the knowledge free each one from a sense of isolation and an injured belief that his children were the worst of all?

This effort to understand life through its dramatic portrayal, to see one's own participation intelligibly set forth, becomes difficult when one enters the field of social development, but even here it is not impossible if a Settlement group is constantly searching for new material. . . .

The dramatic arts have gradually been developed at Hull-House through amateur companies, one of which has held together for more than fifteen years. . . . They present all sorts of plays from melodramas and comedy to those of Shaw, Ibsen, and Galsworthy. The latter are surprisingly popular, perhaps because of their sincere attempt to expose the shams and pretenses of contemporary life and to penetrate into some of its perplexing social and domestic situations. Through such plays the stage may become a pioneer teacher of social righteousness.

I have come to believe, however, that the stage may do more than teach, that much of our current moral instruction will not endure the test of being cast into a lifelike mold, and when presented in dramatic form will reveal itself as platitudinous and effete. That which may have sounded like righteous teaching when it was remote and wordy, will be challenged afresh when it is obliged to simulate life itself. . . .

247   Sheldon Cheney on the Art Theatre Movement and the Little Theatre, 1914

Sheldon Cheney, *The New Movement in the Theatre* (New York: Mitchell Kennerley, 1914), pp. 178–83

The true progress of dramatic art in America is coming in the amateur and semi-professional theatres and dramatic societies which have sprung up in the last ten years, to satisfy a longing which the professional playhouse entirely overlooks, and as a protest against the commercialization of the regular theatre. . . . Their ideal lies in the realm of dramatic art rather than of commercial success, and their methods are experimental rather than traditional and set. They have held themselves free from the conventions and artificial standards of Broadway, and they have pushed out into all sorts of new fields. They have not developed a great American drama, and they have not freed the American theatre from the inartistic faults of setting and staging and acting that was brought to it. But they deserve most of the credit for whatever advance has been made toward either ideal. . . .

The Chicago Little Theatre is perhaps the most typical "art theatre" in the country. From amateur material Maurice Browne, the organizer and director, has whipped into shape an organization which stands today as one of the most vital expressions of the new dramatic spirit in America. . . . The Chicago Little Theatre tends to the literary or poetic drama, rather than to intensive social drama; and it has produced literary plays that are seldom seen on the stage elsewhere . . . The staging is designed according to the newest European ideas of simplicity and suggestion, and the settings as a whole have been remarkably successful in evoking the proper atmosphere for the action. . . .

The Boston Toy Theatre is very similar to the Chicago Little Theatre in its aims and in the breadth of its field. The organization is more truly an amateur one – its activities up to this time have taken place in a converted stable – but it plans to occupy soon a theatre of the "intimate" type in Boston's commercial playhouse district . . . The Theatre's most important achievement, perhaps, has been in stage setting. It was the Toy that gave to Livingston Platt the opportunity to work out in practice his advanced theories of symbolic and suggestive staging. The work of this little playhouse really foreran a movement which promises to revolutionize American stage decoration. . . .

248   Maurice Browne on the Chicago Little Theatre, 1913

Quoted in Karleton Hackett, "The Little Theatre in Chicago," *Theatre Magazine*, 17 (March 1913), vii

We have no special purpose to make propaganda for American playwrights, though, other things being equal, we should give the preference to America over Europe, and to Chicago over any other place; but the important thing is that the play shall be worth something. If we give interesting productions, the future will take care of itself, and we welcome the general public to the full extent of our seating capacity [91]. For our members we charge fifty cents, while the public is asked to pay only a dollar, and if we cannot give them the value we have not the slightest intention of asking for support on the grounds of patriotism, of the elevation of the drama, or in any other form of charity. Meanwhile we are having "the time of our lives."

249   Essay on Chicago Little Theatre Production of *The Trojan Women*, 1915[1]

Maurice Browne, *Too Late to Lament: An Autobiography* (Bloomington: Indiana University Press, 1956), appendix[2]

Barker used a chorus of over twenty as against five used by the Chicago Little Theatre; his was a pageant, dignified, impressive, pictorially compelling if bizarre. His chorus remained remote, detached from the principals and from the movement of the play as a whole, singing their words to the music of an orchestra, keeping always their place in the decorative scheme but playing no intimate emotional part. The Chicago Little Theatre's spirit and technique were different, different indeed from anything I have witnessed on the Anglo-American stage. There was something so poignantly real about the spirit and something so elusively natural about the technique that I found myself forgetting the latter and gripped by the throat by the former – gripped to such a degree that at times it seemed I must cry out against my impotence to help the world suffering they held out in their hands. Theirs was not a pageant but a tapestry of emotions.

The chorus, swaying rhythmically with waves of sorrow, sometimes chanting,

---

[1] The staging of this production by Barbara Winter is compared to that of Granville Barker's, seen first at Harvard Stadium on May 19, 1915.

[2] Browne's autobiography is highly emotional and lacking in objectivity. For a more straightforward account of his career and the Chicago Little Theatre, see Homer N. Abegglen, "The Chicago Little Theatre, 1912–1917," *Old Northwest*, 3 (June 1977), 153–72.

sometimes half-singing, became themselves the height of the emotion of each of the principals, mingling with it, supporting it and finally transfiguring it. At last one saw the Greek chorus as one had dreamed it – and yet, curiously, it is only now that I know this. At the time it was so one with the scheme of things that I almost forgot it; it was the roar of the undertow of the ocean; it was the thing which articulated the pent-up anguish in me: and therefore so fitting that I grew unconscious of it. The play itself drew me into its marrow until I remembered only the ache of the world. Afterward – well, I sat down for hours, not to think, only to sit and stare dumbly.

Barker's technique was familiar to me: the clear, incisive, direct method of "modern stage technique" applied finely to poetry. But this other was still in the process of making. The formalization was complete, crystallized most strongly in the chorus; the tempo was legato; all voices were pitched between *d* and *f*. The chorus was always lyrical, always sculptural, moving from one group of sorrow to another. The principals, not as strongly characterized as Barker's, were partly lyrical, partly characterized. Their transitions from lyricism to naturalism and back again were astonishingly interesting; instead of having a tendency to make the play fragmentary as one might suppose, they welded all parts more strongly together. The ensemble – the choreography, it might justly be called – was the best I have ever seen outside the Imperial Russian ballet. Waves of emotion would run through the players simultaneously, each expressing them in his or her native way but with a harmony that was symphonic. The inevitable psychological effect of this was to sweep the hearer along on the very crest of emotion until he was left as I had been left, stranded – or was it in harbor? – among the things that do not change. There are people – I have talked with them – who will have none of it; but even these, I find, cannot quite forget. To others it has been almost a revelation. And I believe that, in the final analysis, this is the great difference between the Chicago Company – who they are one does not know, as they gave the play anonymously – and Barker's people. One has, with the former, almost the sense of a new religious order – or a white fire being lighted once again, and in these days.

Bibliography

Abegglen, Homer N. "The Chicago Little Theatre, 1912–1917." *Old Northwest*, 3 (June 1977), 153–72.

Alger, William Rounseville. *Life of Edwin Forrest, The American Tragedian*. 2 vols. Philadelphia: J. B. Lippincott Co., 1877.

Allen, Robert C. *Horrible Prettiness: Burlesque and American Culture*. Chapel Hill: University of North Carolina Press, 1991.

Amacher, Richard E. "Behind the Curtain with the Noble Savage: Stage Movement of Indian Plays, 1825–1860." *Theatre Survey*, 7 (1966), 101–14.

"American Playwrights on the American Drama." *Harper's Weekly*, 33 (February 2, 1889), 97–100.

Appelbaum, Stanley, ed. *The New York Stage: Famous Productions in Photographs*. New York: Dover, 1976.
ed. *Scenes from the Nineteenth-Century Stage in Woodcuts*. New York: Dover, 1977.

Archer, Stephen M. *American Actors and Actresses*. Detroit: Gale Research, 1983.
Junius Brutus Booth: Theatrical Prometheus. Carbondale: Southern Illinois University Press, 1992.

Auser, Courtland P. *Nathaniel Parker Willis*. New York: Twayne Publishers, 1969.

Auster, Albert. *Actresses and Suffragists: Women in the American Theatre 1890–1920*. New York: Praeger, 1984.

Bagley, Russell E. "Theatrical Entertainment in Pensacola, Florida: 1882–1892." *Southern Speech Journal*, 16 (1950), 62–84.

Bank, Rosemarie K. "Actor Training at the Mid-point in Nineteenth Century American Repertory." *Theatre History Studies*, 8 (1988), 157–62.
"Louisa Lane Drew at the Arch Street Theatre: Repertory and Actor Training in Nineteenth Century Philadelphia." *Theatre Studies*, 24/25 (1977–79), 37–46.
"A Reconsideration of the Death of Nineteenth-Century American Repertory Companies and the Rise of the Combination." *Essays in Theatre*, 5 (November 1986), 61–75.
"Theatre and Narrative Fiction in the Work of a Nineteenth-Century American Playwright, Louisa Medina." *Theatre History Studies*, 3 (1983), 54–67.

Baral, Robert. *Revue, A Nostalgic Reprise of the Great Broadway Period*. New York: Fleet Press Corporation, 1962.

Barnes, Eric W. *The Lady of Fashion*. New York: Charles Scribner's Sons, 1954.

Barnes, James J. *Authors, Publishers, and Politicians: The Quest for an Anglo-American Copyright Agreement, 1815–1854*. Columbus: Ohio State University Press, 1974.

Barnum, P. T. *Life of P. T. Barnum*. Buffalo, NY: Corier Company Printer, 1888.

Barrett, Lawrence. *Charlotte Cushman*. New York: Dunlap Society, 1889.

Bates, Alfred, ed. *The Drama, Its History, Literature and Influences on Civilization*, Vols. 19 and 20. New York: Smart & Stanley, 1903.

Beers, Henry A. *Nathaniel Parker Willis*. Boston: Houghton Mifflin, 1885.

Belasco, David. *The Theatre through Its Stage Door.* New York: Harper Brothers, 1919.

Bender, Jack E. "The Criterion Independent Theatre." *Educational Theatre Journal,* 28, no. 3 (October 1966), 197–209.

Bergman, Gosta M. *Lighting in the Theatre.* Totawa, NJ: Rowman and Littlefield, 1977.

Bernard, John. *Retrospections of America, 1797–1811, from the Manuscript by Mrs. Bayle Bernard,* ed. Laurence Hutton and Brander Matthews. New York: Harper and Brothers, 1887.

Bernheim, Alfred L. *The Business of the Theatre: An Economic History of the American Theatre.* New York: Benjamin Blom, 1964.

Berthoff, Werner. *The Ferment of American Realism: American Literature, 1884–1919.* New York: Free Press, 1965.

Berson, Misha. *The San Francisco Stage.* San Francisco: Performing Arts Library, 1992.

Binns, Archie. *Mrs. Fiske and the American Theatre.* New York: Crown Publishers, Inc., 1955.

Birkmire, William H. *The Planning and Construction of American Theatres.* New York: John Wiley and Sons, 1901.

Blake, Charles. *An Historical Account of the Providence Stage.* Providence, RI: G. H. Whitney, 1868.

Blum, Daniel. *A Pictorial History of the American Theatre: 100 Years – 1860–1960.* New York: Crown Publishers, Inc., 1960.

Bogard, Travis, Richard Moody, and Walter J. Meserve. *The Revels History of Drama in English, Vol. VIII, American Drama.* London: Methuen, 1977.

Bost, James S. *Monarchs of the Mimic World or the American Theatre of the Eighteenth Century through the Managers – the Men Who Made It.* Orono: University of Maine, 1977.

Bowen, Elbert R. *Theatrical Entertainment in Rural Missouri before the Civil War.* Columbia: University of Missouri Press, 1959.

Brady, William A. *Showman.* New York: E. P. Dutton, 1937.

Briggs, H. E. "The Early Theatre in Chicago." *Journal of the Illinois State Historical Society,* 31 (June 1946), 165–78.

Brokaw, John W. "A Mexican-American Acting Company, 1849–1924." *Educational Theatre Journal,* 27, no. 1 (March 1975), 23–29.

Brown, Jared A. "British Military Theatre in New York, 1780–81." *Theatre Survey,* 23 (1982), 151–62.

"Howe's Strolling Company: British Military Theatre in New York and Philadelphia, 1777 and 1778." *Theatre Survey,* 18, no. 1 (May 1977), 30–43.

Brown, T. Allston. *History of the American Stage.* New York: Dick & Fitzgerald, Publishers, 1870. Reprinted New York: Burt Franklin, 1969.

A History of the New York Stage from 1732 to 1901. 3 vols. New York: Dodd, Mead & Co., 1903.

Browne, Maurice. *Too Late to Lament: An Autobiography.* Bloomington: Indiana University Press, 1956.

Bunce, O. B. "Behind, Below, and Above the Scene." *Appletons' Journal,* 3 (May 28, 1870), 589–94.

Burge, James C. *Lines of Business: Casting Practice and Policy in the American Theatre, 1752–1899.* New York: Peter Lang, 1986.

Caffin, Caroline. *Vaudeville.* New York: Mitchell Kennerley, 1914.

Cairns, W. B. "American Drama of the 18th Century." *Dial,* 59 (July 15, 1915), 60–62.

Cheney, Sheldon. *The New Movement in the Theatre.* New York: Mitchell Kennerley, 1914.

Chinoy, Helen Krich, and Linda Walsh Jenkins. *Women in American Theatre.* New York: Theatre Communications Group, 1981.

Church, V. "Colonial Theatres." *Theatre,* 11 (June 1910), 181–82, 184.

Clapp, Henry Austin. *The Reminiscences of a Dramatic Critic.* Boston: Houghton Mifflin Co., 1902.

Clapp, J. B., and E. F. Edgett. *Players of the Present,* Series 2, Vols. IX, XI, XIII. New York: Dunlap Society, 1899–1901.

Plays of the Present. New York: Dunlap Society, 1902.

Clapp, William W., Jr. *A Record of the Boston Stage.* Boston: James Monroe, 1853. Reprint New York: Benjamin Blom, 1968.

Coad, Oral Sumner, and Edwin Mims, Jr. *The American Stage.* New Haven, CT: Yale University Press, 1929.

Colby, Elbridge. "Early American Comedy." *Bulletin of the New York Public Library,* 23 (July 1919), 3–11.

Cole, Toby, and Helen Krich Chinoy, eds. *Actors on Acting.* New York: Crown, 1954.

Collins, Sherwood. "Boston's Political Street Theatre: The Eighteenth Century Pope Day Pageant." *Education Theatre Journal,* 25, no. 4 (December 1973), 401–9.

Conner, Charlotte Barnes. *Plays, Prose and Poetry.* Philadelphia: E. H. Butler, 1848.

Cosgrave, Luke. *Theater Tonight.* Hollywood: House-Warven, 1952.

Crawford, Mary Caroline. *The Romance of the American Theatre.* 2nd rev. ed. New York: Halcyon House, 1940.

Creahan, John. *The Life of Laura Keene.* Philadelphia: Rodgers Publishing Co., 1897.

Culp, Ralph Borden. "Drama – and – Theatre in the American Revolution." *Speech Monographs,* 32 (March 1965), 79–86.

Curry, Wade. "Steele MacKaye: Producer and Director." *Educational Theatre Journal,* 18, no. 3 (October 1966), 210–15.

Curtis, Julia. "Philadelphia in an Uproar: The Monks of Monk Hall, 1844." *Theatre History Studies,* 5 (1985), 41–47.

   "The Architectures and Appearance of the Charleston Theatre: 1793–1833." *Educational Theatre Journal,* 23, no. 1 (March 1971), 1–12.

Dahl, Curtis. *Robert Montgomery Bird.* New York: Twayne Publishers, 1963.

Daly, Joseph F. *The Life of Augustin Daly.* New York: Macmillan, 1917.

Damon, Samuel Foster. *Thomas Holley Chivers, Friend of Poe.* New York: Harper & Brothers, 1930.

Davis, Allen F., and Mary Lynn McCree, eds. *Eighty Years at Hull-House.* Chicago: Quadrangle Books, 1969.

Davis, Owen. *I'd Like to Do It Again.* New York: Farrar & Rinehart, 1931.

   "Why I Quit Writing Melodrama." *American Magazine,* 78 (September 1914), 28–31, 77–80.

Davis, Peter A. "From Stock to Combination: The Panic of 1873 and Its Effects on the American Theatre Industry." *Theatre History Studies,* 8 (1988), 1–10.

   "Lawrence Barrett and *The Man O'Airlie*: The Genteel Tradition in Performance." *Theatre History Studies,* 7 (1987), 61–72.

Donohue, Joseph W., Jr., ed. *The Theatrical Manager in England and America.* Princeton, NJ: Princeton University Press, 1971.

Dorman, James H. *Theatre in the Ante Bellum South.* Chapel Hill: University of North Carolina Press, 1967.

Dorson, Richard M. "Mose the Far-famed and World-renowned." *American Literature,* 15 (November 1943), 288–300.

   "The Yankee on the Stage – A Folk Hero of the American Drama." *New England Quarterly,* 13 (1940), 467–93.

Doty, Gresdna Ann. *The Career of Mrs. Anne Brunton Merry in the American Theatre.* Baton Rouge: Louisiana State University Press, 1971.

Downer, Alan S. "Early American Professional Acting." *Theatre Survey,* 12, no. 2 (November 1971), 79–96.

Dulles, Foster Rhea. *America Learns to Play.* New York: Appleton-Century-Crofts, 1940.

   A History of Recreation. 2nd ed. New York: Appleton-Century-Crofts, 1965.

Dunlap, William. *A History of the American Theatre.* 2 vols. New York: J. and J. Harper, 1832. Reprint New York: Burt Franklin, 1963.

   History of the Rise and Progress of the Arts of Design in the United States. 3 vols. New York: Benjamin Blom, 1965.

Durang, Charles. "The Philadelphia Stage from the Year 1749 to the Year 1855." *Philadelphia Sunday Dispatch.* (May 7, 1854; June 29, 1856; July 8, 1860). (Also Third Series, 1830/1–1855, beginning July 1860.)

Durham, Weldon B., ed. *American Theatre Companies, 1749–1887.* 3 vols. Westport, CT: Greenwood Press, 1986, 1987, 1989.

Eaton, Walter Prichard. *The American Stage of To-day.* Boston: Small, Maynard, 1908.

   At the New Theatre and Others. Boston: Small, Maynard, 1910.

Eich, Louis M. "The Stage Yankee." *Quarterly Journal of Speech*, 27 (1941), 16–25.

Ellis, Joseph J. *After the Revolution: Profile of Early American Culture*. New York: Norton, 1979.

Ellis, Milton. "Puritans and the Drama." *American Notes and Queries*, 2 (July 1942), 64.

Emery, G. M. "Passing of the Walnut Street Theatre." *Theatre*, 31 (June 1920), 506–8, 572.

Engle, Ron, and Tice L. Miller, eds. *The American Stage*. Cambridge and New York: Cambridge University Press, 1993.

Enkvist, Nils Erik. *Caricatures of Americans on the English Stage Prior to 1870*. Commentationes Humanarum Litterarum, XVIII, 1. Helsingfors: Centraltryckeri och Bokbinderi ab, 1951.

Ernst, Alice Henson. *Trouping in the Oregon Country: A History of Frontier Theatre*. 1961. Reprint Westport, CT: Greenwood Press, 1974.

Faulkner, Seldon. "The *Octoroon* War." *Educational Theatre Journal*, 15, no. 1 (March 1963), 32–38.

Faust, Clement E. *The Life and Dramatic Works of Robert Montgomery Bird*. New York: Knickerbocker Press, 1919.

Felheim, Marvin. *The Theater of Augustin Daly*. New York: Greenwood Press, 1969.

Felton, C. C. "Dramas of N. P. Willis." *North American Review*, 51 (1840), 141–58.

Fields, Armond, and L. Marc Fields. *From the Bowery to Broadway: Lew Fields and the Roots of American Popular Theater*. New York: Oxford University Press, 1993.

Fisher, Judith L. and Stephen Watt, eds. *When They Weren't Doing Shakespeare: Essays on Nineteenth-Century British & American Theatre*. Athens: University of Georgia, 1989.

Ford, George D. *These Were Actors – The Story of the Chapmans and the Drakes*. New York: Library Publishers, 1955.

Ford, Paul Leicester. "The Beginnings of American Dramatic Literature." *New England Magazine*, n.s. (February 1894), 673–87.

Fort, Tim. "Steele MacKaye's Lighting Visions for *The World Finder*." *Nineteenth Century Theatre*, 18 (1990), 35–51.

    "Three Voyages of Discovery: The Columbus Productions of Imre Kiralfy, E. E. Rice, and Steele MacKaye." *Journal of American Drama and Theatre*, 5 (Spring 1993), 5–30.

Fox, D. R. "The Development of the American Theatre." *New York History*, 17 (1936), 22–41.

Foy, Eddie, and Alvin F. Harlow. *Clowning through Life*. New York: E. P. Dutton, 1928.

Free, Joseph H. "The Ante-Bellum Theatre of the Old Natchez Region." *Journal of Mississippi History*, 5 (January 1943), 14–27.

Freedman, Morris. *American Drama in Social Context*. Carbondale: Southern Illinois University Press, 1971.

Freeman, John R. *On the Safeguarding of Life in Theaters*. New York: American Society of Mechanical Engineers, 1906.

Frohman, Charles. "New Phases of Theatre Management." *Harper's Weekly*, 48 (December 31, 1904), 2022–24.

Frohman, Daniel. *Daniel Frohman Presents: An Autobiography*. New York: Kendall and Sharp, 1935.

    "A Manager's View of the Stage." *Harper's Weekly*, 48 (December 24, 1904), 1988–89, 1999.

    Memories of a Manager: Reminiscences of the Old Lyceum and of Some Players of the Last Quarter Century. New York: Doubleday, 1911.

Fuller, Margaret (Ossoli). *Art, Literature and the Drama*. Boston: Roberts Press, 1875.

    Papers on Literature and Art. 2 vols. New York: Putnam, 1946.

Gafford, Lucile. "The Boston Stage and the War of 1812." *New England Quarterly*, 7 (1934), 327–35.

    "Transcendentalist Attitudes toward the Drama and the Theatre." *New England Quarterly*, 13 (September 1940), 442–66.

Gagey, Edmond M. *The San Francisco Stage*. New York: Columbia University Press, 1950.

Gaisford, John. *The Drama in New Orleans*. New Orleans: J. B. Steel, 1849.

Gallagher, Kent G. *The Foreigner in Early American Drama*. The Hague: Mouton, 1966.

Gay, F. L. "The First American Play." *Nation*, 88 (February 11, 1909), 136.

Gilbert, Douglas. *American Vaudeville, Its Life and Times*. New York: McGraw-Hill Book Co., 1940.

Glassberg, Daniel. *American Historical Pageantry: The Uses of Tradition in the Early Twentieth Century*. Chapel Hill: University of North Carolina Press, 1990.

Goodale, Katherine. *Behind the Scenes with Edwin Booth*. Boston: Houghton Mifflin Co., 1931.

Gossett, Thomas F. *"Uncle Tom's Cabin" and American Culture*. Dallas: Southern Methodist University Press, 1985.

Gottlieb, Lois C. "The Double Standard Debate in Early 20th-Century American Drama." *Michigan Academician*, 7 (1975), 441–52.

"The Perils of Freedom: The New Woman in Three American Plays of the 1900's." *Canadian Review of American Studies*, 6 (1975), 84–98.

Graham, Philip. *Showboats*. Austin: University of Texas Press, 1951.

Grau, Robert. *The Stage in the Twentieth Century*. New York: Broadway Publishing, 1912.

Greenwood, Isaac J. *The Circus: Its Origin and Growth Prior to 1835*. New York: Dunlap Society, 1898.

Grimsted, David. *Melodrama Unveiled: American Theater and Culture, 1800–1850*. Chicago: University of Chicago Press, 1968.

Grose, B. Donald. "Edwin Forrest, *Metamora*, and the Indian Removal Act of 1830." *Theatre Journal*, 37, no. 2 (May 1985), 181–91.

Grossman, Edwina Booth. *Edwin Booth, Recollections by His Daughter*. New York: Century Co., 1902.

Hackett, Karleton. "The Little Theatre in Chicago." *Theatre Magazine*, 17 (March 1913), vii.

Harbin, Billy J. "Hodgkinson's Last Years: At the Charleston Theatre, 1803–1805." *Theatre Survey*, 13, no. 2 (November 1972), 30–43.

"Laura Keene at the Lincoln Assassination." *Educational Theatre Journal*, 18, no. 1 (March 1966), 47–54.

"The Role of Mrs. Hallam in the Hodgkinson Hallam Controversy: 1794–1797." *Theatre Journal*, 32, no. 2 (May 1970), 213–22.

Harding, Alfred. *The Revolt of the Actors*. New York: W. Morrow & Co., 1929.

Harris, Laurilyn J. "Extravaganza at Niblo's Garden: *The Black Crook*." *Nineteenth Century Theatre Research*, 13 (Summer 1985), 1–15.

Harris, Neil. *Humbug: The Art of P. T. Barnum*. Boston: Little, Brown, 1973.

Harris, Richard A. "A Young Dramatist's Diary: *The Secret Records* of R. M. Bird." *Literary Chronicle, University of Pennsylvania*, 25 (Winter 1959), 8–24.

Hartman, John Geoffrey. *The Development of American Social Comedy, 1797–1936*. 1939. Reprinted New York: Octagon Books, 1971.

Hartmann, Louis. *Theatre Lighting*. New York: D. Appleton, 1930.

Havens, Daniel F. *The Columbian Muse of Comedy: The Development of a Native Tradition in Early American Social Comedy, 1787–1845*. Carbondale and Edwardsville: Southern Illinois University Press, 1973.

Hawes, David S. "John Brougham as a Playwright." *Educational Theatre Journal*, 9 (1957), 184–93.

Heller, Adele, and Lois Rudnick. *1915, The Cultural Moment*. New Brunswick, NJ: Rutgers University Press, 1991.

Henderson, Mary C. *Broadway Ballyhoo*. New York: Abrams, 1989.

The City & the Theatre: New York Playhouses from Bowling Green to Times Square. Clifton, NJ: James T. White, 1973.

Theater in America. New York: Abrams, 1986.

Herne, James A. "Art for Truth's Sake in The Drama." *Arena*, 17 (February 1897), 361–70.

"Forty Years before the Foot-Lights." *Coming Age*, 2 (August 1899), 121–29.

Hewitt, Barnard. "Mrs. John Wood and the Lost Art of Burlesque Acting." *Educational Theatre Journal*, 13, no. 2 (May 1961), 82–85.

Theatre U.S.A., 1668 to 1957. New York: McGraw-Hill Book Co., 1959.

Highfill, Philip, Jr. "The British Background of the American Hallams." *Theatre Survey*, 11, no. 2 (November 1970), 1–35.

Hill, Errol. *The Jamaican Stage 1655–1900*. Amherst: University of Massachusetts Press, 1992.

Shakespeare in Sable: A History of Black Shakespearean Actors. Amherst: University of Massachusetts Press, 1984.

Hill, Frank Pierce. *American Plays, Printed 1714–1830: A Bibliographical Record*. Stanford, CA: Stanford University Press, 1934.

Hill, George H. *Scenes from the Life of an Actor*. 1853. Reprinted New York: Benjamin Blom, 1969.

Hill, West T., Jr. *The Theatre in Early Kentucky 1790–1820*. Lexington: University of Kentucky Press, 1971.

Hingston, E. P. *The Genial Showman: Being Reminiscences of the Life of Artemus Ward*. London: John C. Hotten, 1871.

Hodge, Francis. *Yankee Theatre: The Images of America on the Stage, 1825–1850*. Austin: University of Texas Press, 1964.

Hoover, Merle M. *Park Benjamin, Poet & Editor*. New York: Columbia University Press, 1948.

Hopkins, Albert A. *Magic: Stage Illusion and Scientific Diversion*. New York: Munn, 1897.

Hornblow, Arthur. *A History of the Theatre in America from Its Beginnings to the Present Time*. 2 vols. Philadelphia: J. B. Lippincott, 1919.

Howard, Bronson. *The Autobiography of a Play*. New York: Columbia University, 1914.

Hufstetler, Loren. "A Physical Description of Booth's Theatre, New York, 1869–1883." *Theatre Design and Technology*, 43 (Winter 1976), 8–18.

Hughes, Catherine. "Women Playmakers." *New York Times Magazine* (May 4, 1941), 10, 27.

Hughes, Glenn. *A History of the American Theatre, 1700–1950*. New York: Samuel French, Inc., 1951.

Hutton, Laurence. *Curiosities of the American Stage*. New York: Harper & Brothers, 1891.

Ireland, Joseph N. *Fifty Years of a Playgoer's Journal, 1798–1848*. New York: Samuel French, Inc., 1860.

Mrs. Duff. Boston: James R. Osgood, 1882.

Records of the New York Stage from 1750 to 1860 2 vols. New York: T. H. Morrell, 1866–67.

James, Reese Davis. *Old Drury: A History of the Philadelphia Stage*. Philadelphia: University of Pennsylvania Press, 1932.

Jefferson, Joseph. *Autobiography*. New York: Century Co., 1889.

Johnson, Claudia. "A New Nation's Drama." *The Columbia Literary History of the United States*, ed. Emory Elliott et al. New York: Columbia University Press, 1988, pp. 324–41.

Johnson, Stephen. "Joseph Jefferson's *Rip Van Winkle* (1865)." *Drama Review*, 26 (Spring 1982), 3–20.

Jost, Francois. "German and French Themes in Early American Drama." *JGE: The Journal of General Education*, 28, 3 (Fall 1976), 190–222.

Kahn, E. J., Jr. *The Merry Partners, The Age and Stage of Harrigan & Hart*. New York: Random House, Inc., 1955.

Kendall, John. *The Golden Age of the New Orleans Theatre*. Baton Rouge: Louisiana State University Press, 1952.

Kimmel, Stanley. *The Mad Booths of Maryland*. Indianapolis: Bobbs-Merrill Co., Inc., 1940.

Kiper, Florence. "Some American Plays: From the Feminist Viewpoint." *Forum* 51 (1914), 921–31.

Knowlton, Dora. *Diary of a Daly Debutante*. New York: Duffield, 1910. Reprint New York: Benjamin Blom, 1977.

Koger, Alicia Kae. "An Edward Harrigan Bibliography." *Nineteenth Century Theatre*, 19 (Summer 1991), 29–44 and (Winter 1991), 105–29.

Kolb, Deborah S. "The Rise and Fall of the New Woman in American Drama." *Educational Theatre Journal*, 27 (1975), 149–60.

Koon, Helen Wickham. *How Shakespeare Won the West: Players and Performances in America's Gold Rush, 1849–1865*. Jefferson, NC: McFarland & Co., 1989.

Korn, Bertram. *The Early Jews of New Orleans*. Waltham, MA: American Jewish Historical Society, 1969.

Krows, Arthur Edwin. *Play Production in America*. New York: Henry Holt, 1916.

Larson, Orville K. *Scene Design in the American Theatre from 1915 to 1960*. Fayetteville: University of Arkansas Press, 1989.

Law, Robert A. "Notes on Some Early American Dramas." *University of Texas Studies in English*, 5 (1925), 96–100.

Lawrence, W. J. "The Rise of Spectacle in America." *Theatre Magazine*, 25 (1917).

Leach, Joseph. *Bright Particular Star: The Life and Times of Charlotte Cushman*. New Haven, CT: Yale University Press, 1970.

Lease, Benjamin. *That Wild Fellow John Neal and the American Literary Revolution*. Chicago: University of Chicago Press, 1972.

Leavitt, Michael. *Fifty Years in Theatrical Management*. New York: Broadway Publishing Co., 1912.

Leman, Walter M. *Memories of an Old Actor*. San Francisco: A. Roman Co., 1886.

Levine, Lawrence W. *Highbrow Lowbrow: The Emergence of Cultural Hierarchy in America*. Cambridge: Harvard University Press, 1988.

Lewis, Stanley. "Classicism in New York Theatre Architecture: 1825–1850." *Theatre Survey*, 6, no. 1 (May 1965), 11–31.

Lochemes, Sister M. Frederick. *Robert Walsh: His Story*. Washington, DC: Catholic University of America Press, 1941.

Logan, Olive. *Before the Footlights and Behind the Scenes*. Philadelphia: Parmelee, 1870.

Lott, Eric. *Love and Theft: Blackface Minstrelsy and the American Working Class*. New York: Oxford University Press, 1993.

Lovell, John, Jr. "The Beginnings of the American Theatre." *Theatre Annual*, 10 (1952), 7–19.

Ludlow, Noah M. *Dramatic Life as I Found It*. St. Louis: G. J. Jones, 1880.

McArthur, Benjamin. *Actors and American Culture, 1880–1920*. Philadelphia: Temple University Press, 1984.

McConachie, Bruce A. "H. J. Conway's Dramatization of Uncle Tom's Cabin: A Previously Unpublished Letter." *Theatre Journal*, 34, no. 2 (May 1982), 149–56.

   Melodramatic Formations: American Theatre and Society, 1820–1870. Iowa City: University of Iowa Press, 1992.

   and Daniel Friedman, eds. *Theatre for Working-Class Audiences in the United States, 1830–1980*. Westport, CT: Greenwood Press, 1985.

   and Thomas Postlewait. *Interpreting the Theatrical Past*. Iowa City: University of Iowa Press, 1989.

McCullough, Bruce Welker. *The Life and Writings of Richard Penn Smith with a Reprint of His Play, "The Deformed," 1830*. Menasha, WI: Banta, 1917.

McDermott, Douglas. "The Development of Theatre on the American Frontier, 1750–1890." *Theatre Survey*, 19, no. 2 (November 1982), 63–78.

   "Touring Patterns on California's Theatrical Frontier, 1849–1859." *Theatre Survey*, 15, no. 1 (May 1974), 18–28.

McGlinchee, Claire. *The First Decade of the Boston Museum*. Boston: Bruce Humphries, 1940.

Macgowan, Kenneth. *Footlights across America*. New York: Harcourt, Brace & Co., 1929.

MacKaye, Percy. *Epoch – The Life of Steele MacKaye, Genius of the Theatre*. 2 vols. New York: Boni & Liveright, 1927.

McKernan, Laura. "A Study of John Brougham as a Writer of Burlesque." M.A. thesis, Indiana University, 1976.

McNamara, Brooks. *The American Playhouse in the Eighteenth Century*. Cambridge: Harvard University Press, 1969.

   The Shuberts of Broadway. New York: Oxford University Press, 1990.

McVicker, J. H. *The Theatre: Its Early Days in Chicago*. Chicago: Knight & Leonard, 1884.

Mammen, Edward W. *The Old Stock Company School of Acting: A Study of the Boston Museum*. Boston: Trustees of the Public Library, 1945.

Marker, Lise-Lone. *David Belasco: Naturalism in the American Theatre*. Princeton, NJ: Princeton University Press, 1975.

Marshall, Herbert, and Mildred Stock. *Ira Aldridge, The Negro Tragedian*. Carbondale: Southern Illinois University Press, 1968.

Martin, Jay. "The Province of Speech: American Drama in the Eighteenth Century." *Early American Literature*, 13 (1978), 24–33.

Mates, Julian. *The American Musical Stage before 1800*. New Brunswick, NJ: Rutgers University Press, 1962.

Mathews, Cornelius. *The Various Writings of Cornelius Mathews*. New York: Harper Bros., 1843.

Matthews, Brander. "The American on the Stage." *Scribner's Monthly*, 18 (July 1879), 321–33.

   ed. *Papers on Acting*. New York: Hill & Wang, 1958.

Mayorga, Margaret G. *A Short History of the American Drama*. New York: Dodd, Mead, 1932 and 1934.

Mays, David D. "The Achievement of the Douglass Company in North America: 1758–1774." *Theatre Survey*, 23, no. 2 (November 1982), 141–50.

Meserve, Walter J. *American Drama to 1900: A Guide to Information Sources*. Detroit: Gale Research Co., 1980.

An Emerging Entertainment: The Drama of the American People to 1828. Bloomington: Indiana University Press, 1977.

Heralds of Promise: The Drama of the American People during the Age of Jackson, 1829–1849. Westport, CT: Greenwood Press, 1986.

An Outline History of American Drama. Totowa, NJ: Littlefield, Adams, 1965.

Miller, Jordan Y. *American Dramatic Literature*. New York: McGraw-Hill, 1961.

Miller, Tice L. *Bohemians and Critics: American Theatre Criticism in the Nineteenth Century*. Metuchen, NJ: Scarecrow Press, 1981.

Montilla, Robert. "The Building of the Lafayette Theatre." *Theatre Survey*, 15, no. 2 (November 1974), 105–29.

Moody, Richard. *America Takes the Stage: Romanticism in American Theatre and Drama, 1750–1900*. Bloomington: Indiana University Press, 1955.

The Astor Place Riot. Bloomington: Indiana University Press, 1958.

Edwin Forest: First Star of the American Stage. New York: Alfred A. Knopf, 1960.

Ned Harrigan: From Corlear's Hook to Herald Square. Chicago: Nelson-Hall, 1980.

Moody, Robert E. "Boston's First Play." *Proceedings of the Massachusetts Historical Society*, 92 (1980), 117–39.

Moreland, James. "The Theatre in Portland in the 18th Century." *New England Quarterly*, 11 (June 1938), 331–42.

Morris, Clara. *Life on the Stage*. New York: McClure, Phillips & Co., 1901.

Morris, Lloyd R. *Curtain Time: The Story of the American Theatre*. New York: Random House, Inc., 1953.

Moses, Montrose J. *The American Dramatist*. Boston: Little, Brown, 1925.

"The Drama, 1860–1918." *The Cambridge History of American Literature*, Vol. III. New York: G. P. Putnam's Sons, 1921, pp. 266–98.

and John Mason Brown, eds. *The American Theatre as Seen by Its Critics, 1752–1934*. New York: Norton, 1934.

Mowatt, Anna Cora. *Autobiography of an Actress*. Boston: Ticknor, Reed and Fields, 1854.

Mimic Life; or, Before and Behind the Curtain. Boston: Ticknor and Fields, 1856.

Mullin, Donald C. "Early Theatres in Rhode Island." *Theatre Survey*, 16, no. 2 (November 1970), 167–86.

Murdoch, James E. *The Stage, or Recollections of Actors and Acting from an Experience of Fifty Years*. Philadelphia: J. M. Stoddart & Co., 1880.

Murphy, Brenda. *American Realism and American Drama, 1800–1940*. Cambridge and New York: Cambridge University Press, 1987.

Myers, Norman J. "Josephine Clifton: 'Manufactured' Star." *Theatre History Studies*, 6 (1986), 109–23.

Nicoll, Allardyce. *A History of English Drama 1600–1900*, Vol. VI. Cambridge: Cambridge University Press, 1959.

Northall, William K. *Before and Behind the Curtain; or, Fifteen Years' Observations among the Theatres of New York*. New York: W. F. Burgess, 1851.

ed. *Life and Recollections of Yankee Hill: Together with Anecdotes and Incidents of His Travels*. New York: W. F. Burgess, 1850.

Odell, George C. D. *Annals of the New York Stage*. 15 vols. New York: Columbia University Press, 1927–49.

Odom, Leigh George. "*The Black Crook* at Niblo's Garden." *Drama Review*, 26 (Spring 1982), 21–40.

Parrington, Vernon L. *The Beginnings of Critical Realism in America, 1860–1920*. New York: Harcourt, Brace, and World, 1930.

Paskman, Dailey, and Sigmund Spaeth. *Gentlemen, Be Seated!* Garden City, NY: Doubleday & Co., Inc., 1928.

Patterson, Ada. "Woman Must Live Out Her Destiny." *Theatre Magazine* (May 1910), 134–35, xxiv.

Peavy, C. D. "The American Indian in the Drama of the United States." *McNeese Review*, 10 (1958), 68–86.

Philbrick, Norman, ed. *Trumpets Sounding: Propaganda Plays of the American Revolution.* New York: Benjamin Blom, 1972.

Phillips, Levi Damon. "Arthur McKee Rankin's *The Danites*, 1877–1881: Prime Example of the American Touring Process." *Theatre Survey*, 25 (November 1984), 225–47.

Pierce, Lucy France. "Women Who Write Plays." *World Today*, 15 (1908), 725–31.

Pizer, Donald. *Realism and Naturalism in Nineteenth-Century American Literature.* Rev. ed. Carbondale: Southern Illinois University Press, 1984.

Poggi, Jack. *Theater in America: The Impact of Economic Forces, 1870–1967.* Ithaca, NY: Cornell University Press, 1968.

Pollock, Stephen B., and Don B. Wilmeth. "The Shuberts and the Syndicate: The Independent Theatre Comes to Providence." *Rhode Island History*, 45 (August 1986), 95–106.

Pollock, Thomas Clark. *The Philadelphia Theatre in the Eighteenth Century.* Philadelphia: University of Pennsylvania Press, 1933.

Porter, Glen. *Encyclopedia of American Economic History: Studies of Principal Movements and Ideas,* Vol. I. New York: Scribner, 1980.

Power, Tyrone. *Impressions of America during the Years 1833, 1834, and 1835.* 2 vols. Philadelphia: Carey, Lea & Blanchard, 1836.

Prevots, Naima. *American Pageantry: A Movement for Art and Democracy.* Ann Arbor, MI: UMI Research Press, 1990.

Pritner, Calvin L. "William Warren's Financial Arrangements with Traveling Stars, 1805–1827." *Theatre Survey*, 6, no. 1 (November 1965), 83–90.

Quinn, Arthur Hobson. *A History of the American Drama from the Beginning to the Civil War.* New York: Appleton-Century-Crofts, 1923 and 1943.

   A History of the American Drama from the Civil War to the Present Day. 2 vols. New York: Appleton-Century-Crofts, 1927, 1937, and 1943.

   The Literature of the American People. New York: Appleton-Century-Crofts, 1951.

Rahill, Frank. *The World of Melodrama.* University Park: Pennsylvania State University Press, 1967.

Ramirez, Elizabeth C. "A History of Mexican-American Professional Theatre in Texas prior to 1900." *Theatre Survey*, 24 (1983), 99–116.

Rankin, Hugh F. *The Theatre of Colonial America.* Chapel Hill: University of North Carolina Press, 1965.

Ranshaw, Molly N. "Jump, Jim Crow! A Biographical Sketch of Thomas D. Rice (1808–1860)." *Theatre Annual*, 17 (1960), 36–47.

Reed, Perley I. *The Realistic Presentation of American Characters in Native American Plays prior to 1870.* Ohio State University Bulletin, no. 26. Columbus: Ohio State University Press, 1918.

Rees, James. *The Dramatic Authors of America.* Philadelphia: G. B. Zieber, 1845.

Reignolds-Winslow, Catherine Mary. *Yesterdays with Actors.* Boston: Cupples and Hurd, 1887.

Richardson, Gary A. *American Drama from the Colonial Period through World War I.* New York: Twayne Publishers, 1993.

   "Boucicault's *The Octoroon* and American Law." *Theatre Journal*, 34, no. 2 (May 1982), 155–64.

Rinear, David L. "F. S. Chanfrau's 'Mose': The Rise and Fall of an Urban Folk Hero." *Theatre Journal*, 33, no. 2 (May 1981), 199–212.

   "'Innocent and Hearty Merriment': The Life and Work of George Holland." *Theatre History Studies*, 12 (1992), 157–72.

   The Temple of Momus: Mitchell's Olympic Theatre. Metuchen, NJ: Scarecrow Press, 1987.

Ritchey, David. "The Maryland Company of Comedians." *Educational Theatre Journal*, 24, no. 4 (December 1972), 355–62.

Robertson, Peter. "Life on the Stage." *Pacific Life* (August 25, 1877).

Roden, Robert. *Later American Plays, 1831–1900.* New York: Dunlap Society, 1900.

Ruff, Loren K. "Joseph Harper and Boston's Broad Alley Theatre, 1792–1793." *Educational Theatre Journal*, 26, no. 1 (March 1974), 45–52.

Rugg, Harold G. "The Dartmouth Plays, 1779–1782." *Theatre Annual*, 1 (1942), 55–57.

Ryan, Pat M. "John Brougham: The Gentle Satirist." *Bulletin of New York Public Library*, 63 (1959), 619–40.

Sachs, Edwin O. *The Fire at the Iroquois Theatre, Chicago, 30th December, 1903.* London: Batsford, 1904.

Sampson, Henry T. *The Ghost Walks: A Chronological History of Blacks in Show Business, 1865–1910.* Metuchen, NJ: Scarecrow, 1988.

Saraceni, Gene Adam. "Herne and the Single Tax: An Early Plea for an Actor's Union." *Educational Theatre Journal,* 26, no. 3 (October 1974), 315–26.

Sarlos, Robert K. *Jig Cook and the Provincetown Players: Theatre in Ferment.* Amherst: University of Massachusetts Press, 1982.

Saxon, A. H. *P. T. Barnum: The Legend and the Man.* New York: Columbia University Press, 1989.

Seilhamer, George O. *A History of the American Theatre, 1792–1797.* 3 vols. Philadelphia: Globe Printing House, 1888–91.

An Interviewer's Album: Comprising a Series of Chats with Eminent Players and Playwrights. New York: Alvin Perry, 1881.

Seller, Maxine Schwartz, ed. *Ethnic Theatre in the United States.* Westport, CT, and London: Greenwood Press, 1983.

Senelick, Laurence. *The Age and Stage of George L. Fox.* Hanover, NH: University Press of New England, 1988.

"George L. Fox and American Pantomime." *Nineteenth Century Theatre Research,* 7 (Spring 1979), 1–26.

Shafer, Yvonne. "George L. Fox and the *Hamlet* Travesty." *Theatre Studies,* 24/25 (1977–79), 79–93.

Shattuck, Charles Harlen. *The Hamlet of Edwin Booth.* Urbana and London: University of Illinois Press, 1969.

Shakespeare on the American Stage. 2 vols. Washington, DC: Folger Shakespeare Library, 1976 and 1987.

Shaw, Mary. "The Boston Museum and Daly's Theatre." *Saturday Evening Post,* 183, 4 (May 20, 1911), 14–15, 34–35.

Shiffler, Harold. "Religious Opposition to the Eighteenth Century Philadelphia Stage." *Educational Theatre Journal,* 14, no. 3 (October 1962), 215–23.

Shockley, Martin Staples. *The Richmond Stage, 1784–1812.* Charlottesville: University of Virginia Press, 1977.

Skinner, Otis, and Maud Skinner, eds. *One Man in His Times, the Adventures of H. Watkins, Strolling Player, 1845–1863.* Philadelphia: University of Pennsylvania Press, 1938.

Smith, Cecil M. *Musical Comedy in America.* New York: Theatre Arts Books, 1950.

Smith, Henry Nash, ed. *Mark Twain of the "Enterprise."* Berkeley: University of California Press, 1957.

Smith, James L. *Melodrama.* London: Methuen, 1973.

Smith, Sol. *Theatrical Management in the West and South for Thirty Years.* New York: Harper and Bros., 1868.

Smither, Nellie. *A History of the English Theatre at New Orleans, 1806–1842.* 1944. Reprint New York: Benjamin Blom, 1967.

Snyder, Robert W. *The Voice of the City: Vaudeville and Popular Culture in New York.* New York: Oxford University Press, 1989.

Sobel, Bernard. *Burleycue, An Underground History of Burlesque Days.* New York: Farrar & Rinehart, 1931.

A Pictorial History of Burlesque. New York: G. P. Putnam's Sons, 1956.

Sogliuzzo, A. Richard. "Edward H. Sothern and Julia Marlowe on the Art of Acting." *Theatre Survey,* 11, no. 2 (May 1970), 187–200.

Staples, F. "History of the Theatre in San Francisco." *Overland Monthly,* 80 (January 1927), 22–23, 25.

Staples, Shirley. *Male-Female Comedy Teams in American Vaudeville 1865–1932.* Ann Arbor: University of Michigan Press, 1984.

Stephens, Judith L. "Gender Idealogy and Dramatic Convention in Progressive Era Plays, 1890–1920." *Theatre Journal,* 41 (1989), 45–55.

Stoddard, Richard. "Aqueduct and Iron Curtain at the Federal Street Theatre, Boston." *Theatre Survey,* 8, no. 2 (November 1967), 106–11.

"A Costume Inventory in Booth's Bankruptcy Papers." *Theatre Survey,* 16 (November 1975), 186–88.

"The Haymarket Theatre, Boston." *Educational Theatre Journal*, 10, no. 1 (March 1975), 63–69.

Stone, Henry Dickinson. *Personal Recollections of the Drama*. Albany, NY: C. Van Benthuysen, 1873. Reprint New York: Benjamin Blom, 1969.

Strang, Lewis C. *Famous Actors of the Day in America*. Boston: L. C. Page and Co., 1900.

Players and Plays of the Last Quarter Century. 2 vols. Boston: L. C. Page and Co., 1902.

Stratman, Carl J. *American Theatrical Periodicals, 1798–1967: A Bibliographical Guide*. Durham, NC: Duke University Press, 1970.

Stull, A. Frank. "Where Famous Actors Learned Their Art." *Lippincott's Monthly*, 75 (March 1905), 372–79.

Styan, J. L. *Modern Drama in Theory and Practice, Vol. 1, Realism and Naturalism*. Cambridge: Cambridge University Press, 1981.

Sutherland, Cynthia. "American Women Playwrights as Mediators of the 'Woman Problem.'" *Modern Drama*, 21 (1978), 319–36.

Tassin, Algernon. "The American Dramatic Schools." *Bookman*, 25 (April 1907), 151–65.

Taubman, Howard. *The Making of the American Theatre*. New York: Coward, McCann & Geoghegan, Inc., 1965.

Taylor, George Rogers. "Gaslight Foster: A New York Journeyman Journalist of Mid-Century." *New York History*, 58 (July 1977), 297–312.

Theatrical Biography of Eminent Actors and Authors. New York: Estate of William Taylor, n.d.

Thompson, Lawrence. "Longfellow Sells the Spanish Student." *American Literature*, 6 (1934), 141–50.

Tichi, Cynthia. "Thespis and the 'Carnall Hipocrite': A Puritan Motive for Aversion to Drama." *Early American Literature*, 4 (1969), 86–103.

Timberlake, Craig. *The Bishop of Broadway: The Life & Work of David Belasco*. New York: Library Publishers, 1954.

Toll, Robert C. *Blacking Up: The Minstrel Show in Nineteenth-Century America*. New York: Oxford University Press, 1974.

Tompkins, Eugene and Quincy Kilby. *The History of the Boston Theatre, 1854–1901*. Boston: Houghton Mifflin Co., 1908. Reprint New York: Benjamin Blom, 1969.

Towse, John Ranken. *Sixty Years of the Theatre: An Old Critic's Memories*. New York: Funk and Wagnalls, Inc., 1916.

Toynbee, William, ed. *The Diaries of William Charles Macready*. 2 vols. New York: G. P. Putnam's Sons, 1912.

Travis, Steve. "The Rise and Fall of the Theatrical Syndicate." *Educational Theatre Journal*, 10, no. 1 (March 1958), 35–40.

Trollope, Frances. *Domestic Manners of the Americans*, ed. Donald Smalley. New York: Alfred A. Knopf, 1949.

"Uncle Ben Baker." New York *Dramatic Mirror* (September 13, 1890), 5.

Vandenhoff, George. *Leaves from an Actor's Notebook*. New York: D. Appleton & Co., 1860.

Vaughn, Jack A. *Early American Dramatists: From the Beginnings to 1900*. New York: Ungar, 1981.

Ventimiglia, Peter James. "The William Winter Correspondence and the Augustin Daly Shakespearean Productions of 1885–1898." *Educational Theatre Journal*, 30, no. 2 (May 1978), 220–28.

Wagenknecht, Edward. *Longfellow: A Full-Length Portrait*. London: Longmans Green, 1955.

Wallack, Lester. *Memories of Fifty Years*. New York: Charles Scribners, 1889.

Warde, Frederick. *Fifty Years of Make-Believe*. New York: International Press Syndicate, 1920.

Watermeier, Daniel J., ed. *Edwin Booth's Performances: The Mary Isabella Stone Commentaries*. Ann Arbor, MI: UMI Research Press, 1989.

Watson, Charles S. *Antebellum Charleston Dramatists*. Tuscaloosa: University of Alabama Press, 1976.

Wegelin, Oscar. *Early American Plays, 1714–1830*. New York: Dunlap Society, 1900.

Weil, Elsie F. "The Hull-House Players." *Theatre Magazine* (September 1913), xix–xxii.

Wemyss, Francis Courtney. *Chronology of the American Stage from 1752–1852*. New York: W. Taylor, 1852. Reprint New York: Benjamin Blom, 1968.

Twenty-Six Years of the Life of an Actor and Manager. New York: Burgess, Stringer and Co., 1847.

West, E. J. "Revolution in the American Theatre: Glimpses of Acting Conditions on the American Stage, 1855–1870." *Theatre Survey*, 1 (1960), 43–64.

Westlake, Neda McFadden, ed. *Caius Marius, A Tragedy by Richard Penn Smith*. Philadelphia: University of Pennsylvania Press, 1968.

Weston, Effie Ellsler, ed. *The Stage Memoirs of John A. Ellsler*. Cleveland: Rowfant Club, 1950.

White, Richard Grant. "The Age of Burlesque." *Galaxy*, 8 (August 1869), 200–02.

Willard, George O. *History of the Providence Stage, 1762–1891*. Providence: Rhode Island News Co., 1891.

Williams, Henry B., ed. *The American Theatre: A Sum of Its Parts*. New York: Samuel French, 1971.

Willis, Eola. *The Charleston Stage in the XVIII Century*. Columbia, SC: State, 1924.

Willis, Richard. "Curtain Down on Theatre Fires." *Theatre Survey*, 13, no. 1 (November 1972), 60–73.

Wilmeth, Don B. *George Frederick Cooke, Machiavel of the Stage*. Westport, CT: Greenwood Press, 1993.

"Noble or Ruthless Savage? The American Indian on the Stage and in the Drama." *Journal of American Drama and Theatre*, 1, no. 1 (Spring 1989), 39–78.

Variety Entertainments and Outdoor Amusements: A Reference Guide. Westport, CT, and London: Greenwood Press, 1982.

and Rosemary Cullen, eds. *Plays by Augustin Daly*. Cambridge and New York: Cambridge University Press, 1984.

The American Stage to World War I. Detroit: Gale Research Co., 1978.

Wilson, Arthur Herman. *History of the Philadelphia Theatre, 1835–1855*. Philadelphia: University of Pennsylvania Press, 1935.

Wilson, Garff B. *A History of American Acting*. Bloomington: Indiana University Press, 1966.

Three Hundred Years of American Drama and Theatre. 2nd ed. Englewood Cliffs, NJ: Prentice-Hall, 1982.

Winter, William. *Life and Art of Edwin Booth*. New York: MacMillan Co., 1893.

Life and Art of Joseph Jefferson. New York: MacMillan Co., 1894.

Life and Art of Richard Mansfield. 2 vols. New York: Moffat, Yard and Co., 1913.

Life of David Belasco. 2 vols. New York: Moffat, Yard and Co., 1918.

Life, Stories and Poems of John Brougham. Boston: James R. Osgood, 1881.

Other Days: Being Chronicles and Memories of the Stage. New York: Moffat, Yard and Co., 1908.

Shadows of the Stage. New York: MacMillan Co., 1892.

The Wallet of Time. 2 vols. New York: Moffat, Yard and Co., 1913. Reprint New York: Benjamin Blom, 1969.

Winton, Calhoun. "The Theatre and Drama." *American Literature, 1764–1789: The Revolutionary Years*, ed. Everett Emerson. Madison: University of Wisconsin Press, 1977, pp. 87–104.

Witham, Barry B. "Owen Davis: America's Forgotten Playwright." *Players*, 46, no. 1 (November 1970), 30–35.

"Owen Gould Davis." *Dictionary of American Biography*. Supplement VI. New York: Charles Scribners Sons, 1980, pp. 149–50.

Wittke, Carl. *Tambo and Bones, A History of the American Minstrel Stage*. Durham, NC: Duke University Press, 1930.

Wolcott, John R. "Scene Painters and Their Work in America before 1800." *Theatre Survey*, 18, no. 1 (May 1977), 57–85.

Wood, William B. *Personal Recollections of the Stage*. Philadelphia: Henry Carey Baird, 1855.

Woodruff, Jack. "America's Oldest Living Theatre – The Howard Athanaeum." *Theatre Annual*, 8 (1950), 71–81.

Woods, Alan. "Frederick B. Warde, America's Greatest Forgotten Tragedian." *Educational Theatre Journal*, 29, no. 3 (October 1977), 333–42.

Wright, Richardson. *Revels in Jamaica 1682–1838*. New York: Dodd, Mead, 1937.

Young, Rose. "Suffrage as Seen by Mary Shaw." *Harper's Weekly*, 60 (May 8, 1915), 456.

Young, William C. *Famous Actors and Actresses on the American Stage: Documents of American Theater History*. 2 vols. New York: R. R. Bowker, 1975.

Famous American Playhouses: Documents of American Theater History. 2 vols. Chicago: American Library Association, 1973.

Zeidman, Irving. *The American Burlesque Show*. New York: Hawthorn Books, 1967.

Index

N.B. City is not given for theatres in New York City.